A Short World History of Christianity

Revised Edition

A Short World History of Christianity

Revised Edition

Robert Bruce Mullin

WJK WESTMINSTER
JOHN KNOX PRESS
LOUISVILLE · KENTUCKY

First edition Published by Westminster John Knox Press in 2008

Revised Edition
Published by Westminster John Knox Press
Louisville, Kentucky

14 15 16 17 18 19 20 21 22 23—10 9 8 7 6 5 4 3 2 1

Book design by Sharon Adams
Cover design by Eric Walljasper, Minneapolis, MN
Cover illustration: Greek temple on old paper, Kos City, Kos Island (Main Square)
© mammuth / www.istockphoto.com.

Library of Congress Cataloging-in-Publication Data

Mullin, Robert Bruce.
  A short world history of Christianity / Robert Bruce Mullin.—Revised edition.
    pages cm
  Includes bibliographical references and index.
  ISBN 978-0-664-25963-1 (alk. paper)
  1. Church history. I. Title.
  BR145.3.M85 2014
  270—dc23

                                                    2014029379

Most Westminster John Knox Press books are available at special quantity discounts when purchased in bulk by corporations, organizations, and special-interest groups. For more information, please e-mail SpecialSales@wjkbooks.com.

To my students,
from whom I have learned so much

Contents

Acknowledgments

*T*his undertaking has grown out of more than three decades of interactions with teachers and students of Christian history. I have been privileged to observe superb teachers who have mastered the craft of explaining important and complicated questions clearly and simply without compromising the integrity of the materials. To my many colleagues at Yale, Wesleyan, North Carolina State, Duke, and General Theological Seminary, from whom I have borrowed unashamedly, I offer my deep gratitude. Likewise to the multitude of students I have taught—many of whom have asked that most frightening of questions a teacher may hear, "I don't quite understand, could you explain it again?"—thank you for your insistence that good history must be clear history.

On a more specific level, several organizations must be acknowledged. The Wabash Center for Teaching and Learning at Wabash College sponsored a seminar on the reinvisioning of the history of Christianity. The seminar leaders, Mark Noll and Grant Wacker, encouraged me to take on this project, and the participants in the seminar—most particularly Robert Wilken, Ronald Rittgers, and Dana Robert—graciously shared their expertise in their given fields. The General Theological Seminary of the Episcopal Church has been generous with its resources and provided me a sabbatical leave to complete this project. In particular I would like to thank Dean Ward Ewing and board chair Robert Giannini for their unflinching support. The St. Mark's Library at General has been conducive to research and writing. Its remarkable collection and supportive staff have been invaluable. Of the many helpful persons there, I must mention in particular Drew Kadel, Emily Knox, V. K. McCarty, and Laura Moore. The members of the American Religion Seminar in the Columbia University Seminar Program have also cogently examined parts of this work, and I thank them for their criticisms.

I have profited from conversations with and insights of many scholars and students of the field. William Adler, Elizabeth Clark, J. Robert Wright, Richard Corney, Randall Balmer, Robert Owens, Catherine Randall, John Koenig, and Ron Young have all given their insights freely. Helen Goodkin carefully read the entire manuscript and offered important suggestions.

The Conant Fund of the Episcopal Church provided generous funds for both research and travel. The Columbia University Seminar Program has also provided resources for help in publication. I am grateful for the generosity of both.

Donald McKim of Westminster John Knox Press was encouraging and patient in the course of this project. I hope the result is worth the wait.

Finally, to Judith Walker Mullin I owe a particular thanks. She has lived with this project more closely than anyone and has lovingly and judiciously offered support, criticism, and insight that have led me into pathways I would have otherwise never undertaken that have resulted in a better book. Her unselfish and loving support has made this work possible.

The occasion of this second edition has allowed me to correct some minor errors readers have graciously noted, to fill in some lacuna in the first edition, as well as to add a new chapter on trends in world Christianity in the twenty-first century. I have also added a time line of key dates. All of my acknowledgments in the first edition are reiterated, along with special thanks to Mary Robison, reference librarian here at GTS, as well as to the many scholars who have charitably offered corrections and graciously offered suggestions for this present edition.

Robert Bruce Mullin
September 2013

Introduction

"Fire upon the Earth"

*I*n the twelfth chapter of the writing that Christians refer to as the Gospel of Luke, Jesus is recorded as saying, "I came to cast fire upon the earth." It is an uncomfortable image. Fire is usually associated with destruction. Commentators believe that the fire spoken of in this text was the fire of judgment through which a new world would be brought about. But fire is a multivalent metaphor. It both destroys and refines; its light illuminates while its smoke conceals.

The same multivalence can be seen in the story of Christianity in world history. For those within the Christian community, the image of fire has another connotation. For them it symbolizes the presence of the Holy Spirit. When the day of Pentecost (often viewed as the birth of the Christian church) is pictured, tongues of fire represent the Spirit. Thus do Christians view their history. Whatever its failures and limitations, they persist in believing that God is doing something in that history: the Christian story is not a series of random events; it has a great purpose.

In taking "fire upon the earth" as the guiding metaphor for the story of Christianity in world history, this book attempts to do justice to the image's multifaceted implications. Friends, enemies, and neutral observers have judged the story of Christianity to be one of amazing creativity and terrible destruction, of fearless accomplishments and grim failures, of highs and lows. Whatever else there is to be said, Christianity has left its mark on the world as surely as any fire. And the story and the mark form the subject of this book.

Indeed, telling this story has become an urgent task in the present age. As the world has grown smaller and as the influence of religion in human affairs has increased (replacing, together with other social forces, the great ideological movements of the past century), a knowledge of Christianity in world history takes on new importance. But these sociological shifts also make telling

Christian history more complex and nuanced. Paradoxically, as more and more details of the story are filled in, people are increasingly without a grasp of its basic outline. Knowledge of the history of Christianity is probably slighter today than ever before. The present volume addresses this lacuna. In this sense it attempts to do for the twenty-first century what the religious historian Martin Marty accomplished in his *Short History of Christianity* fifty-five years ago—to provide a workable overview for both students and general readers that scholars and teachers might also find helpful.

> This book argues that "global Christianity" is one phase in the evolving history of Chrisitianity.

Such a volume must look very different today, however. Marty's *Short History* was written at a time when the Western preeminence in the story of Christianity could still be assumed. Trajectories such as from Paul through Augustine to Luther could still be confidently made in order to link the various stages of Christian history. For the contemporary chronicler, both the world and the Christian community have become far more complex. Older histories gloss over the non-Western world as well as factions within the church that were deemed unworthy of note. To counteract these blind spots, several volumes published in the past decade have billed themselves as "global histories," attempting to recast the story of Christianity in worldwide perspective.

For better or worse, this volume does not claim to be a global history, though I hope it is sensitive to the issues raised by that genre. Rather, it argues that "global Christianity" is one phase (albeit a crucial one) in the evolving history of Christianity. The thesis of the book can be stated simply: Christianity has passed through a series of interconnected phases. Christianity was born in "globalization." It took root in various environments, each of which left its mark on local Christian life and practice. These distinct regional Christianities were the norm for the first thousand years of the Christian era. But starting in the eleventh century, the dynamic of the Christian world began to change. One regional Christianity, that of the Latin West, began to grow more and more vital while the other geographic centers, for a variety of reasons, weakened. If the first thousand years of the story of Christianity is a tale of competing regional Christianities, the next nine hundred years must be understood as the "Latin era," during which the churches of western Europe uniquely shaped the course of the Christian world. But what has made the past fifty years so turbulent and confusing is the ending of Christianity's Latin era and the return to globalism and competing regional Christianities. This volume is not so much a global history as a study of why globalism has emerged and triumphed in the story of Christianity, and of the impact this has had on both Christianity and the world. Students of history may recognize this book's indebtedness to the structure of the late Sydney Ahlstrom's *Religious History of the American People*, where it was argued that a "Puritan era" shaped the central period of American religious history. When that era collapsed in the 1960s, we entered a new age of pluralism. The idea of a "Latin era" implies that we can speak of history as having a center. Yet centers are both artificial and real at the same time. They are artificial because they are merely constructs of a given time and place; they have no ultimate reality. They are real because when they do function, they help to define a community in a given time and place. Western dominance during the Latin era was accidental—and critics may rightfully say that it was an unfortunate accident—but it was real and must be acknowledged.

The goal of this volume is fourfold. The first goal is to offer a new narrative that will make the two thousand years of Christianity comprehensible and interesting to the general reader. There are many ways to shape a historical study, but to cast it as a story is perhaps the oldest. Despite the complications, a common story still holds together the infinite particularity of Christian experience. The second goal is to bring back into the narrative many of the churches that were rejected by the dominant tradition and that consequently have not found a place in general histories. Thus, for example, Nestorians all too often drop out of sight after the Council of Ephesus, and Monophysites (or Copts) disappear after the Council of Chalcedon, yet, as will be seen in these pages, both continued for centuries to play a significant part in Christian history. The third goal is to incorporate into the narrative the great flowering of recent scholarship that has restored women, the laity, blacks, Hispanics, Asians, and many others to Christian history. A short history can only touch on these concerns, but they account for the tripartite shape of the Christian narrative as understood by this book. Finally, the book attempts to balance internal issues, such as prayer and sacrament, with larger questions of Christianity's relationship to its changing political and intellectual world. It looks at Christian history from both inside and outside.

A narrative history allows readers to experience history as a story, but as a genre it suffers from key limitations. To write history as a story is to be an author in search of one plot. Stories are not encyclopedias. Rather, details are rigorously selected to move the narrative forward. So it is with this volume. Important figures from the Christian past have been ruthlessly excluded in the interest of producing a true "short history." If readers finish this book hungering for more in-depth knowledge, it will be the author's dream come true. There are many fine encyclopedic histories they can consult.

The writing of history is a moral act. The lives and reputations of thousands of persons are in the author's hands. This book strives to be as fair and charitable as possible to all. Judgment is at times necessary, but so, too, is humility.

SECTION 1   Shaping a Christian Tradition

Chapter 1

"Who Is This Man?"

*T*he story of Christianity is a vast and complicated tale with thousands of actors—both heroes and villains—but at its heart it is about one man, Jesus of Nazareth. The earliest Christian Gospel posed the question most bluntly, "Who is this man?" and the subsequent story of Christianity has been the attempt to render an answer to this question. People in different times and locations have offered their own interpretations—in theology, in art, in humble devotion—but the question remains. The poet and sage Ralph Waldo Emerson perhaps said it best: the name of Jesus "is not so much written as plowed into the world."

But if the story is about a man, it is also about what people thought about him, what he said and did, and how they responded to his life. This, too, was as true in the first century as it is in the twenty-first. For centuries some have attempted to separate the man from the testimonies and get back to the true "historical Jesus." In the past century alone this Jesus has been seen as a moral prophet, social revolutionary, philosopher, and Cynic teacher of wisdom, as well as in countless other ways. Indeed, in the long history of Christianity people have tended to read into this Jesus the hopes and fears of their age. Although this task has never ultimately been successful, all of these pictures present some important insight. But what is here attempted is to provide a broad historical sketch to begin this study.

Divisions and Conflicts

There are but a few, brief references to Jesus in what has come down to us in the writings of antiquity, apart from Christian sources. There is a fleeting reference to him by the Jewish historian Josephus and an even sketchier reference by the Roman historian Tacitus, but a historical picture ultimately

3

rests on the texts preserved by the Christian community itself. From these we soon learn that the world of the historical Jesus was one where great forces were clashing. There was, to begin with, the world of Judaism. Judaism had grown more complex since the return from captivity in Babylon in 538 BCE. New ideas began to find a place among believers. The notion of an after-life and a day of judgment (both largely absent in the religion of David and Solomon) took on a prominence in some Jewish groups. The interest in judg-ment brought forth a new type of literature, the apocalyptic. Apocalypticism pictured the world as a battleground between God and Satan, in which the oppressing power of Satan would be overthrown by God, who would usher in a new and perfect age. In this age God would rule directly. The instrument of God in this action would be the messiah. He would restore the kingship of David and, with it, Jewish power. The apocalyptic hope led pious individuals to watch for signs to see if the day of judgment was at hand.

The hope for a restoration of national glory was made intensely practical by the political situation Judaism found itself in. Since their return from exile the Jewish people had been under the dominion of one foreign power after another. First there were the Persians. Their rule, though distant, was real. Then came the Greeks, or Hellenists. In his subduing of Persia, Alexander the Great brought the eastern Mediterranean area (including Judea) under the sway of Greek power. After his death (as we will see) the land was contested by various different satraps, successors to Alexander's control. Finally, in 63 BCE, the land came under the control of Rome, and it was under Roman rule that Jesus was born.

These political changes created divisions within the Jewish world. How one should respond to the challenge of Hellenism became a question of great urgency for those Jews living in the larger world. The Christian writer Tertul-lian was to ask the famous question "What has Athens to do with Jerusalem?" and it was a pressing question for Jews confronting Hellenism. Hellenism introduced the Greek language, a culture that was cosmopolitan, and an educational ideal that rested on philosophy. All were challenges. Language was perhaps most basic. Since the time of captivity many Jews had taken residency throughout the Mediterranean world. They were the Jews of the Diaspora. To live and work in the cities of the Mediterranean was to be in a world that spoke Greek. As Greek increasingly became the language of the Jewish Diaspora, Jews recognized that the Hebrew Scriptures needed to be translated. The Greek version of the Hebrew Scriptures became known as the Septuagint (for the seventy scholars who, according to legend, translated it), and it later would become the first Bible of the young Christian community. But the question of Hellenism ran deeper. According to Greek philosophy, the spiritual was superior to the material, and the universal was superior to the particular. What sense, then, could be made of sacred Scriptures given to a single people and filled with earthy images? Must there not be a greater reality behind the literal words of the text? The search for such a meaning was called allegory. The first-century Jewish philosopher Philo of Alexandria, for example, saw the story of the garden of Eden as symbolizing the development of the soul's moral virtues. Greek wisdom and Hebrew revelation, he believed, could work together.

Others were not so sure. The gymnasium, symbol of the Hellenistic world, where naked young men exercised their bodies, and the Jewish Temple, where pious men in long robes prayed to the God of Israel, seemed like different worlds. The question of Hellenism would become particularly sharp in the second century BCE. Judea had become a point of contention between competing parts of the old Alexandrian empire. Both the Ptolemies of Egypt and the Seleucids of Syria coveted the land. In the 160s the Seleucids under Antiochus Epiphanes triumphed, and they attempted to push hellenization to a further degree. Not only was a gymnasium established in the sacred city of Jerusalem, but the Temple itself was dedicated to Zeus. The result was the revolt of the Maccabees, a fight against assimilation. The Jewish holiday of Hanukkah commemorates the cleansing of the Jewish Temple.

The complicated world of Judaism also contributed to the emergence of many competing parties. There were those who saw the center of Judaism to be its Temple. There priests continued to serve and offer sacrifice to God as in the past. The party associated with the Temple was known as the Sadducees. If the Temple was their place, the books of Moses (the first five books of the present Hebrew Scriptures/Old Testament, also known as Torah or Law) were their Bible. They refused to put other works—such as the Prophets or the "Writings" such as Psalms and Proverbs—on the level of the Law of Moses. Sadducees rejected new beliefs such as the resurrection of the dead because they were not to be found in Moses. Opposing the Sadducees were the Pharisees. They had three distinctive teachings. First, they believed that the Scriptures included the Prophets and the Writings as well as the Law of Moses. Second, they put great emphasis on the interpretation of the law. In a complicated world the law needed to be applied to situations for which it had never been intended. The rabbi (or teacher) interpreted the law for the community, and the rabbi was the great figure among the Pharisees. Finally they believed that much of the thrust of the law was to achieve a moral and ritual purity in everyday life. One needed to be pure not merely to be in the Temple but in all aspects of the world.

In addition to Pharisees and Sadducees there existed another group, the Essenes. The Essenes had withdrawn from a world that had become polluted.

In their isolated communities they focused on their communal life and saw their communal body as the temple of the Lord. In their communities the apocalyptic hope burned bright. Their purity within a world of corruption was like Israel of old, a time in the wilderness in preparation for entering the promised land. The Dead Sea Scrolls were most likely part of a library of an Essene community.

The imposition of new ideas and forces changed Judaism, and these changes would have an immense impact on the shaping of Christianity. But the new milieu also involved Judea in an international community, and this international community would have a role in the shaping of Christianity. The emergence of a common linguistic world as a result of Alexander's conquests meant that the Christian Scriptures, written in Greek, could be comprehended throughout the Mediterranean world. The apostle Paul, in one of the earliest of Christian writings, proclaimed, "In Christ there is no longer Jew or Greek," and in this he meant that the message was for both Jews and Greeks. One practical reason this could be so was that Greeks and (most) Jews shared a common language.

If Alexander provided a common language, Rome created a common society. The birth and rise of Christianity took place in the two centuries when Roman power was at its peak. Rome created what was called the Pax Romana, the Roman peace. Rome's governance was certainly brutal at times. The famous phrase of the historian Tacitus, "They created a desert and called it peace," reflected the negative side of the Pax Romana. But Rome also provided an unprecedented communication network linking the known world from Britain to Baghdad. The Mediterranean Sea, once a haven for pirates, was now a Roman lake, filled with communication and commerce. The Roman peace was the backdrop for the rise of Christianity. Indeed, one of the Gospel writers, Luke, claimed it was more. In his account of the birth of Jesus, Luke was to write, "A decree went out from Caesar Augustus that all the world should be registered," and it was for that reason that the parents of Jesus traveled to Bethlehem. There Jesus was born in the city of David. For Luke, prophecy was fulfilled through the action of a Roman emperor. The early Christian community would have an ambiguous relationship with the Roman Empire.

The Story of a Life

Such was the world, but what do we "know" about this man Jesus, born in the Roman-occupied province of Judea more than two thousand years ago? As we saw, virtually the only source of information is Christian sources, and even that is surprisingly spotty. The Gospels record scant information about his early life. He is associated with the town of Nazareth in the region of Galilee, a place far from the religious center of Judaism or the political center of anything. There Jews and non-Jews lived together. His father is recorded as being a carpenter, and in one place Jesus himself is called a carpenter. From the accounts we also learn that at about age thirty his life radically changed. He underwent baptism at the hands of a fiery wandering preacher, John the Baptist. John was a preacher of righteousness, a bearer of the message of the prophets. The relationship between John and Jesus has generated much speculation. Luke states that they were relatives, and the Gospel writers picture John as the one who prepared the way for Jesus, but many modern scholars believe they may have had competing ministries. We also learn that after the baptism Jesus began acquiring a group of followers or disciples and began a public ministry. Luke has this ministry beginning when Jesus went to the synagogue in Nazareth and read from the scrolls. The scene and the passage chosen, if not historical, do capture the spirit of the ministry of Jesus as recorded by the Gospel writers. From Isaiah, he read,

> The Spirit of the Lord is upon me, because he has anointed me to bring good news to the poor. He has sent me to proclaim release to the captives and recovery of sight to the blind, to let the oppressed go free, to proclaim the year of the Lord's favor.

Good news, healing, and the inauguration of a new age in God's relationship with the world (the acceptable year of the Lord) aptly summarize the ministry that was to follow.

The good news he offered was in an arresting style and focused on a central subject. He made use of parables, or simple stories that used everyday imagery: "A man was going down from Jerusalem to Jericho"; "A sower was out sowing the field." Each parable, though, had a pungent point. And the point of many was the kingdom of God. Mark, whose Gospel is the earliest, has Jesus beginning his public ministry by announcing, "The time is fulfilled, and the kingdom of God is at hand; repent and believe in the gospel." The idea of a kingdom of God would have been familiar to those steeped in the apocalyptic hope of the age. Many sought God's intervention in the world and the restoration of Israel's glory. But Jesus' preaching concerning the kingdom presented a paradox. At times he spoke of the kingdom of God as already present. Through his own ministry, he declared, the relationship between God and the world had been altered. God had become closer. The Gospel writers make this point by recording Jesus' name for God: "Abba," or "Father." The use of the word *Father* to describe God was not unique to Jesus—it is found in some of the Jewish literature of the time—yet the standard Jewish term for God was not *Father* but *Lord*. For Jesus the term *Father* suggested a new and closer parental relationship between God and the faithful.

Yet at other times Jesus speaks of the kingdom as coming in the future. In the prayer he taught his followers, known as the "Our Father" or the Lord's Prayer, he stated, "Thy Kingdom come." It is imminent, and the faithful need to prepare for it, because no one knows when it will actually come. The paradox is reflected in the differing ways in which the parables speak of the kingdom. Some parables urged watchfulness: if you are asleep at the time, you will miss the opportunity. Other parables speak of the present existence of the kingdom and of its being like leaven or yeast—tiny yet transforming— or like a mustard seed that over time will become the greatest of trees. Later, scholars would speak of this paradox as "realized/realizing eschatology" or the belief that the kingdom is both present and future. The tension between present and future would become an important part of the dynamics of later Christianity.

The kingdom entailed a radical ethic. The new relationship between God and humanity demanded a distinctive relationship among people. This ethic is most powerfully set forth in the Gospel of Matthew, in a series of sayings known as the Sermon on the Mount. Although the structure of the sermon may be later, the sentiment reflects the vision of Jesus. The world has been turned upside down: the meek are blessed, and not the powerful; the poor are blessed, but not the rich; and blessed are those who are persecuted for righteousness' sake. Jesus emphasizes the internal spirit of a person over form and show, and he teaches the connectedness of humanity. Old divisions are overturned, and he calls for a wider fellowship. Nor did Jesus merely teach these things. The Gospel writers record Jesus in his ministry overcoming and transcending traditional social barriers, and thus incurring the wrath of those who kept the laws of purity. A regular charge made by his opponents was that he associated with "sinners and tax collectors" and all manner of social and religious outcasts.

A second focus of Jesus' ministry was his healings. At first glance some modern readers might assume that all such stories are to be dismissed as legend or accretion, but his contemporaries, even his enemies, all acknowledged that he—like many others—healed. Spiritual healing was something that was expected in the ancient world, as it is still in large parts of the world today. What made the healing stories recorded about Jesus different was that they seemed not to be mere wonders but were linked to the new relationship between God and the world. Matthew records a visit to Jesus from the disciples of John the Baptist in which they pointedly asked him if he were the one sent from God. And Jesus replied, "The blind receive their sight, and the lame walk, lepers are cleansed and the deaf hear, and the dead are raised up, and the poor have the good news preached to them." To be able to heal and cast out demons was a sign of divine authority in the ancient world. The world was viewed as a spiritual battleground, and the holy man showed his power by being able to overcome the demonic powers that sapped mind and spirit. The Gospels, however, record a second type of miracle in which Jesus showed authority over the physical world as well. He fed large crowds with but a few fish and loaves, he stilled storms, and he cursed a fig tree such that it withered and died. These nature miracles would prove to be a problem for many by the nineteenth century.

> In some accounts, more words are spent describing Jesus' last week than are used to report his entire earlier ministry.

The teaching and healings led people to ask who this Jesus was. The question appears again and again in the Gospel stories. Was he a prophet? Was he the coming again of John the Baptist (who had been executed)? Finally, could he be the messiah? The Gospels record Jesus asking his disciples who they thought he was. One of them, Simon Bar Jonah, later known as Peter, announced that he believed that Jesus was the messiah, or Christ. Peter's confession would be an important event in the later Christian story. Jesus then gave him a new name, Peter, or "the rock," and said that upon that rock the church would be built. But it is important that even here the Gospel writers record the confusion of the disciples. The messiah was supposed to bring triumph, but Jesus instead talked of suffering and death. There seemed to be a conflict between the belief that Jesus was the messiah, and his warning that he would soon be put to death.

Of all the parts of Jesus' life, we know most about his death. All the accounts—Christian, Jewish, and Roman—agree that he was executed by crucifixion, that is, nailed to a cross. The death of a peasant preacher such as Jesus was not extraordinary. The Pax Romana rested on crushing all threats to order, and in an unstable province such as Judea, anyone who went around publicly challenging the social order was a prime candidate for elimination. The task of governors such as Pontius Pilate was precisely to keep the peace. Nor did Jesus' treatment of the Temple and the purity laws endear him to the Pharisees and Sadducees. He had many enemies.

But the Gospel writers take great pains to rehearse the events of the last week of his life, later known as the passion. In some accounts, more words are spent describing this last week than are used to report his entire earlier ministry. The Gospels carefully record Jesus' triumphal entrance into Jerusalem before an adoring crowd, which laid palms before him. They write of his intensifying conflicts with the Jewish authorities and of his overturning a table in the Temple where money was changed. They speak of how one of his closest followers, Judas Iscariot, decided to betray him. But more important for the later story of Christianity, they tell of his meeting with his disciples in an upper room, perhaps to celebrate the Jewish Passover meal, and there taking bread and announcing that it was his body, and the cup of wine, his blood. When this event was first recorded, the author (the apostle Paul) added to Jesus' words the phrase "Do this in remembrance of me." The memorial of bread and wine—the Lord's Supper or Eucharist—would become one of the most important rituals for the Christian community, and Jesus' words "This is my body" one of the most debated passages in the Christian Bible. What did he mean, and how literally was the claim to be interpreted? The later Christian community, particularly in the sixteenth and seventeenth centuries, would have bloody wars over the meaning of this meal of bread and wine. Much ink and even more blood would be poured out fighting over these words.

After the meal Jesus retired to a garden to pray, and there he was arrested. His trial has been a source of controversy. His death was at the hands of the Roman authorities, but Jewish leaders, according to all the Gospel writers, had a role. This assertion would be reexamined at length in the twentieth century, since the claim of Jewish culpability would long poison Jewish-Christian relations. At the time of his arrest his male disciples scattered, abandoning him. Simon Peter, who had earlier confessed him to be the Christ, denied ever having known him. But at the cross, faithful women stood by him. In particular two Marys—the mother of Jesus and Mary Magdalene—are mentioned by the writers. The radical nature of Jesus' teaching also included a new role for women, and both Marys and other women are mentioned in a number of places in the Gospels. Indeed, in all of the Gospel accounts, Mary Magdalene is the first person either to see the risen Jesus or to hear of his resurrection. After his death the body is laid in a tomb and sealed.

The Interpretations of Faith

All of the above can be attested by historians to be at least probably true. That Jesus lived, had a ministry, and died on a cross is almost certain. What comes next is where the world of history gives way to the world of faith. All scholars can agree that the death on the cross was not the end of the story, that something happened that turned defeat and desolation into victory and confidence.

The message began to be proclaimed that Jesus' life had not ended in death but that he had been raised from the dead, and that this event was not just an isolated incident but the consummation of Jesus' ministry. The resurrection was the final sign that a new relationship existed now between God and humanity. This was the *euangelion*, the good news, or as the word became known in English, the gospel. History can tell only so much, and the life and death of Jesus became quickly shaped by the faith of the community striving further to answer the question, who is this man?

Mark, the earliest Gospel, spends no time on the early life of Jesus, but Matthew and Luke tell a little. Both tell of his lineage and birth. But their accounts of Jesus' ancestry differ, and their differences reflect different answers to the question "Who is this man?" Matthew carefully traces the family line of Jesus from the patriarch Abraham down

> What was the relationship between Jesus and the God he called Father? Why did Jesus have to die? What was next?

through Joseph. For Matthew, Jesus was the culmination of God's promise to Israel. He was the descendant of Abraham, father of the Jewish nation. When Matthew has Jesus offering the Sermon on the Mount, he is likened to Moses, giving now a higher law and a new set of commandments. His birth is predicted by the stars in the heavens, and magi from the east seek him to offer him gifts—events that suggest he is a true messiah. Luke, in contrast, follows the lineage from Jesus back to Adam. Jesus, for Luke, was the new Adam, offering a new beginning. He records Mary saying, "God has put down the mighty from their seat and has exalted the humble and meek." The old world has passed; humble shepherds and not magi attend his birth. Women play an important part in Luke's narrative, and Gentiles as well as Jews flock to hear the message of Jesus.

These two Gospels add one more important dimension to the question of who this man is. Both speak of his birth as being extraordinary. Although differing in details, both claim that Jesus was not conceived through the natural conjugal actions of Mary and Joseph but rather through the direct action of God, "by the power of the holy spirit." His birth of the Virgin Mary was a miracle, still another sign that God was connected to this Jesus in a new way.

But three overarching questions emerged from the life, ministry, death, and resurrection of this Jesus. What was the relationship between Jesus and the God he called Father? Why did Jesus have to die, and what was the point of his death? Finally, what was next? The accounts speak of the resurrected Jesus being with his followers for a time (traditionally forty days), after which he departed from them and ascended into heaven. But there was a belief that he would return.

Although these questions were addressed in all the Gospels, it is in the Gospel of John, the Fourth Gospel, that we find some of the most thoughtful discussion. John was the last of the Gospels to be written, and in it one sees an important early reflection on who this Jesus was.

From early on the Christian community sensed that Jesus' relationship to God seemed not to fit into traditional categories. The Jewish world knew of prophets; there had been many in recorded history. Some thought that John the Baptist was a prophet. Prophets were called. A classic example is found in Ezekiel: "On the fifth day of the month (it was the fifth year of the exile of King Jehoiachin) the word of the Lord came down to Ezekiel the priest . . . in the land of the Chaldeans by the river Chabar, and the hand of the Lord was upon him there." One could see something of such a call in the stories about Jesus. Each of the first three Gospels (called the Synoptics because they share a common format and many of the same sayings and events) tells of Jesus' baptism at the hand of John the Baptist. They record that at the time the Spirit of the Lord descended upon Jesus, and a voice from heaven announced, "You are my Son, the beloved, with you I am well pleased." Was Jesus' relationship with God like that of a prophet, and was the baptism his prophetic call? The earliest Christians were unsatisfied with such an explanation. Matthew and Luke, one recalls, spoke of a miraculous birth, or that Jesus had been conceived through the power of the Holy Spirit. The special relationship between Jesus and God did not begin at his baptism but at his conception.

John pushed things back even further. In the famous prologue to his Gospel, John speaks of the heavenly preexistence of Jesus: "In the beginning was the Word, and the Word was with God, and the Word was God." This Word (or *Logos* in Greek) was present at creation and was part of the eternal order. It was God in action. John continued, "and the Word became flesh and dwelt among us." In Jesus, the eternal word took on human form. The term that would later be used is *incarnation*, God becoming human.

Likewise there was the problem of Christ's death. What was the connection between the message Jesus preached about the kingdom and his death? Here, too, John offered an interpretation. Near the end of his account of Jesus' public ministry, John (alone) records Jesus saying, "The hour has come for the Son of man to be glorified. Truly, truly I say to you, unless a grain of sand falls into the earth and dies it remains alone; but if it dies it bears much fruit." In the death of Jesus there is the beginning of new life. Speaking of his death Jesus noted, "And I, when I am lifted up from the earth, will draw men to myself." Christ's death on the cross was an act not of shame but of glory. All the Gospel writers include words that Jesus was said to have uttered while on the cross. The first two Gospels record Jesus uttering the lament found in Psalm 22, "My God, my God, why have you forsaken me?" further emphasizing the point by including the orig   sion, Jesus is heard saying f   :riumphant "It is finished!"   stinguishing aspects of later   mbol the instrument of its fo   insformed.

But h   'ould give to Christianity a   great religions: the intercon   ther religions, both ancient   :auty and equanimity. The   king then, and even in the tv   ng out of traditions such as   ontemporary Asian artist re   conography, but as a Christi   is the hardest spiritual con   inking of suffering and divi   later history of the Christia.. ....o... ......g. ... ..., ... o. oeauty, and much of the greatest art would focus on the suffering of Jesus.

[Handwritten marginal notes overlaying text:]
- ☑ Sexual orientation
- ☐ AF and Martyrdom
- ☐ Apologists
- ☐ Early XP Conflicts
- ☐ Jesus
- ☐ Judaism
- ☐ Scripture
- ☐ Further Refinement

Finally there was the question of the future. A good deal of Jesus' teaching was that the kingdom of God was to come in the future, and his followers came to believe he would soon return to finish establishing the kingdom. In some Gospels he is recorded as saying that some of those present would not taste death before he returned. But what was to happen until then? Here as well the Fourth Gospel offers an answer. John's account of Jesus' time with his disciples on the evening before his death includes several long discourses. Jesus speaks of his imminent departure but tells his disciples that they should not be afraid because they will not be alone: "The Advocate, the Holy Spirit whom the Father will send in my name, will teach you everything, and remind you of all that I have said to you." Teaching and remembrance were part of this divine power.

The Gospels are not histories. Rather, they are proclamations by the early community of exactly who this Jesus was. He was the one who had come from God to announce a new order of things. He had preached and done miracles. He had suffered, died, and was buried. He had somehow defeated death and established a new relationship between God and the world. There were many more things to be said; there were many more questions to be asked. But it had begun.

Chapter 2

Going Out into the World

To profess that Jesus of Nazareth had been raised from the dead and was the Messiah promised of God was still to leave many things to be clarified. What exactly was this new religious movement? Was it a reform movement within a multifaceted Jewish world, or was it something else? What should its relationship be with the Jewish community, and what attitude should it take to the Gentile, or non-Jewish, world? What organization should be adopted to give the community structure? All of these questions faced the first two generations of Christians.

One possible model for this new religion can be seen in the ancient church of Jerusalem. Jerusalem was where the Messiah had revealed himself, and it would be to Jerusalem that he would return. So the Jerusalem church watched. But it watched as a remnant of Israel. They should still attend the Temple, and Solomon's Porch was their favorite meeting place. They also should be zealous for the law. The Sabbath was to be kept in a traditional Jewish way. Did not the remembered words of Jesus say as much? It was recorded that Jesus, after predicting the persecution his followers would experience, added, "Pray that your flight may not be in winter or on the Sabbath"; the former because it would make it more difficult and the latter because it would entail violating the laws against travel on the Sabbath. A famous head of the Jerusalem church was the apostle James, the half-brother of Jesus. Like ancient Nazirites, a body of Israelites dedicated to the service of God, he did not drink wine, eat meat, or bathe. So constant was he at prayer that his knees became like those of a camel, it was said. He followed not only the traditional forms of devotion but also the models of leadership. He was often referred to as a bishop, but some ancient sources speak of him as the high priest of the Christian community of Jerusalem. And as with the office of high priest, succession was according to bloodline. James's authority rested on his familial connection with Jesus, and his successor, in turn, was also related through blood.

The Jerusalem church was an extreme example, and few if any followed it in detail, but the question of the relationship between the religion of Jesus and Judaism concerned many. It is one of the overarching themes in the Acts of the Apostles, the biblical account of the growth of the church in the generation after Jesus' ministry. Starting with the apostles huddled in an upper room in Jerusalem and ending with the Christian gospel being preached in Rome itself, it is a self-conscious portrayal of the mighty acts of God. It must be used with caution as a historical text, but it does highlight both the centrality of the "church/synagogue" question in the first generations and the crucial role of one individual, Paul of Tarsus, in giving further shape to the Christian faith.

The original disciples were all devout Jews, and as devout Jews they kept the law of Moses. But from very early on the message of Jesus began to attract people with different attitudes toward the law. Often these were Greek-speaking Jews who were deeply involved in Hellenistic culture. Acts records that the Hellenists who lived in Jerusalem did not believe that their needs were being met by the ruling apostles. Out of this concern the office of the deacon arose. These Jewish Hellenists were the most active in preaching the message of Jesus to the Gentiles, and their mission proved successful. Out of this mission arose the question of the law in general and the practice of circumcision in particular. Did Gentile converts have to be circumcised and become Jews first in order to become Christians? Acts records a meeting of the apostles in Jerusalem (dated around 50 CE by some historians). There it was decided that circumcision was not necessary but that a minimal keeping of the dietary laws was to be enforced. The "Apostolic Council," as it came to be called, would be of decided importance in the later life of Christianity. The belief developed that when the community became divided over a question, a council should be called, and through such a council the Spirit would guide the church. All later ecumenical councils would see themselves as echoing the practice of the first apostles.

The Apostle Paul

The rise of Gentile Christianity is intimately connected with the life, ministry, and writings of Paul of Tarsus. Paul would be central to the development of Christianity. He was the author of the earliest Christian writings we have. He was a great missionary. Finally, he offered profound reflections on the meaning of the death and resurrection of Jesus. His unique theology would do much to facilitate the separation of the church and the synagogue.

According to the author of Acts (usually attributed to the evangelist Luke), Paul was born Saul and was educated as a Pharisee. He further claimed to be a Roman citizen, thus having feet in the worlds of Judaism and Hellenism. He was at first a great opponent of the early Christian movement, yet while traveling to Damascus he had an overwhelming experience. According to one account, a voice from heaven spoke, "Saul, Saul, why do you persecute me?" and when asked who this voice was, replied, "I am Jesus whom you are persecuting." The experience struck Paul with temporary blindness and left him with the lasting conviction that he, too, was now an "apostle," or one called and sent out by Jesus. The other apostles had received their call from the earthly Jesus; Paul's was from the heavenly Jesus. But Paul's call, he would always insist, was just as authoritative.

Paul spent the rest of his life both preaching the message of Jesus to the Gentile world and defending the rights of Gentile Christians. His relationship to the Jewish community was complicated. He still saw himself as a member, yet for him the old dividing line of circumcision, the ritual that had long firmly separated the Jewish and Gentile worlds, had been replaced by the new dividing line of Christ. In Christ there was a new unity for humanity. Baptism took the place of circumcision and united persons in Christ. As he famously put it, "As many of you as were baptized into Christ have clothed yourselves with Christ. There is no longer Jew or Greek, there is no longer slave or free, there is no longer male or female, for all of you are one in Christ Jesus."

At first his ministry was centered in Antioch, where he labored to bring Gentiles into the fold. It is clear from his writings that his view of the law was more liberal than that reflected in the Council of Jerusalem, and in Antioch, Jews and Gentiles may have eaten together without the latter following any dietary restrictions. Paul's views created a scandal, and more conservative people from the church in Jerusalem (including Simon Peter) challenged the practice. The conflict in Antioch led Paul to undertake a traveling ministry to the cities of western Asia and eastern Greece. It was during this period that he penned his "epistles," or letters, which later became part of the Christian New Testament.

Paul's writings are distinctive. They have very little to say about the teachings of Jesus—indeed one can count on one hand the times that Paul quotes the words of the earthly Jesus. It is both as the supernatural Christ and the suffering savior that Paul presents him. The famous hymn in Philippians reflects Paul's teaching: Christ is the preexistent one who humbles himself by taking on humanity, suffers, and is finally exalted to such a degree that every knee must bow.

Paul also speaks forcefully about the accomplishment of Christ and the meaning of his death. One motif he employs is that of Christ as the second

Adam. As he explained, sin entered the world through the disobedience of Adam and enslaved both Jews and Gentiles. The law (whether the law of conscience or the law of Moses) showed a fallen humanity its own sinfulness. For ages, devout souls had tried to free themselves of this burden. The sacrifices in the Temple were an attempt to wash away this sin. All of these attempts had been to no avail. But Christ, in his obedience, overcame Adam's disobedience, and his death brought about a cleansing or expiation of human sinfulness that is now offered as a gift to be received by faith. As Paul wrote in his letter to the Romans, sinful humanity is "justified by grace as a gift, through the redemption that is in Christ Jesus, whom God put forward as an expiation by his blood to be received by faith." Furthermore the crucified Messiah has inaugurated the eschatological age in which the division between Jews and Gentiles has been overturned. The key to all is faith in Christ.

As scholars rightfully note, Paul was writing within the world of Judaism—albeit a Judaism that had been transformed through the work of Christ. Later on in that same epistle he would write of the continuing role of Israel in God's plan for the world. But Paul widened the gap between the infant Christian community and the synagogue by boldly reinterpreting the story of Israel. As all pious Jews believed, God began a new era in his relationship with the world with the special covenant he made with Abraham. The covenant set the children of Abraham apart by making them chosen, and the seal of the covenant was the rite of circumcision. For Paul, God did make a promise to Abraham, but the traditional interpretation misunderstood it. The promise was based not on what Abraham did but on his faith: "Abraham believed God and it was reckoned to him as righteousness." The covenant was one of faith, so it was not tied to circumcision or to Abraham's lineal descendants but was available to all who believe, or "to those who share the faith of Abraham, for he is the father of all of us, as it is written, 'I have made you the father of many nations.'" Reinterpreting the sacred history of Israel in light of the eschatological revelation in Christ, Paul, in effect, "invents" the Old Testament. What is meant here is not that the Abrahamic story originated with Paul. Indeed, for a millennium it had been a cherished part of the Hebrew Scriptures. But to claim that it can be interpreted rightly only through the lens of the work of Jesus is to make it the *Old* Testament, a writing that is properly understood only when read from the perspective of the new Christian revelation. Countless other Christian exegetes would follow

> Paul widened the gap between the infant Christian community and the synagogue by boldly reinterpreting the story of Israel.

Paul's path and offer their own Christian interpretation of the books of the Hebrew Scriptures. From the time of Paul, Jews and Christians would begin to be two religious communities divided by a common text read in very different ways.

It would be Paul's theology of Jesus and not that of James that would largely triumph in the subsequent history of Christianity. The famous *bon mot*, that all Christian theology is merely a footnote to Paul, may be an overstatement (and in any case is truer in Latin Christianity than in other branches) but is largely true. The success of Paul and his theology can be traced to two factors. One is that by the end of the first century Christianity was on the way to becoming a religion of Gentiles rather than of Jews. As we will see, many in the Roman world would be attracted to the Christian life. For them, the connection of Christianity to Judaism had little interest. A second factor is that, through a series of political events, Judaism itself radically changed. The opposition to Roman rule would boil over into two revolts. The first (68–74 CE) resulted in the fall of Jerusalem and the destruction of the Temple. A second revolt in 132 CE was also crushed. The destruction of the Temple profoundly affected Judaism; indeed, some have claimed that it led to the rise of modern Judaism. Without a temple there could be no Sadducees, and they disappear. From out of the old Pharisaic party emerged what is known as rabbinic Judaism. And the focus of the movement came to be the law, now understood as found in Torah (including the Prophets and the Writings) and the Talmud (which contained the "oral law" given by Moses on Sinai and rabbinic commentary). The multifaceted Judaism that existed at the time of Jesus came to be replaced by a more strictly defined Judaism that was less sympathetic with Jewish Christianity. Increasingly by century's end, Jews and Christians found themselves more in conflict than in dialogue. Many have suggested that the negative picture of the Jews found in the Gospels was more reflective of this latter development than of Jewish attitudes at the time of Jesus or for the first generation of his followers.

How Shall We Live?

The questions confronting the young community were not merely lofty theological considerations but very practical ones as well. What rules should the believers follow? If Jesus might return at any moment, was it right to be involved in "the world"? Many of the sayings of Jesus seemed to suggest not. He had counseled, "Lay not up for yourselves treasures on earth," and he had also said, "Do not worry about your life, what you will eat." One option might be to retire from the world and wait for the final days. Was that the duty of the Christian? Others saw in the belief that in Christ there was a new creation a ground for believing that the old laws constraining human activities had been superseded by a new freedom. If faith justified the Christian, then faith alone, and not actions, was all that mattered.

The community, as a whole, chose to follow neither of these options. What appeared instead was an ethic for the interim between Christ's resurrection and his return. Here, too, Paul made crucial contributions. Nowhere can this be more clearly seen being worked out than in Paul's letter to the church in Corinth. The Corinthian epistle, as the English Catholic writer Ronald Knox once observed, is proof that there never was a golden age for the church. The Corinthian community was divided in all sorts of ways. There were tensions over wealth. There were divisions over how much Christians should participate in the social life of the time. There were questions over eating meat that had been sacrificed to idols—which in the Mediterranean world meant almost all meat. Finally, there was the question of to what degree Christians were obliged to keep the moral law. Baptism was understood as a new birth, a dying to one's old self and a commencement of the new. To emphasize the rebirthing, candidates were disrobed completely and baptized naked. This powerful ritual, coupled with the idea of Christ as the second Adam, carried the believer back to the original garden, where Adam and Eve walked naked and unashamed in a world without sin. Was this the true Christian calling?

> The Christian life, like the kingdom of God, was both realized and yet to be realized. Baptism did indeed offer a new life, but it was only the beginning.

In responding, Paul linked three ideas that for him lay at the core of the rightly ordered Christian life. The first was that the Christian life, like the kingdom of God, was both realized and yet to be realized. Baptism did indeed offer a new life, but it was only the beginning. "I could not speak to you as spiritual people, but as people of the flesh, as infants in Christ." As "infants," Christians were to follow all sorts of rules. It might indeed be true that in Christ there was no male or female, but at the present, distinctions still had to be made. Another metaphor he employed was that of the athlete. For a Gentile community, the gymnasium, as we saw in chapter 1, would have been a familiar institution, and sports an important social ritual. They would have known that an athlete needed to exercise discipline in order to triumph. But discipline was also the responsibility of the Christian: "Athletes exercise self-control in all things. They do it to receive a perishable wreath, but we an imperishable one."

The second idea was that the Christian community was a sacred body. The divisions in the Corinthian church, marked by lawsuits and disagreements over the Lord's Supper, indicated that they did not understand this. They believed that if they satisfied themselves, it was sufficient. The reason to abstain from meat sacrificed to idols, Paul explained, was not that it would pollute the eater—for the pagan gods did not exist—but because it could offend a weaker member of the community. Social responsibility was paramount. Here, too, Paul was not merely speaking of ceremonial issues but also of social issues. It was the wealthy who could afford to participate in the banquets where such meat was consumed. The image of the body of Christ was connected with Paul's understanding of the variety of gifts that individuals possessed. God had appointed apostles, prophets, teachers, and others to guide the community. Each possessed different gifts, but all gifts were for the upkeep of the community.

Finally, for Paul the heart of the Christian life was love. It was by love that persons knew God; it was by love that they served God; and it was by love that the community was held together. The Pauline language of love was a revolution in the ancient world. According to classical thought, one could know God only through the mind, and in order for this to happen, the mind had to be carefully purged of all material things. But for Paul it was love that was essential for knowing God, and one knew God through the face of Christ. God's love sent Jesus into the world, and Christ's love allowed him to endure the agony of the cross. The Christian community's love held the body together. Paul's famous hymn to love, found in the thirteenth chapter of 1 Corinthians, has become trivialized by overuse, but it is a powerful statement. In the Christian life, we are at the beginning; we only dimly see in a mirror the true reality that lies ahead. But love is the guide.

The Pauline ethic would be revolutionary for one further reason. It combined two aspects of life that in the ancient world (except for Judaism) were kept separate—religion and morality. Religion in the ancient world simply concerned humanity's relationship with the gods. Rituals were observed and sacrifices were made so that the gods would be pleased and the world would continue. Religion did not instruct people about how they were to live their lives or what constituted the good. Such instruction was the task of philosophers, who were concerned with the question of how we should live. But in the notion of love one finds ethical and moral being tied to the very core of religion. Both were shaped by love. At the center of the universe were not gods who needed to be placated but a God who cared for humanity and called for love in return, including a love for humanity. The early Christian community called its members by strange names: they were "brothers" and "sisters." The Christian community created literally a new family, and the law of love guided it.

Organizing a Community

One Roman observer described Christian practice in these words: "It was their habit on the first day to assemble before daylight, and to recite by turn a form of words to Christ as a god. . . . After this was done, their custom was to depart, and to meet again to take food." The two practices of meeting on the first day of the week and sharing a common meal marked the early Christian community. Together with the practice of baptism, these were the three seminal expressions of early Christian worship.

Worship on the first day of the week (Sunday in English-speaking lands) marked the early Christian community. Christians believed that Christ had risen from the dead on the first day, so each first day was a commemoration of that event. Even Christians who continued to observe the Sabbath as a day of rest worshiped on the first day.

Baptism, as we have seen, was viewed as the new circumcision. In both theory and practice it possessed powerful symbolism. It was a rite of initiation, washing, and regeneration. Through baptism believers entered the church, had their sins washed away, and were reborn in Christ. The practice of fully immersing candidates highlighted the connectedness with burial and new birth. Its waters separated believers from the dirt and contamination of the outside world and offered a cleansing.

The practice of baptism would become more elaborate in the postapostolic era. Its solemnity would be highlighted by elaborate preparation, both through instruction and fasting. Its link to resurrection would be strengthened by baptisms being done on Easter. Then there would be a formal renunciation of the devil and all his works and an anointing with oil.

The solemnity of baptism created a problem for the early community. Believers were required not only to renounce sin prior to being baptized but also to pledge themselves to remain pure. The issue of sin after baptism became a serious difficulty. In a later New Testament writing it was stated, "How much worse punishment do you think will be deserved by those who have spurned the Son of God, profaned the blood of the covenant by which they were sanctified, and outraged the Spirit of grace?" A grievous postbaptismal sin such as murder or apostasy could result in separation of an individual from the community. The bonds of holiness had to be maintained.

Finally, there was the common meal. The earliest recorded words of Jesus are found in Paul's Letter to the Corinthians, and they involve the institution of the Lord's Supper. Indeed, the very way in which Paul presents these words reflects the importance of the action for the early community: "For I received from the Lord what I also handed on to you." The community believed that the common meal was instituted by Jesus himself on the night of his betrayal and that it was no ordinary meal. The bread and wine had a special meaning. As Paul explained, "As often as you eat this bread and drink the cup, you proclaim the Lord's death till he comes."

This breaking of bread, to be known in the next generation as the Eucharist, or thanksgiving, brought the community closer to Jesus in two ways. The breaking of bread was to be done "in remembrance." The Greek term *anamnesis* suggested that it was no mere intellectual process but one that was actually meant to bring back into contact or to re-present (that is, to make present once again). Each time bread was broken, the community was connected with Christ and the first breaking of bread. The remembrance linked them to Christ at the Last Supper and made real his sacrifice. But the meal not only looked backward to connect the community to the past but also looked forward to Christ's second coming. This concept later became known as prolepsis, or a foretaste of the glory to come. As the great ritual that linked people to both Christ's passion and his return, it was not to be taken lightly. Believers were warned that those who partook of the bread and wine "in an unworthy manner" were in great danger of divine judgment.

Just as with baptism, the understanding and practice of the Eucharist developed in the decades after the death of the apostles. It became separated from the common meal and became seen as a rite in and of itself. As such it began to be celebrated in the morning of the first day, linking it more closely to the resurrection and distancing itself from the Jewish Passover meal (which was observed in the evening). Likewise, there were changes in the prayers said over the bread and wine. The Eucharist was not only the means of anamnesis but also a means of thanksgiving for God's acts of creation and redemption, and this began to shape the nature of the prayer. There was also a continued emphasis on the special nature of the bread and wine. As one second-century writer explained, "For not as common bread and common drink do we receive these, but in like manner as Jesus Christ our Savior having been made flesh by the word of God, had both flesh and blood for our salvation, so likewise have we been taught that the food that is blessed by the word of prayer . . . is the flesh and blood of that Jesus who was made flesh." The writer, Justin Martyr, was one of the earliest Christian thinkers to attempt to answer the question of how the "food . . . blessed by word and prayer," bread and wine, were the body and blood of Christ. He would not be the last.

Justin also spoke of a "president" or one who presided over the celebration of the Eucharist. The question of order and leadership was still another question confronting the early community.

During the first century the primary meeting places of the Christian communities were private homes. Public architecture would not emerge as the norm, as we shall see, until the conversion of Constantine in the fourth century. These "house churches" were the homes of prominent men and women, where the larger household of extended family, domestic slaves, and others gathered. The owner of the house acted as host or patron and as such exercised authority. The house churches were the centers not only of worship but also of hospitality. These patrons are regularly mentioned by Paul in his letters and included women as well as men. Paul was quick to recognize the work of pious women. In Corinth, Chloe and Phoebe were noted as major patrons, and in Rome the apostle mentions Aquila and Prisca.

But how was the church to be governed? As we have seen, after the resurrection the apostles stepped into the role of leadership. They had been with Jesus and had witnessed his resurrection. It was they (according to Acts) who adjudicated the question of the law and Gentile Christianity. Furthermore, according to tradition they scattered around the known world and established churches. John was linked to Asia, Peter eventually to Rome, and Thomas to Parthia (and in some traditions India). As founders of churches, the apostles exercised authority as well. Recall that Paul also claimed to be an apostle (and to have apostolic authority) because he, too, had experienced the resurrected Christ. In a famous passage he argues that his experience put him on equal footing with the other apostles: "He [Jesus] appeared to Cephas [Peter], then to the twelve. Then he appeared to over five hundred brothers and sisters at the time. . . . Then he appeared to James, then to all the apostles. Last of all, as to one untimely born, he appeared also to me." Paul asserted that he was on the same plane as Peter, James, John, and the others. Yet his list had a significant omission. Mary Magdalene was not included. Although according to two of the Gospels (Matthew and John) Mary witnessed the resurrected Jesus before any of the male apostles, she is excluded. Contact with the risen Christ was a badge of spiritual authority, and this authority was denied to Mary by Paul. Willing to praise a woman like Chloe for her generosity to the church, Paul was less forthcoming when it came to giving women authority.

Along with apostles there were deacons, who dealt with the social needs of the community. Furthermore, they distributed the Eucharist and assisted in baptism. At the end of his Epistle to the Romans, Paul thanks Phoebe for being not only a benefactor but also a "deacon." It is unclear whether he meant the term technically or rather in the more general sense of being a servant, but from other sources it is clear that female deacons (or deaconesses) did have the liturgical function of preparing female candidates for baptism.

By the end of the first century and with the death of the first generation, there was a gradual shift in the pattern of ministry. The author of the Letter to Timothy talks about a new office, that of "bishop," or literally, overseer. A bishop, it is declared, must be a person of steady character and without moral stain. But the office itself is largely undefined, and the difference between the bishop and the deacon is not elaborated. As we will see in the next chapter, by the early second century the office of bishop had become much more clarified, and scholars speak of monepiscopacy, in which the bishop is understood to be the sole leader of a local church. The development of the office of the bishop was a key part of the emerging "orthodox" tradition in Christianity.

An Alternative Understanding

Yet other paths were possible. One could follow Jesus and not follow the way of Paul and the bishops. Sayings of Jesus that had not been kept in the churches founded by John, Peter, and Paul were nonetheless remembered in other churches and later were collected as the *Gospel of Thomas*. The book was deemed heretical by the leaders of the early church and would find no place in the formal canon of the New Testament as it would develop, but many modern scholars now see in it an alternative view of Jesus and the Christian life.

The Jesus of the *Gospel of Thomas* was no preacher of an apocalyptic kingdom nor a doer of miracles but was more of a moral sage or speaker of wisdom. In *Thomas* there is no cross and passion, no reference to the Jewish Scriptures; instead there are sayings. Some of the wisdom was of an everyday kind. "Love your brother like your soul, protect that person like the pupil of your eye," devotees are advised. Other sayings parallel passages found in the four traditional Gospels. But the overarching theme is that a new wisdom is being revealed. These were "hidden sayings," and "whoever discovers the interpretation of these sayings will not taste death."

The Gospel of Thomas is also different in its idea of the Christian life. While this Jesus does teach a kingdom, this kingdom is within. (If it were in the heavens, *Thomas* explains, the birds would get there first.) *Thomas*'s Jesus teaches his followers the importance of the light of wisdom but states that they already possess the light: "If they say to you, 'Where have you come from?' say to them 'We have come from the light, from the place of light, from the place where the light came into being by itself.'" Furthermore, the communion between Jesus and his followers is direct and immediate. Rather than any sacramental allusions about feeding on his body and blood under the form of bread and wine, Jesus offers a more immediate image: "Whoever drinks from my mouth will become like me; I myself shall become that person, and the hidden things will be revealed to that person." To receive his wisdom is to truly commune with Jesus.

Still another striking contrast is in the way the disciples are depicted. In the traditional Gospels they are the pillars of the church and speak with authority. It was carefully recorded in these Gospels that it was Simon Peter, who when asked who did he think Jesus was, first called Jesus the Christ and in response received a new name. In *Thomas*, in contrast, the disciples do not speak authoritatively but witness to the mystery of Jesus. Here, when Jesus asks them who do they think he is, the disciple Thomas responds, "Teacher, my mouth is utterly unable to say what you are like."

The emphasis on knowledge and wisdom and the intimate connectedness between Jesus and his followers had very practical ramifications. The main tradition of Christianity was moving (and would continue to move) toward the belief that the message of Jesus had to be received by faith. Its elevation of the sacraments of Baptism and Eucharist emphasized that Christ was communicated through physical things, increasingly ministered by the church. *Thomas* offered an alternative vision of wisdom and spiritual communion that is immediate. The apostles spoke with authority for the main tradition because they had witnessed the resurrected Christ. *Thomas* has no resurrection, and there are no intermediaries. Jesus speaks directly to all. The *Gospel of Thomas* was apparently lost in antiquity and only rediscovered in 1945, and then only in fragments. Since then it has resonated for some as a genuine Christian alternative, a road not taken in which immediate spirituality and not ecclesiology marks the core of the message. In the ancient world its influence was minimal, and it would play little role in the development of Christian institutions. Thus we can see that through decisions made in the first generations, Christianity had taken on definitive patterns. It was a Gentile religion. Its worship centered on Baptism and Eucharist. A distinctive ethos was emerging that set it apart from other religions. Yet major questions still lay in the future.

Chapter 3

Defending and Defining

The two centuries after 100 CE would be crucial in the development of Christianity. During these years many vexing questions were addressed, and the answer to these questions in turn shaped the life of the community. The story of these developments has usually been cast as the emergence of "catholic Christianity," or the Christianity of most modern Christian groups. The value of the triumph of this model of Christianity has been questioned by many in the twentieth century. The paths rejected, some now claim, were lost opportunities. However one chooses to evaluate the phenomenon, decisions made would shape the mind and face of all subsequent Christianity.

Defending the Faith

According to tradition, John, the last of the original apostles, had died in the 90s, and the Christian community was bereft of the guidance of the first generation. Instead, several writers emerged who attempted to steer the young community through the shoals of competing beliefs. One was Ignatius, bishop of Antioch, whose letters are some of the very early pieces of Christian literature. As bishop of the city, he kept a sharp eye out for teachings that might lead his flock astray.

Ebionites (from the Hebrew word for poor men) were one such source of error. Ebionites continued the tradition of Jewish Christianity, keeping the law and seeing no contradiction between their profession of Jesus as Messiah and a continuing identification with Judaism. But in their profession of Jesus as Messiah, they rejected the virgin birth and claimed that Jesus was the natural son of Mary and Joseph. He was a purely human figure who was chosen by God to be the messiah. God's spirit had descended upon him at his baptism, but Jesus for them was more like a great human prophet than the bearer of divinity.

Docetism proposed a very different picture of Jesus. For Docetists, it was the material humanity of Jesus that was the scandal. The term *Docetist* came from the Greek word meaning "to seem," and Docetists claimed that Christ's humanity was more apparent than real. Like many in the ancient world, they believed that the spiritual was higher than the material. Hence, if Jesus were truly of God, his nature would have been spiritual and not material. As spirit, he could not actually suffer, so the passion as well was merely an appearance.

Ignatius railed against both errors. He warned his flock to exercise caution, "lest you fall prey to stupid ideas, and [I] urge you to be thoroughly convinced of the birth, Passion, and resurrection, which occurred when Pontius Pilate was governor." Against the Ebionites, he declared that Christ was born of a *virgin*. Against the Docetists he declared that Christ was *born* of a virgin. Christ was both fully divine and fully human. This paradox lay at the heart of the faith. It was further the cherished faith that needed to be held by all: "Be deaf, then, to any talk that ignores Jesus Christ, of David's lineage, of Mary; who was really born, ate and drank, and was really persecuted under Pontius Pilate; was really crucified and died, in the sight of heaven and earth and the underworld. He was really raised from the dead, for his Father raised him." Ignatius in many places presented these summaries of the faith as a check to error. If any teacher denied any of these points that teacher should be shunned.

Ignatius used these creedal statements to protect his flock against error. But even more he used the church itself. As we will see in the next chapter, Christians in the Roman Empire were under countless pressures to adopt the practices of their non-Christian neighbors. The church was the bulwark against false teachings and practices, and believers should use it as their guide. The center of the church was the bishop presiding at the Eucharist. Those who separated themselves from this symbol separated themselves from Christ. In Ignatius the office of the bishop had become far more elevated than it had been thirty years earlier when the Pastoral Epistles had been written. The bishop was the icon, or representative, of God. "You should all follow the bishop," he wrote, "as Jesus Christ did the Father. Follow, too, the presbytery as you would the apostles, and respect the deacons as you would God's law. Nobody must do anything that has to do with the Church without the bishop's approval. . . . Where the bishop is present there let the congregation gather, just as where Jesus Christ is, there is the Catholic Church." For Ignatius, Jesus, the Catholic Church, and the bishop had all become united, and the Eucharist was a sign of unity with all three. Believers must be loyal and faithful to all. Only through such discipline could the church be preserved in the world.

Ignatius wrote from Antioch in Syria, in the heart of Asia Minor. A few decades later another bishop, Irenaeus, wrote from the West, from Lyons (in what is now France). The Christian community had spread throughout the Mediterranean world. The issue for Irenaeus was the question of Gnosti-

> Broadly speaking, Gnosticism was concerned about knowledge that could provide release for human suffering.

cism, and Gnosticism continues to perplex historians. It is a phenomenon that appears in such differing guises and in such diverse places that some despair about even defining it. Broadly speaking, Gnosticism (coming from the Greek word *gnosis*, or knowledge) was concerned about knowledge that could provide release for human suffering. According to gnostics, the key to understanding the present physical world was to know that it was not ultimately real. Behind it was a divine being who was wholly spiritual. The physical world was brought about by a separate "Demiurge," or creator god. This creation, however, was a terrible mistake, imprisoning spirit in matter. Human suffering was rooted in this imprisonment of spirit in matter. The only salvation was to escape from the world of the physical, through knowledge and discipline. Gnostics were those who possessed a spark of the divine and a knowledge of the world as it truly is. Such an understanding was not unique to Christianity; it is found in many religions of the world. It entered the world of Christianity in the second century. For Christian gnostics, Christ was the revealer of the sacred knowledge. But much popular Christianity unfortunately was bound to the world of matter and believed Christianity to be concerned about the material world. They took language about Christ's body and his death literally rather than seeing them as symbolic as those gnostics with "true knowledge" did.

Gnostics claimed that theirs was a superior Christianity to that of the multitude. Irenaeus countered by claiming that theirs was not Christianity at all. They had substituted false stories and vain genealogies for the faith. Irenaeus made two further assertions about the inherited faith. The first was that it was catholic; it was found everywhere. The church by the end of the second century was spread throughout the ancient world. The church could be found in Germany, Spain, France, Egypt, and Libya, but everywhere the same faith was proclaimed: "For although the languages of the world are dissimilar yet the import of the [Christian] tradition is one and the same." In some places the teachings were more elaborated than in other places, but it was the same faith. The gnostic teachings were local; the church's faith was universal.

Second, for Irenaeus, the faith was apostolic. It was linked by strong tradition to the apostles themselves. He went on to trace the lineage of the major church centers in the world and stressed their succession in teaching. This succession from the apostles was a second source of certainty: "Since there are so many clear testimonies, we should not seek for others for the truth which can easily be received from the Church. There the apostles, like a rich man making a deposit, fully bestowed upon her all that belongs to the truth, so that whoever wishes may receive from her the waters of life." The present church was linked to the apostles by this connection of witnesses and was a second source of certainty.

Among the writers Irenaeus addressed by name was a man named Marcion, who offered a particular twist to the basic gnostic message. He had arrived in Rome around 140 CE and after at first being a strong supporter of the Christian community there, broke with it and founded a competing community.

Marcion does not quite fit the traditional gnostic pattern. His concern was not cosmic speculation but reinterpreting the Christian story. Marcion argued that there was a fundamental dichotomy between the Old Testament and the message of Jesus, or between the law and the gospel. For Marcion, the God of the Old Testament, with his wrath and vengeance, had nothing to do with the God about whom Jesus preached. The Old Testament preached an eye for an eye; the New Testament, turning the other cheek. True Christians should eschew the God of the Hebrews. He was the Demiurge, creating the material world. Nor could the prophets be trusted. Their predictions about the coming of a messiah had nothing to do with the Christ. In Marcion's eyes they, too, were tied to the law and oblivious to the new message of grace and love.

Marcion used his insight to evaluate the religious texts. He rejected the Old Testament as a foreign book. Of the Gospels then in circulation he looked with favor only at Luke. It was Paul whom Marcion found most appealing. But even in Paul he was quick to eliminate any passages that stood in variance to his basic thesis. Marcion read the Bible, as one ancient writer observed, with a penknife, cutting out all with which he disagreed.

In contrast to Marcion's pruning, Irenaeus presents the Bible, both Old and New Testaments, as a seamless whole, a narrative of creation, fall, and redemption, from the beginning to the end of time, whose chief actor is God. The history of Israel leads to the life of Christ, and the latter is incomplete without the former. As he wrote, "Almighty God [is] maker of heaven and earth and Fashioner of man, who brought about the Deluge, and called Abraham; who brought out the people from the Land of Egypt; who spoke with Moses, who ordained the Law and the Prophets; and who has prepared fire for the devil and his angels." Just as the witness of the church is catholic (that is, the same everywhere), so, too, is the message of the Scriptures. It is the heretic who attempts to divide it by pitting one part against another. He then argued that the four Gospels of Matthew, Mark, Luke, and John were the only authoritative Gospels. There could be neither more nor fewer since together they reflected the four faces of the heavenly cherubim and the four zones of the world.

In stressing the unity of the Scriptures, Irenaeus offered a distinctive understanding of the place of the Virgin Mary. She is seen as the new Eve, whose obedience allows God to enter the world. Mary's obedience overcame Eve's disobedience, "so that the virgin Mary might become the advocate of the virgin Eve."

Defining the Scriptures

Marcion's criticism reminds us that before the middle of the second century there had been no formal attempt to define the content of the Christian Scriptures. Any definition involved two separate questions. Which, if any, of the Jewish Scriptures were deemed authoritative? And which of the Christian writings then in circulation should be considered scriptural?

The first question was complicated by disagreements within the Jewish community itself. At the time of Jesus, Jewish scriptural writings could be found in both Hebrew and Greek. The original writings of most of the books were in Hebrew, but a Greek translation, the Septuagint, was the Bible commonly used by Hellenistic Jews. Yet for some books, composed in Greek by Hellenistic Jews, there was no Hebrew original. These included Maccabees, Tobit, Ecclesiasticus, and a number of other writings. It was not until the destruction of the Temple that Jewish rabbis began the process of closing their canon of Scripture, and their decision was to exclude these late Greek works. They became known as the Apocrypha, or the hidden books. The early Christian community, however, spoke Greek, used the Septuagint, and felt no compunction to go along with the rabbinic decision to exclude these books. Although there was some sense (particularly in the eastern part of the Christian community) that they were not on the level of the other scriptural writings, they nonetheless became included in the Christian Old Testament. As we shall see, at the time of the Reformation, Protestants would follow the lead of the rabbis and reject these books. Although Christian writings circulated within the community from a very early period, there is no evidence of their being treated as Scripture until the middle of the second century. At that time Justin Martyr spoke of the Gospels as Scripture. Irenaeus, we have seen, took up this theme in his answer to Marcion. He is also the first Christian writer to refer to the Hebrew Scriptures as the "Old Testament."

But what books belonged in the Christian New Testament, and what criteria should be used in making this determination? In about 180 CE (at almost the same time Irenaeus was defending the four Gospels against Marcion, who wanted to acknowledge Luke alone) there appeared the first listing of the books of the New Testament that bears a similarity with the present Christian canon. The Muratorian canon (as the list came to be known) listed the four Gospels, the Acts of the Apostles, the Pauline letters, and the rest of the present New Testament with the omission of Hebrews, James, and the two letters attributed to Peter. The list included, however, the *Shepherd of Hermas*, a popular work of the late first century. No definitive canon was established until the fourth century, and even then there would be disagreement over the Epistle to the Hebrews, but the attempt to form a distinctive Christian canon had begun.

The first criterion of canonicity was apostolicity. If a writing was believed to be from an apostle, it had authority. This could be either direct or indirect. The authority of the Gospel of Mark, for example, stemmed from the evangelist's connection with the apostle Peter. A second criterion was catholicity. Was a given writing found in all parts of the Christian community? If a work found acceptance in all parts of the Christian world, it was deemed authoritative; otherwise, it was viewed as doubtful. A third criterion was antiquity. Works thought to be composed after the apostolic age were excluded. The final category was orthodoxy. Those works that were in accord with the inherited church found favor. Others were rejected. Writing in the fourth century, the historian Eusebius made the point succinctly. He noted that some writings, such as Hebrews, were still being disputed, yet he cautioned, "We must not confuse these with the writings published by heretics under the name of apostles as containing either the Gospels of Peter, Thomas, Matthias, and several others besides these." Heretical works had no place in the emerging canon.

Liturgy and Order

One can see the movement toward hierarchy, orthodoxy, and formalism in the developments in the liturgical life of the community as well. *The Apostolic Tradition* is a text that probably originated in the church in Rome in the early third century (ca. 230 CE). Traditionally attributed to Hippolytus, a minister in the Roman church, it outlines several religious activities. In the twentieth century this work became an important text for the liturgical movement, providing the basis for many modern liturgies.

The text was divided into three sections, each dealing with an aspect of the Christian life. The first outlined ordination practices. The second concerned the laity and gave directions for baptism, while the third spoke of a number of ecclesiastical observations.

The ordination rites reflect the developments in offices of ministry that were occurring at the time. A distinct hierarchy of administration is set forth. Although the people chose the bishop, his ordination was by the hands of other bishops, "and the presbytery shall stand by in silence." The prayer of consecration calls on the same power of the Spirit that Christ had bestowed on the apostles, emphasizing the connection between the apostles and the office of bishop. In turn, when a presbyter was ordained, the presbyters assisted in the ordination by laying hands on the individuals being ordained. But lest that be misunderstood, Hippolytus was quick to add, "On a presbyter . . . the presbyters shall lay their hands because of the common spirit of the clergy. Yet the presbyter has only power to receive, he has no power to give. For this reason a presbyter does not ordain the clergy, but that at the ordination of a presbyter he seals while the bishop ordains." In the prayer it is not the apostles who were invoked but the persons whom Moses chose to assist him. Finally, when the deacon was ordained, it was done by the bishop alone since a deacon was ordained "to serve the bishop and to carry out the bishop's command." Order was clearly delineated.

In this formalized model of ministry little place was left for the leadership of women. In contrast to the elaborate rules he outlined for bishops, presbyters, and deacons, Hippolytus is almost dismissive of the two small roles, those of widows and virgins, he retains for women. Of widows he insists that "she shall not be ordained because she does not offer the oblation, nor has she a [liturgical] ministry." He is equally cavalier about virgins. They do "not have an imposition of hands, for personal choice alone makes them a virgin." Since these functions were not part of the public worship, they did not merit the laying on of hands.

The second section outlines the responsibilities of laity. Three years of preparation are called for before baptism. Gladiators, soldiers, magicians, jugglers, and mountebanks must give up or modify their professions in order to become Christians. The moral life of persons was carefully examined, not only to assure the avoidance of sin but also to assure that they should model the life of charity through caring for the community. Finally, before being baptized, candidates were questioned one last time concerning the substance of their faith:

Doest thou believe in God the Father almighty? . . . Doest thou believe in
Christ Jesus, the Son of God, who was born of the Holy Ghost of the Virgin
Mary, and was crucified under Pontius Pilate, and was dead and buried, and
rose again the third day, alive from the dead, and ascended into heaven, and
sat at the right hand of the Father, and will come to judge the quick and the
dead? . . . Doest thou believe in the Holy Ghost, and the holy church, and
the resurrection of the flesh?

Baptism had become synonymous with the profession of Catholic Christianity, so much so that a belief in the holy church had now become a tenet of
the faith.

The last section treated ecclesiastical practices, and here, too, one sees the
liturgical formalization of trends already noted. The Eucharist and the community meal are carefully separated, and believers are urged to partake of the
former early in the day and the latter in the evening. But even in the latter
meal institutionalization reigns. The guests were to eat in silence, not arguing about the teachings of the bishop, "but if he [the bishop] should ask any
question, let an answer be given him, and when he says anything, everyone in
modest praise shall keep silence until he asks again." And if perchance there
was no bishop present, "if a presbyter or deacon is present they shall eat in a
similarly orderly fashion."

Hippolytus's *Apostolic Tradition*, as scholars have noted, was not a liturgical prayer book but rather an ideal model. Extemporaneous prayers were
still offered, and the formal authority of bishops, presbyters, and deacons was
nowhere nearly as clearly defined as he suggested. But his liturgical model
parallels the developments found in Ignatius and Irenaeus concerning the
formalization of the faith.

The Alternative of the Spirit

But was this move toward institutionalization and a hierarchical ministry a
good thing? The Scriptures reminded those with eyes to see that the prophets and apostles were not elected but called by God, and their authority was
not mediated through institutions but came immediately through the power
of the Spirit. The issue was not merely authority but rather what the church
was. The Acts of the Apostles tells of many mighty acts of God. In a famous
scene, Peter and John aided a crippled beggar not with silver and gold but
with God-given power of healing. Those in apostolic succession from Peter
and John could claim no such powers. Already by the end of the second
century, Irenaeus observed that the power of miracles was fading from the

church. But the Spirit need not be silent. Its direct or "charismatic" power was still available.

These themes came together in a movement known as Montanism. Surfacing in Phrygia in the second half of the second century, Montanists

> Montanists claimed the charismatic power that seemed to have abandoned the rest of the church.

claimed the charismatic power that seemed to have abandoned the rest of the church. The movement took its name from Montanus, described in some sources as a "newly baptized" Christian who began prophesying in the Spirit. On these occasions he would become possessed; the Spirit would take control of him, speaking directly through him to the hearers. The word of God spoke without any human mixing that might dilute it. It also spoke uncontaminated by any hierarchies, since the prophet's authority was directly from God. Through the mouth of Montanus would flow such words as "I am the Lord God Almighty, dwelling in man. It is neither an angel nor ambassador, but I, God the Father, who am come." Those touched by the outpouring of the Spirit saw themselves as a new elite, called to bring the church back to its original purity. Among them the gifts of the Spirit—the gifts of prophecy, speaking in tongues, and healing—were now restored. As a spiritual elite they practiced an even greater rigor than that of Catholic Christians. Fasting was rigorous, second marriages were prohibited, and the Christian was actively to seek martyrdom. They also believed that the heavenly Jerusalem was soon to be brought about.

Montanism was a classic charismatic movement, in which authority came directly from the Spirit rather than through institutions. As in other such movements, traditional patterns were overturned. Several women emerged as important prophetesses, most notably Priscilla and Maximilla. Contemporary Catholic sources were aghast. One lamented, "[The Phrygians] magnify those wretched women above the Apostles and every gift of Grace, so that some of them presume to assert that there is in them something superior to Christ." There is no evidence that such claims were ever made by Montanists themselves, but such allegations did speak to the popular power of charismatic prophecy.

Montanism not only had the Spirit speaking directly through women but also had the Spirit transcending male-gendered metaphors. Thus Priscilla is recorded as saying, "Christ came to me in the likeness of a woman, clad in a bright robe, and He planted wisdom in me and revealed that this place (Pepuza) is holy, and here Jerusalem comes down from heaven." It is by Christ speaking as a woman that the new Jerusalem is announced. Montanism was ultimately rejected, but it remains another example of a way the community might have evolved.

The Successor of Peter

The rise of Catholic Christianity involved a more self-conscious emphasis on order, belief, and discipline than had been the case earlier. The rule of faith would be epitomized in the Apostles' Creed, which still serves as a summary of the faith for a vast number of Christians to this day. The canonical Scriptures would likewise be a point of unity. Yet one development during this time would be a point of debate within the Christian tradition—the role of the bishop of Rome as the successor of Peter in the Christian community.

In the Gospel accounts, Peter plays perhaps the most prominent role of any of the apostles. He was the first to confess Jesus as the Christ. He was the first of the apostles to enter the empty tomb. Likewise, in the Acts of the Apostles he played a key role in the Council of Jerusalem. But the biblical record is ambivalent. He was also the apostle who denied Jesus at the time of his trial. Further, Paul was quick to deny any authority to Peter's teachings concerning circumcision.

Two Gospel passages stood out and provided the basis for attributing a special role for Peter. In the Gospel of Matthew, Jesus rewards Peter's confession by telling him, "You are Peter, and on this rock I will build my church, and the gates of Hades will not prevail against it. I will give you the keys of the kingdom, and whatever you bind on earth will be bound in heaven, and whatever you loose on earth will be loosed in heaven." Christians have long debated the meaning of the rock and the keys and Peter's relationship to them. Likewise, in the Gospel of John, the resurrected Jesus calls Peter aside and asks him three times if he loves him. To each positive response, Jesus answers by asking Peter to feed the sheep. Since the idea of the church as a flock led by a shepherd was a long-standing metaphor, the question became, To what degree was Peter a unique shepherd?

The later history of the apostles is not recorded in the Scriptures, but an early tradition places both Peter and Paul in the city of Rome. Neither founded the Roman church, but each was associated with it. Both suffered martyrdom there in the 60s of the first century, and their presence gave a particular aura to the church in that city.

As we have noted, by the second century the idea that bishops were successors to the apostles became important for Christians. Great value was placed on churches founded by apostles, and these became regional centers of authority. The church of Alexandria was claimed to have been founded by Mark, and this gave it authority in Egypt. Antioch, it was believed, was founded by John, and Jerusalem by James, and they too took on importance. Each of these lay in the eastern part of the empire. Rome alone was in the West. Hence from the second century, Western writers appealed to the continuity of the Roman church as a sign of the continuity of the faith. When Irenaeus, for example, tried to show the continuity of the faith, Rome played an important role. Rome was "that great, oldest, and well known Church," founded by "those two most glorious apostles Peter and Paul." He proceeded to trace the succession of leaders of the Roman church from Peter and Paul through Linus (their successor) to his own day. The example of Rome as a church faithful to the apostolic message led him to conclude, "For every church must be in harmony with this Church because of its outstanding pre-eminence, that is the faithful from everywhere, since the apostolic tradition is preserved in it from everywhere."

It is doubtful that there was a monepiscopate in Rome before the second century, but from early on leaders of the Roman church saw a responsibility in counseling other churches. One of the earliest extant postapostolic writings is a letter from the leader of the Roman church, Clement, to the ever-troublesome Christians in Corinth. Written at the end of the first century, Clement's letter addressed issues of dissension and schism. He urged unity, offering as an example the actions of Peter and Paul. Scholars disagree whether the spirit of the letter is one of fraternal correction or apostolic intervention, but it is nonetheless the earliest recorded example of Roman intervention in the larger church. It was an example to which Irenaeus would appeal in his emphasis on Rome as the source of true doctrine. It was a letter "leading [the Corinthians] to peace, renewing their faith, and declaring the tradition they recently received from the apostles."

By the end of the second century claims by the successor of Peter became more pointed. The flash point was the question of the dating of Easter. In the Gospels, the resurrection was associated with the Jewish festival of Passover, which was firmly fixed in the Jewish calendar. But to what degree, it came to be asked, should the Christian celebration of Easter be dependent on the Jewish calendar? In early Christianity this dependence was assumed, and it continued to be the rule in Asia Minor. But as the Christian community became increasingly Gentile in its makeup, Western Christians began basing Easter on the Latin calendar. The debate over Easter became a dividing point between Greek and Latin Christians. Into this division entered Victor, bishop of Rome, who summarily excommunicated all who continued to follow the older way of dating.

The dating of Easter was not resolved, nor was the claim of the bishop of Rome to be able to excommunicate other Christians. Irenaeus—who had earlier spoken of the authority of the Roman church—thought Victor's actions unwise and attempted to negotiate a peace among the churches. The churches in Asia continued to remain in communion with Rome despite maintaining their different date for Easter, so it is likely that Victor withdrew his threat. Nonetheless, the claim had been made for Roman authority.

A new stage in the idea of central Roman authority, and the ambivalent way in which it was received elsewhere, can be seen in an imbroglio between the church of North Africa and the church of Rome, which took place in the middle of the third century. Persecution had severely weakened the African Christian community by dividing it over the question of apostates, or how to treat those who in the face of persecution had temporarily abandoned the faith. The bishop of Carthage, Cyprian, sought to hold his church together by emphasizing the unity and authority of the Catholic Church. Here he made use of the biblical image of rocks and sheep. On Peter, Cyprian argued, Christ had built his church and fed his flock. Although all the apostles played a part in the building of the church, there was in the end one "chair"—in Latin, one *cathedra*—on which Christian unity rested. "Assuredly the rest of the apostles were also the same as was Peter . . . but the beginning proceeds from unity."

When the issue turned from theory to practice, however, Cyprian spoke differently. A few years later Cyprian and Stephen, the bishop of Rome, found themselves in disagreement over the issue of the validity of sacraments administered by clergy who had abandoned the faith. Cyprian rejected their validity while Stephen supported them. In the controversy that followed, Stephen for the first time claimed his own authority as the successor of Peter and demanded conformity. In response, Cyprian reminded the Roman church of the limitations of its authority. As Paul had felt it necessary to correct Peter, so too might any prelate, or regional leader, who believed that Rome was in error. Each prelate was responsible for the well-being of his own church, "as he shall give an account of his own doings to the Lord." Peter may have been the source of unity, but final authority rested in the hands of regional leaders.

Thus in the third century the successors of Peter are claiming a unique authority in the church. But the credibility of the claim had yet to be finalized.

The church by the third century had become a much more formal organization than it was in the age of the apostles. In questions of governance, doctrine, and countless other ways it had moved in a decided direction, leaving those who opposed this development on the sidelines. Although it was still a persecuted movement in a hostile empire, it was taking a shape that would mark it for centuries.

Chapter 4

Living in a Hostile World

*D*uring the same years that Christian writers and theologians were attempting to work out the implications of their faith, the vast bulk of the Christian community was attempting to negotiate an existence in a world that viewed them as odd and threatening. The practices and beliefs of everyday Christians would also leave their mark on the development of later Christianity.

Christian Distinctiveness

The Christian community was a strange creature in the Roman world. The common charges against it—that Christians practiced atheism, cannibalism, and incest—suggest how it puzzled outsiders. It bore little resemblance to the general paganism of the time. Nor was it like a mystery cult such as Mithraism nor like Judaism, limited to one ethnic community. It was a close-knit society, with members from diverse races and peoples, linked by definite practices and teaching.

Christian distinctiveness flowed from some interlocking beliefs and practices that set Christians apart. The first was the incarnation, the belief that in Jesus, God entered the world. In contrast to Judaism, the gap between God and the world, and between God and humanity, had been radically reduced. For Christians, the unpictured God of Judaism took on the human face of Jesus. God and the world were no longer separate. Yet in contrast with paganism, the incarnation was the act of the true God. The interconnection of the spiritual and the material was not a problem for ancient pagans. They believed that the world was filled with semidivine spirits—daimons— and these spirits made their influence felt in countless ways. But for Christians it was the true God who came to earth and the world of daimons was condemned. The old religions of the ancient world were the work of these spirits, and Christians were to have no connection with them. The religions were to be shunned.

To say that God had entered the world in Jesus was to make the world a different place. For the classical philosophers, the knowledge of God was hard, and to speak about God was even harder. As Plato wrote in the Timaeus, "Now to find the Maker and Father of this universe is difficult, and after finding him it is impossible to declare him to all men." Such a God could only tentatively be approached through a mind purged of the senses, but an incarnate God could be known sensibly. More important, that incarnate God spoke. Through Christ, believers could know God. As the historian Robert Wilken has put it, "For the Greeks, God was the conclusion of an argument, the end of a search for an ultimate explanation, an inference from the structure of the universe to a first cause. For Christian thinkers God was a starting point, and Christ the icon that displays the face of God." This belief inspired the Christian community with a certainty and confidence.

A second distinctive note was the Christian concept of love. The ultimate reality for classical philosophers was pure reason, and love had nothing to do with such a God. The God of the philosophers was beyond such mortal things. But for Christians God gave the world a son out of love. Christ endured the cross because of love. The first command of Jesus was that people were to love God with all their hearts, minds, and souls. The knowledge of God was impossible without such love. The heart could not be separated from true religion.

"See how they love one another" was an observation made by both Christians and non-Christians.

Love would engender within the Christian community values that were to be found almost nowhere else in the ancient world. One was humility. Pride was an essential virtue in the Roman world. Humility was associated with the ignoble. But for Christians, God humbled God's self to take on human form. Believers should practice the same virtue. Connected with humility was the valuing of poverty. Poverty was not viewed as a curse or a weakness but as a symbol of a dependence on God and a trust in God's love.

But the effect of love was perhaps most dramatic in how it shaped the treatment of others. The second of Jesus' commands was that his followers love their neighbors as themselves. Love was the law of life, encompassing the entire community. "See how they love one another" was an observation made by both Christians and non-Christians. Christians were supposed to extend hospitality to other Christians for up to three days without question.

Care was extended to widows and orphans and those unable to support themselves. In the mid-third century the church in Rome alone supported more than fifteen hundred widows and orphans. The sick were tended in their distress; prisoners were visited in their incarceration. Some have suggested that the practice of tending the sick—a radical idea in the ancient world—was a major factor in the expansion of the Christian community. Numerous times during the second and third centuries plagues swept through the Mediterranean world, killing up to 25 percent of the population. The willingness of Christians to minister to plague victims not only demonstrated Christian love in practice but also increased the survival rate of those ministered to. In this, Christian actions stood in marked contrast with pagans, who in the plague of 262 CE abandoned their sick at the first sign of disease. Another practical fruit of the love command was the providing of burial spaces for believers. Finally Christian churches raised money to ransom fellow Christians who had fallen captive to pirates or invaders.

Christians were distinguished not only for their ethic of love but also for their organization. The church, or *ecclesia*, was in many ways a unique organization. The urban world of antiquity was a society with strong social divisions. Rich and poor had separate sets of laws. Women and men belonged to separate spheres, and slaves made up still another division. The religious cults of the classical world reinforced these divisions. Women and men on the whole worshiped separately. Class distinctions were reinforced. Mystery cults, such as Mithraism, in which a bull was sacrificed and its blood poured upon the initiates, were horribly expensive and excluded all but the upper class. Even the civic rituals enforced these divisions. Sacrifice was offered to the gods for the sake of one's city. A wealthy patron would endow these offerings and would receive honor and deference from the multitude.

Christian worship was strangely different. As a community it transcended local boundaries. Christians were in connection with fellow believers throughout the empire. Their fellowship crossed class boundaries. The small number of wealthy Christians worshiped along with the rest of the community. And although Christians did not formally oppose the institution of slavery, the gap between slave and free largely disappeared within the fellowship. The manumission or freeing of a slave was seen as a good work, and Christian communities often raised money to help free slaves who found themselves in difficult circumstances. Unlike the Roman Empire, the church accepted marriages between free persons and slaves. Indeed we even have records of freed slaves being selected as bishops, most notably Callistus, bishop of Rome, around 220.

The sense of equality was also reflected in the way Christians went about charitable acts. The act of charity was not a thing of pride for wealthy

Christians as it was with pagan patrons. No honor and deference were involved. It was rather an act of humility, in imitation of their savior who humbled himself to take on human flesh, and it was administered not by the patron but by the church officials. The nature of the church community provided important roles for women. Their place in ministry was increasingly questioned, but their place in the community was central. Both Christians and non-Christians commented not only on the large number of women in the Christian community but also on their high social status. Indeed, the disproportionate number of wealthy women—and the far smaller number of male counterparts—led some Christian communities to reassess the Roman taboo against the association of free persons and slaves and to permit any woman to live in chaste union with a low-born or even a slave man.

In other ways as well, Christianity was extremely hospitable toward women. It rejected the practice of female infanticide. It preached against divorce, incest, infidelity, and polygamy. It called for chastity before marriage and faithfulness in marriage for men as well as women. It also provided three public roles for women. The first, the deaconess, has already been mentioned. They assisted in baptism and also ministered to other women. A second was the office of widow. Widowhood was a constant problem in the Roman world in which marriages typically took place between mature men and young girls (often no older than twelve). Mortality rates among these older husbands assured that there would be a steady supply of young widows. To address the problem, the emperor Augustus urged that all unmarried widows should be fined after two years to encourage remarriage and to ensure that they did not become a burden on the society. In contrast, the Christian community discouraged second marriages and honored widowhood. "Ecclesiastical widows" were distinguished from others; they were set apart and played an active role in the church. Finally there were "virgins." Perpetual virginity was an alternative to marriage and reflected for the community a reclaiming of the purity lost in the original fall of Adam.

The Christian community was constructed as a tightly knit fellowship, with strong and fixed boundaries between inside and outside. To belong to a pagan cult was not an exclusive identification or an onerous obligation. To sleep in the great shrine of Asclepius in Pergamum, patrons were only expected to have abstained from sex for two days, and there were other shrines that were far less rigorous. Some merely called for a one-day interval if the sex had been with one's wife, and two days if the sex had been with someone else's wife! In contrast, the Christian community demanded great discipline, and those guilty of serious postbaptismal sin were dealt with accordingly. As one contemporary wrote, "Christian sinners spend the day sorrowing, and the night in vigils and tears, lying on the ground among clinging ashes, tossing in rough sack cloth and dirt." Different levels of sin resulted in different disciplinary actions. Some sins kept one from Communion. Others compelled the penitent to stand on the porch of the building. Still more grievous sins compelled the penitent to grovel and ask for prayer. A major issue for the second- and third-century church was whether a fallen sinner could ever regain a place in the community.

Finally there was the Christian confidence in the last things. By the second century the expectation of Christ's imminent return had begun to fade, but the confidence in the resurrection did not. Unlike their pagan neighbors, Christians did not see death as either annihilation or merely a shadow realm. The departed were asleep waiting for resurrection. Christian burial grounds began to take on a new name — cemeteries (from the Greek, a place of sleep) — since it was there where the departed waited. Resurrection hope took away much of the scandal of death. Tombs for the dead became places of worship because they were connected to this hope.

How the Romans Saw Them

What did the classical world make of this new religion? Many of its practices were condemned from afar. Its rejection of the pagan gods was considered rank atheism. Its sacramental eating of bread and wine and its claim that these were the body and blood of their savior were viewed as cannibalism. Its language of love and brotherhood sounded like incest. Satirists laughed at the gullibility of Christians who would offer hospitality to any charlatan who darkened their door. But the Christian threat could not be ignored. In many ways the Roman world was extremely tolerant yet in other ways quite rigid. The Roman Empire was made up of many ethnic groups. A multitude of cults were accepted, since religion and ethnicity were intertwined. But the empire was held together by some distinctive religious practices. These were called the "traditions of the fathers," and their presence gave to the culture a strong conservative streak. Concerning things religious, the emperor Augustus was advised, "You should abhor and punish, not merely for the sake of the gods, but such men by bringing in new divinities in place of the old, persuade many to adopt foreign practices, from which spring up conspiracies, factions and political clubs." The abandonment of the old religion was both a religious and a social challenge. Religion and society complemented each other. Religion held all together; indeed the very root of the word *religio* was to bind. Religion defined and bound its people to the cosmos, the city, and the social order. All of this the Christian, in the name of his or her faith, rejected. The Roman writer Tacitus referred to Christians as the "enemy of mankind." Christians belonged to no people and had no ancient traditions as paganism did. One could not reject the religion of the fathers in the name of a new god.

The Martyrs' Path

Christian differences formed the background to the waves of persecution the church suffered during these centuries. Persecution was intermittent in the early period, but in some reigns, such as those of Nero and Domitian, it was fierce. Nero (54–68) had Christians attacked for being allegedly behind the burning of Rome. With Domitian (81–96) the issue involved the cult of the emperor. As emperor he assumed the title "Lord and God" and insisted on being reverenced. Christians (and Jews) objected to such language as well as the obligatory oath "by the genius of the emperor."

Domitian's successor, Trajan, attempted to establish a policy for determining on exactly what grounds Christians should be persecuted. An official in Asia Minor, Pliny the Younger, wrote to Trajan around the year 112 for advice. He reported that he had found a number of people condemning their fellow citizens as Christians. Were these so-called Christians to be judged guilty simply by the allegation of belief or only by their participation in Christian acts? Anonymous condemnations were a particular problem since there was no accountability. Pliny suggested that those charged should be questioned as to whether they were indeed Christians. If they denied it, they should be released. If they admitted it, they should be given the opportunity to renounce their faith in order to avoid execution. They could go free by reciting a prayer to the gods, offering wine and incense to a statue of the emperor, and cursing Christ.

> If the Christian life entailed imitating Christ, no one did so as faithfully as the martyr.

Trajan approved this plan, and the policy was largely followed by the magistrates of the empire until the middle of the third century. Pliny's policy sheds light on the famous martyr accounts that were a powerful genre of early Christian literature. Two of these accounts are particularly illustrative of the idea of martyrdom. The first concerns the Christian bishop Polycarp of Smyrna, and the second involves two holy women of North Africa, Perpetua and Felicity.

Christians spoke of martyrdom with the metaphor of witness or testimony. The martyr was one who followed the way of Christ. If the Christian life entailed imitating Christ, no one did so as faithfully as the martyr. The pattern was established in the death of Polycarp, one of the oldest accounts extant. As the author of the account noted, his was a "martyrdom conformable to the gospel." As the persecution intensified, many fled the city, but Polycarp calmly awaited his capture. When the authorities arrived to arrest him, he ordered food and drink for them and asked only that he might be granted an hour of undisturbed prayer. According to the account, many of his arrestors repented on the spot. Under examination, his judges asked Polycarp to compromise and offer sacrifice to Caesar in order to save his life. The dialogue became a devotional classic: "The proconsul was insistent and said, 'Take the oath and I shall release you. Curse Christ.' Polycarp said, 'Eighty-six years I have served him, and he never did me any wrong. How can I blaspheme my king who saved me?'" Nor did the threats of wild beasts or fire disturb him. "The fire you threaten burns but an hour. . . . For you do not know the fire of the coming judgment and everlasting punishment that is laid up for the impious." While tied to a stake he offered a final prayer, and then to the amazement of all, his body could not be consumed by the fire. The account concludes that Polycarp was "crowned with the wreath of immortality, and had been borne away to an incontestable reward."

Perpetua and Felicity met their fate around the year 200. Perpetua was of noble birth and only twenty-two when persecutions came, and Felicity was her servant and was pregnant. Perpetua's father pleaded that she should renounce her faith, but she replied, "Can I call myself aught other than that which I am, a Christian?" When arrested, they were taken along with other Christians and asked to sacrifice to the emperor, but they refused. The account of the martyrdom of Perpetua and Felicity included a series of mystical visions, in which they understood that their conflict would not involve fighting wild beasts but rather the devil. Because of her pregnancy, Felicity was originally not to be executed, but just before the execution day, she gave birth, and she joined the others to be tortured by wild animals and later killed by the sword. On the day of their martyrdom (which the text referred to as her day of "victory") the account explained that Perpetua showed no fear but urged her fellow Christians, "Stand fast in the faith, and love ye one another."

Explaining the Faith

Accounts such as those of Polycarp, Perpetua, and Felicity were cherished by the early community and were often read on the anniversary of the martyrs' deaths. But they were not the whole story. Martyrdom was an individual response, but how were other Christians to respond to the charges made against them? This task belonged to the apologist. The apologist did not apologize in the modern sense of the term but defended Christianity using resources from the classical world itself. The apologists began the process of engaging the world and in some ways translating biblical categories into forms that outsiders could understand.

Some apologists did so simply through the use of classical rhetoric. The best-known example is Tertullian (c. 160–c. 225). A North African and probably trained as a lawyer, Tertullian was masterful in answering pagan claims that Christianity upset the peace of the empire. Christians, he argued, had been made scapegoats for all the ills of the empire; if anything went astray, Christians were to blame. He was the master of ridicule. "If the Tiber reaches the walls, if the Nile does not rise to the fields, if the sky does not move or the earth does, if there is famine, if there is plague, the cry is at once, 'The Christians to the lion.'" He then added contemptuously, "What, all of them to one lion?" He argued that Christians were not disloyal. They prayed for the emperor, were moral, and in most things were extremely loyal. All they wanted to do was to practice their religion. But instead they underwent suffering and persecution. The persecution, he noted, was unlike any other. Normally evildoers attempted to escape notice and, when caught, to avoid punishment. But Christians did neither. They were defiant because they were innocent. "What sort of evil is that which has none of the native marks of evil—fear, shame, shuffling, regret, lament?"

If Tertullian made use of classical rhetoric, he had little patience for classical philosophy or reason. He has come down in history as the one who set the church's faith and the wisdom of the world in stark contrast, although his own writings are far more nuanced than you might expect. "What indeed has Athens to do with Jerusalem? What has the Academy to do with the Church?" he asked. "Away with all attempts to produce a Stoic Platonic Christianity and dialectic Christianity! We want no curious disputation after possessing Christ Jesus, no inquisition after receiving the gospel! When we believe we desire no further belief." Tertullian suggested that faith was ultimately independent of reason or philosophy.

Yet the majority tradition would not be shaped by Tertullian's rejection of philosophy and instead came to believe that there could be a fruitful interchange between Athens and Jerusalem. By the middle of the second century other apologists began to suggest that although it was flawed, philosophy could be used to explain the Christian faith. Justin Martyr led the way. Writing in Alexandria, a center of classical learning, he suggested that the Greek philosophical category of Logos could be used by Christians to explain to outsiders who Jesus was. According to philosophy, the Logos was the rational governing principle of the universe. It was in some sense a divine principle. It was that which connected the divine to the world. The term *Logos* had already been used by the fourth evangelist to describe Jesus' preexistence: "In the beginning was the Word [Logos], and the Word was with God." As Justin explained, the preexistent Christ was indeed the Logos that the philosophers had identified. That the Logos was divine, but not one with the Father, could explain to citizens of the ancient world the divinity Christians proclaimed in Christ. The Logos also connected human beings with God. In their participation in reason, Christians have existence in Christ the Logos. In Justin one finds one of the earliest attempts to use philosophy to understand the nature of Christ.

The task would be taken up by two of Justin's famous successors in the city of Alexandria, Clement and Origen. Clement (160–215) is a figure we know little about. He described himself simply as a Christian questing for understanding about God. He probably headed an independent school in Alexandria, presenting Christianity as the true philosophy. There he sought to forge the connection between Christianity and Greek culture.

Clement expanded on Justin's use of the category of Logos. God and the Logos were the Creator and Creative agent that planned and made the cosmos. The Logos planted the seeds of true knowledge or gnosis in the world and made the world a place that God cherished. Human beings were created in the image of the Logos but only grew through disciplined education. Through education (*paideia*) humans learned more of God's will. Philosophy was a preparation for true knowledge. It was given to the Greeks to assist in true education just as God gave the law to the Hebrews. "Philosophy . . . is a preparation, making ready the way for him who is being perfected."

In his use of the Logos, Clement combined Platonic and biblical themes. Greek philosophy had taught that the goal of human life was "likeness to God" through the acquiring of habits and education. In this Christ would agree, but it was only possible because of the work of the Logos in creation. Human beings were created in the likeness of God, according to Genesis, and hence the ability to know was a divine gift. *Paideia*, or education, was only possible because the likeness had already been created.

Finally there was Origen (185–254). Origen was not technically an apologist. Rather he was the greatest mind in the pre-Constantinian church, and perhaps the most controversial. He was a biblical exegete, theological speculator, and much more. His writings were steeped in the Platonic philosophy of his age, though strictly tethered to the Scriptures. The result was an interesting amalgam. In his interpretation of Scripture, the spiritual meaning or interpretation of a passage often took precedence over the literal or historical. The literal sense, he argued, was not the reason for which the Spirit gave the Scriptures. The true sense was the spiritual sense.

He applied this to his view of creation. Genesis for him was a cosmic myth, and the fall occurred not in history but before the ages. Out of free will, the preexistent souls fell away from God. Satan, possessing free will, chose to resist. Other souls fell to greater or lesser degree and became demons and angels. For the remaining souls, God created the physical world. But there would be a final redemption, and at that time even Satan, since he possessed freedom and reason, would find redemption. The gospel was the working out of this cosmic redemption; it brought to actuality what had only existed in potential. Philosophers had caught glimpses of this, but in the person of Jesus it was achieved.

Origen's speculations showed how far the basic teachings of the Scriptures could be expanded and evolved through creative contact with the classical world. Within two centuries of his death Origen would become a controversial figure, and many would claim that speculation had gotten the better of him. Jerusalem must always be to a degree suspicious of Athens.

The Renewal of Persecution

As previously noted, there was no systematic campaign by the Roman authorities against the Christian community until the middle of the third century. Things changed under Decius (249–251). In order to bolster the empire he ordered that every citizen demonstrate his or her loyalty by performing public sacrifice. Upon doing so they would receive a certificate (*libellus*). The demand for universal sacrifice created a crisis. The refusal to sacrifice had serious implications, particularly for Christians who owned property. They could lose all they possessed. Some did perform the sacrifice while others bribed officials to give a certificate without their performing the deed. Decius's policy also focused on church leaders. In Rome, Bishop Fabian was executed. In Alexandria, the bishop was jailed, and in Carthage, Cyprian was forced to flee. All told, hundreds died.

Decius's death in 251 eased the immediate crisis, but in 284, with the accession of Diocletian, persecutions returned. Diocletian was concerned with revivifying the empire, and defense, currency, and taxation were all reorganized. But he also began a large-scale attack on Christian churches.

Christian houses of worship were dismantled, and clergy were jailed. He also demanded surrender of Bibles, liturgical books, and sacred vessels and forbade all Christian worship. The Diocletian persecution became known as the Great Persecution, and particularly in the eastern part of the empire it caused great suffering. It, too, led some to compromise. To surrender sacred books at the behest of the magistrate seemed prudent to some. But others saw such compromises as betraying the faith. Those who did so were "*traditores,*" traitors to the faith. In North Africa the church became bitterly divided over the fate of the *traditores*, and the division would have momentous consequences.

The State of Christianity on the Eve of Constantine

The two centuries stretching from 100 to 300 witnessed a remarkable spread of Christianity. The sociologist Rodney Stark has estimated that at the beginning of the period there were perhaps as few as eight thousand Christians, and by the year 300, over six million. The church had moved from being a mere speck in the ancient world to making up 10 percent of the Roman Empire's population. The growth rate has been estimated at 40 percent per decade.

Although the center of the Christian world was the Mediterranean, Christianity had grown outward. By the year 300 CE it was found in almost all parts of the Roman Empire. It found a home in Britain, France, Spain, Italy, North Africa, and Egypt. Probably the greatest concentration of Christians was in what is now Turkey. But if the center of the religion was the Roman Empire, it had established important outposts elsewhere as well. From Egypt Christianity moved south along the Nile River to Nubia or what is now Sudan. It had early taken root in east Syria, which was the contested border between the Roman and Persian empires. The city of Edessa, for long periods outside of the empire, became an important Christian center. There, according to legend, Agbar, an Edessene king, on hearing accounts of Jesus' persecution in Jerusalem, wrote to him offering sanctuary. The legend continued that Jesus wrote back thanking Agbar but declining his offer, yet he promised to send an apostle to Edessa. Although the legend is almost certainly false, Edessa did become a center of Christianity, and one of its citizens, Bardasian (or Bar-desenes), was among the most learned figures in the early Christian world. Another center of Christianity outside of the Roman Empire was Persia or what is now Iraq and

> By the end of the third century, Christianity was as much an Asian religion as anything else.

Iran. More than twenty bishops served the church in Persia, and Persian missionaries brought Christianity to Arabia. Farther east there was a Christian community in India. The origins of Indian Christianity remain something of a mystery. According to one tradition, the apostle Thomas traveled to India, established a Christian community there, and converted the king, Gandapher. There is still another tradition of an interconnection of the Indian community and that of the church of Alexandria.

By the end of the third century, Christianity was as much an Asian religion as anything else. The geographical center was Asia Minor, and it had vibrant communities even farther east. The apologist Tatian, writing from Assyria over a hundred years earlier, could proclaim, "In every way the East excels, and most of all in its religion, the Christian religion, which also comes from Asia and which is far older and truer than all the philosophies and crude religious myths of the Greeks."

SECTION 2   Embracing the World

Chapter 5

The Constantinian Revolution

*T*he first decade of the fourth century was not a happy time for the Roman Empire or the young church. Both struggled with conflicts that threatened their well-being. But few if any could have predicted that within a few years the course of church and empire would be profoundly changed in a way that would mark their subsequent histories for more than a thousand years.

The empire had teetered on the brink of disarray toward the end of the third century. Its borders were threatened by invasion, and its army seemed out of control. Diocletian (emperor from 284 to 305) had restored order. He stabilized the empire and reorganized its administration. He divided the governance of the empire into two sections, the Greek-speaking East (where most of the wealth lay) and the Latin-speaking West, each with a separate governor. In addition he created two new governing offices so that four men, or a tetrarchy, effectively administered the empire. The system worked well as long as Diocletian maintained control, but when he abdicated in 305, discord erupted.

But Diocletian did not abdicate until he had inaugurated the "Great Persecution," attacking Christian communities and their institutions in an unprecedented way. As we have seen, his demand that Christian leaders surrender their sacred texts had divided the community. The church in North Africa, which had always had a rigorist streak and had nearly divided over the question of apostasy during the time of Cyprian, became hopelessly divided between those who said that the *traditores* could be forgiven and those who claimed they could not. A similar controversy raged in Rome. Bishop Marcellinus had handed over the Scriptures in accordance with the imperial edict. When he died shortly thereafter, his successor Marcellus, believing his predecessor's actions to be apostate, removed his name from the official episcopal list. The action angered many Roman Christians, and Marcellus was forced into exile. For a number of years there was no bishop in residence in Rome.

The Conversion of Constantine

In 306, on the death of the Western tetrarch Constantius Chlorus, his army proclaimed his son Constantine emperor. A struggle for power ensued between the competing tetrarchs. A great battle was to be fought at the Milvian Bridge to determine whether Constantine would in fact succeed as emperor. But on the eve of the battle an event occurred that would change the course of history: the "conversion" of Constantine. Constantine had always shown a consideration for Christians. In 306 he had decreed that property confiscated during the periods of persecution should be restored to Christians, although personally he had shown little interest in the movement. But on the eve of the battle Constantine claimed he had received two signs. The first was a cross of light in the sky together with the words "In this conquer." The second was a vision with a special insignia. He was instructed to make a copy of it and use it as his standard in the forthcoming battle. Whether this image was the labarum, the famous Chi-Rho (formed from the first two letters of the word Christ), or the *stauros*, which symbolized the cross, is not clear. But with the Christian symbol displayed, Constantine's forces were victorious, and he became emperor of the Latin West.

It must be stressed that Constantine was not the first political ruler to embrace Christianity, and the Roman Empire was not the first Christian land. In the Caucasus Mountains lay the kingdom of Armenia. It had early been visited by Christian missionaries. In the early fourth century its king, Tiridates III, had converted to Christianity through the labors of Gregory the Illuminator, and Armenia has the claim of being the oldest Christian nation. Tiridates had also appointed Gregory as "Catholicos" or head of the Armenian church. But the conversion of Constantine would have a monumental impact, because through it Christianity entered the public arena of one of the world's great empires.

Much has been written about Constantine's conversion, and some question whether he ever expressed exclusive loyalty to Christianity (he was only baptized on his death bed—but that had more to do with questions of sin than belief). In 313 he and his fellow emperor, Licinius, issued the Edict of Milan, granting Christians (and others) freedom of worship, "that whatever divinity is enthroned in heaven may be gracious and favorable to us and all who have been placed under our authority." Constantine never swayed from either a policy of religious toleration or a personal identification with Christianity.

Changes for the Church

The conversion of Constantine had immediate implications. The first was that large resources began flowing into the church. He endowed and had built large-scale Christian churches. He also gave the palace of his second wife, Fausta, as an episcopal residence for the bishop of Rome. In order to replace the sacred books destroyed during times of persecution, he financed the production of new copies of the Bible. Clergy and church lands were exempted from taxation. Clergy were also given monetary compensation for persecution. Finally he set up a system of gifts of food so that churches could administer charitable support. All of these actions, as we shall see, transformed a small, poor, marginal community into a powerful social force.

Laws were also affected. Crucifixion and gladiator shows were abolished, and the branding of the faces of criminals was forbidden, because "man is made in God's image." The old Roman laws against widowhood and perpetual chastity were abandoned out of respect for Christian sensibilities. Sunday was mandated as a day of rest. Bishops were given judicial authority. Slaves could now be manumitted in a declaration before a bishop, and churches became important centers for the manumission of slaves.

Two actions of Constantine stand out. The first was the restoration of Jerusalem as a Christian city. In the 320s he sent his mother, Helena, on a visit to the Holy Land. There she had one great church built in Bethlehem, where Jesus had been born, and a second on the Mount of Olives in Jerusalem, where he had died. While in Jerusalem, she is said to have discovered the cross upon which Jesus had been crucified.

The second action was Constantine's own. From 312 to 323 Constantine shared the governance of the empire with Licinius, who controlled the eastern half while Constantine ruled over the west. Gradually the two men became rivals, and religion played a key factor. Although both had approved the Edict of Milan, their subsequent developments had been different. As Constantine moved more and more into the Christian camp, Licinius became more hostile, evoking the pagan gods and persecuting the Christians. In 324 Constantine invaded the east and defeated his rival, thus controlling for the first time the entire empire. This allowed him to lay the foundation of a "New Rome," but one rooted in Christianity. In 324 Constantinople was established as a Christian city. In 330, when construction was complete, Constantine took residence there, and the city became the symbol of the new Christian Roman Empire. Great churches were constructed there, dedicated to the apostles and to peace.

> Constantinople became the symbol of a new vision of empire and a new vision of Christianity. With Constantine, the movement of the empire to Christianity had begun.

Constantinople became the symbol of a new vision of empire and a new vision of Christianity. With Constantine, the movement of the empire to Christianity had begun. It was a slow process, particularly in the countryside. There, the rural community—the *pagani*—resisted the new religion, and their name became associated with all defenders of the old religion, pagans. During the course of the fourth century the Christianization of the empire would continue in intervals—and under the reign of Julian (known as Julian the Apostate in later Christian accounts) it was temporarily reversed. But the empire became increasingly identified with Christianity.

Constantine's actions also had their effect on the church. As patron, the emperor wielded influence. If Constantinople were indeed a Christian city, the center of both the city and the new Christian empire was the emperor. The church surrendered some of its sovereignty. Within a few hundred years the Christian community would be fundamentally divided, and a key division would be between those who looked toward Constantinople and the emperor and those who looked toward Rome and the papacy. For the former the acts of Constantine constituted an unmixed good thing; for the latter there would be more ambivalence.

Imperial support for the Christian community increased over the course of the fourth century, and gifts and special favors continued to be received. Finally, by 380, Emperor Theodosius would issue the following decree: "It is our will that all the peoples who are ruled by . . . Our Clemency shall practice that religion which the divine Peter the Apostle transmitted to the Romans, as the religion which he introduced makes clear even unto this day. . . . We command that those persons who follow this rule shall embrace the name of Catholic Christians." But as we will see in the next chapter, the imperial embrace of the church made any divisions within the Christian community a political as well as a religious concern. Theodosius went on to state, "The rest, however, whom we adjudge demented and insane, shall sustain the infamy of heretical dogmas, . . . and they shall be smitten first by divine vengeance and secondly by the retribution of our own initiative, which we shall assume in accordance with the divine judgment."

Developments in Worship

The granting of official status to Christianity profoundly affected Christian worship. During the pre-Constantinian period the church had been a small community, and the standard place of worship was the house church. These were regular houses with rooms grouped around a central court. There would often be a meeting area and a separate baptistery. After Constantine, larger spaces were needed, and thus the basilica was adopted. The style originated in the pagan world. The size was royal (hence the term, *basilike*, or pertaining to a king). The earlier Roman basilicas included an entrance hall, a central hall, and an apse or semicircular construction on one end where an image of the emperor or some deity would be placed. The style was taken over by the Christian community and became the first public Christian architecture. Often they were very large; the Church of St. John Lateran in Rome, begun in 313, was 312 feet long, 180 feet wide, and 95 feet tall. There the bishop would have his chair, or *cathedra*, and from it he would teach the people. It would also be the place where divine services would be offered. The basilica provided an architectural model that Christians would follow for centuries as well as a vocabulary that continues to this day: *nave* for the central section, *transepts* for the side entrances, *apse* for the location of the altar, and *narthex* for the entrance porch.

With their size and monumentality basilicas influenced the nature of worship. The simple worship of the pre-Constantinian church was transformed both to impress and instruct the new larger crowds. Care was taken about how clergy entered into worship, and processionals began to find their way into the services. Ceremonies developed for presenting the bread and wine at the time of Communion. Litanies, chants, and hymns began to find a place so that congregations could better participate. A formal dismissal was added at the end of the liturgy (*ita missa est*), and this over time would give still another name to the Eucharist: the mass. A movement toward set prayers began. Even with Hippolytus, the liturgies found in *The Apostolic Tradition* were only ideal models, and clergy were free to extemporize. Prayer now became more formal. One example of this was the rise of a prayer tradition that merged Roman oratorical tradition and Christian piety. The result was the "collect," a short prayer for a particular need addressed to the Father in the name of Jesus, which became the classic form of prayer in the Christian West. Still other actions were added to elevate the liturgy's solemnity, such as a ritual washing of the officiating minister's hands at the celebration of the Eucharist (the lavabo). Likewise the angelic hymn found in the prophet Isaiah ("Holy, Holy, Holy," or the Sanctus) was incorporated to emphasize the interconnection of the earthly and the heavenly in worship. Candlesticks and special books lent an added dignity to the service.

The solemnity of basilica worship also led to the use of special clothing for clergy for the first time. Constantine himself presented to the cathedral church in Jerusalem in 330 a sacred robe of gold tissue to be worn by the bishop while presiding at solemn baptism. The clergy as persons of status wore the dignified dress of upper-class Romans, and these articles of clothing, preserved in the face of changing fashion, over the years became the basis of a distinctive clerical dress.

Another development that emerged in the Constantinian church was the formation of a "church year," or annual celebration of festivals. Christians had always celebrated Easter, the festival of the resurrection of Christ, although, as we have seen, they argued over its date. But the whole year was now invested with symbolism. We have an account of fourth-century worship practices in the diary of Egeria, a pious woman from Spain who recorded a pilgrimage to Sinai and Palestine. The center of the Christian year, she explained, was the Easter cycle. But to prepare for Easter a period was set aside for special devotion. The length of this period differed in different parts of the church. "In our part of the world," she wrote, "we observe forty days before Easter, but here [in Jerusalem] they keep eight weeks." During that time the "bishop and presbyters are at pains to preach, to ensure that the people will continue to learn God's law." From the Thursday before to the Sunday of Easter numerous services were observed, and baptisms were administered. Forty days after Easter the ascension of Christ was celebrated, and ten days after that (or fifty days after Easter) was the feast of the Holy Spirit or Pentecost.

One festival not mentioned by Egeria was Christmas. Christmas developed first in the West in the mid-fifth century. A celebration of Christ's manifestation, or Epiphany, had been long-standing and continued to find favor in the East. But in the West the celebration of the birth of Christ began to be separated from the Epiphany (which now began to be seen as a celebration of Christ's manifestation to the non-Jewish magi). The date December 25 was probably chosen to counter an existing Roman holiday, *Dies Natalis Solis Invicti*, or the celebration of the birth of the invincible Sun. Through all of these festivals the church year took on a teaching function.

Christians also tried to shape the week as well. The idea of a seven-day week only slowly emerged in the classical world, and its roots were not the Genesis creation account but astrology. Popular astrology taught that each of the seven planets (including the sun and moon) controlled a day. From this not only developed a seven-day week but names of the days of the week linked to celestial bodies. Constantine had established the first day of the week, Sunday, to be a day of rest. Christians attempted to rename the days of the week with new Christian names so as to break with paganism. They succeeded in the East, but in the West (with the exception of Portugal) they failed. But Latin-speaking Christians did succeed in shaping the language by christening the first day—*Dies Dominica*, or the Lord's Day—which has continued in Romance languages.

Space, too, was sanctified. Christians had long been ridiculed for their devotion to the dead, particularly their veneration of the bones of martyrs. The narrative of Polycarp's martyrdom records that his bones were carefully collected and distributed to the faithful. Shrines were established at the tombs of martyrs, where the faithful could sit and reflect on the dead. As one writer noted, "When the faithful look at the relics it is as though with the eyes, the mouth, the ears, indeed all the senses they embrace the living body itself, still blooming with life." The doctrines of the incarnation and resurrection taught that spirit and matter were not separate but profoundly interconnected. In the period after the conversion of Constantine the veneration of relics continued, often linked with the practice of pilgrimage. The city of Jerusalem was "restored" as a Christian city, and the sites of Christ's earthly ministry were marked by great churches. Pilgrims would travel to Jerusalem, where the true cross found by Helena was venerated on Good Friday, the day of the crucifixion. Egeria described this event and how the wood was taken out of a gold and silver box for the faithful to kiss. She also records how the deacons would stand guard lest anyone try to take a bite of the precious wood and carry it away. Rome also became a destination for pilgrimage because of its association with Peter and Paul.

Shifting Fortunes

The support of the emperors assured that the church would grow. The resources that poured in came to a large degree at the expense of the old pagan religion. Fewer and fewer patrons could or would finance the great pagan sacrifices and feasts that had earlier been the custom. To be a Christian was no longer a detriment in the empire but rather an advantage. To profess Christianity opened doors to a career in the administration of the empire, and such positions could be quite lucrative. Enterprising towns could win better charters by proclaiming that they had become Christian. To profess Christianity now became for some not simply a path for doing good but for doing well. The inevitable result of this shift in fortune was that insincere conversions began to be reported. By early in the next century (the fifth) it is recorded that when Synesius was elected a bishop in Egypt, he agreed to the office only if he could continue to hold on to his non-Christian philosophy

> To profess Christianity now became for some not simply a path for doing good but for doing well.

and to his wife. Later writers have speculated whether there was anything noticeably Christian at all in his writings. Synesius was an extreme case, but preachers in their homilies began to complain of a shallowness of faith.

But if the conversion of Constantine was a boon (albeit a problematic one) within the empire, it created grave problems for Christianity outside of it. Persia was the historic enemy of the Roman Empire, and the romanization of Christianity had a devastating effect on the Christian community there. Constantine's conversion left Persian Christians open to the charge that as Christians they were more loyal to the Roman emperor than to the Persian state. Their religious competitors, the Zoroastrians, adherents of the ancient faith of Persia, made much of the charge, and during the period between 340 and 379, as the imperial church waxed, more than sixteen thousand Persian Christians are believed to have suffered death by persecution. The Persian church, though wounded, would continue. It established a degree of independence, and, as we shall see, became an important missionary source for planting Christianity in East Asia, but it would always be on the margins as a foreign religion. Tatian's claim that Christianity was an "Asian" religion was less true in the fourth century than it had been when he said it. The center of Christianity was the empire, and those outside of it were marginalized. As we will see in the next chapter, Constantine would call a great council in 325 to meet in Nicaea, and the council has been called to this day an "ecumenical" or universal council. But in attendance were only two bishops from churches outside of the empire.

Fleeing the World

The worldly success of the church in the fourth century led some in a very different direction—to retreat from the world. It became necessary for them to take flight physically from civilization and psychologically from desire. Asceticism took on a new vigor. Asceticism, or the belief that one must discipline the physical in order to empower the spiritual, was not a uniquely Christian movement. It is found in many religions. But it took on a new urgency among Christians in the fourth century. The battle was now not in the society but within the person. One needed to strive to overcome desire in order to achieve that tranquility where one could find God. The soul required exercising and discipline. In an earlier age the world disciplined the Christian through persecution; now Christians must discipline themselves. Extreme mortification became the mark of the ascetic. One hermit, Symeon, spent thirty-five years living alone on a pillar. Others practiced extreme fasting, mixed ash with their food, and burned their fingers rather than give way to temptation.

In some ways the ascetic was the successor to the martyr. Like the martyr, the ascetic was a mirror of Christ. In achieving such holiness one also achieved the power of holiness, particularly the power to do miracles. In this way the wandering holy man became an important figure in the fourth century. These persons were crucially important in the conversion of the countryside. Their spiritual power could offer victory over the demonic, which meant power over sickness, evil, and weather. The spiritual power of the holy man impressed those of the countryside in a way that apologetical treatises could not. One contemporary account witnessed to this power: "All the citizens together ran to see [him]. 'We ask to see the man of God' for so all called him. For there also the Lord through him cleansed many from demons, and healed the mad. Many Greeks asked only to touch the old man, believing that they should be helped."

Syria was the great center of the wandering holy man. It was in Egypt that the ascetical call would become reflected in the institution of monasticism. Egypt was a province shaped by the Nile River. The Nile's waters produced a teeming civilization along its banks. But where the water ended the desert began. It was to the desert that Egyptian ascetics began to withdraw. There they dedicated their lives to asceticism, contemplation, and service to God. Some of them lived singly as hermits. They were known as anchorites. The paradigmatic anchorite was Antony of Egypt. Antony was reared in an economically comfortable Christian home but abandoned it for a life of seclusion. Athanasius's *Life of Antony* recounted his physical withdrawal from the world: from home to the outskirts of the village, then to a nearby tomb, and later to the distant desert. But where he went, crowds would follow, drawn by his spiritual power. He was the healer of the sick and the consoler of the troubled. The life of Antony was a constant spiritual struggle, but his discipline allowed him to succeed. As his biographer noted, "The devil watched Antony closely and (as David sings) gnashed his teeth against him."

Women also fled to the desert. The "ammas" or desert mothers, like Antony, sought a life of simplicity and prayer. Typical among them was Amma Syncletica. Born around 300 to wealthy Christian parents in Alexandria, her early life was one of ease. With the death of her parents she sold all and gave the proceeds to the poor. Retiring to the tombs outside of Alexandria she lived as a hermit with her blind sister. Eventually other women joined her, and she became their spiritual mother. In some ways her community can be seen as a bridge between anchorites and later monasticism.

The other form of monasticism was communal, called cenobitism. Monks lived together in a common community under a common rule. The founder of cenobitic monasticism was another Egyptian monk, Pachomius. He had received a vision that told him to "dwell in this place and build a monastery, for many will come to you to become monks, and they will profit their soul." Pachomius derived a rule in which monks, while living in separate cells, spent their days in prayer, worship, and labor. Peace and order were the greatest of virtues, and the community was to work together and encourage one another in the attainment of spiritual goals. Pachomius's community would become the model for most later Christian monastic communities.

Eusebius and the Meaning of History

The conversion of Constantine had one other effect. It gave to some an answer to the problem of history, or God's plan for the world. The first generation of Christians believed that Christ would return quickly and establish his kingdom. In the interim they were living in a period of expectation. As the years accumulated, however, it became harder to hold onto this expectation, and the question of the divine plan for the world became acute. What was God doing while the community was undergoing persecution? The conversion of Constantine seemed to offer an answer. The first church historian, Eusebius of Caesarea, wrote his celebrated history in the wake of Constantine's action. His story of Christianity began in Jerusalem and ended with Constantine, for in Constantine the church had finally triumphed. Destruction had now overtaken God's enemies, and "from that time on a day bright and radiant . . . shone down with shafts of heavenly light on the churches of Christ throughout all the world." The rule of Constantine confirmed the blessing that God had showered upon the church. The emperor was God's great "Commander in Chief," spitting on dead idols, trampling the lawless rites of demons, and laughing about the old stories about the gods. His subsequent triumph over his rival Licinius was further proof of God's providence, and Eusebius ended his history by proclaiming how the work of God was finally accomplished through the emperor Constantine and his son, who "having made it their first task to wipe the world clean from hatred of God, rejoiced in the blessings that He had conferred upon them, and by the things they did for all men to see, displayed love of virtue and love of God, devotion and thankfulness to the Almighty."

The triumph of God and the triumph of Constantine were one. Spiritual and temporal power had now become united. As Eusebius wrote, "This is . . .

what God himself, whom Constantine honored, by standing at Constantine's side . . . confirmed by his manifest judgment, putting forward this man as a lesson in the pattern of godliness to the human race." Constantine was "God-beloved" and "Thrice-blessed."

Such a theological linking of the political order and the divine would have serious repercussions in the later course of Christian history and would find as many critics as defenders. But Eusebius's reading of history also left the faith vulnerable to any change of circumstances. If it was God who led the empire to support Christianity, and God who allowed Constantine to triumph, what could one say about any reversal of fortune? Would a crisis in the empire be a failure by God? This was a question a Western writer, Augustine, would take up about a century later, when the future of the Roman Empire was not as rosy as it had seemed to Eusebius.

The Christian community entered a new era with Constantine. It had embraced the world—for weal and woe—in ways that would have been unfathomable for earlier generations. Throne and altar were joined, and both were dedicated to shaping the social order and creating a new society. The task would be neither simple nor easy.

Chapter 6

Defining and Dividing

*T*he church profited from the munificence of Constantine and his successors, but the imperial bounty gave a practical turn to a question that was as
old as Christianity itself—exactly what was the church? In the decades after
Constantine's conversion Christians wrestled over a myriad of issues and
often found themselves divided. If the empire supported and defended the
"church," when believers divided, to which group did the "church" adhere?
Intraecclesial debates began to have great political significance. In the East
the questions were about theology, while in the West the issue was ecclesiology. The decisions made would both clarify key ideas and divide the
community.

The Question of God and Christ

The question of the relationship between Christ and the God whom Jesus
called Father had been long-standing. From the beginning Christians had tried
to hold three claims that seemed in tension: There was but one God; God was
in Christ; and the Father and the Son were distinct. Throughout the first three
centuries various attempts had been made to reconcile these claims, but none
was successful. Some proposals, such as Adoptionism, tended ultimately to
subordinate the Son to the Father. Others, such as Sabellianism, merged the
Father and the Son so closely that the true identity of Christ became lost.
Both, it was generally agreed, were errors to be avoided.

In Egypt in the early fourth century the question was taken up again.
Arius, a presbyter in Alexandria, thought he had found the answer. If the Son
were truly the Logos, it followed that the Father was the fundamental unitary
principle that lay behind the Logos. The Logos was derived from the Father.
Christ then could not be coeternal with the Father: "There was a time when

65

he was not," Arius argued. The Logos or Christ was part of the created order. Although Arius's solution was condemned by his bishop, he found supporters, and a theological scuffle began. The disturbance caught the attention of Constantine, who sent his chief theological adviser, Hosius of Cordova, to investigate.

The controversy spread. Arius appealed to clergy outside of Alexandria and won the support of the noted historian (and friend and biographer of Constantine) Eusebius, who was a power not to be trifled with. When a local council in Antioch voted to excommunicate Eusebius for his support of Arius, Constantine acted quickly. He called for a general council to examine the question. It was to meet in Nicaea, near the yet-unfinished Constantinople. There Constantine himself would chair the proceedings.

Nicaea has been called the first ecumenical council, and about 220 bishops attended. But it was largely a council of the imperial church. Only two bishops from outside the empire attended—one from Persia and another from Scythia (on the Black Sea)—and they were something of an oddity. No Armenian bishops were reported attending (though Armenians have claimed that their Catholicos was in fact present). The presence of the emperor dominated. As Eusebius reported in his *Life of Constantine*, "All rose at a signal, which announced the Emperor's entrance, and he finally walked between them, like some heavenly angel of God." Constantine urged unity and peace. In the course of the debates Eusebius was rehabilitated, and the bishops crafted a creed to define the official faith. The council's decision to issue a creed was an innovation. Heretofore creedal statements had been associated with baptism. As such they were directed to catechumens and served to instruct. This new creedal statement was directed to clergy and served to define.

On the surface the Nicene statement clearly rejected the teachings of Arius. Christ was defined as begotten not made, and of "one substance with the Father." This last phrase and the Greek term *homoousion* (one substance) were key. However, it was a term not found in Scripture but borrowed from Greek philosophy. Christ and the Father shared a common substance or *ousia*. This made some bishops uneasy. They found the term discomforting because it could be understood to being very close to the Sabellianism (or the merging of the distinction between the Father and the Son) that had been condemned in the previous century. Nonetheless the creed was signed by almost all of the bishops present, though a number did not sign the condemnations, or anathemas, that accompanied it. It seemed as if peace had been achieved.

The Nicene council also passed a series of canons or rules that befitted the new situation in which the church found itself. The date of Easter was finally set. Rules for the consecration of bishops were formalized. The regional authority of the bishops of Antioch, Alexandria, and Rome was affirmed, and rules for admitting lapsed members were set forth. Discipline as well as doctrine were being formalized.

Post-Nicene Developments

Nicaea did not end the controversy over Arianism; it was but the first round. Powerful political forces in the empire, including the emperor Constantius himself (son of Constantine), were determined to at least modify, if not undo, the position decreed at Nicaea.

Early opposition to Nicaea was led by Eusebius of Nicomedia (not to be confused with the historian Eusebius). Although he had formally signed the creed (though not the anathemas), he was not really convinced of its rightness and labored hard to undermine the decision of the council. His closeness to the emperor (indeed, it was he who baptized Constantine on the emperor's deathbed) gave him great power. His strategy was both to remove the key defenders of the creed and to stir up doubts among the conservative Eastern bishops who found the term *homoousion* unbiblical and suspiciously Sabellian. Among those he attempted to eliminate was Athanasius, the bishop of Alexandria.

Athanasius was one of the most forceful and resourceful figures of the fourth century, and he needed all his forces and resources to survive. Five times would he be exiled. He was accused of many crimes and often feared for his life. Particularly after 337 he faced constant battles. Many wanted a compromise that would involve the replacement of *homoousion* with the term *homoiousion*, which merely claims that Christ and the Father were of similar or like substances, rather than the same. This would ease the concerns of many of the conservative critics. The battle hung over the iota, the smallest of Greek letters, and seemed trivial to many.

For Athanasius the debate about the *homoousion* was not an arcane speculative disputation as to the Son's place in creation; it was crucially involved in the matter of salvation. God had created human beings in his own image, but sin brought about not only disobedience but also corruption, a corruption that was the source of human woe. The heavenly God could not remove this corruption: "The Word perceived that corruption could not be got rid of

> If Christ were not truly God, then his sacrifice could not erase the corruption of human nature. Only God could do that.

otherwise than through death, yet He Himself, as the Word being immortal and the Father's Son was such as could not die." The meaning of the incarnation for Athanasius was that God truly entered the world in Christ. The identity (*homoousion*) of the Father and the Son was crucial. If Christ were not truly God, then his sacrifice could not erase the corruption. Only God could do that. "By the offering of His own body, He abolished the death which they had incurred, and corrected their neglect by His own teaching." Only by taking on humanity could God suffer death, and through this death the relationship between God and humanity was restored.

Repeatedly exiled, Athanasius was forced to take refuge in the Western church, and there he found favor, particularly with Julius, who was bishop of Rome. The Western church was somewhat impatient with the theological debate. They viewed it as stemming from an overly subtle Greek vocabulary.

Eventually the great power of the Arian party under the reign of Constantius alarmed many and precipitated a rapprochement between the conservatives (still fearful of Sabellianism) and the defenders of Nicaea. It was recognized that the term *homoousion* standing alone could cause confusion. The term could theoretically mean either one substance or one person. Hence to avoid confusion it was asserted that although there was in God but one substance (*homoousion*), there were three persons (*hypostasis*). This breakthrough was the accomplishment of three individuals: Basil of Caesarea, Gregory of Nazianzus, and Gregory of Nyssa. Together they were known as the Cappadocian fathers. But they also appealed to the prayer life of the community to defend their compromise. On the liturgical or sacramental level, the church had always been Trinitarian; it both baptized and blessed in the name of the Father, Son, and Spirit. Any theological definition would need to reflect this fundamental reality. The Father and the Son were at the same time one and separate. But by arguing so, a clarification of the Spirit became necessary. In all of the careful discussion of the relation between the Father and the Son at Nicaea, the Spirit was merely mentioned in passing. Indeed some claimed that the Spirit was something of an angel, or merely a messenger. If one were to claim a triune God, the third person would have to be defined.

In 379 Theodosius became emperor. A staunch foe of Arianism, he called for a council to meet in Constantinople in 381. There 186 bishops gathered. The language of Nicaea was reaffirmed, and a clause on the Holy Spirit was added to the creed, stating that the Holy Spirit proceeded from the Father and was to be glorified. This modified creed—technically the Nicene-Constantinopolitan Creed but today generally referred to simply as the Nicene Creed—would become the fundamental Christian statement on the nature of the Godhead. God, though a mystery, was one substance in three persons. Through theological acumen and the power of the emperor, Arianism was finally defeated. Although it would find a home among the Germanic tribes outside of the empire, through the labors of the missionary Ulphilas, in the Roman world it was rejected.

The Nature of Christ

Athanasius had claimed that the eternal Christ had to take on humanity so that the human race could again be reconciled to God. But what did this mean? What was the relationship of humanity and divinity in Christ? This question would consume Christians in the eastern half of the empire and would result in two more ecumenical councils, another creed, and painful divisions.

The complicated theological question was still further complicated by politics. The sixth canon of the Council of Nicaea reaffirmed the dignity and authority of the metropolitan jurisdictions of Alexandria, Antioch, and Rome. But among those three, which had precedence? Rome was in some ways geographically detached. Few denied its place in the Latin-speaking church, but the West was a backwater. Rome was a big fish in a very poor pond. But the East was different: it was the center of the empire and the center of Christianity, and there Alexandria and Antioch were rivals. Each saw itself as the primary metropolitan center, or see, of the Eastern church. Each viewed the other with suspicion, and both cast a wary eye on the upstart church in Constantinople. If dignity was a matter of apostolical descent, they had nothing to fear. Constantinople could match neither St. Mark of Alexandria nor St. John of Antioch. But Constantinople did have something neither of its rivals possessed: the presence of the emperor and the center of imperial administration. The bishops at Constantinople in 381 had added a vague canon recognizing the dignity of the bishop of Constantinople, but no one was sure exactly what this implied. Hence the christological debates (as the discussion concerning the relationship of Christ's humanity and divinity came to be called) would be in the context of a three-way duel among Alexandria, Antioch, and Constantinople.

The theological traditions of Alexandria and Antioch were in many ways different. They marched to different philosophical drummers and had different concerns. Alexandrian theology was fundamentally Platonic in nature. Plato is the philosopher of unity rather than of classification, and Alexandrians shared this emphasis. As Platonists, Alexandrian theologians had a predilection for the permanent rather than the transient. The Logos for them was the unchanging nature of God. And they showed a Platonic understanding of the human person by seeing people as bodies animated by souls, with the soul being the far greater reality.

Antiochene theology was much more Aristotelian in nature. These theologians tended toward observation and classification rather than synthesis and metaphysical unity. They likewise shared Aristotle's understanding of humanity as being a psychophysical unity and not merely a soul in a body, as Platonists thought. And the Aristotelian concern for potentiality and becoming made a sense of development a key part of their understanding.

Philosophical differences led the two groups to use the Bible differently. For Alexandrians, the core of Scripture was its eternal, unchanging meaning. Such a meaning, more often than not, was not to be found in the letter of the text, which all too often was tied to a changing, ephemeral existence. Scripture accordingly was to be read allegorically. Antiochenes took an opposite approach. Theodore of Mopsuestia, the leading biblical interpreter among the Antiochenes, eschewed a mystical or allegorical interpretation of Scripture in favor of an emphasis on the particularity of the historical narrative.

All of these presuppositions shaped their differing approaches to Christology. Their differences, though subtle, are important. Both agreed, contra the Arians, that in Christ God entered into the world. For Alexandrians the eternal Word of God became *flesh*. The Logos was present in Jesus Christ in a way that formed a single entity or person. That unity was the key to the incarnation. In the incarnation the Logos did not take on the identity of a particular human in union but created a complete union with human nature. As they stated, "He was himself personally the Son of God and took human nature in vital union with himself." This implied that there was a complete interchangeability between Christ's humanity and divinity.

Antiochene writers framed the question differently. Christ did not merely become *flesh* but became *human*. Human nature was important, and Christ needed to possess a true human nature. In part this flowed from their Aristotelian understanding that a true human must possess both a body and a soul. But it also followed from their reading of Scripture. According to the Gospels, Jesus had all the marks of full humanity; he hungered, wept, expressed limitations in knowledge, and displayed other human attributes. The Antiochene approach did protect the historical Jesus, but to their Alexandrian critics, the Antiochenes threatened the unity of Christ's person. If Christ had a human nature and a divine nature, what was to be the revelation between them? Did the two natures exist in tandem, or was there a true union?

These differing approaches can be best seen in the issue that made their disagreements public. Throughout the fourth century the devotion to Mary, the mother of Christ, had grown. Her place in the narrative of salvation was essential. Mary was the one who assented to God's plan and thus gave birth to the savior. A Greek term, *Theotokos*, or God-bearer, had entered into popular devotion to describe Mary's role. Opponents of Arianism latched on to the term to defend the full divinity of Christ. Furthermore, the *Theotokos* gave a regal honor to the virgin. A popular image was the adoration of the Christ child by the magi, and in it a baby Jesus rested on the lap of a queenly Mary. The image was particularly attractive to recent converts from paganism, who would have undoubtedly found the absence of female imagery in Christian iconography peculiar.

But on the theological level, in what sense could one say that Mary was the God-bearer or the Mother of God (as the term was rendered in Latin)? From the Alexandrian point of view, with its idea of the divine/human unity, it was perfectly appropriate to ascribe characteristics of humanity (such as being born) to Christ's divinity. Antiochene writers were not so sure. Truly Mary was the mother of the earthly Jesus (*Anthropotokos*), but to what degree could she be called the Mother of God?

These philosophical and exegetical questions were soon compounded by bitter church politics. To ensure their preeminence, patriarchs of Alexandria needed a weak archbishop of Constantinople. At the end of the fourth century they had successfully intrigued to have the Antiochene monk John Chrysostom, one of the great preachers in Christian history, removed from his office as archbishop of Constantinople. The selection of another Antiochene monk—Nestorius—as his successor made the Alexandrian patriarch, Cyril, all the more worried. Nestorius combined an Antiochene discomfort with language of *Theotokos* with a willingness to involve himself in the affairs of the church of Alexandria. He was seen as a threat, and in Cyril he met a formidable opponent—a man who combined theological acumen with a love of brass-knuckle ecclesiastical politics. He accused Nestorius of denying the *Theotokos* and claimed Nestorius did so because he did not believe that Christ was God (an untrue claim). Nestorius, as archbishop of Constantinople, had the emperor on his side, but Cyril could count on popular piety, as well as influential members of the imperial court, to support his attacks. He also had the support of Rome. He issued "twelve anathemas" that condemned the Antiochene claim that Christ had two natures. In 431 a third ecumenical council, in Ephesus, was called to deal with the issue.

The core of Nestorius's support came from Antioch and the surrounding Syrian bishops. They arrived at Ephesus late, and in the interim Cyril had convinced the council to excommunicate Nestorius. When the Syrians finally arrived, they in turn excommunicated Cyril. Which vote was authoritative? Rome and eventually the emperor backed Cyril; hence the third ecumenical council went down in history as condemning Nestorianism. Nestorius was forced from office and retired to a monastery in Antioch.

But Nestorius's condemnation alienated the Antiochene church and threatened ecclesiastical unity. Through pressure, Cyril retreated. He withdrew his twelve anathemas and signed a formulary affirming the fundamental principles of Antiochene theology. A peace (albeit an uneasy one) reigned in the [...]os, wanted to complete the [...]vas to resurrect the twelve [...] would not only be a blow [...] the Alexandrian church. A [...] here Dioscuros carried the [...] *ophusis*) was asserted, and [...]dria had triumphed, and the [...] Alexandrian position. [...] nd no longer supported the [...]ten a letter, or tome, objecting to the Monophysite position. The letter, however, was never read at the council. An angry Leo refused to accept the authority of the council and condemned it as "a den of robbers" (*latrocinium*).

[Handwritten margin notes:]
o Rome backed Cyril +
Nestorius was gone
o Cyril wanted unity
so he backed down
↳ successor is Dioscuros
↳ Antioch bishops condemned
Settlement of Chalcedon:
o reversed - condemned Dioscuros

The Settlement of Chalcedon

Alexandria's hope rested on imperial acquiescence, and in 450 the emperor Theodosius II fell from a horse and died. His successor was leery of the Alexandrian cabal. Instead, a new council was called to meet in Chalcedon in 451, where it soon became clear that the extreme Alexandrian position of Monophysitism no longer held sway. The bishops at Chalcedon reversed the decisions made two years before at Ephesus, and instead condemned Dioscuros. Leo's tome was publicly read. A new creedal statement was issued, condemning the errors of both the Nestorians and the Monophysites. Christ, it was said, was "born from the Virgin Mary, the *Theotokos*, as touching the manhood, one and the same Christ, Son Lord, Only-begotten, to be acknowledged in two natures, without confusion, without change, without

The quest for christological clarity may have resulted in the crystallization of a key element of Christian theology—and Chalcedonian Christology would remain unchallenged in most of the church for fifteen hundred years—but it introduced a three-way division among Eastern Christians.

division, without separation; the distinction of natures being in no way abolished because of the union." Chalcedon claimed doctrinal closure for the question of Christology just as Constantinople had claimed it for the Trinity. The emperor had once again spoken.

But had su~~ch closure occurred? The ch~~ ~~in E~~ (Alexandrians) may have bee~~n~~ ~~ey continued to hold fast t~~ ~~ority of Chal~~cedon. The d~~ ~~ce Chalcedon precipitated b~~ ~~ypt and Con~~stantinople. T~~ ~~Ethiopia who were connect~~ ~~ans any hap~~pier. The con~~ ~~ault on all of Antiochene th~~ ~~nded outside the empire to~~ ~~rian dissatis~~faction with i~~ ~~v. They were willing to acc~~ ~~ed at accept~~ing Ephesus, ~~ ~~os. The divi~~sions that had~~ ~~ristological clarity may have resu~~ ~~the crystallization of a key element of Christian theology—and Chalcedonian Christology would remain unchallenged in most of the church for fifteen hundred years—but it introduced a three-way division among Eastern Christians. A dominant Constantinople (backed by the emperor) confronted disgruntled Egyptians and Syrians, supported by their nonimperial allies.

Chalcedon further resulted in the ascendancy of the church of Constantinople. The council in its canons asserted that the bishop of Constantinople was to have not only the "prerogative of honor" second only to the bishop of Rome but also power and privilege. Constantinople was granted jurisdiction and authority over Thrace, Asia, and the Pontic dioceses. Rome refused to accept this elevation of the power of the new see and rejected the canon, to little avail. As long as the emperor exercised authority, Constantinople would hold sway.

The Problem of Donatism

If in the Eastern part of the Christian world the dividing issues were those of Trinity and Christology, in the West they involved the nature of the church. The Diocletian persecution, one recalls, led many to make compromises. The church, some claimed, must ride the waves of the crisis and not drown in martyrdom. Such compromising struck more rigorous souls as a betrayal of the Christian faith. Those who made such compromises, critics continued, forfeited the right to be ministers of the gospel.

Mensurius was one such culprit. As bish[op] ... e cooperated with authoritie[s] ... d of persecution. He died i[n] ... r, Caecilian, who showed th[e] ... sed of being a *traditor* for h[is] ... self unfit for leadership. His ... thage found itself with two ...

Who knows w... rred earlier, but, as it was, it ... empowering the church. T... tored property and paid co[mpensation] ... epresented the true church? ... e, particularly since North Africa, the breadbasket of the Western empire, was a crucial province to keep placated. Both Caecilian and his opponents made their case, and for reasons both high and low Caecilian and his supporters were judged to be the true church while his opponents, known as the Donatists, were deemed schismatic. The Council of Arles reaffirmed the decision, as did the emperor himself in 316. None of this persuaded the Donatists. Foreign churches, they claimed, could not interfere in the deliberations of a regional church. In the confrontation, Constantine, the first Christian emperor, in 317 inaugurated the first Christian persecution of fellow Christians.

The split between Catholics and Donatists was not about theology per se. Both read the same Bible and affirmed the same creeds. Rather it hung on a number of questions concerning the nature of the church and its ministry. The first was that of connectionalism versus purity. In appealing to other churches Catholics claimed that a regional church was part of a network of churches. Since both Rome and Jerusalem recognized their claim, they, the Catholics, must be the true church. Donatists instead emphasized the purity of the church. Digging deeply into their African tradition, they claimed that the true church must be unstained. Cyprian had earlier taught that apostate ministers were invalid, as were their sacraments. Donatists, they claimed, were true to the African principle of purity. A second issue involved the holiness of the church. Donatists believed that holiness was the responsibility of each member. Those who failed, such as the *traditori*, must be excluded. For Catholics the holiness of the church was not so much empirical as structural. Noah's ark was dark and dirty, yet it was nonetheless an ark of salvation. So too was the church. Jesus had spoken in one of his parables of a field of wheat that

had been marred by   plants.
Rather than trying to   t, Jesus
counseled that they   d only
then were they to be   vays be
a mixed community   e question of sacraments.   ded on
the worthiness of th   uld be
invalid. Catholics ne   e hands
of *traditori* were inv   aments
depended on God's   . When
they were correctly

[Handwritten margin note:]
Sacraments?
D: worthiness of minister
C: God's promise

Augustine of Hippo
- against his will ordained
  a priest
- became Bishop of Hippo
° famous writer/philosopher
  ⤷ Donatist controversy

The full shape of these divisions evolved over a long and bitter controversy, but it was in the Donatist debates that Augustine of Hippo would make his mark. Augustine is the greatest theologian Latin Christianity has ever produced. Indeed, some call him the greatest theologian of all. He was born in 354 in what is now Algeria to a pagan father and a Christian mother. A brilliant student, he was little attracted to the religion of his mother, Monica, preferring to focus on fame, fortune, sensuality, and a career in Italy (as he was later to lament in his autobiographical *Confessions*). Only later did his driving intellect and questioning spirit lead him through various philosophies and back to the faith of his mother. Baptized in 387, he returned to Africa to establish a lay ascetic community. In 391, while visiting the town of Hippo, he was seized by the people

> Augustine is the greatest theologian Latin Christianity has ever produced. Indeed, some call him the greatest theologian of all.

and, against his will, was ordained a priest. To add insult to injury, in 395 he was made assistant bishop and shortly thereafter, after the death of his aged predecessor, was made bishop of Hippo.

Augustine's corpus of writing is monumental, and no short discussion can do it justice. He wrote dazzling theological works and sublime biblical commentaries, but his writings on the Donatist controversy helped crystallize his understanding of the church, and this would become foundational for Western Catholicism. For Augustine the Catholic Church was a body held together by the Spirit, which gave to it a unity in faith, hope, and charity.

Such a unity was the greatest of miracles and proved that the church was not a mere human creation. Furthermore, it was in the church that the Spirit worked. The movement of the soul was a pilgrimage toward God. Individual souls might be mutable and unreliable, but when connected to the church by the bonds of love, they followed this path. Last, the church was an institution. It was a communion within whose bonds God worked through appointed sacramental means. Infused with divine grace, the soul moved toward the final union with God in the heavenly kingdom. For Donatists to break away from such a church was baffling to him. The church was the realm of Christ. There was no salvation apart from it.

Through Augustine, the Donatist controversy gave to Western Catholicism two additional principles. The first was an elevated doctrine of the sacraments. The sacraments were the means by which God infused grace into the believers. Augustine was perhaps the first to use the phrase "Word and sacrament" to describe divine action through the Bible and the sacraments. For him these two means of grace were inextricably linked. Both were objective means that left a mark on the soul. The second principle is perhaps harder to swallow today. This was the willingness to use force to defend true religion. At first Augustine believed that only reason and moral suasion should be used to influence the Donatists, but gradually he came to believe that sinfulness made coercion sometimes justifiable. Human beings, he argued, perished in error not simply for principled reasons but by misperception. Jesus in his parables had said, "Compel them to come in." For Augustine, sin was a strong force, and hence a strong force was necessary to correct it.

Discussion of coercion points again to the changed world of the fourth century. The conversion of the empire brought the force of the sword into alliance with Christianity, and deviant Christians would find it used against them as well as outsiders. Rome, in establishing the church, claimed the right to determine who were the true Christians and also the right to enforce that judgment.

Augustine's view of human sinfulness and its effects would have a further ramification. The idea of "original sin" had a long tradition in earlier North African Christianity, but Augustine would make it central to understanding the human predicament. Human nature was broken. It suffered from "concupiscence," or the love of and desire for the wrong things. This false love turned humans away from God and was the source of unhappiness. For those called to faith, baptism began the correction of this. It freed one from sin. But the disorder remained, just as a physical deformity might remain from a broken limb even when the bone had been healed. The subsequent Christian life was a long process of reordering, and there were no short cuts. As he argued against the Donatists, one could not avoid sin by walling oneself up in a pure community (even if such a one existed). But neither could one avoid sin by trusting in one's own will. This was the error of the British monk Pelagius (350–425). He taught that a human being could freely choose the good, and he urged others to do so. Augustine was dubious about such counsel. Sin was a strong enemy. The battle against sin began at the very beginning with infant baptism (a practice that would have been unthinkable a century earlier, when baptism was linked to human choice) and continued in a life marked by grace, struggle, and growth. God offered grace, but human beings needed to accept it, and even so, some grew faster than others and some seemed not to grow at all. It was all a mystery of God.

Augustine beats Pelagius

Pelagius would be condemned at the Council of Ephesus—the same one that condemned the Donatists—but his influence did not go away. In many ways the optimistic Pelagius was closer to the way Greek Christians saw God working than was Augustine. Augustine's ideas would formally triumph in the Latin West, and Pelagius was buried. But he never stayed buried.

One hundred and forty years after Constantine's conversion, Christianity would find itself in a far more organized and defined state than it ever had been, but it was also more divided. The great questions of the triune Godhead and of the nature of Christ had been set forth. The church had become an important—if not the most important—institution in the empire. But it had become so at the cost of serious and lasting divisions. The church of the Eastern empire was in three pieces, with the Christian communities outside the empire (as we shall see) more in sympathy with the "losers" at Ephesus and Chalcedon than the victors. The church of North Africa remained divided despite the best efforts of Augustine. The community was both stronger and weaker, and both aspects—strengths and weaknesses—would come into play in the next centuries.

° CHURCH IS EVERYTHING
Western Catholics:
1.) elevated doctrine of sacraments
2.) willingness to use force to defend religion

Chapter 7

Out of One, Many

*T*he great dream of the Christian emperors was that there might be a united Christian church that would serve to strengthen the empire. This too had been the vision of Eusebius of Caesarea, the early church historian. But it was not to be. The failure of Chalcedon to provide a foundation of unity as the Council of Constantinople had done meant there was no longer a unified Christian community. Instead there were a number of regional bodies, each claiming to be the true church. These regional Christianities would continue to flourish in the three centuries after 451, but all would be affected by the changing political fortunes of the empire and by the rise of a new religious force in the seventh century—Islam—which would profoundly influence the course of Christianity.

The Church of Constantinople

If one regional church could still claim the mantle of the true church, it would be Constantinople, often known simply as the Eastern Orthodox Church. There the union of church and empire, forged by Constantine, continued to hold sway. Canon 28 of the Council of Chalcedon had assigned to Constantinople, the New Rome, an order of rank second only to old Rome. To symbolize its power, in 537 the great church of Hagia Sophia was dedicated, and it, along with the great Sacred Palace of the emperor, was the center of the city. The unity of church and empire was reflected in other ways. In the palace there stood a throne that contained an open Gospel book, to remind all of the nature of imperial authority. In public worship, emperor and patriarch together led worship. As one er. peror was said to proclaim, "The greatest blessings of mankind and the gifts of God which have been granted us by the mercy on high are the priesthood and the imperial authority. The priesthood ministers to things divine: the imperial authority is set over and shows diligence in things human, but both proceed from one and the same source and both adorn the life of man." Church and emperor worked in tandem for the glory of God.

> A later account reflected the impressiveness of Byzantine worship: "We knew not whether we were on heaven or on earth."

This did not mean that the lot was always easy for the Christian emperor. When it appeared that God had turned his back on an emperor, the reaction of the people could be fierce. Of thirty-eight emperors who served between Constantine and the fall of Byzantium in 1453, thirty met violent deaths. One poor discredited emperor, before being tortured to death, was dragged through the streets with his head under the tail of a sick camel.

As the imperial church developed, worship began to take on a special role. The church was a holy place, and divine worship was an occasion for an encounter with the holy. As one leader wrote, "The Church is an earthly heaven in which the supercelestial God dwells and walks about." A building like Hagia Sophia was seen as symbolic of the cosmos. The great dome and the presence of light gave glimmers of the heavenly sanctuary. A later account reflected the impressiveness of Byzantine worship: "We knew not whether we were on heaven or on earth. For surely there is no such splendor or beauty anywhere upon earth. We cannot describe it to you: only this we know, that God dwells these among men, and that their service surpasses the worship of all other places. For we cannot forget that beauty." The liturgy practiced in these great churches contained processions, chanting, and music, all to bring the persons assembled into a sense of the sacredness of the place and moment. But worship was not circumscribed by church buildings. Processions were a major part of Byzantine religious life and brought a sense of holiness to the city at large. Processions that began in the streets would end in the church. Some evening processions in which the faithful carried torches led observers to describe the streets as being filled with rivers of fire.

Worship was solemn and elaborate, required great effort, and could easily become excessive. To counteract this, the patriarch Sergius mandated that the worship be simplified and decreed that the staff of Hagia Sophia be reduced to 80 priests, 150 deacons, 40 deaconesses, 70 subdeacons, 160 readers, 25 cantors, and 100 doorkeepers! Such a simplification would have puzzled earlier Christians.

Monasticism was still another institution central in the life of Byzantium. Monasteries were not only centers of worship and hospitality but also sources for higher clergy. In the Orthodox tradition, monks could not be married, but parish priests could (if they were married before being ordained). Since bishops also had to be unmarried, most bishops were drawn from the monasteries. By the fifth century monasticism was no longer purely rural, and by the end of the sixth century there were sixty-eight monasteries in Constantinople alone. The presence of monks would only increase in later years. A century later, in part because of persecution in the countryside that forced many monks to flee to Constantinople for safety, observers would note that there appeared to be as many monks in the city as there were laypeople.

Along with worship, Byzantine Christianity was characterized by its continuing emphasis on the conciliar tradition. The ecumenical nature of the councils, they believed, guaranteed that they would be a source of true teaching. After Chalcedon there were three more ecumenical councils: the second council of Constantinople (553), the third council of Constantinople (681), and the second council of Nicaea (787). The first two addressed issues festering about the nature of Christ. The last, however, dealt with the question of icons.

Icons, or images of Christ and the saints, were still another fundamental part of the piety of Byzantine Christianity. As such, they reflected a continuing move away from the older Jewish tradition. Judaism, strictly interpreting the Mosaic commandment against idolatry, was strongly opposed to the use of any graven images. Byzantine Christians, in contrast, believed that Christ's incarnation had modified this ban. In Christ the unpictured God of the Old Testament had taken on human form, and the incarnation put pictorial images in a new light. If God had chosen to take on human form, human form could be represented pictorially. Images taught the truth of the incarnation, but even more, they made Christ and the saints present in a special way. They were not mere pictures but heavenly images that had been miraculously recorded here on earth, and as such, they were gateways to the divine. They could appropriately be venerated as objects of worship and be touched and kissed.

The nature of Byzantine Christianity can perhaps best be seen in the life and labors of the emperor Justinian (483–565), who, when he became emperor in 527, saw the unity of his empire challenged both politically and theologically. In this regard he was assisted by his wife, the empress Theodora, who was a strong power in herself. During the fifth century Roman imperial authority had largely collapsed in the western half of the empire as a result of the migration of Germanic tribes into the empire. Rome itself had been sacked in 410. As we will see, the sack of Rome led some Western Christians such as Augustine to rethink the meaning of God in history. For

Justinian the collapse of the Western empire was simply a political problem to be corrected. Theologically, Justinian inherited an empire divided by the decisions at the councils of Ephesus and Chalcedon. His task was to make his empire truly Christian and truly united. In 528 he announced to the remaining pagan citizens of the empire that they had three months in which to be baptized. He closed the Academy in Athens, a center of pagan philosophy, in 529 and decreed that all knowledge taught must be Christian. He also reorganized the legal system. The result was the *Codex Justinianus*, or the Justinian Code, which translated Roman law into a Christian context and would be the foundation of much later law. It was he who oversaw the construction of Hagia Sophia. Justinian was likewise bent on restoring the unity of "the Fortunate race of Romans," by restoring imperial authority over the lost western provinces. In the 530s he began a campaign to take back Carthage, Sicily, Rome, and Ravenna from their Germanic conquerors. Finally he strove (unsuccessfully, as we shall see) to reconcile the Monophysites.

Justinian was in many ways the ideal Christian emperor: pious, orthodox, interested in theology, and anxious to support the church. But his agenda was ultimately a failure. By draining the empire's resources in his bid to reconquer the West, he left his realm vulnerable to the attacks of old enemies such as Persia. His attempts to restore doctrinal unity were also of no avail. Nor were the fates kind to him. In the 540s a plague devastated Constantinople, killing, according to some estimates, a third of the population. After this the empire could never muster the strength it once had. In 600 Constantinople could claim to be the leading center of Christianity, but its position was not as strong as it seemed.

Critics of Chalcedon

The decisions at Chalcedon had created a breach between the church in Egypt, known as the Coptic Church, and the empire. The bishops meeting in Chalcedon had not only rejected Monophysitism by adopting the "two nature" language but also deposed the Alexandrian patriarch, Dioscuros, and his successor, Timothy. An alternative bishop, Proterius, was set up as patriarch by the emperor in Constantinople, but his tenure rested on imperial support. To the populace of the city of Alexandria, Proterius and his few supporters were merely "Melchites" (from the Syrian for imperial), or minions of the emperor. When, in time, imperial support faltered, the Alexandrian mob made short work of the emperor's patriarch. According to one account, they hunted Proterius down and, in the baptistery of the church in which he was serving, murdered him. Then they dragged his body through the city, ate of it, and burned the remains, scattering the ashes to the wind.

The emperor continued to maintain an orthodox patriarchate in Alexandria, but it was the Monophysite clergy who enjoyed the support of the populace. The conflict between Melchites and Monophysites was often bitter. Constantinople did everything it could to keep Egypt—a major source of grain for the Eastern empire—in line both politically and religiously. One tactic involved trying to solve the divisive theological issues. Various attempts were made to rethink the decisions of Chalcedon. The *Henoticon*, or act of union, was sponsored by the emperor Zeno and issued in 482 as an attempt to bridge the impasse. It reaffirmed the inherited faith, concurred with the condemnation of Nestorius, and included the twelve anathemas of Cyril, while remaining diplomatically silent concerning the nature or natures of Christ. A century and a half later, still another compromise was floated under the name of Monotheletism. This position tried to sidestep the Chalcedonian quagmire by shifting the issue from the nature of Christ to his will. Monotheletism claimed that Christ had but one will.

The compromises, however, failed to restore unity. On the religious level, Rome, deeply committed to the language of two natures as set forth in the Tome of Leo and affirmed at Chalcedon, balked at any compromise, and Constantinople resisted alienating Rome. On the political level, Constantinople was never quite clear whether it wanted to reconcile its opponents or crush them. The seventh-century imperial appointee Cyrus was not only the Melchite patriarch but imperial prefect of Egypt as well, and in the latter role he embarked on a vigorous policy of persecution to defeat the Monophysite movement. Flogging, imprisonment, and death began to rain upon Monophysite clergy. The result was, however, only a further alienation of the Egyptian church.

The Egyptian Copts were not alone in rejecting Chalcedon. So did a large part of the church in Syria. The position of Syrian Christianity is complicated because the Syrian church was made up of three distinctive groups. There was first a Greek-speaking community centered in Antioch that largely followed the patterns of the rest of the classical world. A second group was the Syrian-speaking Christians of the countryside of west Syria (in the area that is now present-day Syria). Third, there was a community of Christians in east Syria, largely outside of the Roman Empire (in the area that is now Iraq) that, as we shall see, stood out in its own way. Of the first two groups, Greek-speaking Syrians tended to accept the Chalcedonian settlement while Syrian speakers sided with the Monophysites. These two groups were often in competition.

The religious conflict in Syria evoked a mixed response from Constantinople. The political importance of west Syria led the empire at times to attempt to reach an accord between Orthodox and Monophysites there. The empress Theodora was both religiously and politically sympathetic to the Syrian Monophysites and even sheltered a Monophysite monastic community in the Grand Palace in Constantinople. However, her husband, the emperor Justinian, had other views. Under him, the policy was to enforce conformity. Believing that there could be only one church in the empire, Justinian's agents harrowed the Monophysite clergy.

It was during this time of persecution that one of the legendary figures in Syrian Christianity was to emerge, Jacob Baradeus (also spelled Baradaeus; 500–578). In the midst of the Monophysite persecution he was consecrated metropolitan, or chief bishop, of Edessa. Eschewing any fixed headquarters, he began a memorable ministry traveling through Syria, Armenia, Cappadocia, and many other places. His vestments were made of old saddlecloths, not only because of poverty but to elude imperial agents. His feats were storied. Apocryphal accounts state that he ordained 102,000 priests and 89 bishops in the course of his ministry. Even when these numbers have been reduced by modern scholars to priestly ordinations in the thousands and 27 episcopal ordinations, his labors were impressive. To this day, Monophysite Syrian Christians are called Jacobite Christians.

The split over the Council of Chalcedon would extend beyond the confines of the old empire. The churches of the Nile were offspring of the Coptic Church, and they too would reject Chalcedon. In the area of what is now the Sudan, the Nubian church took root. Although Christianity had been known there earlier, the traditional date given for the formal organization of the Nubian church there is 543, when a Coptic priest named Julian convinced the empress Theodora to send missionaries to the region. Indeed, both Orthodox and Monophysite missionaries were dispatched. A competition developed over who would set the pattern for the new church. The Monophysites triumphed, and the Nubians became still another church to reject Chalcedon. Nubian Christianity became strongly influenced by the indigenous culture of the region, in particular the emphasis on the office of the king as a sacred office. Nubian Christianity later disappeared. However, it was an early example of Christianity finding favor in a part of Africa that had never been part of the Roman Empire.

Even more important was the church of Ethiopia. The connection of Ethiopian Christianity to the biblical record is intriguing. The first book of Kings tells of the Queen of Sheba, who came to study with Solomon, bringing him magnificent gifts. Later tradition associated her with Ethiopia. In another ancient tradition, the ark of the covenant, when lost to history with the destruction of the first Jewish Temple, found its way to Ethiopia, where it allegedly still resides. Likewise in the Acts of the Apostles one of the early conversion narratives entailed an Ethiopian eunuch. Archeologists have documented a long-term connection between Ethiopia and Arabia, which were separated only by the narrow Red Sea. It was through this connection, claims still another ancient account, that Christianity entered Ethiopia. Early in the fourth century, two Syrian Christians returning from India were part of a crew captured by barbarians. Taken to the court of King Ella-Amida of Aksum, they eventually became important assistants in the governance of the country, where they established a small Christian community. On their release, one of them, Frumentius, traveled to Egypt to convince Athanasius to send a bishop. Athanasius ordained Frumentius, who returned to labor in Ethiopia.

Whatever the status of the tradition, the linkage between the churches of Egypt and Ethiopia became important, and the churches became interlinked. Christianity acquired increased popular support, particularly with the arrival of the "nine saints" who built numerous monasteries and churches. Perhaps the most famous was Debre Damo, which is the oldest existing church in Ethiopia. As a church in the Coptic orbit, Ethiopians would also reject the authority of Chalcedon.

The Armenian church was somewhat anomalous. Though often classified as a Monophysite church, its story has to do more with language and culture than theology. Its Catholicos participated in both the councils of Nicaea and Constantinople, and, though not present, Catholicos Parthiev approved the conclusions of Ephesus. But the church had a sense of independence from its early stages. Not being part of the Roman Empire, it rejected the idea of a universal church so important for the Roman Christian world. The creation of a written Armenian language in the late fourth century contributed to this as Scripture, philosophy, and liturgy became recorded in Armenian. The break was complete by 554/5 when the Armenian church formally severed its ties with both Constantinople and Rome. Although on one level one could call the division theological, since Armenians refused to accept the technical language of the Chalcedonian settlement, it had in fact far more to do with fears of political domination by Constantinople.

The Nestorian East

If the Christian communities of Egypt, Ethiopia, and West Syria found themselves at odds with the church of the empire as a result of the decisions at

Chalcedon, the Christian communities farther east objected to the condemnation of Nestorius at Ephesus. East Syria, or what is now Iraq, had been for
centuries almost wholly outside the Roman world and looked to Persia as the
dominant power. The identification of the Eastern Syrian church with Nestorius is complicated. The condemnation of Nestorius led his supporters (along
with many other proponents of Antiochene theology) to take refuge in Edessa,
on the easternmost fringe of the empire. One of these exiles, Ibas, became
head of the theological college there and in 435 became bishop of Edessa.
Imperial persecution of Nestorians and the closing of the theological college
by the emperor Zeno in 489 led the community to seek refuge in Persia.

What attracted the small Persian Christian community to Nestorianism
was less doctrine and more practical politics. Since Constantine, Christians
in Persia had been viewed with suspicion as potential subversives. A religion identified with the Roman Empire had little chance flourishing among
Rome's long-term adversaries. Nestorianism provided a critical distance.
Since it was officially condemned by the Roman Empire, Nestorianism could
not be seen as a Western stalking horse. Nestorian theology and Persian independence were brought together under Acacius (486), bishop of Seleucia-
Ctesiphon, when the Persian church condemned both Monophysitism and
Chalcedonian orthodoxy and formally accepted a Nestorian understanding
of Christ's natures. Persian monarchs encouraged the growth of Nestorian
Christianity in their realm. The bishop of Seleucia-Ctesiphon was viewed
by Persian Christians as the patriarchal see, and this claim was ratified by
the Persian King Yazdegerd. Persian Christianity was now separate from the
other branches of the church.

The lot of the Persian church was never easy, and it suffered periodic
episodes of persecution. Persecution imbued the church with an austere
monastic discipline and a missionary zeal. The latter made Nestorians the
mother community of Asian Christianity. Cut off from the Mediterranean
world yet open to the great trade routes of the East, Nestorian missionaries
planted churches from Arabia to China (reaching the latter as early as 635).
Although these communities were small, they represented an area of growth
in a largely stagnant Christian world, and they constituted what some have
called the most dramatic expansion of Christianity since the early centuries.

The Dormant West

But what was happening in the West, in that part of the old Roman Empire
later to be known as Europe? A survey of Christianity circa 600 CE showed

that no part of the church was as weak as the Latin-speaking West. Yet ironically, in its weakness lay seeds of revitalization.

The Western empire had for centuries been the weaker part of the empire. Egypt provided grain; the cities of Asia Minor offered commerce; Constantinople was the jewel through which all was ruled; but the West had little to offer. Because of this, by the late fourth century the empire had begun to shift its resources so as better to protect its valued provinces. This imperial downsizing resulted in a power vacuum. Just at this time the Gothic Germanic tribes that had for centuries lived in peace along the empire's borders began to move into the imperial lands. Some of these tribes, particularly those in the area of the Danube, which had long-standing contacts with Roman society, entered peacefully. Others, including those along the Rhine who were much less Romanized, entered with more conflict. But the twofold combination of imperial withdrawal and Germanic occupation overturned the fragile economic order of the Western empire. This "invasion," if less violent than it is often pictured, was a traumatic one nonetheless.

In 410, Alaric, a Visigothic king, captured and sacked Rome. The capture of Rome, the "eternal city," was shocking. Some recalled that Rome had been preserved under the old gods. What was now happening, and why did the new Christian God allow it to happen? Alaric's conquest occasioned Augustine of Hippo's greatest work, *The City of God*. In that volume Augustine not only answered these charges but also in the context of the collapse of the empire set forth a theology of history acutely different from the triumphalistic account of Eusebius. Augustine's worldview would be central to the development of a distinctive Western Christianity.

> For Augustine, the entire world of humanity was made up of two great cities—the city of God, directed by true love and moving toward heaven, and the city of the world or humanity, inspired by lesser loves and heading toward perdition.

The problem with the critics, Augustine explained, was that they did not know the real issue at hand. The ultimate goal of humanity, he taught, was the journey toward God. In that sense, Rome, like any political body, was beside the point. It was an instrument God could, but did not have to, use. For Augustine, the entire world of humanity was made up of two great cities—the city of God, directed by true love and moving toward heaven, and the city of the world or humanity (or in Augustine's language, the city of man), inspired by lesser loves and heading toward perdition. But at present they inhabit the same society—and indeed perhaps the same household. Consequently no political organ, not even a Christian empire, could be identified with the city of God. All political organizations were mixed beings. They could do good things, such as restrain evildoers, but were not *ultimately* good. Although never explicitly referring to Eusebius, it was clear that there could be no union of church and empire in the city of God. But even the church, he continued, could not be equated with the city of God. It too was mixed. At best it was an ambiguous anticipation of the city of God. Until the end of history Christians must be reconciled to living with ambiguity, because only at the end of history would the two cities be finally separated.

New Institutions

Augustine's sober realism would shape the mind of Western Christianity for a millennium and provide a rationale for a political theory very different from that of Byzantium. But a more pressing immediate need was to fill the vacuum left by the ebbing of the imperial order. Into this vacuum moved the Western church with its developing ecclesiology. This can be seen in the expanding role of the papacy. We have already seen the important role of the bishop of Rome in the Western understanding of Christianity. The ecumenical councils had been clear in their canons that the bishop of Rome was the first among the patriarchs of the church. The Roman church's reputation for orthodoxy had meant that its opinions were given great respect, such as in the reception of the Tome of Leo at the council of Chalcedon. But there had been both theological and political limits to this preeminence. Rome's claim to authority was always held in check by claims of patriarchs, and all ecclesiastical power was curtailed by the overarching authority of the Christian emperor, which Rome acknowledged. Throughout the fifth century Roman bishops dutifully dated their official documents by the regnal year of the emperor in Constantinople.

But the new political situation began to create new roles for the successors of Peter. When Attila and his Huns were intent on sacking Rome, it was Leo (author of the Tome) who led the delegation out to Attila's camp to plead for the city. His presence so impressed Attila that the city was spared.

But the new vision of the papacy can best be seen in the pontificate of Gregory the Great (590–604). Gregory came from a wealthy, prominent family and had been groomed for public office. Upon the death of his father, however, Gregory spurned the world to follow a monastic vocation, establishing a number of monasteries. In 590 he was called to public service and elected bishop of Rome. In Gregory one would see three developments that increased the profile of the papal office. First, he expanded the role of the Roman church in civil affairs. The invasion of Italy by outsiders—both Ostrogoths and Byzantines—had left central Italy in shambles. The papacy alone had the energy and resources to respond. Gregory became engaged in the military defense of the city and took up the negotiations with the invaders. Gregory provided the leadership, but the papal estates supplied the resources. The pope was landlord of properties in Italy, Africa, and France, and the income from these lands allowed him to help the poor, ransom captives, and support other works of social charity. Second, he was diligent in strengthening papal primacy and was vigilant against any encroachments by the patriarch of Constantinople. Finally, he took upon himself the responsibility of sending missionaries to various places in the West. Some were sent to correct error. The Germanic tribes were on the whole Arian, and Gregory sent missions to convert them to Catholic Christianity. Others were sent to those peoples, such as the Anglo-Saxons, who were completely outside of the Christian faith. The mission to Britain, according to a famous account, began when Gregory saw fair-haired children in the slave market in Rome. When told they were Angles, he famously replied, *"Non Angli, sed angeli"* (Not Angles, but angels). Through Gregory the papacy began to assume increased centrality in both Italy and the larger Western church.

Two other movements would emerge. The first was a model of monasticism associated with Benedict of Nursia (480–550). Coming of age during this time of dislocation, Benedict feared for the continuation of civilized life. "Rome will not be depopulated by the barbarians," he wrote, "but will be worn out by tempests, lightning, storm and earthquakes." In the face of a collapsing society, Benedict proposed a monastic vision based not on the desire for perfection, to be achieved by heroic self-denial and sacrifice, but on a concern for stability. "The Rule of Benedict" offered such a stability. Benedict's rule was simple, moderate, and centered on corporate prayer. Benedict's communities would become centers of stability and order in a world in which many fixtures of the social order were disintegrating.

Also at this time the influence of Irish monasticism became felt. The Irish were known for their learning and their missionary zeal. On the borders of the Roman Empire but never part of it, theirs was the first Western land to become Christian without first becoming Roman. This absence of a Roman tradition gave them the freedom to adapt the new situation. Irish Christianity was organized around the monasteries, not the bishop, whose office was often tied to an urban setting. If the hierarchical diocese reflected the administrative units of ancient Rome, the monastery mirrored a Celtic spirit of tribal organization. The abbot was more a chieftain than an aristocratic administrator.

The great missionary to the Irish was Patrick. A Christian from Britain who had been captured by Irish pirates and sold as a slave to an Irish chieftain, Patrick eventually became a priest and a missionary to the Irish. His labors were enormously successful, and the Irish church soon distinguished itself by the rigor of its discipline and its missionary zeal. Its rigor was inspired by the belief that all sin—even the most horrendous—could be atoned for by penance. From the Irish monks came the practice of confessing individual sins to a spiritual guide, who in turn would assign a fixed penance of prayer, fasting, and mortification. Such a discipline was not merely for the monks but for all the faithful. Through this method the burden of sin became manageable. Likewise the zeal of the Irish monks led them far and wide. Seeing themselves as exiles in this world, they were content to live among those far from the center of the civilized world. Irish missionaries spread the Christian faith throughout Britain and northern Europe.

Thus by the year 600 there were regional Christianities in Constantinople, Egypt, Ethiopia, Armenia, western Syria, Persia, and Latin Europe. Each differed from the others on key points, but each claimed continuity with the Christianity established in the apostolic age. Although there was no clear center of the faith, demographics still tipped the scales toward Asia Minor.

The Rise of Islam

Constantinople had been defending its empire for centuries and hoping to restore the lost Christian unity. If Constantinople had a chief political rival, it would have been Persia. Persia and the Christian empire had dueled for decades, and as recently as the 620s the former had wrested away Jerusalem and Alexandria from the latter. It took a decade for the emperor to restore control over these important provinces. But in the 630s a new force emerged that would transform the world, and Christianity in particular.

To say that Islam burst upon the world scene would be an understatement. The movement seemed to occur in the blink of an eye (particularly in contrast with the rise of Christianity). Muhammad is said to have received his first

> To say that Islam burst upon the world scene would be an understatement. The movement seemed to occur in the blink of an eye.

revelation in 610, and these revelations continued until his death in 632. The message of these revelations (collected as the Qur'an soon after the prophet's death) was simple and epitomized in the *Shahadah*, the Islamic statement of faith—"There is no god but Allah, and Muhammad is the prophet of Allah." There was one true God, all-powerful and unpictureable. It was the role of humanity to submit to this God (the root of the term *Islam* is "to submit") and to follow the right path. This submission would provide a new order for the society. The relation of Islam to Judaism and Christianity is delicate. According to the Qur'an both Abraham and Jesus were prophets, but their messages were corrupted by later Jews and Christians. In the case of the latter, Christians had turned Jesus from a prophet into a God, thus violating the oneness of God and transforming Jesus from a teacher of God's truth into a supernatural savior. The Qur'an offered the perfect and complete revelation of God's message to humanity, and those who followed and submitted were promised the glories of paradise.

The message of the prophet unified what had been heretofore a mass of competing Arab tribes and set them on a course of expansion. Starting in 632, they began a campaign of conquest that was perhaps the most dramatic in history. Islam emerged at a propitious time. The great empires of Byzantium and Persia had exhausted themselves in decades of conflict. Within the Roman imperial world intra-Christian divisions (exacerbated by continuing persecution) were rampant. Both factors worked to the advantage of the Arab forces. In quick succession Damascus and Syria fell in 635; Jerusalem, in 638; and Egypt, between 639 and 641. In the next few decades all of North Africa succumbed, and in 708, Arabs began the invasion of Spain. At the same time Arabs successfully conquered Iraq in 637 and Persia between 640 and 649. Almost all of the great centers of the ancient world were now under the control of the followers of Allah.

The triumph of Islam would have a profound effect on the history of the world. It brought to an end a civilized order that had been established by Alexander the Great and advanced by imperial Rome, in which a Hellenistic culture centered on the Mediterranean dominated and shaped the Western world. The Islamic triumph would also shape the future of Christianity. Those conquered provinces—Jerusalem, Antioch, Alexandria, and Carthage—had been the center of ancient Christianity. It was there that Ignatius, Athanasius, Augustine, and countless others had lived and taught. Of course in many of these provinces the unity of Christianity had already been sundered. Monophysites in Egypt and West Syria found the Islamic Arabs far less onerous as sovereigns than had been the Chalcedonians. Although subject to a special tax and other legal limitations, the non-Chalcedonian churches found more freedom under Islam than under Constantinople. The Monophysite patriarch in Egypt could now show his face in public after being in seclusion for years. Indeed, since the Arabs treated all Christians the same, non-Chalcedonian Christians became eligible for governmental service in a way they had not been for centuries. Christian medical doctors became an important part of the Arab world, and Syriac Christians became the conduit of classical knowledge into the world of Islam.

But the erosion of the Christian communities under Islam was marked. Some communities, such as those in North Africa, largely disappeared. Others found themselves reduced in numbers. The poll tax was seen as being onerous and led to a number of (failed) tax revolts. Other laws that Christians were subject to were also debilitating. Finally there was the question of language. The Arab invaders brought with them not only the Qur'an but also the Arabic language, and within a few centuries Arabic had triumphed over the local dialects. Because of the connection between the language and the religion, where Arabic triumphed, Islam was not far behind.

The Question of Icons

The Chalcedonians of Constantinople weathered the Islamic assault but found themselves on the defensive. In the early eighth century Muslim armies had reached the gates of Constantinople. Although turned back by the emperor Leo III (who also successfully recaptured some of Asia Minor) the Islamic conquests had taken their toll. Byzantium's richest provinces (Egypt and Syria) had been plucked from it, and the task of survival would hang like a pall over the remaining centuries of its existence.

The challenge of Islam, however, was not merely military. Why, many asked, had God allowed such defeats to happen? As required by Mosaic law, the Islamic God was unpictured. But in the Christian churches, God's image was everywhere. Icons adorned Orthodox churches, and their worship had become deeply embedded in Orthodox piety. Increasingly, however, icons had their critics. According to Emperor Leo, the Muslim victories had been a judgment upon the church's impiety, and he ordered the destruction of all the icons. Thus began the iconoclastic controversy. Opposing icons were the emperor and the army, for whom icons represented a falling into the sin of idolatry, and their destruction exhibited a return to purity. Leo had even destroyed the image of Christ that stood above the doorway of the imperial palace in Constantinople. The defenders of icons were found among the monks and many of the common people. For them, icons were symbols of the foundational truth of Christianity—that God had come to earth and taken on human form. To attack icons was ultimately to attack the incarnation itself.

The battle between opponents and defenders of icons (iconoclasts vs. iconodules) would rend the Orthodox Eastern Church for over a century. In the long run the iconoclasts were defeated, and the place of icons was restored, but not before causing discord in Byzantium and (as we shall see in the next chapter) division between the churches of the East and the West.

By 750 it was clear that the world that gave birth to ancient Christianity was over. The communities that had weathered the challenges of the seventh century were weaker than they had been a hundred years earlier, but they were still standing. What the future would bring, however, was uncertain.

SECTION 3   The Shifting Center

Chapter 8

The Emergence of Christian Europe

As Christianity in the ancient centers was undergoing stress and tribulation, Christianity in the old Latin West was beginning to take a new shape. Although still probably the poorest and weakest corner of the Christian world, it was beginning to find its legs.

Rise of the Franco-Papal Alliance

Western Europe only slowly recovered from the breakdown in order following the collapse of Roman rule. One crisis seemed to follow another. Italy was devastated by a decades-long conflict between Byzantines and Ostrogoths. Spain's fragile post-Roman order was overturned by the Islamic invasion beginning in 710, which quickly swept over most of the Iberian Peninsula. Thus, if almost by default, it was France that would become the center of a developed Christian social order. The French king Clovis had been converted in 496, and the Frankish kingdom had become part of Catholic Christianity. But it was not until the eighth century that there began to be advances in both church and state. The rise of Charles Martel (who was technically only the "Mayor of the Palace") inaugurated a new royal line, the Carolingians. Charles himself in 732 defeated the invading Muslim armies at Tours, checking the Islamic advance into Europe. Under his son, Pepin, the Carolingian leaders began to press for reform of the church and for a strengthening of the relationship of the church with the papacy. One sees this in the ministry of the great missionary Boniface, whose labors were supported by both the papacy and the Carolingians. Thus reform and "Romanization" became the rule of the Frankish church.

When ascending to the kingship, Pepin asked for papal support, which he received. The Carolingians would establish a new model for Christian kingship. The earlier French kings had claimed that their authority stemmed from

Pepin – 1st French King anointed

their descent from the gods. Pepin saw kingly authority as sacral and was the first French king to be anointed. In 751, Boniface, acting as the papal representative, anointed Pepin with holy oil, thus confirming the sacral nature of the kingship. It was sacred oil and not descent by blood that made one a king. Pepin was later to be reanointed by the pope himself.

Pepin, in turn, offered his support to the papacy. In 754 the pope asked Pepin to defend the Roman church against still another Germanic invader, the Lombards. Pepin invaded Italy and defeated the enemy. He then gave the papacy the land he had acquired in central Italy, which became an important part of the Papal States, or those sections of the Italian peninsula ruled directly by the papacy. These actions were to have a revolutionary significance. Until the eighth century the papacy had seen itself as one of the westernmost parts of the eastern Roman Empire. The emperor in Constantinople was the recognized political authority. But the events of the middle of the eighth century changed all this. The traditional papal/Constantinopolitan axis was gradually supplanted by a new Franco-papal alliance. The papacy had a new foundation for political support, and the Frankish church had become more self-consciously Roman in liturgy, law, Sunday observance, and many other ways.

Reforms

The new spirit can perhaps best be seen in the policies of Charlemagne (742–814). Charlemagne's reforms assumed that the present affairs of the church were badly disordered, and to bring about reform, the guidelines must be based on the "ancient customs." Thus part of the Carolingian task was the compilation of ancient canon law and the careful reproduction of classical texts. The concern for order would also produce two further innovations that have continued to this day. The first was the standardization of dating. It was in the scholarly courts of Charlemagne that the practice began of dating history from the incarnation—or the *Anno Domini*. This both unified and organized history. There was also the attempt to bring order to the written word. A new minuscule, or way of writing, emerged (with differentiations between capital and lowercase letters), and it became the foundation of all modern European typescript.

Other reforms were more practical in nature. Carolingians strove to improve the moral and educational discipline of clergy. They attempted to unify liturgical practice according to Roman models. To encourage the laity, the faithful were organized into small, defined religious communities, which became known as parishes.

Theological Developments

The revival in learning also led to a new interest in theology, and a theological debate broke out that would consume Western Christianity. In 831 the Benedictine monk Paschasius Radbertus published what was perhaps the first doctrinal monograph about the sacrament of the Holy Eucharist. In it he claimed that the Eucharist involved not merely a general presence of Christ but that the flesh born of Mary was present in each consecration of the Eucharist. Ratramanus, another monk, challenged the literalism of Paschasius's formulary. The elements, he claimed, were contained in the figure of a mystery. One needed to distinguish between "that which appears to the bodily sense" and that "which faith beholds." Without realizing it, Paschasius and Ratramanus were beginning a debate that would echo throughout Western Christianity—exactly how Christ was present in the Eucharist. Whereas earlier writers had spoken of Christ's presence in the breaking of bread, there had been little attention to precisely how this took place. By the ninth century the focus had shifted from the rite to the elements. Here theology followed practice. The language of the liturgy, Latin, made it impossible for all but the most educated to follow the prayer of the Eucharist. Popular focus instead turned to the "elements," or bread and wine. As such they were viewed as holy objects. The ninth-century eucharistic debate was over how these objects were holy.

The theological revival of the Carolingian era sparked an additional conflict between the Eastern and Western churches. In the debate over icons, the West was firmly iconodule, or pro-icon, and critical of iconoclastic emperors. Now the issue moved to the creed. When the bishops at the Council of Constantinople (381) crafted an additional paragraph for the earlier Nicene Creed dealing with the Holy Spirit, they declared that the Spirit "proceeds from the Father, who with the Father and Son together is worshipped and glorified," and this became the official wording of the ecumenical creed. The text remained (and remains) unchanged in the East, but in the West new theological concerns reopened the issue. In response to the reemergence of the old heresy of adoptionism (that Jesus only became the Christ at some point in his earthly ministry), the Spanish Council of Toledo in 589 authorized an addition to the creed. The new wording declared that the Holy Spirit proceeds "from the Father *and the Son*." The addition became known as the *filioque* (Latin: and [from] the Son). The council further stated that the creed should be recited at the Eucharist.

In 798 Charlemagne adopted the new wording and the practice of reciting the creed at the Eucharist for use throughout his dominion, and it became (as it remains) a regular part of the Western liturgy. Frankish monks then carried the practice to their monastery in Jerusalem, where it was noticed by Eastern clerics. They were shocked that any local church could have the temerity to alter an ecumenical creed.

divided church

> Rome held that God spoke through the church. The great preserver of truth was not ecumenical councils but the office of the papacy.

The filioque controversy divided the church East and West. Yet the controversy was actually twofold: first was the teaching of the double procession (or the Spirit's proceeding from both the Father and the Son) permissible, or did it (as Eastern writers maintained) upset the balance of the Trinity; and second, could the teachings of an ecumenical council be modified? The first question raised theoretical questions about the nature of the Trinity, but the second question cut to the core of a long-smoldering dispute between Rome and the East. The East had a lofty veneration for ecumenical councils, believing that through them God spoke. Rome, in contrast, held that God spoke through the church. Ecumenical councils could speak the truth but did not necessarily do so. The great preserver of truth was not ecumenical councils but the office of the papacy. Thus the pope, while personally maintaining the old usage, defended the right of the church to refine its liturgy. Although practical ecclesiastical politics (such as which church would control the Christian communities in southern Italy and the Balkans) played a major role in the dispute, the filioque controversy did reflect two very different theological trends.

The Carolingian revival was an impressive movement. The new hopefulness was symbolized when on Christmas day, 800, while at prayer in St. Peter's in Rome, Charlemagne was crowned by Pope Leo as emperor, the successor to Constantine. Other contemporaries referred to Charlemagne as the "New David," the leader of Latin Christendom. But the revival was a movement that was led by a handful of learned individuals, a very thin layer over a very primitive society. It rested precariously on the stability that Charlemagne and his successors could provide. But Charles's successors could not fill his mighty sandals. His son, Louis the Pious, lacked the reputation as a warrior on which much of Charlemagne's authority rested. Louis eventually partitioned the empire among his three sons so that the preciously gained political unity was lost. But damage was inflicted not only by Charlemagne's heirs but by marauding bands, which in eighth- and ninth-century Europe made devastating raids. In the north these raiders were the Vikings, pagan plunderers from Scandinavia. In the south they were Saracens, Muslim raiders. Defenseless monasteries were a prime target, and the effect was tragic. As one contemporary wrote, upon hearing of the looting and destruction of one of the famous Irish monasteries, "The misfortune of your destruction saddens me every day, even though I am far away. The pagans defiled the sanctuaries of God and shed the blood of the saints in the vicinity of the altar, they ravaged the home of our hope, they trampled the bodies of the saints in the temple of God as if they were dung in the street." These centuries witnessed the physical destruction of much of the carefully accumulated art and scholarship, the breakdown of political culture, and the decline of both clerical discipline and the office of the papacy. The reputation of the papacy had fallen so low that some later historians have referred to the discredited mid-tenth-century papacy as the "pornocracy."

Struggle between Pope and Emperor

The middle of the tenth century brought the beginning of an upturn, first in the political realm and then in the church. Otto the Great (936–973) from Germany revived the office of the Holy Roman Emperor. Otto exemplified the ideal of the theocratic king, or the monarch who both supported and controlled the church. He restructured ecclesiastical organization, giving it imperial support yet also using the resources of the church to finance his court. His "advocacy" system provided secular managers for ecclesiastical properties, as well as a cut for the monarch.

Otto next turned his concern to the papacy. The emperor, he claimed, was the protector of the papacy and stood guard over the office; hence he felt free to oust one pope and have another elected. Popes, he declared, were only to be elected with the consent of the emperor and were to swear allegiance to the emperor. Otto's vision of imperial power dominating the church was that of the Byzantine East, in which the emperor was the preeminent figure. To emphasize the sacral nature of the imperial office he wore robes like those of a bishop and occasionally accepted the title of vicar of Christ.

Otto and his successors did their work too well. Not only did the office of the papacy revive, but by the early eleventh century, popes began to chafe at the pretensions of emperors. There had been a long tradition in the Western church of rejecting the subservience of the church to the emperor. An earlier pope, Gelasius, had set forth the concept of the "two swords": both church and state had authority, but the church must always have prominence. A document called "The Donation of Constantine" began to be cited; it alleged that the emperor Constantine had awarded to Pope Sylvester, in gracious appreciation for being miraculously cured of leprosy, authority over all other ecclesiastical patriarchs and superiority over the emperor himself. "The Donation of Constantine" was undoubtedly a forgery—being clearly a product of the ninth and not the fourth century—but it reflected a growing desire to assert the superiority of the papacy over the emperor. It was perhaps not accidental that it was at this time that the pope began to abandon his old title, "Vicar of St. Peter," and claim a new one—the same title that the emperor had assumed, the "Vicar of Christ." The role of the papacy was not simply to preserve the tradition of Peter but to do Christ's will in the world.

The policy of papal reform (known as the Hildebrandian reforms, since the prepapal name of Pope Gregory VII was Hildebrand) involved an assertion of the independence of the church. Papal elections were taken out of the hands of the mob at Rome (as well as those of the emperor) and entrusted to senior clergy known as cardinals. Gregory VII also initiated a vigorous campaign against simony. Simony had originally been understood as the buying or selling of church offices, but it was now interpreted as any lay interference in the affairs of the church, including that of the theocratic emperor.

> Gregory and his allies attacked the practice of lay investiture, demanding that the emperor relinquish that power and that clerical authority be seen as being derived from the church alone.

A clash between emperor and papacy was inevitable. An occasion produced itself in 1075 with the issue of investiture. The influence of emperors (and other political leaders) over bishops and other higher clergy stemmed in part from the fact that the political leaders were the source of clerical authority. The powers of office were symbolized in a ceremony known as investiture, in which certain gifts were given by the emperor, and clergy in return pledged their loyalty to the sovereign. The cleric was ultimately the emperor's man. Gregory and his allies attacked this practice. They demanded that the emperor (Henry IV) relinquish that power and that clerical authority be seen as being derived from the church alone. When Henry refused, the pope excommunicated him and freed his feudal vassals from any loyalty to him. This created a political crisis in the empire; it was reconciled only when the emperor confessed his sins to the pope—doing so at Canossa in 1077, having stood for days barefoot in the snow. Although Gregory would have preferred to have seen Henry removed by his vassals, and thus make absolute papal power over imperial, as a priest he could not refuse a penitent absolution.

One must see the investiture controversy as part of a wider campaign to replace the model of theocratic kingship (with the church as the subservient institution) with the vision of a unified, independent Christian church with the pope as its head. A second aspect of the campaign was enforcement of clerical celibacy. The question of celibacy, or whether clergy could be married, was an old one, and there had been many compromises. Canons had been on the books since the fourth century insisting on clerical celibacy, but by the eleventh century they were seldom enforced. Gregory's insistence on celibacy was not simply for moral reasons. Marriage (or cohabitation) bound local clergy to their social and political environment. In practice, clerical positions were often passed on from father to son. Celibacy laws removed clergy from this nexus and reinforced their association with the larger church. It made parish clergy more like monks, with vows of poverty, chastity, and obedience. Further, by bringing monks and clergy together by a common rule of celibacy, it emphasized the division between clergy and laity. Under the Hildebrandian reforms the church became not only more independent but more clerical.

The Medieval Reformation

The investiture controversy was but one part of a fundamental transformation of Western Christianity during the period between 1050 and 1300. During these years European society took on a vitality not seen earlier. Urban life reemerged; commerce and trade became reinvigorated. The population increased, and the society expanded to the east (into what is now Poland) and south (with the *Reconquista*, or the reconquest of the Iberian Peninsula from Islam). A unified society was gradually emerging, with a common language (Latin) and a common law. Scholars had been revising the Justinian code to provide a common church law. In the mid-twelfth century, Gratian issued his *Decretum*, which cataloged and harmonized earlier legal documents. If canon law provided the universal law for this new society, Rome was the court of appeal, and the pope, the final authority. Like the emperor in the East, the papacy was the center of authority in the West.

But what characterized Europe during these years was not merely new organization but a new spirit and vitality. Some scholars have called this period the "medieval reformation," in which a spiritual hunger demanded new forms and insights. This is evident in a new piety. Earlier, much of European Christian piety was influenced by the Old Testament. The world of the Old Testament—with its warfare and conquest, anointed kings, and formal rituals—seemed more relevant than the world of the New. The famous historian Henry Adams once suggested that in the world of Charlemagne, the sword-bearing archangel Michael was a more empathetic figure than was the suffering Jesus. After the year 1000, however, things began to change.

The figure of Jesus, particularly as the one who suffered on the cross, became more popular. These images transformed Christian imagery and views of beauty. Holidays such as Christmas that had had comparatively little importance became far more popular. Francis of Assisi, for example, introduced the use of the crèche, or models of the nativity, to better teach the mystery of the incarnation. To make a broad generalization (which books such as this must do), piety turned inward, with a concern for how persons felt and thought, and not merely for what they did.

All of this interest can also be seen in an intensified devotion to the Virgin Mary. Almost all the great cathedrals built at the time were dedicated to her, and her image appeared in almost every local church. In a world where God at times could seem either distant or stern, Mary symbolized love.

The goal of the new piety was to follow Jesus, and the *vita apostolica* (apostolic life) became the ideal. Church art became more didactic in teaching the New Testament stories. Individual prayer books (often illustrated) began to appear to direct the faithful. Hymns also reflected the new intensity. To cite but one example (known as the *Stabat Mater*):

> At the cross her station keeping, stood the mournful mother weeping
> Where he hung, the dying Lord: for her soul of joy bereaved
> Bowed with anguish deeply grieved, felt the sharp and piercing sword.

The point of religion was to directly experience the union of God and the soul. But to do so required a higher devotion.

This new intensity led some to explore new ways of imagining Christ. Christ's compassion was sometimes pictured in feminine terms. The theologian Anselm of Canterbury wrote of Jesus as a mother who gathered up his people. This image would be picked up by later mystics such as Julian of Norwich (1342–ca. 1416), who was to write, "Jesus is the true mother of our nature because he created us. He is also our mother in grace, because he took our created nature."

The *vita apostolica* also demanded poverty. The turn to the New Testament led faithful persons to rediscover Jesus' message concerning poverty. The story of the rich young man (Matt. 19:16–22) whom Jesus told to sell all and give the money to the poor, began to haunt many and to be seen as a way to become closer to God. Some have observed that an interest in poverty could only take root in the comparative prosperity of these years, when poverty was a choice. The new prosperity created a new appreciation for poverty.

The *vita apostolica* also suggested a new activism. The New Testament pictured Jesus again and again calling people to *do* things, and in particular to go into the world and spread the good news. The combination of the call for poverty and the call for evangelical action resulted in a new movement, the rise of the mendicant orders such as the Franciscans and the Dominicans. These offered a different model of religious life from that of Benedict and his rule. Benedictine monks retired from the chaotic world and were regular in prayer while moderate in lifestyle. The friars, as the mendicants came to be known, shaped their common lives around poverty and evangelistic zeal. The life of Francis, founder of the Franciscans, is illustrative. Born into a prosperous family, he abandoned wealth and chose instead to serve "Lady Poverty." He attracted a group of followers who called themselves the "Little Brothers" (*fratres minores*, hence friars). They lived by begging and lived for preaching. In 1209 he sought papal permission for his new order. Francis became the symbol of a new dedication toward following the way of Christ. Tradition records that Francis was so intent on following Christ that he ultimately received the stigmata, the same wounds by which Christ suffered. Although in a less dramatic way, Dominic, founder of the Dominicans, likewise dedicated his order to poverty and preaching.

Scholasticism

Another aspect of this reformation was a flowering of theology known as scholasticism. As the name suggests, scholasticism was associated with the schools then emerging. Its aim was to reconcile Christian belief with Hellenic thought, meaning at the time the works of Plato. As Anselm of Canterbury (c. 1033–1109) put it, the task of theology was "*fides quarens intellectum*" (faith seeking understanding). By the use of logic (usually in the form of questions and answers) topics such as the existence of God and the meaning of Christ's sacrifice could be explained even to those outside the Christian orbit. The typical method was to set out authoritative statements from the Bible and church authorities for comparison, and any apparent contradictions became the "*quaestio*" (question) to be addressed. Some like Peter Lombard (c. 1100–1160) used the scholastic method to refine ideas concerning sacraments and ministry. Others such as Peter Abelard (1079–1142/3) used it to question easy reconciliations.

A New Role for Women

This spiritual revival had a major effect on women's religious life. During the earlier Middle Ages there had been large and important nunneries and even "double monasteries" of both women and men headed by an abbess.

But these catered largely to noble widows and daughters and were declining by the tenth century. By the late eleventh century women began turning to the *vita apostolica*. Clare, a close friend and follower of Francis, was given permission to organize a second order of Franciscans for women. Because of social restrictions, women could not be friars out in the world, but instead they became organized as "Poor Clares," a cloistered community of sisters dedicated to poverty. Groups of laywomen in the Low Countries, known as Beguines, did attempt to follow the way of the *vita apostolica* out into the world. There, wearing secular dress, they renounced property and dedicated themselves to works of charity. Hildegard of Bingen (1098–1179), abbess of Rupertsberg, near Bingen, also became an important voice. Her mystic visions attracted the attention of both popes and emperors.

All of these differing movements made European Christians conscious of their unity. The church was by far the most powerful of social organizations. They proudly called their society Christendom, or a society organized around a distinctive Christian vision. Places like the University of Paris were international institutions, training leaders for this larger society. But the language of Christendom suggested a new attitude toward other Christian communities. Western Christianity was no longer subservient to Byzantium. Competition rather than deference now marked the relationship between Christians East and West. Conflicts that had begun over iconoclasm and the filioque had not lessened, and in 1054 the two churches excommunicated each other. As one historian has put it, the rise of a self-conscious Western consciousness changed forever the relations between the churches. Eastern churches "began as 'us' and ended as 'them.'" Increasingly Latin Christians saw their church as the center of the Christian world.

The Crusades

This new Western vitality was the background for the Crusades. The waves of crusading that began in the middle of the eleventh century and continued intermittently for centuries both reflected a new power relationship in the Christian world and served as a catalyst for even greater changes. By the 1070s the Byzantine Empire had suffered some crushing military reversals. A new Islamic invader, the Seljuk Turks, was again threatening Constantinople. The Byzantine emperor (Michael VII) sought the assistance of the West, but the investiture controversy prevented any immediate action. Not until 1095 did Pope Urban II call on the West to aid the Byzantine church.

The response was staggering; from all over France and Italy noblemen volunteered for the cause, and in this response one sees at work the trends that have been mentioned. Its multinational nature reflected the appeal of a unified Christendom and the moral authority of the papacy that called forth the crusade. The added hope that the massive enterprise might result in a reunified Christianity under Roman suzerainty also testified to the new Western vitality.

In 1096 the force set out, and in the short run it was militarily successful. Sharp divisions within the Islamic world allowed the crusaders to capture Edessa, Antioch, and eventually Jerusalem. In these places they established Latin kingdoms, much to the consternation of the Byzantines, who still deemed these their lost provinces.

Historians have often commented on the mixed motives behind the Crusades, as well as the atrocities the crusaders committed in the name of their religion. The relatively short life span of these Latin kingdoms is also well known. The last Latin outpost, Acre, fell in 1291, less than two hundred years after the beginning of the Crusades, and Jerusalem had fallen far earlier. Although there were seven separate crusades in the two centuries between 1096 and 1272, except for the first they accomplished very little.

The impact of the Crusades on the Christian churches of the East was particularly harmful. Certainly they exacerbated Latin-Byzantine tensions. The Byzantine emperor saw the crusaders as a dangerous threat, while the crusaders saw the Eastern Christian community as ungrateful. The animosity boiled over in the infamous Fourth Crusade (1202–1204). In it a group of northern European troops were redirected by the son of a deposed Byzantine emperor (Alexius Angelus) to help him regain the imperial throne. For this he promised a large payment and the submission of the Greek church to Latin authority. Though the pope forbade the undertaking, the bulk of the crusaders agreed. Alexius, however, was not able to keep his bargain, and angry Latin forces captured and plundered Constantinople. The new Rome that had successfully defended itself for centuries from non-Christian attacks had succumbed to a Latin Christian force. The Byzantine Empire was turned into a series of Latin kingdoms, and a Latin patriarch, subservient to the pope, was placed at the head of the Greek church. Many of its great treasures were carried away as booty by Western crusaders. Although Latin control lasted for less than sixty years and the Greeks recaptured Constantinople in 1261, Byzantium would never recover its strength, and the long-festering Latin-Greek antagonism would become permanent.

The Latin invasion would adversely affect the other Eastern churches as well. In both Syria and Egypt the Crusades worsened the relations between

Oriental Christians (as the non-Chalcedonian churches have come to be known) in this area and their Muslim governors. All "worshipers of the cross" became suspect, and extra taxes were placed on the communities to pay for campaigns to recapture the lost provinces. The communities were already reeling from the acute persecution of the Muslim caliph al-Hakim. Al-Hakim (996–1021) had not only destroyed the venerable Church of the Holy Sepulcher in Jerusalem but ordered mosques to be placed on the flat roofs of Christian churches and required Christians to wear five-pound wooden crosses around their necks. The delicate position of Christians under Islamic rule became more precarious as a result of the Western Crusades.

Innocent III and the Western Medieval Ideal

The fullness of the development of a Latin Christianity can perhaps best be seen in the pontificate of Innocent III, pope from 1198 to 1216. By 1198, the new pan-European Latin Christian culture was in full bloom. Trade, education, and crusading zeal linked the society. The new canon law organized it, and the papacy, exercising its fullness of power (*plenitudo potestatis*), acted as supreme governor. Innocent embraced many of the trends earlier discussed. He endorsed the *vita apostolica* and gave permission to Francis to form his order. According to a later tradition, on the night before his interview with Francis, Innocent dreamed that the walls of the Lateran Basilica were collapsing and were being propped up by the endeavors of a little man. Francis alone, he came to believe, could save the church. Innocent was a strong proponent of both crusading and canon law.

Innocent would be most remembered for his extension of papal authority over the political leaders of Europe. He viewed the papacy as the greatest office on earth and acted accordingly. "No king can reign rightly unless he devoutly serves Christ's vicar," he explained. He exercised authority over the Holy Roman Emperor, to guard against any threat to papal influence in Italy. He actively pursued the principle that the pope had the right to act in the political world when a question of sin was involved. This led him to force a French king (Phillip II) to return to his wife. He aggressively maintained papal authority over national churches. He clashed with King John of England (bad King John of the Robin Hood stories) over the appointment of the archbishop of Canterbury. To enforce his will Innocent made use of the greatest weapon in the papal arsenal, the interdict. When a nation was put under an interdict the sacramental system was shut off. The interdict was the

WMD (weapon of mass destruction) of canon law. Used in the cases of both Phillip and John, in both instances the punishment worked.

Perhaps the culmination of Innocent's pontificate was the Fourth Lateran Council (1216). The Fourth Lateran was deemed by the Latin West an ecumenical council, but almost all the bishops were Western. The council formalized some of the developments that had begun earlier. One issue was the presence of Christ in the Eucharist. Since the time of Charlemagne theological debate had raged over this question. The Fourth Lateran officially approved the doctrine of transubstantiation. It was declared that in the Eucharist the substance (or underlying essence) of the bread or wine was miraculously transformed into the body or blood of Christ without any change in physical properties. The mass was a miracle. Transubstantiation also reflected the sacral quality of the mass and became reflected in certain practices. The elements were so holy that many went to mass simply to look on them rather than partake of them. To prevent the elements from being profaned, the cup began to be withheld from the laity; only the priest drank from it. The tendency to see the mass as something to be witnessed was so strong that the council had to mandate annual Communion. The bishops also took up the question of auricular confession, popularized by the Celtic monks. All faithful Catholics were obligated to confess their sins to a priest at least once a year.

The Fourth Lateran formulated many of the developments that had made Europe Christendom. It also authorized some of the less sympathetic elements. Much energy was directed against heretics who broke from the church. Crusades against heretical movements within the Christian world were duly authorized. Care was also taken to "protect" the Christian society from "outsiders." Jews and Muslims were to wear distinctive dress and to keep themselves separate from Christians. Jews, for example, were forbidden to appear in public during Holy Week so as not to scandalize devout Christians. In a Christian society, they were declared outsiders and were treated accordingly.

The Beginning of the Latin Era

In the period this chapter has examined—and in particular in the years between 1050 and 1300—the Christian world underwent a sea change. At the time of the beginning of the Franco-papal alliance the Western church was small, weak, and arguably the least developed of the regional Christianities. The Greeks, Copts, Syrians, Armenians, and Persians could all claim to be at least as important in the Christian world as were the Latins. By the year

1300, this pecking order was reversed. Now the Latin church was emerging as the dominant community, both because of its own growing strength and the declining fortunes of the other regional churches. During this period the "Latin era" of Christianity was developing. As we shall see, it would only be finalized at the end of the fifteenth century, but the course had been struck. The center of Christian intellectual and social vitality had moved west and north. The story of Christianity was beginning to be directed by the Latin West. The older centers of regional Christianity would continue to exist, but the center stage had become Europe. For weal or woe, Western Christendom had become the center of Christianity.

Chapter 9

Endings and Beginnings

*P*eople have looked back at the thirteenth century as a remarkable time. Almost a century ago the historian James J. Walsh wrote a book called *The Thirteenth, Greatest of Centuries* and spoke glowingly of the century's accomplishments in art, literature, education, commerce, and music. In the West it marked the high point of medieval Latin Catholicism. But as ages go, it was short, and succeeding centuries were far less "great." Indeed, by 1460 the Christian world was in its most precarious position since the time of Constantine.

Medieval Order

When people speak of the achievements of the thirteenth-century renaissance, they are often referring to the genius for synthesizing that people of this age possessed. The Western medieval mind was fascinated by the idea of gradational order and hierarchy. Through right ordering, everything could have a place, and there could be unity. Innocent III had proclaimed a great unified Christendom with the pope as Christ's vicar reigning supreme, and the vision of ordered unity was seen as undergirding all reality. Gothic architecture encapsulated the sacral universe in its design, with each part of the building reflecting a truth. Resurrection was illustrated in the east and judgment in the west; Old Testament patriarchs were found on the north wall and Christian figures on the south; a building's iconography displayed the hierarchy of existence. The greatest of the medieval poets, Dante Alighieri, structured his masterpiece, *The Divine Comedy*, in three books of thirty-three cantos each. In it he sketched the order of the cosmos from the pit of hell to the presence of God, and in each level of Inferno, Purgatorio, and Paradiso there were further gradations. Dante's reality encompassed all.

> Nowhere was the idea of synthesis more significantly displayed than in the theological accomplishments of Thomas Aquinas.

Dante's poem furthermore reflected a unique Western understanding of the church. The church was envisioned as encompassing heaven and earth. On earth the "church militant" labored, and in heaven the "church triumphant," the saints, resided, and their prayers and intercessions were sought by the faithful. Between these two lay the "church expectant," or the souls in purgatory. Although the idea that the dead were in an intermediate state awaiting the resurrection had been an old Christian belief, the Western church had developed a distinctive understanding of this intermediate state. After death, the effects of sin were purged from the souls of believers, preparing them for heaven. The prayers of those still living, it was believed, could benefit them in their purgation. All three levels of the church were interrelated.

But nowhere was the idea of synthesis more significantly displayed than in the theological accomplishments of Thomas Aquinas (1225–1274). The work of Aquinas represented the epitome of scholasticism. But Aquinas faced a distinctive challenge. Beginning in the twelfth century, Europe experienced an information explosion, largely due to the rediscovery of Aristotle. Plato had been the great philosophical source for the Latin West, particularly as mediated through Augustine, and was the philosophical foundation of earlier scholasticism. Aristotle had been largely lost. But Aristotle had been kept alive among Arab scholars who had been instructed by Nestorians and Jacobites. Aristotle entered Western consciousness in places like Sicily and Spain, where Christian and Islamic cultures intermingled. Aristotle was a serious challenge to centuries of earlier Christian thinking. His was a philosophy far more empirical and naturalistic than anything Western thinkers had theretofore encountered. Furthermore he offered virtually a complete system of knowledge: an ethics, a politics, a logic, a physics, a metaphysics, as well as other areas. Yet it was an intellectual system in which God barely figured, and the soul was largely absent. It did not start (as did Plato) with eternal unchanging ideas but with the stuff of nature. How, if at all, could it be made to fit in with traditional Christian claims? If it could not, then Christianity would lose its ability to claim itself as a source of true knowledge, or at best would be forced to admit that there existed multiple and nonreconcilable truths. The latter was the solution offered by the Muslim philosopher Averroës (Ibn Rushd).

Aquinas rejected Averroës's idea of multiple irreconcilable truths. His great works—*Summa Contra Gentiles* and *Summa Theologiae*—were intended to bring together the biblical (or evangelical) and the Aristotelian. The strength of Aristotle, for Aquinas, was that he allowed one to see the world as it truly was and not merely as being symbolic, as was the case with Plato. Aquinas's greatness lay in his rejection of easy dichotomies such as spirit versus flesh, reason versus revelation, and nature versus supernature. The path to truth was in seeing how these contrasting realities were to be ordered.

One sees this in his discussion of the relationship between reason and revelation. For Aquinas, human knowledge began with the natural as perceived by the senses, and upon this empirical knowledge was employed the power of reason. This was a natural power from God: "If a man is to know anything whatsoever, he needs divine help in order that his intellect may be moved to its act by God. But he does not need a new light added to his natural light in order to know the truth in all things, but only in such things as transcend his natural knowledge." Thus through natural reason we conceived of God's existence. But there are other aspects of reality that cannot be perceived through the senses, such as a knowledge of the angels, and to know these things a person must depend on revelation. Once one understood how reason and faith operated, one could see how they worked together. Revelation had one other function: it could offer truth to the many who had neither the time nor the proclivity for careful reasoning.

Aquinas's method was to ask questions and pose apparent contradictions found in Scripture, the writings of the church fathers, and philosophy, and in turn to show that a right posing of the question inevitably demonstrated that the contradictions did not exist. The intellectual world, like Dante Alighieri's poetry, was one of light, order, and gradation. It was perhaps fitting that in his *Paradiso*, Dante has Thomas in the Heaven of the Sun.

Decline in Christian Europe

The cosmos might be wonderfully ordered, but as the thirteenth century progressed, Latin Christendom became less so. As we have noted, the society was in theory held together by the church, with the pope on top. But authority was ultimately moral. When Urban VI called for a great crusade, Europe seemed to arise en masse. As later popes continued to call for arms, the enthusiasm began to ebb. So too did the force of the threat of the interdict wane through overuse, particularly when used for overtly political ends.

The revitalization of European society resulted as well in the strengthening of nation-states. Increasingly monarchs began to chaff at the subservience of kings to popes, as established through the investiture controversy. Another test of wills occurred at the end of the thirteenth century when Philip IV of France decided to tax his clergy to help finance a war with England. When the clergy appealed to Rome, Pope Boniface VIII in a bull, *Clericos Laicos*, threatened excommunication of all who demanded or paid such taxes. Rather than submitting, Philip responded by banning the export of gold and silver to Italy, thus threatening papal finances. Boniface backed down, but his blood was up. When Philip provoked him again by arresting a papal representative, Boniface in 1302 solemnly issued the bull *Unam Sanctam*, the most elevated statement of papal authority to come out of the Middle Ages. The church was like the ark of Noah: the only source of safety in a drowning world. And the head of the church was the successor of Peter. It was an authority "not human, but rather divine, given at God's mouth to Peter . . . whoever therefore resists this power . . . resists the ordinance of God." But unlike Henry IV during the earlier investiture controversy, Philip did not back down. Through a national assembly, he charged Boniface with a series of crimes and called for him to be tried. Furthermore, Philip's agents in Italy gathered a force and took Boniface prisoner. Although soon freed, Boniface died a short time later. On one level, the struggle between pope and monarch was simply a testimony to the growing power of the new monarchs. Yet Boniface's disgrace was also seen as a fruit of the church's overinvolvement in the political order. Dante was later to place Boniface in one of his levels of hell as a symbol of the worldliness into which the church had fallen:

> Ah Constantine! what ills were gendered there—
> No, not from thy conversion, but the dower
> The first rich Pope received from thee as heir.

Dante's criticism centered not on the political pretensions of the papacy but on its worldliness and riches. It stood in marked contrast with the ideal of apostolic poverty espoused by the mendicants. A century and a half earlier, one story goes, the pope had tried to impress Dominic (founder of the Dominicans) with the church's wealth. When the pope commented, "Peter can no longer say 'silver and gold have I none,'" Dominic (it was said) tartly replied, "No, and neither can he now say 'Rise and walk.'"

Both external and internal factors contributed to a great decline in the office of the papacy in the fourteenth century. During much of this time it was under the control of the French kings. In 1309 Pope Clement V, himself a Frenchman, moved the formal papal residence to Avignon in France. Although the action was allegedly taken to free the papacy from the political environs of Rome, it was viewed with disfavor. Technically Avignon was not a French province; it was under papal control. But to many the move signified French dominance over the church. The poet Petrarch referred to the transfer of the papacy to Avignon as the "Babylonian captivity of the Church." The loss of revenues from the Italian Papal States forced the church to find other sources of revenue. An "annate," or tax, of approximately one year's income was levied on each new appointment of a bishop or head of a monastery. Taxes for papal documents also rose. By the next century it was common to say that the old adage that avarice was the root of all evil (*radix omnia malorum avaritia est*) could be abbreviated as Rome (ROMA).

By the 1370s there was a movement to bring the papacy back to Rome, and in 1377 Pope Gregory XI did so. Much of the credit must be given to Catherine of Siena (1347–1380), a third-order Dominican (i.e., a layperson who voluntarily adopted Dominican discipline) whose great spirituality and insight made her a valued resource in mediating church conflicts. It was she who convinced Gregory to return. Unfortunately Gregory's successor, Urban VI, in his desire to free the papacy from French control, alienated a majority of the cardinals, who then returned to Avignon. There they invalidated Urban's election and chose another to replace him. Thus Christendom had two popes—one in Avignon and one in Rome. Europe divided, and those nations in league with France (Scotland, Spain, Naples, etc.) backed the Avignon pope, while France's opponents (England, northern Italy, most of Germany, and Poland) proclaimed loyalty to the Roman pontiff. The schism would last for thirty years, and before it was resolved, there would emerge a third claimant to the papal office.

The disarray in the papacy was not the only sign of crisis in Latin Christendom. Throughout the Middle Ages there had been protest movements, faulting the church for its worldliness. In the fourteenth century these protests intensified. In England, John Wycliffe (ca. 1330–1384) was an Oxford-trained theologian who lashed out at the church's great wealth. God was the true owner of the church's wealth, and the church was merely the steward. Clergy who were not righteous forfeited their claim to their possessions. Eventually he would also claim that the church was merely a spiritual society. Furthermore, he began to argue that the Bible was the only true authority and that the doctrine of transubstantiation was unscriptural. Wycliffe's followers became known as "Lollards" (from Dutch, one who mumbles). In Bohemia (the present Czech Republic) Wycliffe's teachings inspired further unrest. John Huss (ca. 1372–1415; in Czech, Jan Hus), a faculty member at the University of Prague, took up Wycliffe's ideas (though not his condemnation of transubstantiation) and began to attack the morals of the present-day clergy. Eventually he became entangled in the labyrinthine politics of a church with three popes, and after being promised safe conduct to the Council of Constance (1414–1418), he was imprisoned and burned at the stake. Huss's supporters continued his protests for decades.

If all these human problems were not enough, nature began to take its revenge. During the same century there began a systematic cooling of the climate of Europe, which had disastrous effects. Shorter growing seasons meant reduced food supplies, and a series of famines engulfed the continent. Even more catastrophic was the great plague that swept over the continent. Starting in Asia, it entered Europe in 1347, and in the three years between 1348 and 1351 it is estimated that between one-fourth and one-third of the European population died, with the mortality rate in parts of Italy even higher. Settlements were abandoned, commerce was broken up, and social and economic disorder ruled. Throughout Europe peasants saw this as a moment to protest their lot. Dutch historian Johan Huizinga aptly called this period the "waning of the Middle Ages."

The presence of multiple popes presented a peculiar dilemma for Latin Christians. As the law had developed, it asserted that there was no power greater than that of the papacy. Hence there was no institution empowered to fix a papal crisis. Some writers, such as Marsilius of Padua, questioned the entire theory on which the religio-political edifice rested, and argued that sovereignty came from the people themselves, but few were willing to accept such a radical claim. Instead what developed was a renewed idea of the authority of a general council. In 1409 the cardinals met in Pisa to exercise this authority. There they deposed both popes and chose a third. Finally, still another council was called to meet in Constance. There two of the three popes were deposed and the third resigned. A new pope, Martin V, was elected. It appeared that the conciliarism had triumphed. Yet Martin and his successors fought against it as threatening the power of the papacy, and by the mid-fifteenth century, the conciliar ideal began to languish.

Hope and Disappointment in the East

As Christians of the West were struggling with their assorted woes, Eastern Christians were suffering even more dire crises. Although the fourteenth and fifteenth centuries would prove to be destructive for Eastern Christians, there were nonetheless points of light and a bevy of might-have-beens that would have changed both the story of Christianity and world history itself.

As it has been noted, the great missionaries to Asia were the Nestorians. Strategically situated on the Silk Road, which connected the Mediterranean world with China, Nestorian merchants and missionaries carried Christianity into central Asia. Christianity had taken root in China as early as the seventh century, but over the succeeding centuries it seemed to have disappeared. There, as elsewhere in the East, the challenge of planting the church in such a vast geographical expanse without the political support such as that which Constantine and the Roman emperors provided, proved daunting.

By the thirteenth century it seemed that this level of support might be forthcoming, and from the unlikeliest of sources. When modern-day students think of the Mongolian Empire, their thoughts tend toward cruelty, pillage, and destruction. Yet for a time it looked as if the Mongols might be the means of putting Christianity on a new footing in Asia.

> For a time it looked as if the Mongols might be the means of putting Christianity on a new footing in Asia.

The people of central Asia consisted of nomadic tribes. Most were shamanists, believing in the various powers of the spiritual world, but thanks to Nestorian labors, some were Christians. One such tribe was the Keraits, who lived south and east of Lake Baikal. Toward the end of the twelfth century, their chief, Toghrul Wang-Khan, took under his wing a young man who would later be known as Genghis Khan. Genghis Khan would become one of the greatest military leaders of all time, and he founded an empire that stretched from Korea to Kiev. He forged the disparate Mongolian tribes (including the Kerait) into a unified force for conquest. But Genghis Khan was not simply a military leader. His religious policy, for example, was enlightened and displayed interest and toleration toward all religions. He also set forth a written law, the "Great Yasa," by which Mongols were to be governed. Some have seen possible Nestorian influence in this document. One law, for example, stated, "All men are to believe in one God, Creator of Heaven and earth."

But Christian influence on the Mongolian leaders came chiefly through royal marriages. Particularly the Kerait princess, Sorkaktani-beki, wife of Genghis Khan's fourth son, Tolui, was influential in finding a place for Christianity in the Mongol court. Even more important, three of her sons became, in turn, the Great Khan of the Mongols, the emperor of China, and the emperor (or ilkhan) of Persia. Each would be sympathetic to Christianity.

Mongol interest in Christianity had its practical side. As the Mongol Empire expanded west and south, it found itself in conflict with Muslim realms and eagerly sought allies. The Christian community was an obvious possibility, and this may have promoted some of the Mongol openness to Christianity. But the interest was not one-sided. Western Christians also dreamed of a coalition that could frustrate Islamic advances, and during the thirteenth and fourteenth centuries popes sent a number of missionaries to the court of the Khans.

Of the sons of Sorkaktani-beki, Hulegu was the most successful in bringing such an alliance about. Whether he ever became a Christian himself is doubtful, although there were rumors that he planned on being baptized. He nonetheless was eager for Christian support and presented Asian Christians with a great possibility. In the 1250s he began a major campaign against Persia. His leading general, Ked-Buka, was a Christian, and his army began to swell with Nestorian Christians, hoping to return to their native Persia. In 1258 he captured Baghdad, the center of the Islamic caliphate. In the slaughter that followed, only those Christians who took shelter in Nestorian churches were spared. A year later Damascus in Syria was captured. For the first time in five hundred years "Oriental Christians"—the name commonly given to the heirs of Nestorians and Monophysites—were free from Islamic control. Indeed, one of the palaces of the caliph was given over to the leader of the Nestorian church, for the building of a new church. After success in Syria, the next goal was Egypt, the final Islamic stronghold. Ked-Buka's army continued to draw Christian volunteers. Riding along with the general were both the king of Cilicia, or lesser Armenia, and Count Bohemund VI of Antioch. The former represented the oldest national church in the Christian world while the latter was one of the last remaining Latin crusading presences in the Holy Land (Bohemund I was a leader of the First Crusade). Despite his ruthlessness, many believed that Hulegu might be the deliverer of the Eastern Christian communities and the defeater of Islam. As one Muslim chronicler wrote, "He [Hulegu] visited the Christian church, and paid deference to their clergy. The governor was a Kerait and a Christian."

But it was not to be. Hulegu was not to be the Mongol Constantine. Almost immediately after the victory at Damascus, Hulegu retired with the bulk of his army back to central Asia. His brother, the Great Khan, had died, and a successor had to be chosen. When Ked-Buka led his reduced forces forward, they were soundly defeated at the battle of Ain Jalut (the Springs of Goliath), near Nazareth in 1260, by a much larger Islamic force. In the battle the Christian general went down in death saying, "From my birth I have been a slave of the King." The high-water mark of a new Christian order in the Middle East had passed.

The defeat of Ked-Buka and his partially Christian army near the place where Jesus had spent his boyhood offers an opportunity to observe how, ironically, culture can be a stronger force than religion. The Latin Christian crusaders were initially fearful of the advancing Mongols because of their reputation. The treatment of Christians in Baghdad convinced some crusaders that these forces were indeed friendly to Christianity. But the Mongols' reputation could not be eradicated, and ultimately the Latin Christians feared the "barbaric" Christian Mongols more than they did the "civilized" Muslims. After some hesitation, Latin leaders permitted the Islamic troops to pass through their territories unmolested before the battle of Ain Jalut. The Muslim victory rested on Christian cooperation.

Although the Mongols retreated, they continued to occupy Persia, and historians have referred to the thirty-seven years between 1258 and 1295 as the last flowering of Nestorian Christianity. The Mongolian ilkhans offered protection to the Christian minority, and some, such as Arghun (1284–1291) actively tried to establish an alliance between Mongol Asia and the Christian West against Islam. He sent an ambassador (who was also a bishop) to speak to the papacy and to the kings of England and France. He pleaded in a letter to Edward I of England to renew the Crusades and promised that Latins and Mongols together could recapture Jerusalem. But nothing came of it. The year of Arghun's death (1291) also witnessed the loss of the last crusaders' fortress in the Holy Land.

The ilkhans after Arghun became less sympathetic and protective of Christians. They also began to abandon the hope that Christianity might be used to stave off a Muslim encirclement. By 1295, the office was occupied by a Muslim, and unofficial and official persecution began. By the fourteenth century the Nestorian church began to recede from history.

The Church in China

A similar pattern of initial hope, yet ultimate disappointment, can be seen in the case of China. There Sorkaktani-beki's third son, Kublai Khan, governed. Although not a Christian himself, Kublai Khan was a friend of Christians. He is the famous figure recorded by Marco Polo. In his conversations with the Italian explorer, the Khan offered to send a letter to the pope asking for a hundred missionaries to try to explain by reason "that the Christian faith and religion is better . . . and more true than all the other religions, and if they proved that, [Kublai Khan] and all his potentates would become men of the Church." Two monks were eventually sent out from Europe but soon returned home. By the time a monk finally reached Beijing in 1294, Kublai Khan had died.

Marco Polo also recorded the presence of Nestorian Christians in China. He had heard rumors that there were secret Christian communities. Many were along the Silk Road in western China, but some were to be found along the coast and may have been remnants of earlier Chinese Christianity.

Kublai Khan's policy (as well as that of his immediate successors) was the toleration of all religions, and Christians benefited. When the first Latin Catholic missionary, John of Montecorvino, finally reached Beijing, he was allowed to proceed with his mission. Prospects for a Chinese church seemed so bright that in 1318 Pope John XXII divided Asia into two missionary districts: one for China and the other for Persia. But already Mongol power was slipping away, and as it did, the lot of Christianity worsened. To the Chinese the Mongol dynasty was viewed as foreign (and hence suspect), and Christians—whether Nestorian or Latin—were also so regarded. As one scholar has put it, with the defeat of the Mongols, "China turned Chinese in religion," and the Christian communities again began to disappear.

The Eastern churches would suffer one final blow. In the late fourteenth century still another conqueror emerged, Timur (1336–1405), often known in the West as Tamerlaine. His ferocity was legendary. In one battle he had the heads of seventy thousand victims piled in a pyramid. Unlike the earlier Mongols, Timur was a Muslim, and he dreamed of an Islamic force that would crush the infidels. Oriental Christian communities have long remembered his outrages. In Armenia, he had four thousand people buried alive after they surrendered, since he had cunningly assured them that if they surrendered, no blood would be shed (with no mention made of other forms of death). His atrocities against Muslims were equally abhorrent and made Islamic writers wonder whether he was indeed a Muslim. His campaigns, as we shall see, actually prolonged the life of Byzantium by weakening its enemies, but the effect on Christian life was catastrophic. Already weak Christian communities were unable to endure his blows and became shadows of their former selves.

The End of Byzantium

The fourteenth and fifteenth centuries were even more catastrophic for the Byzantine empire and church. The earlier Latin conquest was a terrible blow and a grievous outrage. The emperor was forced for a time to rule from Nicaea, and large parts of the once-proud empire were conquered and Latinized. These losses hurt the empire economically, which weakened the church, but popular opposition to the Latins kept their ecclesiastical changes from taking root. Such was the hatred that Byzantine clergy were solemnly forbidden to celebrate at altars that had been used for Latin services until they had been cleaned and disinfected. Greek rule was eventually restored to Constantinople in 1261 under the emperor Michael Paleologus, but the defeats had sorely damaged the empire.

In the latter decades of the thirteenth century, Byzantium found itself in a horrible dilemma. The emperors recognized that their only way forward was to restore relations with Rome. This would end the continuing strife between Byzantium and Latin barons intent on further peeling off the empire's riches, and it would allow resources to be shifted to the defense against Islamic incursions. But such a course of rapprochement was anathema to the large majority of clergy and laity, for whom it was seen as an abandonment of the faith and a succumbing to the hated Latin foe. This dilemma lay behind the failure of the Second Council of Lyons (1274). Reckoned an ecumenical council by the Western church, it was the first meeting of East and West in centuries. Emperor Michael Paleologus did all he could to bring about concord. He professed a belief in the "supreme and full primacy and governance" of the Roman or universal Catholic Church. He also accepted the Latin teaching on the filioque. The great schism could now end. But the emperor's church would not follow. The agreement was between pope and emperor; the reigning patriarch of Constantinople refused to accept it. Abdicating his office, he became the center of opposition to any compromise with the Latins. Lyons resolved nothing.

Throughout the fourteenth century the Byzantine Empire continued to shrink. By 1300, the great bulk of Asia Minor, which in Constantine's time had been the heart of Christianity, was captured by Muslims. Still another marauding group, the Ottoman Turks, by the end of the century had invaded the Balkans and had overcome the Christian communities in Serbia and Bulgaria. On the seas, the once-proud Byzantine merchant fleet was overtaken by Venice and Genoa. Politically and economically the bottom was falling out. Ironically, however, these same years witnessed a cultural and spiritual revival. Scholars of Byzantium have called the late thirteenth and fourteenth centuries the "Paleologian renaissance." A burst of creativity occurred in the production of both churches and icons. The writing of saints' lives, which had declined earlier, was revived. So, too, in monasticism, the practice of *hesychia*, solitary contemplation, flourished. Prayer, it was taught, had the power to transform persons and bring them closer to God. Hesychasm would revitalize Byzantine piety and would best be reflected in the popularity of the "Jesus prayer" ("Lord Jesus Christ, Son of God, have mercy upon me, a sinner").

By the fifteenth century Byzantium's political situation had worsened

> The Council of Florence was a decision made out of political necessity, was distasteful to most, and resulted in no Western military support.

even more. In 1422, the Turks (who had been distracted for more than a decade by struggles with Timur) besieged Constantinople. A revolt in Asia Minor forced them to temporarily lift the siege, but all knew that their success was a matter of time. One final attempt was made to achieve Western support. The Latins had been asking for still another council, and in 1438 one was called. Meeting first in Ferrara, it soon ran out of money and was forced to move to Florence, where it received the hospitality of the wealthy Cosimo de' Medici. The Council of Florence (as it came to be known) was important for many reasons. It provided the final blow to the earlier conciliar theory that General Councils were superior to popes, and it defined several doctrines. But its chief task was an attempted reunion of a divided Christian world. The filioque and the other points of disagreement were again addressed. Byzantine representatives, pressured by the Latin assertion that "the saints cannot err in faith," reluctantly accepted the Latin teachings concerning the filioque, papal primacy, and other disputed questions. A Decree of Union was signed July 5, 1439, and all Greek bishops present (save one) acquiesced.

The Council of Florence officially solved the Great Schism, and both the Greek church and empire dutifully ratified its teachings, but it had little impact. It was a decision made out of political necessity and was distasteful to most. It resulted in no Western military support, and in 1453 Constantinople finally fell to the Ottoman Turks. No official document could ever hope to overcome centuries of animosity, and one Byzantine nobleman supposedly said, as the Turkish army massed before the walls of the city, "It would be better to see the Turban of the Turks reigning in the center of the City, than the Latin mitre."

Russia: The Third Rome

The Ottoman policy was that of earlier Islamic rulers—the concern was not so much to destroy the Orthodox Church as to isolate it, and most of the Byzantine churches reluctantly acquiesced to this new situation. There was, however, one exception. In Russia, Orthodoxy would have a new place to grow. The Christianization of Russia was a gradual affair. A Russian prince had been so impressed by the beauty of Orthodox worship that he had invited Greek priests into his realm. By the eleventh century the Russian church was firmly in the Byzantine orbit, siding with it at the time of the Great Schism. It readily adopted the Eastern monastic tradition. Sergius and Germanus founded an important monastery at Valamo, and later Sergius of Radonezh (ca. 1314–1392) helped reform and spread monasticism. Russian princes suffered greatly for their faith during the various invasions the land underwent in the thirteenth and fourteenth centuries. In the early fourteenth century, the metropolitan, or head of the church, moved from Kiev to Moscow.

Until the middle of the fifteenth century the Russian church was but a subservient part of the greater Byzantine church. However, unlike the latter, Russians would accept neither the Council of Florence nor reunion with the Latin West. Hence in 1448, when it came time to elect a new metropolitan, one was chosen without reference to Greek authority. The estrangement over the Council of Florence led the Russian church down the path of independence to become autocephalous, or self-governing. Thus it stood when Constantinople fell.

With the fall of Byzantium, both Russia and its church began to see itself in a new light. In 1472 Ivan III (known to history as Ivan the Great) married the niece of the last Byzantine emperor. Although the marriage had little practical significance, psychologically it suggested a continuation of Byzantium in Russia. The leader of the Russians took the title of tsar (a corruption of the word *caesar*) and adopted the emblem of the double-headed eagle from Byzantium. This continuity was not lost on the church. Early in the next century a monk was to write that the tsar was now the leader of the apostolic church and that Moscow had now become the "Third Rome."

New Beginnings

By the 1460s the Christian world was in a precarious position. Byzantium had fallen; the old Oriental churches were barely holding on; smaller outlying churches like that of Ethiopia were isolated; and Europe was still recovering from the collapse of the medieval papacy. The Balkans were occupied by the Ottoman Turks, who threatened to extend their European conquests. The Christian world felt besieged and was far smaller than it had been a millennium earlier. But there was some hope. In the twelfth century tales had begun to circulate about "Prester John," a monarch descended from the race of the three wise men who visited the infant Jesus. He was said to rule over a fabulously rich land and to combine military judgment, saintly piety, and great wealth. Some identified him with St. Thomas of India and believed his realm was there. Others placed it farther east, and still others in Africa. But there came to be the hope that if a connection could be established between the Latin church and Prester John and his kingdom, the Muslim threat could be overthrown, and the Holy Land could be reclaimed.

But to reach him it was necessary to master the sea. During these troubling years in the fifteenth century, in the small realm of Portugal men began to do so. Henry the Navigator was their king. He was in many ways a typical medieval figure. It was said that he lived like a monk and died a virgin. He still harbored the crusading vision. But he combined all of these attributes with a spirit of exploration. He worked to improve the ships of his fleet and sent them outward for exploration in the hope of finding Prester John. His captains did not find Prester John, but what they did find (as we will see in chap. 12) would transform Christianity and the world. But, as we will see in the next two chapters, other changes were afoot, changes that would likewise remodel the Christian world.

Chapter 10

The Dividing of Western Christendom

*B*y the beginning of the sixteenth century the fate of Christianity rested on the Christian community of Europe more than ever before. The once-great churches of the East had either been overwhelmed by conquest or existed under the dominion of Muslim overlords. European churches alone possessed the autonomy to act, and they would soon act in ways that would add a new wrinkle to the Christian story.

As in the eighth century, the Islamic invasion (now by the Ottoman Turks) seemed almost irresistible. Powerful Muslim armies marched up the Balkans threatening central Europe. Between 1512 and 1541 the forces of the kingdom of Hungary suffered defeat after defeat, and the great city of Buda was captured. Soon after, the Ottomans would be at the gates of Vienna, and all Europe trembled. Islamic power had made the Mediterranean a Muslim lake, and Christian communities were threatened. Between 1530 and 1640 Islamic raiders took around one million Christians into slavery (approximately matching the number of Africans enslaved during the same period).

Not only was Islam a military threat, but its advance had theological ramifications. Many Christians viewed the Turkish invasion as a divine judgment against the sins of the Christian nations. Others believed it to be a sign that history was coming to an end. Augustine had long ago written (interpreting the always opaque book of Revelation) that

> Were these, then, the last days? Was the church in need of reform? Many sensitive people thought so.

God would enchain Satan for a thousand years to allow the church to flourish, but then Satan would be released and there would be a time of tribulation before Christ's return. Were these, then, the last days? Was the church in need of reform? Many sensitive people thought so. Worldliness and concern for wealth were threatening the church and needed to be addressed. In Spain, through the work of Ximenes de Cisneros, archbishop of Toledo, reform was initiated, and apostolic poverty was preached, learning was pushed, and religious houses were renewed in discipline.

New Factors and Forces

The beginning of the sixteenth century bore some resemblance to the eleventh century, when hopes and fears led to the medieval reformation, but there were important differences. One was a new political reality. The eleventh century had seen the defeat of the theocratic monarchs and the triumph of the international church; by the beginning of the sixteenth century these trends had been reversed. As papal power waned, the power of key nation-states in western Europe grew. By 1500 the kings of Spain, Portugal, France, and England were consolidating authority in their lands, and this shifted the balance of power between Rome and the monarchs. The Pragmatic Sanction of Bourges (1438) was an early example. Through it the French church (and in actuality, the French monarch) was given the right to administer its temporalities independent of Rome, and the papacy was denied the right to make nominations for empty benefices.

Another difference was a new intellectual spirit afoot, which later became known as humanism. Humanism is a distressingly murky yet necessary category historians must employ. Broadly speaking, humanism involved a recovery of the classical world of Greece and Rome and the elevation of the classical as the ideal in art and learning. Unlike scholastics who focused on logic and reconciliation of competing views, humanists emphasized reading texts in their original Greek and Latin. The movement began in Italy in the fifteenth century and spread northward. For humanists, the intervening centuries were at best a middle age, a time when the purity of the ancient world—whether it be in art, literature, or philosophy—was corrupted by outside forces. The rediscovery of ancient texts and the recovery of languages long forgotten in the Latin West inspired a new perspective. Whereas Italian humanists focused largely on the art and literature of the ancient world, in northern Europe Christian humanists applied the new learning to the study of the Bible and Christian antiquity. The greatest of the religious humanists was Desiderius Erasmus (1466–1536). Through his knowledge of Greek, he rediscovered many church writers who had been lost for centuries. Perhaps his greatest achievement was the publication of the Greek text of the New Testament in 1516.

Erasmus shared the humanist emphasis on right living and deeds rather than doctrine, and this shaped his view of true Christianity. His vision of reform was a simple Christ-centered faith with much of the physicality of Christian devotion—with its emphasis on relics, rituals, and monasticism—purged away. The Bible and the practices of the early church were at the heart of his reforming vision. But the witness of the ancients could lead in other directions. An interest in antiquity led some to read Augustine afresh. There they found neither the religious teaching of the times nor the simple, rational faith set forth by Erasmus, but a powerful sovereign God and a picture of humanity mired in sin. In Augustine, human beings were in a desperate state, and only the grace of God could rescue them. Augustine furthermore spoke of an omnipotent God who predestined who would be saved.

All of these factors—a sense of crisis over the events of the world, impatience with the worldliness of the church, an interest in the Bible and the early church as a source of renovation, and the influence of Augustine—would be the background of the Reformation. They would be catalyzed in a distinctive way in the life and thought of Martin Luther. Indeed, it is not too much to say that through Luther a spirit of reform became the Reformation.

Luther and the Reformation

Luther (1483–1546) was a product of his times. He was born into a family that had benefited from the economic changes then sweeping Europe. His father, emerging from the peasantry, had prospered in the mining industry of Saxony in Germany. There Martin was nurtured, and his father expected great things of him. Yet Luther himself had different plans. Caught in a violent thunderstorm, he made a vow to St. Anne (the nonscriptural mother of the Virgin Mary) that if he were to survive, he would become a monk. True to his word, in 1505 he joined the Augustinians, a strict religious order. Luther was a good monk, bright and obedient. He soon took priestly orders and became learned in the Scriptures. In 1511 his order sent him to teach at the University of Wittenberg.

> How could we be certain that we were striving fully? The idea that the Christian life depended on our actions was a tar pit for the souls of the overscrupulous.

Luther was a successful monk, but he had a problem, and it was not his alone. The problem was assurance of salvation. What was God's part, and what was humanity's part in salvation? Augustine had balanced his view of God's omnipotent grace with his understanding of the role of the church. According to the Augustinian tradition, the church, through its sacramental system, administered or infused grace into the faithful. Grace was made stronger by human cooperation through works of charity. To use the technical phrase, it was grace "formed by love." This concept lay behind the great medieval vision of the Christian life as a pilgrimage toward God. Our loving response to grace transformed us, and as we became transformed we became more acceptable to God. This process began on earth, and for most, it was completed in purgatory. Yet exactly how did this process begin? In classical theology the first step was God's; grace must come first. Yet in the fourteenth and fifteenth centuries, others (who were later called the neo-Pelagians) suggested a different answer. Human beings possessed the power to initiate the journey. If they strove with all they had within them, God would respond with grace. The technical phrase was *facere quod in se est* (to do that which is in you).

Yet the problem became, how could we be certain that we were striving fully? Ideally clergy and confessors could give assurance, but their assurance was only probable, and for those with greater scruples, the lack of certainty resulted in a "terrified conscience." The idea that the Christian life depended on our actions was a tar pit for the souls of the overscrupulous.

For Luther (who was overscrupulous) this was both a personal and theological problem, and to resolve it, he was led to a fundamentally different understanding of the human predicament. In 1513–1514 he undertook a study of the Psalms and Paul's Letter to the Romans and there began to perceive that the act of reconciliation was not a goal to be achieved but a gift from God. To quote his famous words, "There I began to understand that the righteousness of God is that by which the righteous live by faith. . . . Here I felt that I was altogether born again and had entered paradise itself through open gates." The saving act was God's alone, purely by grace, and was not tied to human participation but was freely given, to be received by faith. Lying behind Luther's discussion was an understanding of grace different from Augustine's and with great implications. The grace of the "passive" righteousness was a gift from God that covered sinful humanity like a cloak. The sinful individual was enshrouded by Christ's righteousness so that he or she might find favor with God.

Luther's "Reformation breakthrough" (as it came to be called) was one of conceptualization or theory. It necessitated no change in action but merely change in understanding. But by 1517 he began to use his insight to criticize one of the more problematic aspects of late medieval Catholicism, the indulgence system. Indulgences, in theory, were based on the belief that even a forgiven sin still carried a penalty that had to be addressed through penance. Defenders of indulgences claimed that the church possessed the power to remit these penalties, and an indulgence was the means. By doing a designated good work of the church, the penalty of a sin could be removed. Indulgences involved both theoretical and practical issues. The whole system was based on speculation for which there was little certain evidence. That sin entailed a penalty and that the church had the power to remit such a penalty were both open to question. Furthermore, on the practical level, indulgences were not only granted but sold, and their sale became an important source of ecclesiastical revenue. To finance the rebuilding of St. Peter's in Rome (whose fourth-century basilica had fallen into ruin), Pope Leo X issued a license or permission to sell indulgences. The indulgence question impelled Luther to act, and on October 31, 1517 (or possibly November 1), according to tradition, he nailed a set of propositions on the church door of the cathedral at Wittenberg, challenging the practice. These propositions have gone down in history as the "Ninety-Five Theses" and are seen by many as the beginning of the Protestant Reformation.

On the question of indulgences Luther was on comparatively safe ground, for he was not alone in questioning the practice. But the issue soon moved from an abstruse point of theology and practice to questions about the nature of the church. In a series of debates, culminating with one at Leipzig in 1519, Luther's protagonists successfully shifted the debate from indulgences to the authority of the church, and they forced Luther to express doubts about the authority of ecumenical councils. As a result, in 1520 he found himself condemned for heresy by the bull *Exsurge Domine*. Yet Luther did not submit. In response he published three treatises that both fleshed out his theology and indicated the future course of his movement. The first was an address to the Christian nobility of the German nation, which called for the civil rulers to reform their churches. The second was *The Babylonian Captivity of the Church*, which reassessed the sacramental system and argued for reducing the number of the sacraments from seven to three. The third treatise, *The Freedom of the Christian*, developed his understanding of passive righteousness and offered a new understanding of Christian duty.

In 1525 Luther took one other step that would have great later significance. He wed Katharina von Bora, a nun who had abandoned the cloister as a result of Luther's teachings. Luther had come to oppose both monasteries and celibacy, and his reformation rejected the women's religious orders that had been an important part of medieval Catholicism and provided a role for women. But in Katharina von Bora a new role emerged, that of pastor's wife. In the history of Protestantism, that would play an important, albeit unofficial, role in parish life.

Luther's theology struck a chord in Germany, and much excitement ensued. He had challenged the authority of the Roman church in the name of justification by faith and the authority of the Bible. But were there limits to what should be reformed? Among Luther's followers there were moderates (associated with Philipp Melanchthon) and radicals (associated with Andreas Karlstadt). Luther, who was himself conservative in nature, favored the moderates and rejected the radicals. But other reformers were willing to push reformation further. In the Swiss city of Zurich another seedling of the Reformation also took root, under the leadership of Huldrych Zwingli.

Switzerland and Huldrych Zwingli

Zwingli and Luther were contemporaries and were both born into a similar comfortable social position. But whereas Luther chose the path of the monastic cloister, Zwingli's life was much more worldly. He was educated in the humanist fashion and shared Erasmus's confidence that right learning could transform the world. After serving as a parish priest, in 1518 he was appointed to the Great Minster at Zurich. While there he gradually became attracted to the spirit of reform. In 1519 he began to preach directly from the Bible, shunning the medieval scholastic commentaries, and he was so successful that the city council required all Zurich preachers to follow suit. With Scripture as his guide, he began to question the veneration of saints, purgatory, images, vestments, and music.

From early on, Zwingli's reformation was more radical than Luther's. Much had to do with how they read the Bible. Both Luther and Zwingli appealed to the unique authority of Scripture (*sola scriptura*), but they differed as to how Scripture should be applied. For Luther the core of Scripture was the doctrine of justification by faith. Where justification by faith was maintained, he was tolerant of traditions and customs even when they had no scriptural warrant. They were as such *adiaphora*, things indifferent. Zwingli was more insistent on using the Bible as a guide for right reform. This would eventually lead to a difference in the numbering of the Decalogue, or Ten Commandments. Western Christians had generally followed the numbering of the commandments set forth by Augustine, which listed the first commandment as being about God ("I am the Lord thy God . . .") and included the subordinate injunction against "graven images." This, it was understood, did not imply a rejection of all graven images but only those that challenged the lordship of God. Based on this reading, the Western church had firmly sided with the defenders of icons in the Iconoclastic debate, and its churches overflowed with pictures and statues. Luther followed this reading and was sympathetic to the pictorial tradition. Zwingli and his supporters, however, demanded a new numbering of the Decalogue that made the injunction against graven images stand as a separate commandment. The rejection of images was not subordinate but absolute. Like the Iconoclasts earlier, Zwingli and his followers called for the removal of all images and statues in the churches. These divergent attitudes on traditional images led the Lutheran and Swiss Reformations in strikingly different directions.

An even more divisive issue was the Eucharist. Luther rejected many medieval errors concerning the mass: the elements should not be adored; the cup should be restored to the laity; and transubstantiation was a dangerous mixture of the gospel and Aristotelian piffle. But he was adamant that Christ was truly and locally present in the bread and wine. Zwingli objected to such a teaching. Not only was transubstantiation to be rejected but so, too, was any talk of a real presence. The meaning of the sacrament for Zwingli concerned the spirit rather than the flesh. A sacrament was a sign, and a sign was distinct from that which it signified. The sacrament was like a ring a lover might bestow at the beginning of a long journey. It served as a reminder of a presence, but the presence was at best a spiritual one and rested in the hearts of the faithful. Luther found such reasoning unpersuasive. If Christ became spiritually present only through human belief, then there was no certainty, and the dilemma of the terrified conscience returned. The objectivity of Christ's presence in the sacrament paralleled the objectivity of Christ's saving grace. Both rested on divine promise and not human effort.

The division between Luther and Zwingli threatened to split the young protest movement. At a time when the Holy Roman Emperor, Charles V, was marshalling military forces to suppress the ecclesiastical discord in his realm, intra-Reformer unity seemed essential. The leading Protestant prince, Philip of Hesse, sought a confessional alliance between Germany and Switzerland, and thus Luther, Zwingli, and their followers met for formal discussion in 1529 at the Colloquy at Marburg to see if they could overcome their disagreements.

There, they avoided discussions of images to concentrate on the Eucharist. The meeting was, however, to no avail. Zwingli believed that "eating" was interchangeable with "believing" and that in the sacrament, one ate the physical bread while feeding on Christ's true body by faith. Luther insisted that when Christ proclaimed, "This is my body," it must be taken literally.

For Zwingli there existed a wide gap between the physical and the spiritual; he doubted whether the physical could truly convey grace. For Luther, God worked through the physical. No agreement resulted, and by 1530 Lutheran and Swiss Protestants began going their own way.

The Radical Alternative

Zwingli died in battle in 1531, and his name would not be immortalized by any Christian community. But his distinctive emphases have influenced non-Lutheran Protestantism. Strict scripturalism, a suspicion of idolatry, a preference for spirit over matter, and discomfort with talk of eucharistic real presence would be taken up by many later Protestants. He pushed the Reformation of Luther into directions that Luther himself would not take. But did even Zwingli go far enough? Throughout sixteenth-century Europe there were those, inspired by Scripture, who believed it possible not merely to reform the church but to restore the primitive model of Christianity. Collectively this group has been known as the Radical Reformation. Its proponents offered an alternative vision of what Christianity might be.

Despite their theological disagreements, both Luther and Zwingli accepted the Christian system inaugurated by Constantine in the fourth century that led to the emergence of Christendom. Constantinian Christianity rested on two foundations. The first was that Christianity was to be the religion of the land. All persons in the society were (ideally) members of the church. Baptism was a social ritual and not an act of independent choice. The second was the interconnection between the crown and the cross. Many would differ (as we have seen) on just how they were related, but all agreed that they were interconnected. By 1523 a number of early supporters of Zwingli—Balthasar Hubmaier, Felix Manz, and Conrad Grebel—began to question both foundations. They became convinced that infant baptism lacked scriptural warrant, and in 1525 they and a small band of followers underwent a new baptism, or a "believer's baptism." Their action gave to them a name, Anabaptists (literally, re-baptizers).

> Baptism should be limited to believers who had repented and chosen to follow Christ. The church must be a voluntary community of true believers.

A few years later, in 1527, Swiss Anabaptists (along with some from southern Germany) came together to issue the Schleitheim Confession of faith, which offered a theological summary of their vision. Baptism should be limited to believers who had repented and chosen to follow Christ: "This excludes all infant baptism, the high and chief abomination of the pope." The church must be a voluntary community of true believers. A second Anabaptist concern was church discipline. Through the use of the "ban," or the shunning of members who had fallen into sin, and by limiting the Lord's Supper to those who were in good fellowship with the community and excluding all others, discipline was to be maintained. Still a third concern was the relationship between the church and the world. No fellowship was to be struck with the sinful world; the church must remain pure. This meant that true Christians could not participate in the coercive activities of the state, since "the sword . . . is ordained of God outside of the perfection of Christ." Here the Anabaptist broke decisively from Constantinian Christianity's joining of church and state. Finally, the true Christian must never swear an oath, as was required in courts of law. In all of these points the Anabaptists saw themselves as carrying the principle of biblicism to its logical conclusion.

The city leaders of Zurich, appalled by these principles, ordered that the Anabaptists be drowned, in mockery of their call for rebaptism. Persecution spread the movement into south Germany and Moravia as well as other parts of Switzerland. As the radical movement expanded, it began to exhibit a broader theological spectrum. Some, such as Kaspar Schwenkfeld, pushed the movement in a more spiritual direction, claiming that Christ must be received spiritually and directly, not mediated through preaching, sacrament, and Scripture. Others, such as Bernardino Ochino and Michael Servetus, used biblical radicalism to question the doctrine of the Trinity. In both cases they were viewed as threatening the idea of a Christian society as it had developed over a thousand years. Luther denounced them as *Schwarmers* (crawling things), and both Protestants and Catholics joined in their persecution.

The symbol of the radical threat became the town of Münster (in northern Germany), where in 1530 radical Anabaptists attempted to set up a theocratic Old Testament community under an inspired prophet. In their "New Jerusalem" they exiled dissenters and reinstituted polygamy. Münster was eventually captured by a combined force of Lutherans and Catholics, who publicly executed its prophet, displaying his body (and those of his associates) in an iron cage on the church tower. Religious revolutions were a serious business. The remnant of the radicals was reorganized by Menno Simons, a former priest who joined the movement after the collapse of Münster, leading it away from apocalypticism and toward a consistent pacifism. He also indirectly gave to them another name by which they are still known, Mennonites.

The Lutheran Reformation triumphed (at least in the short run) in most of Germany, and eventually in Scandinavia as well. By 1530 it gained its classic theological shape in the Augsburg Confession. In 1529 the movement would receive a name. At the Diet of Speyer the reforming princes and cities of the Holy Roman Empire issued a "Protestatio," a united declaration of faith, to answer their opponents. From this developed the term "Protestant," which became the standard term to designate the Reformers of the sixteenth century. Outside of Germany the Protestant message found its most vigorous proponents not among the followers of Luther but in a different group that has come to be known as the "Reformed." The Reformed churches attempted to find a middle ground between the sacramentalism and traditionalism of Luther and the radical thrust of Zwingli. In particular, its leaders would advance Zwingli's scripturalism and fear of idolatry while modifying his sacramental teachings.

Calvin and the Reformed Vision

Although there were many Reformed figures in different communities, the greatest was the French theologian John Calvin (1509–1564). He was of the generation after Luther, and in his life and thought he reflected both Reformed understandings and the attitudes of many second-generation Protestants who had no memory of a united Catholic Church. He was born in Picardy, northeast of Paris, into a politically and socially well-connected family. Family resources allowed him to receive a thorough education at the University of Paris. After his father's death he shifted his study from law to Greek and Hebrew, and his first publication, *A Commentary on Seneca's Treatise on Clemency*, was a model of humanistic erudition. But in the France of the 1520s, humanism was allied with the forces pushing for religious reform. In the 1530s Calvin underwent what he later called a "sudden conversion," and he became committed to religious reform. To advocate religious reform was to live precariously. In 1534, in an incident known as the Affair of the Placards, irreverent signs were pinned not only in the city streets but even in the king's own bedroom. The affront led to a royal crackdown on religious dissent.

Calvin fled to Basel in Switzerland. He intended to settle eventually in the Protestant city of Strasbourg, but as he passed through Geneva in 1536, a Protestant leader, Guillaume Farel, pleaded for him to stay and lead the city as it struggled to define its Protestant identity. Geneva was a Swiss city under control of the House of Savoy, administered by a prince bishop. In the 1520s it had revolted against Savoy and gradually moved toward religious reform. But its policies were not set, and Calvin would shape Geneva, and over time Geneva would influence all of international Protestantism.

In 1536 Calvin published the first edition of his most famous work, *Institutes of the Christian Religion*. The *Institutes* shows Calvin at his most typical: organized, logical, and thorough. Much ink has been spilled on how Calvin and Luther differed as theologians. On one level there was little formal disagreement (except on the question of the Eucharist), but Calvin and Luther were very different kinds of thinkers. Calvin's theology flowed logically from his starting point, the glory of God and the correct human response. The *Institutes* begins with the question of the knowledge of God and ends with how the right community is to be governed.

True knowledge of God, argued Calvin, can only come from the Scriptures. Sin made it impossible for natural human beings to know of God in any other way, such as through reason, as Aquinas had claimed. Scripture, furthermore, was important in and of itself. For Luther, the heart of Scripture was the good news or gospel. This led him to put differing weight on various parts of the Bible. The Epistle of James, which seemed to contain little about justification by faith, he dismissed as an epistle of straw. For Calvin, all Scripture was authoritative. Calvin's belief in the unity of the Bible led him further to put more emphasis on the Old Testament than had many earlier figures. The Old Testament had authority in itself and was not merely a preparation for the New Testament. The practical implication of this was that Calvinist communities took seriously the laws of the Old Testament. Opposition to the use of graven images and a desire to maintain the sanctity of the Christian Sabbath marked the Calvinist world. For Calvin the Bible was a positive law by means of which the church and society could be rightly ordered.

> For Calvin, all Scripture was authoritative. Calvin's belief in the unity of the Bible led him further to put more emphasis on the Old Testament than had many earlier figures.

Calvin's sense of the sovereignty of God led his logical mind to emphasize the idea of predestination. The view that God must initiate salvation through an act of grace was indeed an old one. Both the apostle Paul and Augustine (to name but two) admitted such, as did Luther. But predestinarian teaching was usually counterbalanced with other scriptural themes, such as God's call for all to believe. Calvin pushed the doctrine of predestination further, claiming not only that God chose whom he wished to save but that God also chose those he wished to condemn. The technical name for the teaching is "*double* predestination." Calvin believed that predestination was scriptural but had little pastoral implication, and though the question of determining whether one was predestined would consume many later Calvinists, it was not one of his concerns. People need not worry whether they were chosen, only whether they were following Christ. Over time, however, it did have strong pastoral implications, and the question of knowledge of one's predestined state would become all consuming.

Divine sovereignty also shaped Calvin's understanding of human response. Decades later, the Westminster Catechism pithily summarized Calvin. To the question of what was man's chief end, the answer was, "Man's chief end is to glorify God." The glorification of God involved the "third use of the law." The divine law was not only used as a mirror for human sinfulness (the first use) and as a restraint for evil (the second use), but it had a positive purpose for edification (the third use). Faithful obedience to the law allowed God to be glorified and allowed individuals and communities to grow in grace. This building up of the body of Christ through obedience is what Calvinists called edification. Individuals, churches, and societies all had the obligation to move ever closer to God's law.

God's law, finally, offered an outline for the right ordering of the church. In contrast with Luther, who was not particularly interested in exactly how the church was to be organized, for Calvin church order, or polity, was of crucial importance. The Scriptures, he claimed, revealed a fourfold ministry of pastor, teacher, elder, and deacon. Elders and pastors met together in the consistory and were in charge of ecclesiastical discipline, including excommunication. They were assisted by "certain persons of good life" from each quarter of the city appointed by the city council to monitor any actions of impropriety. Thus Geneva was to be a model Christian commonwealth, in which "edification" would rule civil as well as ecclesiastical life. Calvin's agenda, to be sure, was controversial. At one point he was exiled, and even after his return in 1541 he often struggled against opposition. Yet by the 1560s Calvin's (and the consistory's) control was secure, and Geneva became a destination for dedicated Protestants. The vigor and discipline of Calvin's Geneva would inspire similar attempts throughout Europe, and eventually in the New World.

A Stumbling Start in England

The final Reformation movement was unlike the others, though drawing on many common strands. England's Reformation was rooted in political concerns but spawned competing parties who struggled to give it direction. Because of this it would not be finally determined until the next century.

Although England had experienced the Lollard movement in the fifteenth century and did have some individuals keenly interested in the reform movements that were shaking the continent, there was little popular interest in reform during the early decades of the sixteenth century. Indeed King Henry VIII received the title Defender of the Faith (*Defensor Fidei*) for a work he (allegedly) authored defending the seven traditional sacraments against Martin Luther. A political crisis opened the door for religious change. Henry's house of Tudor had ruled the land for only two generations, and to continue, it needed a male successor. Henry's wife, Catherine of Aragon, had been able to provide only one surviving child, a daughter, Mary. Henry convinced himself that this situation stemmed from the sinful nature of his marriage. Catherine had earlier been betrothed to his brother Arthur, and only a papal dispensation allowed Henry and Catherine to wed. Such a marriage, he now believed, violated the teaching found in Leviticus (18:16). Accordingly, Henry sought another papal action to annul his marriage and allow him to marry the conveniently attractive Anne Boleyn.

Catherine of Aragon was not without influence. Particularly after her nephew, the emperor Charles V, occupied Rome, it became evident that no annulment would be forthcoming. Henry then turned to England and, after subduing the clergy, had Parliament pass in 1533 the "Act of Restraint of Appeals" that forbade all appeals to Rome in matters spiritual or temporal. Significantly, the act also began by defining England as an "empire," thus laying the legal groundwork for the king of England to exercise imperial control over the church. Other acts followed, and in 1534 the break was completed. Henry was proclaimed the "Supreme Head of the Church of England." Henry's actions led to opposition from the noted humanists Thomas More and John Fisher, who refused to concur with Henry's break from Rome. Both were executed for refusing to affirm Henry's new authority. Yet the first phase of the English Reformation did little more than separate England from Rome. It called for changes neither in practice nor in doctrine.

Henry's activities provided a small but real opening for those with a Protestant agenda. Two of these were Thomas Cromwell and Thomas Cranmer. Cromwell was eventually named vicar general for ecclesiastical affairs. Although personally interested in Protestantism, his greatest accomplishment was the suppression of the English monasteries, allegedly because of their decay and corruption. Cromwell's act both destroyed an important link with the religious past and created a party of individuals (who took possession of these properties) who then had a vested interest in preventing any return to the old order that might threaten their newly gained wealth. Cranmer (as we will see in the next chapter) would become the formulator of the new English liturgies. Henry (on the whole) tolerated these Protestant partisans, but he carefully balanced them with strong traditionalists. At different times during the 1530s and 1540s the English Reformation moved to the left and the right, but it was unclear where it would ultimately end.

By 1540 the unity of Western Christendom had become shattered. Protestantism had taken firm root in Germany and Switzerland and was gathering force in other places as well. Yet much was still uncertain. Europe would experience a century of violent conflict before any religious peace could be secured.

SECTION 4   Contesting Boundaries

Chapter 11

The Battle for the Soul of Europe

The rush of events in the opening decades of the sixteenth century left many wondering about the state of Western Christianity. The church had been for over a millennium the unifying force in society, and now it was divided. What would the future bring, and could unity be restored?

The problem, however, was that the Reformation was about a number of things. It was a protest over worldliness and corruption. It was a rejection of several decisions the church had made over the preceding centuries. A formal insistence on clerical celibacy only went back to the eleventh century, and the decision to remove the cup from the laity and have the priest alone receive wine at Communion was an even more recent change. Protestants overwhelmingly rejected both. Finally there were new theological understandings, such as Luther's teaching concerning justification. Could these critiques be incorporated into a reunified Catholic Christianity?

Attempting Reunion

Some hoped so. Particularly in the Holy Roman Empire, where the religious divisions were most acute, there arose voices calling for reform and reconciliation. Herman of Wiede, archbishop of Cologne, attempted to tighten clerical discipline and introduce liturgical reform in the hope of restoring unity. In Italy throughout the 1530s there were also those who sought a way out of the impasse. There, Jacob Sadoleto and Gasparo Contarini labored to bridge the theological gap opened by Luther and bring Protestants back into the fold. In 1536 Pope Paul III created a special commission on the need for reform. Its membership included Sadoleto and Contarini, along with other voices for reform. Their report criticized the current state of the church and called for a strengthening of the episcopacy. It also questioned the economic structure of the church that was again slipping into simony. Reform was in the air.

But perhaps the boldest undertaking was a colloquy, or formal discussion, at Ratisbon in 1541. There, three Catholic theologians and three Protestant theologians, chosen by the emperor Charles V, were charged by him not merely to defend their own theologies but to explore whether their theologies could be reconciled. The Protestant party included Melanchthon, and the Catholic party was led by Contarini. The Catholic emperor was willing to concede both clerical marriages and the restoration of the cup in the Eucharist to Protestants if the theological differences could be met. The participants did reach agreement on the question of justification, but on other contested issues the discussion broke down. Catholics would not budge on transubstantiation, and Protestants would not allow a necessary role for confession to priests. The attempt failed.

The failure of Ratisbon led to a collapse of the reformist party within the Latin church. Critics had always argued that the reformists were willing to give up too much to reconcile the dissidents, and now it seemed as if compromise was fruitless. Contarini was placed under house arrest after his return from Ratisbon, and he died shortly thereafter. Other reformists were quieted while still others eventually abandoned the old church. The few remaining reformists in the Latin church saw their influence continue to erode.

The Rise of the Jesuits

In contrast, those who argued that the old church needed to stop the Protestant movement began to grow in prominence. No group was to become so associated with this new combative spirit as the Society of Jesus, or the Jesuits, founded by Ignatius Loyola.

Ignatius (1491–1556) was of the same generation that produced Luther and Zwingli, but he came from an entirely different background. Born in Spain, he was trained as a courtier and soldier. He was seriously wounded in 1521 at the battle of Pamplona. During a long period of recuperation, Ignatius, whose literary tastes had theretofore been limited to chivalric romances, became enamored of the life of Christ and the *Golden Legend*, a collection of the lives of the saints. Through his readings he became converted; he would no longer be a soldier for Spain but a soldier for Jesus. While making pilgrimage at the shrine for the Virgin Mary at Montserrat (near Barcelona), he dedicated himself to the vocation of spiritual knighthood. Other mystical experiences gave him added certainty and contributed insights that would be reflected in his masterpiece, *The Spiritual Exercises*. After an unsuccessful mission to Jerusalem, he returned to Spain and undertook a course of education that would lead him to the College de Montaigu in Paris (where Calvin had studied but a few years earlier), from which he graduated in 1534.

In Paris, a group of young men gathered around Ignatius, and in 1534 they made a vow of poverty and service to others. Among these persons was Francis Xavier, who would find fame in the mission field. The band intended to begin a mission in the Holy Land, but a war raging there would not permit it. Instead they labored in and around Rome (where they were encouraged by Contarini, who believed them to be a tool for furthering church reform). In 1540 the Society of Jesus was recognized by the pope as a new religious order.

The Jesuits were a new kind of religious order. They did not recite the elaborate daily prayers or canonical office, as monks did, nor did they wear a special habit. Their piety was far more internalized and less institutional. Most important, their order reflected the military background of its founder. Hierarchy and discipline were paramount. The Jesuit mind-set reflected the spirit of Ignatius's *Spiritual Exercises*.

Although not formally directed against Protestantism, the *Exercises* offered a radically contrasting view of both the human predicament and the path of grace. Human beings did not

> Jesuits were set apart from other religious orders by a special vow of loyalty to the papacy.

suffer from a terrified conscience (à la Luther) but from a will that was not adequately bound to God. If people truly loved God, they would ideally want to serve him, but in actuality most people were confused about the love and the service. The *Exercises* was carefully constructed to place individuals in a position where they could see what their duty was and how they could act on it. Human will was not bound by divine action (as predestinarians might claim) but clouded by human sin. Furthermore, in the *Exercises* Ignatius used Scripture in a different way. For Luther, Zwingli, and Calvin, the Bible, as the word of God, was a source of theological truth, a guide to doctrine, and an ultimate judge of the church. Ignatius focused not so much on the doctrines of Scripture as on the images. He urged his exercitants (those being led through the exercises) to enter into the world pictured in the Gospels and to relate to the scenes not only intellectually but affectively as well. To place oneself imaginatively at the foot of the cross made Christ's sacrifice far more real than merely being told about it. The emotive power of Scripture for Ignatius was like that of the most moving religious artwork, yet because it was imaginative and not physical, it was internal and portable. Through

the *Exercises* the exercitant took away all the teaching embodied in the iconography of a medieval cathedral and carried it with him wherever he went.
This portability was essential because the goal of the *Exercises* was action.
Ignatius did not teach meditation for meditation's sake, or for the edification
of an individual soul, but to empower activity in the world. Finally, there was
obedience to the church. Jesuits were set apart from other religious orders by
a special vow of loyalty to the papacy, and the *Exercises* underscored that
loyalty. Perhaps its most famous line is "What I see as white, I will believe to
be black if the hierarchical Church thus determines it."

The growth of the Jesuits was phenomenal. In 1540 there were ten members of the society. By the time of Ignatius's death in 1556 there were five
thousand. In 1640, after a century of growth, there would be twenty-two
thousand. Jesuits would be known for their work as educators and as missionaries both inside and outside of Europe. Their message of discipline and
obedience combined with a willingness to interact with the world made them
a potent force in the revival of Catholicism. Their vision of a reunited church,
however, did not involve a rapprochement with Protestantism but its defeat.

Calling a Council

As the Jesuits were being organized, a movement to call a general council
began. The church of the Holy Roman Empire was eager for a council, but the
papacy (although supportive of such a gathering) worried about the emperor
taking control of it. A council was finally called in 1545, and Trent—an imperial city in Italy—was chosen as a compromise location. The eclipse of the
reforming party ensured that no Protestant representatives would be invited
to attend and that the first agenda item would be a clarification of the theological issues separating Catholics and Protestants, not the reform of abuses.
In choosing to focus on the definition of doctrine, the bishops at Trent not
only set themselves against what they saw as the fundamental errors of the
Protestants but also pushed Latin Catholicism in a particular direction. Up to
this point many beliefs had not been formally defined. The precise number of
the sacraments, for example, although commonly understood as seven, had
never been officially delineated. Medieval Catholicism was a period of rich
theological discussion in which different schools of thought presented varia-
tions on common themes. Trent set out to define official Catholic teaching
much more explicitly.

Three of the early questions concerned ecclesiastical authority, the sacraments, and justification. The idea of *sola scriptura* (Scripture alone) was

rejected, and the church was set forth as the true interpreter of Scripture. Whereas Protestants had questioned the validity of the Apocrypha (those books in the Old Testament without Hebrew originals, which were rejected by the rabbis), the council defined them as fully canonical. The sacraments (including the doctrine of transubstantiation) were reaffirmed, and the number of sacraments was formally defined as seven. Baptism, Eucharist, confession, confirmation, marriage, ordination, and unction (or anointing the sick) were all defined as sacraments. Justification by faith alone was rejected, and the traditional idea of faith formed by love asserted. Also rejected was the carefully worked-out compromise on justification coming out of the colloquy at Ratisbon. The time for compromise had passed.

Having settled doctrine, the council addressed church discipline in later sessions. Bishops were required to reside in their diocese and make periodic pastoral visitations. Their authority was strengthened by giving them much more direct oversight over their dioceses than they had previously possessed because of numerous and long-standing exemptions from episcopal control. Clerical celibacy was reaffirmed, the use of a distinctive clerical dress code was required, and the education of clergy was regularized. A unified Latin eucharistic liturgy, which came to be known as the Tridentine mass, was set forth, and this liturgy was mandated to be used uniformly in all places. This discipline was necessary to meet the needs of the present crisis of the church. Nor were the laity ignored. A new catechism was drawn up, and greater concern was directed toward the education of laity.

The old Latin church emerged from the Council of Trent reinvigorated and with a new sense of direction. Clergy became much more conscientious in instructing and governing the laity. Reforming figures, such as Charles Borromeo, archbishop of Milan, illustrate the change in spirit. Originally he was attracted to the church as a lucrative career, but he became a strong agent for reform. He regularly preached, practiced great austerity, revised the catechism, and dedicated himself to the education of his clergy and the pastoral care of his diocese. To encourage the sacrament of confession, he created the confessional box, where the sacrament could be undertaken in comparative privacy.

A Reinvigorated Latin Catholicism

By the 1560s observers could witness a real change in Catholicism, particularly in the Mediterranean world. A new vitality and confidence quickly eliminated any traces of Protestantism. This was made easier by the tool of the Inquisition. The Inquisition had developed in Spain to root out hidden but continuing Jewish and Islamic sympathies after 1492. In 1542 it was established in Italy and became an important weapon for crushing dissent.

But one must quickly note that there were other and more positive tools. In the life of Teresa of Avila (1515–1582) one sees elements of both new piety and new organization. Teresa was a Spanish Carmelite nun. Her christocentric piety emphasized good works as the fruit of disciplined prayer ("God deliver me from people so spiritual that they want to turn everything into contemplation, no matter what," she commented tartly about her friend and fellow mystic John of the Cross), but her piety was also manifested in intense mystical experiences that she recorded in detail, in particular the piercing of the heart and the mystical marriage of the soul with the divine bridegroom. Her works became a guide for others. Further, she believed that only by a reform of religious life could the church be prayed into a new life and overcome the Protestant threat. She established a number of houses of "Discalced [barefoot] Carmelites," which attempted to restore the original poverty and rigor of the order.

> The Catholic revival was in key ways the work of the Mediterranean churches of Italy and the Iberian Peninsula. Their influence was so great that one can now speak of a "Roman Catholicism" that recognizably differed from the earlier Western Catholic heritage.

Much of the reinvigoration was on the local level. Just as the Council of Trent had strengthened the authority of the bishops in their dioceses, so too did it strengthen the authority of priests in their parishes. Responsibility for preaching and hearing confessions, which in the Middle Ages had often fallen to wandering Dominican and Franciscan friars, now rested on a more thoroughly trained parish clergy. The reinvigorated confidence was reflected in a new architectural style—the baroque. If the earlier gothic style had accented light and reason, baroque style paid homage to solidity and mass. Particularly throughout Italy, great new sanctuaries were erected that overwhelmed the worshipers, letting all know that the church was here to stay. The baroque's indebtedness to the Counter-Reformation could be seen not only in its massiveness and solidity but also in its use of color and picture, which offered a visualization of *The Spiritual Exercises*.

The Catholic revival was in key ways the work of the Mediterranean churches of Italy and the Iberian Peninsula. Their influence was so great that one can now speak of a "Roman Catholicism" that recognizably differed from the earlier Western Catholic heritage. It was more defined; it was more unified; it was more directed; and it was more Latin than it had been since the time of Augustine.

Yet it was not clear what the fate of this revived Roman Catholicism would be outside the Mediterranean milieu. As late as 1555 Protestantism was still expanding. Austria, Bavaria, and Bohemia in Central Europe were places of intense Protestant activity. Poland had a vigorous Protestant movement among its aristocracy. There seemed to be no stopping its growth. But gradually the tide began to reverse. In the lands controlled by the Habsburgs, there was a continuing campaign to shift the allegiance of princes and peoples away from Protestantism and toward a renewed Catholicism. The Peace of Augsburg (1555) had theoretically established a truce between warring Protestants and Catholics, and each dominion was to follow the religion of its ruler. But covert and overt Catholic pressure helped reverse Protestant advances. Much credit here must go to the Jesuits. Although not originally envisioned as a tool in the battle against Protestantism, by the mid-1540s the order had entered on this task with gusto, as seen in the career of Peter Canisius (1521–1597). He became celebrated for answering Protestant charges and establishing educational institutions through which a new generation could be introduced to the old faith. Canisius and other Jesuits were also diligent in combating those practices within the church that had provoked Protestant criticisms. As a papal nuncio observed, "The best way to fight the heretics is not to deserve their criticism." By the end of the sixteenth century, it became clear that the tide had turned in a Catholic direction throughout the contested areas of Europe.

In Poland, a combination of royal authority and Jesuit persuasion determined the contest. The king, Sigismund III, reversed an earlier policy of religious toleration. He conferred no offices on Protestant subjects, encouraged his Catholic nobles to evict Protestants from their estates, and used the influence of his court to advance the Catholic agenda. He also bestowed on the Jesuits much of the responsibility for education. Poland would become a solidly Catholic nation, though more tolerant of non-Catholics than other central European countries.

To face the renewed Catholicism became the task of followers of Calvinists rather than Lutherans. By the 1550s the Reformed church represented the most vital part of the Protestant world, and its more militant and comprehensive form of the faith seemed a better tool to answer the Catholic challenge than did Lutheranism. In the Holy Roman Empire, the Reformed were hampered by not being included in the Peace of Augsburg, and accordingly having no legal status. But outside the empire they were vigorous and shaped the religious developments in the Netherlands, France, and the British Isles.

The Netherlands and France

The Netherlands was something of an anomaly in the sixteenth century. Although located in the heart of Europe, it was not part of the Holy Roman Empire but was directly under the control of the king of Spain. It was composed of what at present are Belgium and the Netherlands. The southern Netherlands (today's Belgium) had at first been a welcoming place for Protestants (indeed, it had been a center for the Anabaptists), but through Spanish pressure Protestantism was eliminated, and the land was brought into line both religiously and politically. The northern Netherlands was a different story. There, Spanish policy came into conflict with a strong tradition of local liberties. Dutch opposition began as a defense of political liberties against Spain, but by the 1560s, the conflict became a religious one. As Spain used the Latin church to enforce its own authority, defenders of local liberty increasingly turned toward Protestantism. The Protestantism they identified with was Reformed, and in 1573, William of Orange, the leading figure in the anti-Spanish struggle, formally became a Calvinist. Spanish forces were able to crush the Protestant forces in the south but could not subdue the north. The conflicts lasted throughout the sixteenth century and into the seventeenth. In the struggle, the Reformed faith became both the rallying cry of the Dutch opponents of Spain and a justification for other Protestant leaders to ally themselves with the Dutch against the Spanish. By the early seventeenth century the Netherlands had become divided between a Catholic south and a Protestant north.

Religion and politics created a deadly mixture in France as well. Although many of the Protestant leaders (such as Calvin) had been forced into exile in the 1530s, the cause of Protestantism was not forgotten, and expatriates such as Calvin continued to hope and pray for the conversion of France. An interest in Protestantism could be found in many corners of the land, but the royal policy was continued harassment and persecution of any surfacing of Protestant organization. France, however, was no political monolith, and country gentry (particularly in the south of France) and many influential merchants continued to support reform. Persecution kept French Protestantism below the radar, but worshiping communities could be found in increasing numbers, many ministered to by clergy trained in Geneva. By the 1550s this Protestant community had received a distinctive name—Huguenot (though scholars are still unclear as to its origin).

The situation markedly changed in 1559. In that year King Henry II died in a freak accident, and power devolved to his sons, who all proved to be weak rulers. Real power, in fact, rested with his widow, Catherine de Medici. The political uncertainty allowed Huguenots to come out into the open and hold their first national synod. Competing factions appeared within the nobility, and religion became a point of division. The Guise family were adamantly Catholic, while the Bourbons were Protestant. Beginning in 1562, France suffered through thirty years of intermittent religious civil war. The brutality of the conflict was shocking. To the Huguenots, Catholicism was idolatrous, and mobs would invade Catholic churches destroying the images. For Catholics, Protestantism was a blasphemy, a horrid stain on the nation. The result was repeated atrocities. The most gruesome example was the St. Bartholomew Day massacre of 1572, where Catholic mobs (instigated by Catherine de Medici) killed between five and ten thousand Huguenots.

> To the Huguenots, Catholicism was idolatrous; for Catholics, Protestantism was a blasphemy.

The bloody conflict in France raised a new question for Christians. Was it defensible to take up arms against a lawful monarch? The apostle Paul had long ago written that Christians must be subservient to governing authorities, and that had long been the Christian practice, but in the heat of the Protestant-Catholic civil war, some were not so sure. Some began to advocate the right of Christians to resist tyrants. Still another question was what role Catholicism should play in the struggle. The Catholic side contained a strict party who wanted a complete destruction of their opponents and moderates who worried about the cost such a policy would have on the nation. What should Catholic policy be?

After 1589 the situation began to change. With the death of the last son of Henry II, the heir to the throne became a Protestant, Henry of Navarre. Realizing he could never govern the nation without the support of the strongly Catholic population of Paris, in 1593 Henry submitted to the old church and took an oath renouncing heresy. Although he probably never said the famous phrase attributed to him, "Paris is worth a mass," it reflected his concern to move beyond religious division. To the Huguenots he issued the Edict of Nantes in 1598, granting them freedom of worship in traditional Protestant centers, the ability to establish schools and cemeteries, and other protections. France would continue to be a Catholic nation, but a Protestant minority was (for the foreseeable future) to be tolerated.

The British Isles

Nowhere was the Reformation more convoluted than in the Atlantic isles of Britain and Ireland. For more than 150 years the religious situation there was in flux. England's Henry VIII died in 1547, leaving the church in a peculiar position. Politically it had separated from Rome, but doctrine and worship (save for the suppressing of the monasteries) remained unchanged. During the last years of the king's reign, both Protestants and traditionalists lobbied for influence, but a balance was maintained.

Henry had sired three children, and each in turn would try to shape the English church. The first was Edward. Coming to the throne as Edward VI in 1547, he was hailed by the Protestants as the new Josiah, who would cleanse the temple. Being only ten years old, he was assisted in his governance by Protectors, who were firm Protestants as well. Together they aimed to bring the English church into the Protestant camp.

One of the first tasks was the reform of the liturgy. In 1548, Thomas Cranmer, the archbishop of Canterbury, and others began the process of creating an English liturgy. The first English Prayer Book was issued in May of 1549. Although the book was Protestant in its theology—justification by faith was a common theme—in other ways it was very traditional. The older vestments were maintained; the shape of the baptismal and eucharistic liturgies was kept; and the real presence in the Eucharist was affirmed. The book received criticism for its conservatism. Hence, a much more thoroughly Protestant version was issued in 1552. In it the liturgy was recrafted and stripped of most of its traditional trappings, and the real presence was rejected. Liturgical change was only part of Edward's protestantizing agenda. Articles of Religion that reflected Protestant theology were also composed. Images were removed from the churches, and marriage of priests was made legal.

But in 1553, after a scant six years on the throne, Edward died and was succeeded by his half-sister Mary, daughter of Catherine of Aragon. Mary's intent was to bring the English church back to Rome. The Latin liturgy was resumed; monastic houses were reestablished; and finally, in 1554, papal authority was restored. The popularity of these actions has been debated for centuries, but Mary in her reign undertook two actions that over time would profoundly (and negatively) affect English perceptions of the old religion. The first was her marriage to Philip II of Spain; the second was the inauguration of a campaign of persecution against Protestant heretics. Although both actions were defensible as part of a campaign to undo the work of her brother, they imbued the popular perception of Roman Catholicism with two strong beliefs: that it was a foreign religion (and conversely, that Protestantism was English) and that it was built on persecution.

Mary died in 1558 and was succeeded by her half-sister, Elizabeth. Although a Protestant—as the daughter of Anne Boleyn she was considered illegitimate by Rome—Elizabeth's religious policy was to stress inclusivity.

The "Elizabethan compromise" combined Protestant theology with traditional practices. As much as possible the church was to look like the church of the past. Furthermore, in key ways the liturgy of 1552 was modified to allow flexibility of belief. The eucharistic prayer was rephrased to allow, but not necessitate, a belief in the

> Elizabeth's religious policy was to stress inclusivity. The "Elizabethan compromise" combined Protestant theology with traditional practices.

real presence. Finally, Elizabeth insisted that what would hold together the church was practice and not doctrine. If subjects practiced the religion and conformed to the established church, they might have a degree of freedom of belief. As she stated, "I do not wish to make windows into the souls of my subjects."

Elizabeth's religious policies stood in marked contrast with those of England's northern neighbor, Scotland. Calvin's message and the leadership of John Knox (ca. 1513–1572) led the Scottish nobility to reform their "kirk." In 1560 the Reformed Church of Scotland was established along Presbyterian lines, and a confession and a Book of Discipline were adopted. It was this reformed church that greeted the young Queen Mary (known to history as Mary Queen of Scots), who ascended to the throne in 1561 as a Catholic. Mary's stormy seven-year reign was riddled with increasing conflict with her Protestant subjects. Unlike the case in England, the Scottish church refused to be dictated to by its monarch.

Elizabeth's religious policy was motivated as much by foreign policy considerations as by religious factors. Her aim was to avoid foreign Catholic intervention and await the eventual pacification of her realm. By the 1570s both aims had failed. In 1570 the pope excommunicated her, and Mary Queen of Scots, who had fled to England after the loss of her throne, became the center of Catholic intrigue. Similarly, the more Protestant-leaning members of Elizabeth's realm became increasingly frustrated by the continuation of the older practices. Particularly those who had fled to the Continent during the reign of Queen Mary believed that the English church was only partially reformed. Its liturgy was filled with remnants of the old religion; its discipline was lax; and Elizabeth's policy of control prevented many earnest persons from preaching. A movement developed that called for the church to be purified and refashioned after the model of the Reformed churches of the Continent. Calvin's Geneva was seen as the ideal. The movement came to be known as Puritanism, and in the latter part of the sixteenth century it grew in popularity.

In reaction there began to develop a positive defense of the Elizabethan compromise. Perhaps the most famous spokesperson was Richard Hooker (ca. 1554–1600), who defended the use of reason in the interpretation of Scripture, the value of forms in religion, and other aspects of the Elizabethan compromise. Still others defended the office of the bishop. Episcopacy had continued in the English church almost by accident, but no special claims were made for it during the first generation. But by the 1590s some were arguing that the threefold ministry of bishop, priest, and deacon was the polity of the ancient church and marked a true church. It was a particular blessing of the Church of England to possess it.

Thus a division developed within the English Protestant community. Some wanted Elizabeth's compromises eliminated and the church to move in the direction of the continental Reformed churches. Others saw in these compromises a "via media" that combined the best of both churches, old and new.

Whereas versions of Protestantism succeeded in taking root and winning over the majority of the inhabitants of England and Scotland, in Ireland Protestantism proved to be a failure. During Henry's reign there was a hesitant acceptance of the new religious policy, but it did not last. The English policy of sending Protestant immigrants into Ireland (the most famous being the Ulster Plantation in what is now Northern Ireland) turned the Irish against any compromise and solidified their loyalty to the church of Rome.

Religious Wars

The 1555 Peace of Augsburg had tried to establish religious boundaries in the Holy Roman Empire, but by the early seventeenth century they were badly fraying. Protestants and Catholics continued to clash, and Catholics continued to chip away at earlier Protestant gains. A sign of the growing tensions was the witch craze that swept a polarized Europe between 1560 and 1660. Any beliefs or practices smacking of deviance were viewed as being possibly diabolical. During these years fifty thousand persons (80 percent women) met their death as accused witches.

> After years of death and destruction, the attempt to restore Europe's religious unity by force had failed. Europe would continue to be divided by religion.

By 1608 a number of Protestant princes had formed a defensive union, and in the following year Catholic princes followed suit. Conflict finally broke out in Bohemia in 1618, where Protestants revolted against an attempt by a Catholic monarch to assume control. An angry mob tossed two Catholic representatives from an upper window at the Hradčany Castle in Prague (an event known to history as the Defenestration of Prague). The result was thirty years of warfare between Protestants and Catholics, with first one side in ascendance and then the other. Although the war was about religious policy in the Holy Roman Empire, it attracted wide interest. Spanish troops aided the imperial Catholic forces, while Swedes under Gustavus Adolphus supported the Protestant union, and France (although a Catholic power) did what it could to weaken both Spain and the empire, its historic enemies. All in all, the destruction was horrific. Some estimates suggest that 40 percent of the population of the affected lands met with an early death. And the conflict destroyed not only life but cherished beliefs. Both Protestants and Catholics at first believed that the struggle would be the occasion of the divine triumph of their causes. After thirty years, no divine triumph was evident. After years of death and destruction, the attempt to restore Europe's religious unity by force had failed. The Peace of Westphalia in 1648 recognized that Europe would continue to be divided by religion.

In many ways the wars on the Continent mirrored a similar struggle in the British Isles. Elizabeth was succeeded by James of Scotland (son of Mary Queen of Scots), and he attempted to keep the religious peace in England, draw together the English and Scottish churches, and solidify the unity of international Protestants. But tensions only increased. Some defenders of the English church, such as Lancelot Andrewes, attempted to bring back some of the discarded practices of the old religion. Theological issues also began to surface. Some members of Reformed churches by the early seventeenth century began to question the Reformed emphasis on predestination. A movement known as Arminianism began to suggest that human beings had free will to respond to God. In response, the majority of the international Reformed community pushed the definition of predestination at the Synod of Dort (1619) to its logical conclusion. Only the elect would be saved, and they would be saved through the overwhelming grace of God. Some in England, in reaction to Dort, began to move away from Calvinistic rigor and defend the free will of Arminianism.

The tensions continued in the reign of James's son and successor, Charles I. The English Protestant church became polarized, and the religious divisions were reinforced by political disagreements over claims of king and Parliament. Ultimately, in the 1640s England experienced a series of civil wars pitting the king and the defenders of the Elizabethan compromise against Parliament and its Puritan allies. The crisis proved disastrous for the former. The Prayer Book was rejected, episcopacy abolished, and theology made rigorously Calvinistic. The king's chief ecclesiastical adviser, William Laud, and eventually King Charles himself were executed. Government was in the hands of Oliver Cromwell and the insurgents, who proclaimed England a commonwealth. For eleven years the land was without a king, and Cromwell enacted a religious policy that allowed for all sorts of religious experimentation. Some, such as the Baptists, took up believer's baptism; others, such as the Quakers, claimed that God spoke directly to them; still others in the name of religion rejected all social distinctions.

With the death of Cromwell in 1658 it became clear to many that the commonwealth could not continue. In 1660 the son of Charles was invited to take the throne as Charles II, and in short order both bishops and the Prayer Book were restored. The Elizabethan compromise ultimately triumphed, and Anglicanism (as the tradition came to be known) in key ways would remain different from both Roman Catholicism and continental Protestantism. But it no longer claimed to include the entire nation. Some refused to accept the changes. Those Puritans who refused to conform were expelled from the church, thus becoming Nonconformists, and as such were barred from the halls of power. They would continue to exist and in time would become leaders in business and trade. A small Roman Catholic community also continued to exist, still barred from power but no longer overtly persecuted.

Thus by the 1660s the great battle over the soul of Europe had reached a stalemate. Roman Catholicism predominated in southern and much of central Europe. Protestantism, in its various forms, triumphed in northern Germany, Holland, Scandinavia, and Britain (save, of course, Ireland). There was still much suspicion and dislike, but the era of religious warfare had passed.

Chapter 12

The Reinternationalization of Christianity

*T*he sixteenth and seventeenth centuries were years of brutal civil war among Western Christians and witnessed a divided Christendom. But during this time other events were taking place that would ultimately have a greater impact on the history of Christianity. These years saw a reinternationalization of Christianity. By the end of the seventeenth century, Western Christians had planted their churches on all the inhabitable continents with the exception of Australia. The internationalization, however, would be unlike that of the earlier centuries. In the past the expansion of the church had flowed from the various regional centers; in the sixteenth century it was almost exclusively from Western churches. The new churches would be shaped in the image of Western Christendom, mirroring both its strengths and faults. Furthermore, this expansion was intricately connected with the imperial expansion of European power, hence Christianity and Western hegemony became linked, challenging and displacing old cultural models, which would prove troublesome in the future.

The New Missionary Impulse

The vast outpouring of missionary endeavors was a striking change. For almost a thousand years Christianity had been losing population and territory. The missionary impulse (save for the Nestorian Christians of the East) had all but disappeared, but by 1500 it had returned. Catholics, and particularly Catholics of the Iberian Peninsula — Spain and Portugal — were the great champions of this outreach. Iberian Christians had spent seven hundred years reclaiming their homeland from the invading Moors. Only in 1492 had Grenada, the last Moorish stronghold, fallen. As almost all schoolchildren know, this victory allowed the Spanish monarchs, Ferdinand and Isabella, to finance

Christopher Columbus in his voyage of exploration. But the Iberian sense of expansion did not begin here. As noted in chapter 9, Henry the Navigator throughout the fifteenth century had improved Portuguese navigation and pushed his ships farther down the coast of Africa. Clearly one reason was gold, for which the Gold Coast of West Africa (now Ghana) was already famous. But the Portuguese also sailed to outflank their Muslim enemies. Islam controlled North Africa and all the land routes east, but southern Africa and the seas were up for grabs. They could, to use Arnold Toynbee's famous phrase, "conquer the ocean." Furthermore, there was still the legend of Prester John. Somewhere in the East lay a fabled Christian kingdom.

The activities of Spain and Portugal flowed from ambition and piety and were not directed by Rome. Rome did, however, become involved in the Treaty of Tordesilles (1494), in which the pope divided the world between Spain and Portugal, giving to Portugal authority over Brazil and all to the east (i.e., Africa and Asia), and to Spain the rest, or the New World. But both powers were required to propagate the Christian faith among the inhabitants they might find. They would do so in a way largely independent of Rome. The "*padroado*" system gave to the monarchs of Spain and Portugal full patronage and almost complete control of the churches in their colonial empires.

The Portuguese in Africa

The Portuguese moved along the coast of Africa in search of trade, particularly slaves, and as they advanced, they built coastal forts. To these forts they brought their Catholic religion, but there was comparatively little religious contact with the native populations. The one exception was in the kingdom of the Kongo. In the 1480s they made their first contacts, but the real advance occurred after 1491. Landing at that year on the coast, they were welcomed, and the head of the coastal province was at once baptized along with his son. Two months later they reached the capital, Mbanza, where the king himself, Nzinga Nkuvo (or Nkuvu), was baptized, taking the name João I in honor of the reigning king of Portugal. João and others, however, eventually grew critical of and abandoned a Christianity that burned the traditional religious objects as fetishes and preached that a person should have only one wife—both of which had political as well as moral and theological implications. One of João's sons, however, Mvemba Nzinga, refused to renounce his Christianity and continued to serve as a connection between Christianity and the royal family. In 1506, upon the death of his father, Mvemba defeated pagan opponents and took control of the throne. His reign of almost forty years was marked by a concern for the educational, social, religious, and medical improvement of his land and for fostering connections with the Europeans. Reigning under the name Alfonso I, he strove to shape his kingdom according to Christian principles, but he was continually hampered by a shortage of priests and teachers. In 1596 the pope made the Kongo a diocese, and a Kongolese ambassador was sent to Rome in 1608. This, however, was the high-water mark of the Christian Kongo, for during the seventeenth century changing political winds made Christianity (and a European presence) less welcome. By century's end, both the church and the Portuguese were compelled to abandon the realm.

The Portuguese also established contact with the ancient church of Ethiopia, one of the last remaining relics of a once-Christian Africa. The Ethiopian church had close connections with the Coptic Church of Egypt (and along with it, its Monophysitism), which continued to appoint the Abuna, or patriarch, of the Ethiopian church. As the Egyptian church weakened under Muslim domination, the Ethiopians became more and more isolated in a sea of Islam. In isolation they continued to practice their distinctive Christianity, which included such Hebrew elements as Sabbatarianism, dietary laws, and a reverence for the ark of the covenant. The church experienced something of a revival in the thirteenth century, and it was then that the famous rock-hewn churches of Roha were constructed. Several reforms date from the same period. When the Portuguese established contact with Ethiopia in 1520, they believed they had found the legendary land of Prester John. Ethiopia was a Christian nation in the middle of Africa, filled with churches and monasteries and possessing a highly developed musical tradition. In many ways the kingdom of Ethiopia was notable: it could boast of an advanced literary tradition and a strong imperial government. But its economy and technology were much less developed, and the emperor Lebna Dengel hoped that contact with the Portuguese could lead to advances in these areas. The Portuguese presence was even more important because of changing political currents. In the 1520s an Islamic jihad of tremendous force was unleashed on Ethiopia and its church under the leadership of Ahmed Gran. Churches and monasteries were systematically destroyed; such was the destruction that few, if any, pre-1530 Ethiopian Christian manuscripts survived. The Ethiopians appealed to the Portuguese for assistance, and eventually, in 1543, the Muslim opponents were defeated at the battle of Woguera, at which Ahmed Gran was slain. For the next sixty years Portuguese representatives labored to bring Ethiopia and its church more closely into the Latin orbit. At first the policy seemed effective. By the 1620s the emperor, Susenyos, was willing to submit to Rome and to abjure the Monophysitism that had marked Ethiopian Christianity since the fifth century. But such changes were too much for the monks and clergy of the land, and within a few years Susenyos was forced to abdicate, the Portuguese clergy were expelled, and Ethiopia slipped back once again into isolation.

Christianity in India

Asia, not Africa, was the goal of the Portuguese mariners, who were drawn to the great wealth of the ancient civilizations. Vasco da Gama reached India in 1498, carrying with him a missionary and a cannon. When locals asked him what he sought, he simply responded "Christians and spices." The Christians he found were descended from the ancient "Thomas Christians," the old community by tradition founded by the apostle Thomas under the authority of the Christian patriarch of Baghdad. They at first welcomed the Portuguese as fellow Christians, but soon disputes began over worship, authority, and other issues. For their base, the Portuguese established Goa on India's west coast, and Goa became the center of transplanted Latin Christianity. It quickly became an episcopal see (and later an archiepiscopal center) and was given missionary authority from the east coast of Africa to the Indonesian archipelago.

The Portuguese were at best only moderately successful in their missionary endeavors. Their few successes, such as the mass conversion of the fishing villages of the Paravas, were exceptions rather than the rule. Many have noted that the behavior of the Portuguese "Christians" provided little evidence of the moral superiority of Christianity. As one observer noted, "There are innumerable Portuguese who buy droves of girls and sleep with all of them. . . . This is carried to such excess that there was one man in Malacca who had twenty-four women of various races . . . all of whom he enjoyed."

Things would change in the 1540s with the coming of the Jesuits. The Portuguese monarchs were early patrons of the Jesuits, and hence Jesuits shaped sixteenth-century Portuguese missions as they did no other nation's missions. The great figure in Jesuit missions to India was Francis Xavier (1506–1552). Like the founder of the Jesuits, Ignatius Loyola, Francis Xavier was of Basque stock. Unlike the young Ignatius, however, he was from an early age more interested in learning than in military glory. To prepare for an ecclesiastical career he began his studies at the University of Paris. For a time he was attracted to Protestant teachings. Yet the influence of Ignatius triumphed, and Francis Xavier became one of the original members of the Jesuit order.

Soon after the papal approval of the Jesuits, Ignatius received a request from Portugal's King John III for missionaries to the East. Francis Xavier was selected, and with two others he made the thirteen-month journey from Portugal to Goa. Upon arrival, he began an active ministry of preaching and teaching. After learning the necessary languages, he visited the Paravas Christian settlement. Although they had earlier converted, this had been largely motivated by the hope of securing Portuguese protection against Muslims. Xavier found them with only the most nominal understanding of the faith. He spent two years with them, administering the sacraments; translating the Apostles' Creed, Ten Commandments, and catechism into their language; and instructing the youth. Through his labors Paravas became one of the strongest outposts of Latin Christianity in India. Francis would also travel to other places in south India and Sri Lanka, meeting with success there as well. As we will see, he would also travel to Japan and attempt to enter China.

Other Jesuits began to appear, and by 1560 the Jesuits were said to have baptized nearly thirteen thousand people around Goa alone. But Catholic missions in India faced a difficult dilemma. In the areas the Portuguese came in contact with, the dominant religion was Hinduism. Hindu society was marked by a rigid caste system, which divided the society into separate hierarchical groups. Elaborate rules defined how members of different castes could interrelate. Indians viewed Christians as another caste, the Portuguese caste. The early converts to Christianity, such as the Paravas, were outcastes (technically, Panchamas, but now commonly called untouchables or Dalits) and as such outsiders to the caste system. For them, Christianity represented liberation from social and cultural marginalization. Christianity made almost no inroads, however, among the Brahmin, who were the social and religious elite and to whom Christianity seemed barbaric. The question arose whether Christianity could be adapted to be made more acceptable to the Brahmin community. Robert de' Nobili (1577–1656), another Jesuit missionary, believed it could. He adopted many of the practices of the Brahmins. He lived in a hut in the Brahmin quarter, abandoned Western dress for that of an Indian teacher, practiced vegetarianism, and compromised with

> The success of Christian missionary endeavors depended on three factors: the extent of European involvement in a given society, the geographic size of the society, and the nature of the existing religion.

the caste system. His methods proved successful; between 1607 and 1611 he converted over a hundred high-caste Hindus, but he did so by allowing worship to be divided according to caste lines. De' Nobili was criticized because of his compromises not only with the caste system but with Hindu worship practices that struck many Christians as idolatrous. Eventually exonerated by Rome, de' Nobili argued that only his method could bridge the gap between Christianity and traditional Hindu society.

Of course caste was not the only problem for Christian missionaries. India set a pattern that would be repeated in the story of Christian expansion in Asia and Africa throughout the Latin era. The success of Christian missionary endeavors depended on three factors: the extent of European involvement in a given society, the geographic size of the society, and the nature of the existing religion. Where European presence was strong (as it was in Goa), Christianity took deep roots. Where Christians encountered traditional religions, they were far more successful than when they confronted an advanced or sophisticated religion such as Hinduism. Finally, the larger the geographical area, the more diluted was the presence of the missionaries. The last two factors hampered the growth of Christianity in India. Advanced religions like Hinduism (and even more so Islam, which Christians would encounter in other parts of India) were rocky soils providing very few converts, and the vastness of the land presented the missionaries with a daunting challenge. One sees this by contrasting the cases of India and Sri Lanka. The latter was a small island, easily accessible to the sea-based Portuguese. The religion there was a depressed state of Buddhism that offered far less effective opposition to missionary inroads than did the Hindus in India. Christianity during the sixteenth and seventeenth centuries made gains there that were proportionately greater than anywhere else in Asia save for the Philippines.

The Rise and Fall of Japanese Christianity

Japan represents the great "might have been" in the story of Christianity in Asia. Scholars often refer to the "Christian century" in Japan's history, when the Christian church flourished. Japanese religion in the sixteenth century was dominated by Buddhism, which was closely connected to the imperial office, and by the native Shinto. But Japan in the mid-sixteenth century was in a state of political turmoil. The old governing order of the emperor and shoguns, or feudal leaders, had lost its grip on the society, and three warlords battled for control. Below these three there were many lesser feudal lords, or daimyo.

Into that culture went Francis Xavier in 1549. He was assisted by two fellow Jesuits and three native Japanese, including a convert named Anjiro, who referred to himself as the "Paul" of Japan. One of the warlords, Oda Nobunaga, became friendly to Christianity. The political situation led Francis Xavier to adopt a different mission strategy than the one he devised for India. Whereas in India he focused his labors on outcastes such as the Paravas, in Japan he sought out social and political leaders. The strategy worked. Nobunaga and others like him chafed against a Buddhism that was closely linked to the old imperial order. They were also impressed by the technology and learning the Jesuits brought with them. Finally, they anticipated trading with the Portuguese. All these factors helped the cause of Christianity.

The Christians developed their major base in the southern part of the kingdom, and the center was the port city of Nagasaki, whose daimyo gave great power to the Jesuits. By the time Francis Xavier departed in 1552, there were an estimated 2,000 Christian converts. Twenty-nine years later (1581), at the death of Nobunaga, the number of Christians had grown to an estimated 150,000, or almost 1 percent of the entire population. A bit more than twenty years later (1605) the Christian community had increased fivefold. Not only did numbers increase, but educational institutions were also taking root.

But the political climate of Japan began to change, and with it the fate of the Christian community also changed. Nobunaga's successor, Hideyoshi, while at first friendly to Christians, gradually came to prefer the old religion of Shinto. Native Shinto and Buddhists were contrasted pointedly with the foreign Christian community. Hideyoshi began a persecution of the Japanese Christian community. The position of the Christians was further weakened by the introduction of a Spanish Franciscan mission. The presence of a second Christian mission not only divided the Christian community but raised the threat of European military intervention when some of the Spanish unguardedly spoke of the need for greater Spanish control in Japanese affairs. By 1612 the antiforeign reaction entered a new phase. European missionaries were compelled to leave, church buildings were destroyed, and Japanese Christians were ordered to abandon their new religion. After a group of Christians rose up in what became known as the Shimabara Rebellion, persecution intensified. All contact with the West, except for a tiny trickle, was cut off, and Japan would remain isolated from the West for more than two hundred years. Christians were hunted down. Those suspected of Christianity were required to trample on a cross or an image of Christ. Well into the eighteenth century, all inhabitants of Nagasaki were still required to perform an annual ritual of stepping on a cross. Although, as we will see in chapter 17, Christianity was not completely eliminated and it would resurface in the nineteenth century, the Jesuit hope of a vibrant Japanese Christian community came to a crashing end.

China and the Rites Controversy

The situation in China paralleled that of India. Here, too, was a society inhabiting a vast land, with ancient religious customs deeply intertwined in the social order. Twice before had Christianity been planted there, and twice it had died out. But the Jesuits made a determined effort to anchor the faith. The great figure in the Jesuit mission to China was Matteo Ricci (1552–1610), but he was not alone. Ricci had been preceded by another Jesuit, Michael Ruggieri. Ricci was yet another talented young Jesuit, trained not only in theology but in mathematics and astronomy. Entering China from Macao in 1582, he undertook an intense study of Chinese. Soon he became a master, and he was able to commit to memory large portions of the Chinese classics. He also put his scientific training to use and created a new and highly accurate map of the world that did not place China at the center.

Ricci was convinced that Christianity could triumph in China only if it could adapt to a Chinese idiom. He wore Chinese clothing—first that of a Buddhist monk and later that of a Confucian scholar. In choosing a Chinese word for God he purposely selected *Tianzhu* and *Shangdi*, both of which had been used in classical texts and hence had pre-Christian meanings. He believed that Confucian ceremonies that honored ancestors were social rather than religious in nature and thus posed no conflict with Christianity. He also recognized that the key to success was winning over the emperor, and in 1601 he established a mission in Beijing for that purpose. Although his mission to the emperor was not a success, he continued to attract learned converts. Perhaps the most important was Paul Hsu, who would become known as one of the "three pillars of the Chinese church." Hsu was a high-ranking intellectual, but his attraction to Christianity was more for its moral teachings than its intellectual tradition. Christian morality could easily fit into China, he said, because it "supplements Confucianism and displaces Buddhism." After the death of Ricci, Hsu became the acknowledged leader of the Chinese Christian community.

> The policy of adapting Christianity to Chinese practices increasingly came under fire by other Christians.

Other Jesuits followed Ricci's example by using Western scientific knowledge as a gateway into circles of influence and stressing the parallels between Christianity and China's traditional Chinese Confucianism. The Jesuits' knowledge of mathematics and astronomy was so respected that they were authorized to revise the Chinese calendar. As in Japan, some in China feared Christianity as a foreign threat, yet the support of Chinese intellectuals allowed missionaries to pursue their work through the early decades of the seventeenth century. However, the policy of adapting Christianity to Chinese practices increasingly came under fire by other Christians. Dominicans and Franciscans accused the Jesuits of compromising true belief. Throughout the second half of the seventeenth century, the "Rites Controversy" (as the debate became known) was hotly debated. Of particular concern were the terms used to translate the word "God." Did the Chinese names truly represent the Christian understanding of God? Also under contention was whether Christians could participate in Confucian ceremonies without undermining the faith. Appeals made to Rome took varying positions, but eventually in 1704 the contested terms for God were forbidden, and Christians were ordered to refrain from participating in sacrifices to either Confucius or their ancestors.

The condemnation of the Jesuits and their practices weakened the Chinese mission, as did the eventual suppression of the entire Jesuit order in 1773. But the missions to both China and India had lost vigor long before that. Both were outgrowths of Portuguese imperial activity, but the Portuguese "empire" was at best a string of trading posts. By the early eighteenth century, as Portugal's national power began to seriously wane, the missionary activities began to wane as well. In some places, such as Sri Lanka and what is now Indonesia, Dutch forces expelled the Portuguese. The Protestant Dutch did not look with favor on Catholic missions. The eighteenth century was an age of decline for Catholic missionary endeavors in Asia.

Spain and the New World

If Portugal looked east, Spain looked west and left a far more significant mark. The Spanish came not just to trade but to establish an empire, and the church was a central part of its imperial policy. The reunification of Spain in 1492 was predicated on a unity of church and state. Forced conversion and the expulsion of non-Christians went along with the triumph of the Catholic forces, and these religious policies would be transported to the new Spanish domains. A rigid, crusading Catholicism was linked to a church completely dominated by the crown. As was the case in the Portuguese colonies, the crown was granted the right of *patronato* (the Spanish version of the *padroado*), giving the monarch complete control over church matters.

The Spanish Empire, starting from a few small islands in the Caribbean, spread to Cuba in 1515, Mexico in 1519, and Peru in 1532. Eventually it was to encompass all of South America (save for Portuguese Brazil), Mexico and Central America, much of the American Southwest and far West, and the islands of the Philippines. In most of these places the pattern was the same. It was said of the Spanish conquistadors that they were inspired by "God, gold, and glory." Usually the latter two dominated, and the concern for God came in third. Particularly in the cases of the Aztecs in Mexico and the Incas in Peru, great native civilizations were cruelly and systematically destroyed in the voracious quest for gold. Christianity seemed to play little if any role in these conquests. Yet even here the record is actually more ambiguous. The conqueror of the Aztecs, Hernando Cortez, was certainly cruel, ruthless, and desirous of gold, but he was regular at mass, devoted to the Virgin Mary, and topped his flag with a cross. He was also horrified by the religion he found practiced among the Aztecs, with its emphasis on human sacrifice. For him the Spanish victory was a victory for God.

The real work of Christianization was undertaken by the religious orders, at first Franciscans and Dominicans and later Jesuits. The fervor of sixteenth-century Spain assured that there would be a flood of missionaries to serve in the new provinces. Peter of Ghent, a relative of Emperor Charles V, abandoned the life of a courtier for a religious calling. Refusing high clerical rank, he instead served in Mexico as a lay Franciscan brother, and there were others like him. In many places the labors of the missionaries met with great success. Peter of Ghent reports baptizing fourteen thousand people in a single day. Other reports noted that in the two decades after the conquest of the Aztecs, some one and a half million people had been baptized. Such mass baptisms may raise questions (as they did at the time) as to the seriousness of the commitment of those baptized and how far sixteenth-century Christians had moved away from the rigorous idea of baptism in the early church, but the numbers are notable nonetheless. But not all provinces were as amenable as Mexico, and missionary endeavors in Peru met much opposition.

The Spanish were conscientious not only in mission but also in creating institutional structures for the church. A diocese of Santo Domingo was established as early as 1504, and by the early seventeenth century Spanish America boasted five archbishops, twenty-seven bishops, two universities, and countless seminaries and religious houses.

The church in New Spain (as the Spanish colonies came to be known) was shaped by the social structure of the colonies. At the highest level were those officials sent from Spain. Like the viceroys who exercised royal governance, bishops throughout the seventeenth century were invariably Spanish. Below the Spanish aristocracy were many creoles, people of Spanish descent who had been born in the colonies. This group dominated the church and made up the bulk of the lower clergy. The Council of Trent had called for parish churches to be staffed by secular clergy (those who did not belong to any religious order), and in New Spain the priesthood became a desirable occupation for creoles. Below the creoles was the indigenous Native American population. During the sixteenth century their lot was perilous. Mistreatment by civil leaders and disease led to death on a massive scale. Some estimate that the native population declined from twenty million to two million people in the course of the sixteenth century. The church's attitude toward this population was ambivalent. Although many were baptized, there was a fear that pre-Christian beliefs and practices continued to find favor. Native Americans were only slowly admitted to Communion, and it would be a century and a half before they were allowed to be ordained as priests. This did not stop clergy, especially members of the religious orders, from advocating for them. Although in many ways unique, Bartolomé de las Casas (1484–1566) was noteworthy in defending the rights of the Native Americans. He reported on the cruel ways in which they were treated and labored long to change Spanish policy and laws. One strategy in defending the native populations was the establishment of "*doctrinas*," separate geographical areas where they were ministered to and kept separate from Europeans for their protection. The most famous example of this was the Jesuit mission in Paraguay, known as the *Reductions*, which at its height included more than one hundred thousand people living in villages and united in prayer. With the suppression of the Jesuits, these declined.

Although the Christianity of New Spain was divided between creoles and natives, connections were possible. One famous example was the apparition of the Virgin of Guadalupe. According to tradition, on December 9, 1531, she appeared at Tepeyac (in what is now Mexico) to a poor native named Juan Diego, instructing that a church be built. A miraculous image appeared, which mirrored earlier pre-Christian imagery, and in it the Virgin herself was depicted as Native American. The miracle convinced the local bishop, and the chapel was built. The old religion had taken on the face of the new land, and the Virgin of Guadalupe became a powerful force in Spanish American Catholicism.

The extension of Latin Catholicism to Quebec, or New France, followed lines similar to that of New Spain. From the late 1620s, here too Roman Catholicism was the dominant religion, Protestantism was not tolerated, and the religious orders were crucial in propagating the faith. Through leaders such as François de Monmorency Laval (1623–1708) and Jean Baptiste de

Saint Vallier, the church became disciplined, conservative, and French. Men and women such as Marguerite Bourgeoys (1620–1700) undertook education and mission work.

England and North America

A different pattern is to be found in the English colonies in what is now the United States, and that pattern was to have major ramifications. The English entered the campaign of imperial expansion almost a century after Spain and Portugal. Although there were some abortive attempts in the sixteenth century to establish English colonies, it was not until 1607 that permanent settlements began to take root. More important, the English (and eventually British) colonies did not possess the religious homogeneity of the Portuguese, Spanish, and French plantations but instead became a haven for the disparate voices that appeared during the Reformation period.

The role of the Protestant Reformation was crucial. During the first two centuries of their existence, the English colonies were overwhelmingly Protestant. A Catholic colony was established in Maryland in 1634, but within two decades even there Protestants dominated. It would not be until the nineteenth century that there would be a significant Catholic population in what is now English-speaking America. This factor gave the struggle for empire a religious dimension, and the British saw their battles with Spain to the south and France to the north in religious terms.

During the seventeenth century three separate religious patterns developed in these colonies. In the southern colonies of Virginia, Maryland, the Carolinas, and Georgia colonists brought the Elizabethan compromise of the sixteenth century to the New World. In each colony, to varying degrees, the Church of England was established by law. In Virginia, the legislature divided the colony into parishes and arranged for the building of churches and the support of ministers. Worship was according to the Book of Common Prayer, and attempts were made through ritual, furnishings, and actions to stress the continuity between the colonial church and the mother church. The churches were governed by the church law of the Church of England, and they were technically under the authority of the bishop of London. But in one way they were profoundly different from their English counterparts. No bishop resided in any of the colonies. The absence of bishops left a power vacuum and resulted in a far greater voice for laity. Lay councils or vestries were created that had the power to appoint clergy and to monitor the financial affairs of the parish. By the end of the seventeenth century the bishop of

London did begin appointing personal representatives to the colonies, known as commissaries. These men could exercise authority over clergy but had no power over laity, nor could they perform those sacramental actions, confirmation, and ordination reserved for bishops.

Of greater importance were the other two models. The first arose in the northern colonies of New England. As was noted in chapter 11, by the 1570s many in the Church of England found the Elizabethan compromise flawed. It permitted traditional yet unscriptural practices and did not possess an effective means of church discipline. Finally it was made up of all types of people and not just those who had experienced saving grace. The latter, these Puritan critics went on, were the true church; they were the visible saints whom God had called. During the late sixteenth and early seventeenth centuries the Puritans struggled to hold their beliefs within the confines of the Church of England. Some actually urged separation, claiming that the Church of England was irredeemably fallen, but most did not. It was these Puritans who migrated to New England in the 1620s and 1630s. The Separatists (known to history as the Pilgrims) came first, landing in Plymouth, Massachusetts, in 1620. But by 1630 the religious policy of Charles I convinced many of the Non-Separatist Puritans that only in the New World could they organize the church as it was meant to be. Between 1630 and 1640, twenty thousand of these Puritans flocked to the New World, an event that later historians called the "swarming of the Puritans."

The society they established was called the Holy Commonwealth and was based on Puritan principles. It was to be an example to the world. As Governor John Winthrop announced in his famous Arabella Sermon (named after the ship that carried them to the New World), "We must consider that we shall be as a city upon a hill, the eyes of all people are upon us." Convinced that they were living at the end of history and that Christ would return shortly, the Puritans offered new understandings of church, society, and the individual. Each was based on the insistence that God and his people were joined by means of a covenant. As with ancient Israel, God offered a conditional promise: if the people followed in his ways, they would be blessed. With few exceptions, the Puritan colonies made church membership depend on the narration of an individual experience of divine grace. Others might (and indeed must) attend the church and support it, but only these visible saints could be full church members. But since

> As with ancient Israel, the Puritans believed that God offered them a conditional promise: if the people followed in his ways, they would be blessed.

church membership was required for citizenship, these same visible saints were responsible for governance. New England was accordingly "holy" in ways very different from those of European societies. As Christianity had developed in the centuries after Constantine, the Christian nature of a society was seen in the clergy's role in legislation and the judicial process. Old England proudly possessed its House of Lords, which included bishops and ecclesiastical courts that could administer justice. Both were lacking in New England. Holiness was rather to be seen in the way lay governors exercised their authority in a Christian way. Governance was a religious calling, as was citizenship itself. If the society were to be a covenanted society, then it was the responsibility of every person to maintain the holy discipline, and citizens were dutifully reminded in election sermons that voting was a religious act.

In their own way New England Puritans were as insistent as Portuguese and Spanish Catholics that religious heterodoxy was a threat to the community and should be punished. But some among them thought otherwise. Roger Williams (ca. 1603–1683) rejected the idea of a covenanted society and argued for religious toleration. Anne Hutchinson (1591–1643) challenged the authority of the Puritan clergy, saying that they were not truly spiritual. Banned from Massachusetts, both found refuge in the colony of Rhode Island, which saw itself as a "shelter for persons distressed for conscience."

Ultimately it was in the middle colonies that a pattern of church life developed that would become normative in America. These colonies, founded by Swedes, Dutch, and English individuals, were a panoply of different groups. In the early seventeenth century the Dutch governor of New Amsterdam (now New York) reported that eighteen languages were spoken in his city. Likewise in religion, the diversity was so great that no center could emerge. Diversity was a fact, but in one colony, Pennsylvania, it became a principle as well. There William Penn (1644–1718) established a "holy experiment" unprecedented in European history. Penn belonged to one of the radical religious movements that emerged in Commonwealth England: the Quakers, or Society of Friends. Quakers believed that within every person was the Inner Light of God, which both revealed truth to each person and gave intrinsic worth. Quakers believed the use of force was antithetical to true Christianity, as were distinctions based on class, race, or sex. Penn's vision was reflected in the name he chose for the chief city of the colony, Philadelphia, the city of brotherly love. His policy was to extend religious freedom to all. That policy, coupled with the cheap land he willingly sold, made Pennsylvania a magnet for many. Scots-Irish came from Ulster in Northern Ireland, bringing their Presbyterianism with them. Displaced German-speaking Protestants flocked to Pennsylvania as a haven. These included many of the scorned

Anabaptists, who found there a freedom to practice their ways. They became known as the Pennsylvania Dutch (for *Deutsch*, or German), and there they lived their retired life. Pennsylvania would become the most ethnically and religiously diverse colony in the New World and would serve as a model for later generations.

By 1700 Christianity could again claim that it was a world religion. In some places it was strong and in some places weak, but it was to be found in all the inhabitable continents save Australia. In many places it was represented by outposts of the divided Latin church. Russia was an exception: as the Russian tsar began pushing his empire eastward into Asia and ultimately across the Bering Strait and into Alaska, the Russian Orthodox Church followed. Through these labors North Asia became Christianized. But everywhere else the expansion of Christianity, for better or worse, was an expansion of Europe.

Chapter 13

Reason and Faith

*T*he world of the Christian West looked and felt different by the 1660s. The decades of religious strife had exhausted the nations, disturbed the sensitive, and disabused almost all from the belief that religious unity could be restored by force. The Anglican cleric Jonathan Swift, writing a few decades later in his satire *Gulliver's Travels*, had Gulliver carefully explain to the Houyhnms that part of the greatness of European society could be seen in the proclivity for religious war. They fought great wars, he explained, over whether "Flesh be Bread, or Bread be Flesh; Whether the Juice of certain Berry be Blood or Wine . . . whether it is better to kiss a Post [i.e., a cross] or cast it in the Fire." He concluded by observing, "Neither are any Wars so furious and bloody . . . as these occasioned by Difference of Opinion, especially if it be in things indifferent." Killing vast numbers of people for "things indifferent" somehow no longer seemed to make sense. It did not seem to be what Christianity was all about.

But what was Christianity all about? In the years between 1660 and 1760 many began to ask that question anew. Once raised, the question suggested others as to the nature of God and humanity and the ultimate foundation of the Christian faith.

Catholic Concerns

This questioning was stronger among Protestants than Catholics. Roman Catholicism by the end of the seventeenth century was both suspicious of the new intellectual trends and caught up in internal issues. As we saw in the previous chapter, by this time Spain and Portugal possessed but a shadow of their former glory. The leading Catholic power was France, which under Louis XIV reigned supreme militarily, culturally, and intellectually. Louis's policy was to centralize authority and to elevate the absolute power of the monarch, and this affected religious life. In 1685 he revoked the Edict of Nantes, which had protected the Huguenots, and compelled them to conform or leave. He also condemned as heretical such movements within the church as Quietism, which strove for a mystical union between the soul and God. But Louis's absolutism took aim at not only Protestants and heretics but also the papacy. He encouraged the theory of Gallicanism, which denied the pope any authority over the temporal affairs of the French church, and subordinated the pope's religious authority to that of general councils.

The French church was further weakened by a bitter debate between the Jesuits and a group known as the Jansenists. Jansenism was a revival of Augustinian theology, which emphasized both the power of God and the sinfulness of humanity. Without grace, they claimed, natural human beings, corrupted by sin, could do nothing to please God. Jesuits, in contrast, de-emphasized the effects of sinfulness and taught the importance of human freedom and responsibility in the work of salvation. Jansenists viewed Jesuits as lax; Jesuits saw Jansenists as crypto-Protestants rejecting classic Catholic teaching. The fight was bitter. One of the great intellectuals of France, Blaise Pascal (1623–1662), in *Lettres Provinciales*, acidly satirized the Jesuit position. The rigor of Jansenist piety attracted many, and the convent of Port Royal became famous for its religious life and studiousness. Although Jansenism was condemned by the papacy in 1653, it tenaciously held on. It was condemned again in 1713 and began to suffer occasional persecution. Eventually the movement was to wither, but the effect of the controversy engulfed the larger church. Jansenist attacks on the Jesuits contributed to their loss in favor and eventual suppression in 1773. The Jansenist-Jesuit debate left no victors; all parties were casualties, and the Catholic Church was weaker because of it.

The Appeal to Reason

In rethinking Christianity, some began with the idea of human beings as creatures who reason, that is, who could examine phenomena and reach conclusions that were universally demonstrable without reference to divine revelation. While armies were fighting over the fine points of belief and practice, others were making strides as to the knowability of the world. The philosopher Francis Bacon had earlier suggested that to know the world, one must begin with its causes, since the world was rational and orderly. The Royal Society for Improving Natural Knowledge was founded in England in 1645 with the active support of leading clergy and laity. Their confidence was that Bacon's method provided a better way of understanding the world and improving it than did the old religion.

The work of the Royal Society was based on two assumptions. The first was that a regular law and plan, flowing from God, governed the universe. God was a great architect. Because of

> In discovering the rules of cosmic order the scientist rethought the original thoughts of God in the act of creation.

this, they did not talk much about divine intervention in the world. Rather, they believed that God's "presence" could be seen in the world's order and symmetry. As the poet Joseph Addison put it,

> The spacious firmament on high, with all its blue ethereal sky
> And spangled heav'ns a shining frame,
> Their great Original proclaim.
> The unwearied sun from day to day does his Creator's power display;
> And publishes to every land
> The work of an almighty hand.

The second assumption was that we could know and discover the order of the universe because there was a profound parallel between human and divine reason. In discovering the rules of cosmic order the scientist rethought the original thoughts of God in the act of creation. The great symbol of this insight was the physicist Isaac Newton (1642–1727), whose writings on gravitation, optics, and the motion of heavenly bodies made the heavens and earth fit together like a seamless garment. Such was his reputation that Alexander Pope could pen his famous couplet:

> Nature and Nature's laws lay hid in night,
> God said let *Newton* be! And all was light.

Human reason bound humanity closer to God.

In many ways the center of this rationalist trend was England, and it had political as well as religious implications. Part of the appeal of absolutism (which was triumphing at the time in France) was that only absolute power could preserve truth and prevent error. Human beings in themselves could not be trusted to know the truth. The philosopher John Locke (1632–1704) fought against the appeal to absolutism in both politics and religion. For him enlightened reason and not blind authority was the better guide. Natural reason pointed humans in the direction of truth and helped them recognize error. To violate a moral precept in the name of either an absolute king or an absolute church was to contradict our moral nature. This did not mean that Locke rejected all revelation. Revelation could give humans knowledge that was above reason, but it could never contradict reason. Locke called for toleration in religion because the great truths of Christianity could stand by themselves; they did not need an absolute church to protect them. Locke here stands in direct opposition to Ignatius Loyola, who was prepared to believe white black and black white on the church's word. Locke urged Christians to question the church and not their senses, since the senses were a surer guide.

As the appeal to reason developed, it spawned a whole school of apologetical literature. "Natural theology" attempted to prove God's existence and define God's nature through an appeal to the natural world. Other theologians used the natural world to prove the reasonableness of Christian claims. Still others defended the credibility of the New Testament by evaluating its testimony as one would judge the testimony of witnesses in a court trial. In all these approaches, Christian claims were to be judged and defended by reason.

But there were some who wished to push the appeal to reason even further. Why did one need revelation at all? Earlier in the seventeenth century Edward Herbert of Cherbury argued that true religion rested on five truths known directly through reason and nature. There was a God; humans had an obligation to worship that God; there was an ethical law associated with God; humans failed at times to keep this moral law and needed to repent when they failed; and there would be a final reward for good and punishment for evil. These five principles constituted the essence of religion and were found in all the great religions of the world. Revelation was divisive and unnecessary. This thinking produced a movement known as Deism that emerged at the end of the seventeenth century. Writers such as John Toland in *Christianity Not Mysterious* and Matthew Tindal in *Christianity as Old as Creation* popularized the Deist cause.

The rise of Deism coincided with a growing awareness of the religions of the world. The expansion of European influence brought wider contact with other religions, and relatively impartial accounts of them began to appear. The religion of China in particular grabbed the imagination of many in the early eighteenth century. The ancient culture and high ethical teachings provoked questions about whether all religions might not be undergirded by similar assumptions. Deism was an early attempt to address this question.

Deism became an international phenomenon, but its influence would vary. In England it had only little effect. The earlier move toward the linking of religion and reason blunted the Deist critique of revelation, and writers like Joseph Butler, in his *Analogy of Religion*, demonstrated that Deism had as many intellectual problems as traditional Christianity did. In France Deism found favor with persons like Voltaire and the Encyclopediasts, and it took on a strongly anticlerical tone. It was viewed as an alternative to a Roman

Catholicism that seemed oppressive and reactionary. Voltaire's famous cry concerning the Catholic Church, *"Écraser l'infâme!"* (Crush the infamy!), reflected the tension between Deism and Catholicism in France. In Germany rational religion developed only later, but it produced a major impact on the intellectual life of the nation, and the critical and constructive work of German rationalists laid the groundwork for many developments in Protestant theology in the next century. Christian Wolff (1679–1754) did not deny that there might be revelation but claimed that nothing contrary to reason could be held to be true. Reason was the necessary guide to any certain knowledge. Wolff's teachings were eventually to triumph in the new German universities, but in the short run were so controversial that Prussia's King Frederick Wilhelm ordered him to leave his university in forty-eight hours or be hanged. He chose the former. H. S. Reimarus (1694–1768) rejected miracles and revelation in the name of reason and criticized the Bible's historicity. His works were only posthumously published, but in his edition of them, Gotthold Lessing (1729–1781) made an even more radical claim: No event in history ("accidental truths," as he called them) could convince a person about a truth of reason, since the facts of history and eternal truth were completely independent of each other. Although such critical ideas found little favor on the popular level, they helped transform German intellectual life.

Religion of the Heart

Reason was one answer to the question of how to ground religion in this new world. Yet others thought there was an alternative. The place to start was in the transformed heart. Christianity's problem was that it had become formal and external. Theological disputes between Protestants and Catholics had led to more care for logic than for the spirit. The wars of religion had placed the cross on the banners of military legions, but somehow they had drained it of its power in the hearts of men and women. European society might boast of the name Christendom, but there was little that was genuinely Christian about the culture and mores of the lands.

The turn to a religion of the heart was one of the great religious movements of the age. It would have a tremendous effect on virtually every nation in the Protestant world, and in its own way it would impact Roman Catholicism as well. This religion of the heart had different names in different lands. On the continent of Europe it was known as Pietism. In Britain, since it was associated with John Wesley, it was known as Methodism. In America it would eventually be known as evangelicalism.

In Germany Pietism grew out of a sense that the Reformation had some-how stalled. The Reformation of the sixteenth century had dealt with the question of reforming doctrine, but the task remained to reform Christian life. What was needed was a revitalized interior life stressing the transform-ing power of God's love. Pietism can perhaps best be seen through one of its most important figures, Philipp Jakob Spener (1635–1705). In his studies at Strasbourg, Spener became acquainted with both the mystical piety of an ear-lier writer, Johann Arndt, and the Puritan emphasis on the transformed heart as a sign of true religion. In both he saw the means of revivifying a cold Lutheranism. Spener's great work was *Pia Desideria*, which analyzed the failures of current Christianity and pointed a way toward reform. Worldli-ness among magistrates, clergy, and laity, he argued, prevented the power of Christianity from breaking forth. Magistrates were forgetting their Christian responsibilities. Clergy preferred disputing doctrine over encouraging piety and sought after prestige rather than humble service. The laity believed that if they avoided major sins and attended church regularly they were respectable Christians. Spener called all to a higher standard. Externals in religion were not enough. "Your God has indeed given you Baptism," he wrote, "and you may be baptized only once. But he has made a covenant with you . . . [that] must last through your whole life." Only when the church was truly trans-formed would it be able to convert the world. To achieve this goal Spener urged greater study of the Bible, a concern for practical Christianity, and the use of small groups for encouragement and discipline.

> For over a century and a half after the Reformation Protestants were pointedly absent from missionary outreach. With Pietism the mis-sionary impulse blossomed.

Pietism had a revolutionary impact on continental Protestantism. Worldly amusements that had long been tolerated, particularly the use of alcohol, began to be questioned. The active responsibility of all Christians in good works and the stewardship of wealth were stressed. Finally the responsibility for mission entered into Protestant consciousness. As we have seen, for over a century and a half after the Reformation Protestants were pointedly absent from missionary outreach. With Pietism the missionary impulse blossomed.

One of the groups influenced by Pietism was the Moravians. Their reli-gious dedication made them willing to go anywhere to serve Christ, and they became famous for their missionary labors. But ironically it was through their decision to start a community in the American colonies in the early 1730s that they became most famous in the later history of Christianity. In Georgia, they made a strong impression on a young Anglican cleric, John Wesley. Moravians became the conduit between continental Pietism and English Methodism.

Wesley and the People Called Methodists

John Wesley (1703–1791) is arguably the most important eighteenth-century religious figure in the English-speaking world. Born into a clerical family, he and his brother Charles followed their father's profession. While at Oxford, John, always disciplined in his religious devotion, gathered a small group of like-minded souls who fasted, prayed, and did works of mercy so methodically that they were derisively called "Methodists." In 1735 the Wesley brothers traveled to the colony of Georgia, an eighteenth-century experiment in philanthropy where debtors were given a second chance. A Moravian leader there, August Spangenberg, asked John the pointed question "Do you know Jesus Christ?" Wesley could only respond, "I know he is the Saviour of the world." But when the Moravian pressed him, "True, but do you know he has saved you?" Wesley could not honestly answer yes.

Spangenberg's question centered on personal certainty. Did Wesley possess not only the church's faith but a true and lively personal faith? The question would dog him. His ministry in Georgia turned out to be a failure, not only because of an unfortunate love affair but because it raised questions as to whether true religion could be achieved by rigorous religious practice alone. Two years after returning to England, on May 24, 1738, in a chapel on Aldersgate Street in London, Wesley achieved this certainty. Writing in his diary, he stated that his "heart was strangely warmed" and that he had experienced that personal saving faith he had felt he had lacked. He traveled to the Moravian community in Germany, and there he vowed to promote "vital practical religion" and to increase the life of God in the souls of men. Although influenced by the Moravians, Wesley differed from them

> For Wesley, without a transformed heart a person was at best only an external Christian. Without it one could not truly know spiritual things.

in his emphasis on activity in the world. Wesley himself lived up to his call for action. Over the course of his long life he is said to have traveled 225,000 miles on horseback and given 40,000 sermons!

The transformed heart became Wesley's message. Without it a person was at best only an external Christian. Without it one could not truly know spiritual things. As with the earlier Puritans, the transformed heart was the mark of a true Christian, but unlike the Puritans—whose Calvinism attributed this conversion to an act of God—Wesley claimed that anyone could choose to believe. He was a firm defender of free will, or Arminianism. Wesley's emphasis on free will made him much more willing to appeal to the emotions than earlier preachers, since emotion could move the will. Wesley would add one new element to Protestant thinking: Human beings not only had the power (through God's grace) to ask forgiveness for sin but to triumph over the sin as well. Sanctification was now in reach of the true believer.

Wesley's message was both popular and controversial. His message of the transformation of the heart appealed to many for whom the old church was losing its sway, particularly those who were being economically displaced as Britain shifted from being an agricultural society to an industrial one. The discipline that Wesley saw as necessarily tied to the new life—like the Pietists, Wesley frowned on alcohol and urged stewardship—offered a sense of purposeful discipline to this population. So too did Wesley's adoption of the small-group system advocated by Spener, known as the "class system," which aided in maintaining discipline. Religion in the Methodist societies was closer to the ground than in the older churches; it was found in the transformed heart and in the encouragement and discipline of the small group rather than in the vision of the Christian society.

Yet for those who believed that religion and reason should be linked, Wesley's emphasis on emotion seemed dangerous. For a person like Anglican bishop and philosopher Joseph Butler, Wesley's belief that God communicated directly seemed dubious. He is reported to have told Wesley, "Sir, the pretending to extraordinary revelations and gifts of the Holy Spirit is a horrid thing—a very horrid thing." Similarly, for those who believed in order and decorum in worship, Wesley's adoption of field preaching (or preaching outside) and lay preaching were disturbing. The Methodist movement both attracted and alienated, and his relationship with the Church of England was strained. In 1784 he decided that for the sake of his followers in the New World he would ordain Thomas Coke as superintendent or bishop of the Methodist community there. This action sealed the split between Methodists and the Church of England (which held that only bishops could ordain persons to ministry). Methodists organized an independent church in America in 1784 and one in England almost immediately after the death of Wesley.

John Wesley was aided in his labors by the work of his brother, Charles Wesley, who wrote some of the best-known hymns in the English language. Hymn singing, an innovation in English-speaking Protestantism, became an important part of evangelical religion. Wesley's great hymn "O for a

Thousand Tongues to Sing" paid homage to the power of singing. It united persons, binding their individual faiths into a common voice while speaking with a directness and passion that earlier forms of church music often lacked. Evangelical hymns made use of the first-person singular— *my* redeemer's praise—to reinforce the intimate relationship between the believer and her Lord.

Although Wesley and his followers were the best-known example of the evangelical revival in eighteenth-century Britain, they were not alone. Some split with Wesley because of his emphasis on free will. George Whitefield (1714–1770), one of the great preachers of all time, continued to maintain a Calvinistic view of grace, and many gathered around him. He was helped immensely by Selina, Countess of Huntingdon, a wealthy supporter of evangelicalism. She used her fortune to establish a series of chapels around England, where the religion of the heart could be preached. Still others, such as John Newton and Charles Simeon, preached the evangelical message within the Church of England.

In the grand struggle between reason and faith, England and Germany followed diverging patterns. In England rationalism appeared first, and Wesley and the evangelicals can be understood as responding to it. In Germany Pietism appeared first, and rationalism represented a critique of Pietism as well as the older orthodoxy. In America, Pietism and rationalism arose at approximately the same time and helped to give the American religious scene its distinctiveness.

The Great Awakening in America

As the previous chapter describes, the English-speaking colonies in the early eighteenth century followed three religious patterns: the southern attempt to reproduce the established order of the Church of England (albeit without bishops), the New England covenanted communities, and the religious pluralism of the middle colonies. In the early decades of the eighteenth century elements of both rational religion and heartfelt religion began to appear in the New World, but until the 1740s neither was strong enough to upset the earlier patterns. In the southern colonies the message of rational religion, with its emphasis on reason and morality, found much favor. Likewise in maritime or eastern New England there were signs of interest in a religion of reason. Already by 1701, Harvard College (an institution founded by the Massachusetts Puritans and still in existence) began moving away from strict Puritanism. In response, the Connecticut Puritan churches in 1701 founded the world-famous Yale University. At the same time continental Pietism began to take root in the middle colonies, brought there by immigrants from Germany and the Netherlands, and Pastor Theodore Jacob Frelinghuysen taught the necessity for personal conversion. But there were few active signs of a groundswell for either rationalism or the religion of the heart. Indeed in New England there was more concern that the vigor of religion was declining and that worldliness was triumphing over the faith of the forbears.

All of this was to change by the late 1730s. Beginning then, colonial America (and English-speaking Canada) experienced decades of religious turmoil known as the Great Awakening (or Awakenings; historians differ), which swept away the old religious patterns and created a new religious landscape.

The Awakening occurred in a series of phases. The first, often referred to as the Frontier Revival, was rooted in western New England (which was then the frontier). By the late 1730s preachers began to notice a new seriousness in religion and a large number of conversions. As one wrote, "a great and earnest concern about the great things of religion . . . became universal . . . and among persons of all degrees and all ages." The Frontier Revival saw the emergence of Jonathan Edwards as a powerful preacher and thinker. Edwards, who is often considered the greatest American theologian, chronicled the course of the revival in *A Faithful Narrative of the Surprising Work of God*. Although it was only a brief and relatively small affair, Edwards's account of the revival generated great excitement. The British hymn writer Isaac Watts noted, "Never did we hear or read, since the first ages of Christianity, any event of this kind so surprising as the present narrative has set before us." Mass conversions had not occurred since the time of the apostles, yet they had now returned. Was the Spirit acting again as it had in biblical times?

The Frontier Revival was but a prelude to the great stir caused by the preaching of George Whitefield. Whitefield made many visits to the New World, but it was his second visit (1739–1741) that was most celebrated. His dramatic and forceful preaching style and his emphasis on the new birth offered a baptism by immersion into heartfelt religion. Crowds flocked to hear him, and his final sermon on the Boston Common was said to have been heard by thirty thousand listeners. Whitefield brought not only the message of the new birth but also its ramifications: that without it one lacked true Christianity. In his journal (later published) he lamented the lack of vital piety among the faculties of Harvard and Yale and many of the clergy he had encountered.

Others took up both Whitefield's itinerating ways and his criticism of the clergy. The Presbyterian Gilbert Tennant preached on the dangers of an unconverted ministry and urged believers to abandon churches where the minister did not show signs of vital piety. When others followed suit, great controversy engulfed New England. Inevitably a reaction occurred. One Boston minister, Charles Chauncy, in *Seasonable Thoughts on the State of Religion in New England*, blamed the disruption of religious life on the new heartfelt religion, which jettisoned all constraints of reason. The emotionalism of the Great Awakening was a destructive thing. Edwards in response published a *Treatise on Religious Affections*, defending the role of emotion in religion.

If the Awakening was disturbing in New England, it would revolutionize the South. There, the message of heartfelt religion created a social as well as religious crisis. The established Anglican Church had attempted to maintain an ordered society shaped by reason and morality. But particularly in the newer settlements along the frontier, the heartfelt religion proved more attractive and served as a challenge to a hierarchically ordered society. Presbyterians and Methodists joined in preaching this message, but the Baptists were its great apostles. Missionaries from the northern colonies, such as Shubal Stearns, preached the new message with warmth and fervor. The success of these groups seriously weakened the established Anglican churches of the South. In maritime Canada the cause of heartfelt religion was advanced through the labors of the evangelist Henry Alline.

In America, supporters of the heartfelt religion came to be known as evangelicals, and from them a common religious culture began to be forged. Evangelical Protestantism became the glue that bound together the different parts of the colonies. The older religious establishments were ultimately undermined by the new vision (although some of the New England established churches would continue for a number of decades). Evangelicalism also created an impetus to spread the Christian message to the outcasts of society. David Brainerd (1718–1747), the son-in-law of Jonathan Edwards, began a mission to Native Americans, though with comparatively little success. Of greater importance was the spread of the message to the African slave community. The evangelization of the slave community had been a thorny question, since some believed that Christian baptism entitled a slave to emancipation, and before the middle of the eighteenth century there were at best only modest attempts. But the new religion of the heart found favor among African Americans, and increasingly it became the common religion of both blacks and whites.

The Great Awakening stirred up not only its defenders but its critics as well. Among the churches of eastern New England, Charles Chauncy's attack on emotionalism and defense of the authority of reason became the starting point for a reassessment of many Calvinist/Puritan doctrines. Some involved the doctrine of original sin. Did sin destroy natural virtue, and were human beings culpable for the sins of Adam? Others involved human freedom. Did human beings have moral freedom, or were they bound by predestination? A relatively new question was the work of Jesus. Reason demanded the rejection of the idea of God as an autocratic king, exacting retribution from his son to pay the human debt of sin. Instead, Jesus was pictured as the embodiment of divine love and the teacher of righteousness. Eastern New England was on its way toward embracing Unitarianism, which it would do by the early nineteenth century. Reason was to be the judge of all inherited doctrines.

A similar drift can be seen in southern Anglicanism, though it is less documented and harder to specify. In the period of the Great Awakening some Southerners began to push the cause of reason in religion toward a Deism that jettisoned much of traditional Christianity. The division is unclear, and as late as the 1770s one can find many examples of persons both interested in Deistic literature and still committed to the established Anglican Church. But the interest in rational religion advanced, at least among men. The Masonic order (which in the eighteenth century advocated rational religion) was more devoutly attended by some men than were parish churches. The attraction to Deism was far less frequent among women.

Herein lay the paradox of the American Revolution, a paradox that has bedeviled students of history for centuries. Was the Revolution the work of rationalists or evangelicals? The answer is both. On the level of leadership, New England and southern rationalists provided crucial support, yet on the ground much of the struggle was carried out by evangelicals who saw the Revolution as the throwing off of the tyranny of the British government and the British church. Rationalists and evangelicals united to overturn the established Anglican churches of the South. Both could claim to be the driving force of the Revolution, and they worked surprisingly smoothly together—far more smoothly, indeed, than do their twenty-first-century heirs.

The religious ferment of the late seventeenth and eighteenth centuries was in some ways below the surface. In 1760 the religious world of Western Christianity looked little different than it had a century earlier. Wherever one looked the Constantinian union of throne and altar was firmly in place. But the defenders of the religion of reason and the religion of the heart had done their work. They had brought the questions of religion down to the individual level. Were *you* persuaded? Was *your* heart warmed? These became key questions. The stage was set for the challenging of the Constantinian world.

SECTION 5 Placing Christianity in a New World

Chapter 14

Challenging Christendom

The end of the eighteenth century brought a revolutionary fervor that would challenge almost all of the carefully constructed Christian order that had been forged during the reign of Constantine and that had held sway for fourteen centuries. The result would be not only a questioning of Christianity's place in the social order but of the grounding of Christianity itself.

Cracks in Christendom

Although Christian Europe was at war with itself almost continuously throughout the eighteenth century, nothing much seemed to change. The religious divisions that had been accepted at the Peace of Westphalia (as noted in chap. 11) continued to mark the boundaries. The king of France was still the "most Christian" king; the king of Spain, the "most Catholic" king; and the king of England, the "Defender of the Faith." The Catholic Habsburgs ruled triumphantly in central Europe as they had done since the thirteenth century, more secure since the 1690s when the last Turkish threat was beaten back. Catholic prince bishops still governed their little pieces of Germany as they too had done since the Middle Ages, and Lutheranism (though now tinged with rationalism) still undergirded the Prussia of Frederick the Great. Spain, though weakened, still ruled a quarter of the earth, while France, Britain, Portugal, and the Netherlands all tended their far-flung colonies, attempting to balance religion and profit. The Enlightenment praised peace and balance, and Christendom appeared supremely balanced. But looks were deceiving, and by century's end violent waves of political, social, and religious revolution would wash away this sense of peace. If sensitive souls in the 1660s had begun to inquire about the basis of Christianity and what was to be its place in society, by 1800 these questions had taken center stage, and for the first time since the age of Constantine, the Christian state found itself under assault.

Like the lost horseshoe nail of the adage, the path to crisis appeared innocent enough. The wars of the eighteenth century pitting France and its allies against Britain and its supporters were carried out not only in Europe but all over the world. They usually ended unremarkably, but in the 1760s Britain was successful in pushing the French out of Canada. The conquest of French Canada would have immediate consequences. The century-long North American struggle between England and France had always had a religious dimension; would Protestantism or Catholicism dominate the continent? The Treaty of Paris of 1763 put virtually all of French-speaking Canada under British jurisdiction. But the British success resulted in a new colonial policy that had important religious ramifications. The lower colonies were to be brought more in line with British practice, and this entailed, at least for some, the introduction of Anglican bishops. In Canada it necessitated coming to terms with the powerful French Catholic Church, and the Quebec Act of 1774 restored key privileges to the Catholic Church. Both actions enraged the Protestant sensibilities of the English colonies, particularly in New England, and were viewed as part of a plot to undermine Protestant liberties. These fears gave a religious zeal to a general dispute about taxes, and many on both sides of the Atlantic saw the conflict between Britain and her colonies as but a second phase of the English civil wars of the seventeenth century in which religion and politics were intertwined. The result was the American Revolution, through which the thirteen colonies found themselves free from the bonds of England.

It is sometimes hard to realize how radical the American Revolution was and how much it broke from older models. Religion had a far different public place than had ever been the case before in the Western world. America was the first nation in the Christian world without an established church. In part this was because the diversity that had arisen was so great that no one church could predominate, and it is true that religious establishments did continue in some states in New England. But others saw this separation of church and state as a positive thing and an important part of the accomplishment of the revolutionary generation. Thomas Jefferson, in defending the Virginia Statute of Religious Freedom, which he wrote, argued that religion had no place in public policy. Religious belief was a purely private matter: "To say there are twenty gods or no God,"

> "To say there are twenty gods or no God," declared Thomas Jefferson, "neither picks my pocket nor breaks my leg."

he declared, "neither picks my pocket nor breaks my leg." The absence of an established religion, however, left open some questions. What would be the symbols of civil authority if the traditional Christian ones were rejected? How would public rituals, such as state funerals, be conducted? And who would now be the stewards of morality? For civic symbols the founding generation reached back to Greece and Rome. For rituals the Masonic order filled the gap. Morality, however, was the rub. Who would be the moral stewards?

Revolution in France

But the indirect effects of the loss of New France did not end here. To avenge France's shame, Louis XVI poured its wealth into the cause of the American war of independence. He did so for reasons of empire, but others in France saw in America a vision of the future. In this, they needed all their imaginative powers. France seemed solid and secure, and the Catholic Church appeared the same. For a thousand years France had been the heart of Christian Europe, and in 1785 the French church still lay at the center of French society. It was the "First Estate," the most honorable part of the realm. Since the revocation of the Edict of Nantes, only Catholics could be citizens. Catholic clergy were a privileged class. They were exempt from taxation and possessed enormous wealth. They had their own courts of law and a monopoly on marriages, education, and care of the sick. Yet despite (or because) of this worldly power, the church's spiritual state was not strong. The higher clerical positions were monopolized by the aristocracy, and often these positions were viewed more as wealthy sinecures than as pastoral responsibilities. It was said that all too many bishops administered more provinces than sacraments. A wide disparity of income existed between the higher clergy and the lower, and many of the latter silently favored radical reform that would redistribute power. Among the laity there was still a respect for the church, but the skepticism and anticlericalism of Voltaire and others had left its mark. The church had its enemies as well as its friends.

The French Revolution would overturn the old order in both church and state. The crisis started innocently enough. In 1789 Louis XVI, bankrupt from his support of the American cause, called the Estates General (the national Parliament, which had not met for 175 years) to address the financial crisis. In the assembly, the increasingly radical middle-class representatives vented their frustrations with the aristocratic dominance of society, and this included the church. The assembly passed the Civil Constitution of the Clergy, which redistributed clerical incomes. But the Constitution went further and also eliminated the authority of the pope, called for the popular election of bishops and priests, and imposed on all officeholders an oath of compliance. The Civil Constitution became a symbol of an increasingly radical French Revolution, one sharply at odds with the old church, and the oath of compliance became a litmus test of loyalty to the Revolution. It bitterly divided the French clergy, particularly after it was rejected by the papacy, between those who would and would not sign it. Those who refused to sign found themselves subject to ejection from office and even deportation.

By 1793, the year of Louis XVI's execution, the Revolution entered its most radical phase. As the nations of Europe began to press on France to destroy its Revolution, the Catholic clergy were seen as enemies of the people and executed by the hundreds. A policy of extreme de-Christianization was undertaken. The Christian Sunday and the biblical seven-day week were suppressed. All references to the birth of Christ as beginning the present era were dropped, and a new era of history was said to have commenced with the Revolution. Churches were turned into "temples of reason," and the ceremonies performed there caricatured the mass. In Notre Dame in Paris an actress/courtesan was enthroned on the high altar as reason's goddess. Still later Robespierre called for a cult of the "Supreme Being" that would reflect the new republican sympathies. Other religious alternatives were also offered but never struck deep roots, and a proposed republican version of the Lord's Prayer that included the petition "Give us this day our daily bread, in spite of the vain attempts of Pitt, the Coburgs, and all the tyrants of the Coalition [i.e., foreign opponents of the Revolution] to starve us out" never caught on.

All of this profoundly broke up the old religious order. A reaction to the excesses of the Revolution eventually occurred; Catholicism was again tolerated; and indeed, under Napoleon Bonaparte, part of the public role of the church was restored. But the church's power was greatly reduced. It had to forgo all its property confiscated during the Revolution and have clergy who were paid by the state. It also had to submit to the naming of all bishops by the government. Finally, religious freedom was granted to non-Catholics. Catholicism was no longer the religion of France but simply the largest religion in France. In less than a generation the very heart of Catholic Europe had been transformed.

The impact of Napoleon was even greater than this religious transformation. The famous image of him crowning himself emperor as the pope stood and watched reflected a new relationship between the secular and the sacred. With Napoleon, the nation began to emerge as the preeminent and all-powerful category. The cry of the Revolution, "*Liberté, Égalité, Fraternité*," would make a new social order. The idea of a land being made up of many formal "estates" or classes, each having its own rights and privileges, was replaced by the idea that a common law placed each individual on an equal basis. The state was the *fraternité*, or brotherhood. It demanded the highest loyalty, greater even than religion. One of Napoleon's famous acts was the opening up of the Jewish ghettoes, or special places, where Jews as outsiders were required to live. But when he did so, he posed to the rabbis of France a simple question: Did they consider all Frenchmen to be brothers? Were they willing to accept that now French nationality and not their religion was the source of unity and identity? Peoplehood and not religion held together the nation-state. If the idea of nationhood was startling in France, it was even more revolutionary in places such as Italy and Germany that had long been divided into minor principalities, many governed by the church. The age of the nation-state had begun.

In the new nation-states Christianity was not simply displaced as the source of unity but was robbed of many of its historic responsibilities as they began to be taken on by the state. For millennia the church had been the record keeper of society, dutifully chronicling births and deaths. This now became a function of the state. It had been responsible for marriage, but the new Napoleonic Code not only legitimized civil marriage but even made divorce legal. The church had also been the guardian of the final resting places of the people. Cemeteries, a distinctively Christian institution that developed in the early centuries, had for centuries served as an indirect means of church control since the church had the final say as to who might be buried there. In the wake of Napoleon's conquest of Europe, public cemeteries began to appear; it was the state and not the church that determined inclusion.

The revolutionary impulse was not just confined to the political; many other aspects of the inherited order found themselves under scrutiny. In 1792 Mary Wollstonecraft (1759–1797) wrote *A Vindication of the Rights of Women*. Equality could not be limited to the rights of men but must transcend gender. Women should have the opportunity for education so that the relationship between men and women could be put on a new footing.

Affairs in France divided Europe. If some were excited by the ideals of the Revolution, others were appalled. In Britain, conflict with France pushed many of the churches sharply to the right. Anglicans, Methodists, and many others joined in supporting the struggle against France and opposing radicalism in both politics and religion.

Struggle in America

The American response to the French Revolution followed a different pattern. For some the French struggle represented a continuation of America's revolution, but for others it was an abomination. Early American politics became polarized between pro-British Federalists and pro-French Democratic Republicans. A religious division could not be avoided. Tom Paine, pamphleteer of the American Revolution, had argued in *The Age of Reason* that the struggle for liberty must involve not only battling kings but clergy as well. In Thomas Jefferson was found an individual combining the political ideals of the French Revolution and a confidence in a religion of reason. Such a combination worried conservatives, and Jefferson's election as president in 1800, over the furious objections of the New England clergy, indicated that perhaps the religion of reason was becoming the religion of the republic. The religious free thinker Joel Barlow, who had earlier organized a Deistical Society for the advancement of the ideals of the French Revolution and those of free religion, was so inspired by Jefferson's election that he began publishing a weekly newspaper, *The Temple of Reason*.

But rational religion was not to triumph. Instead the early nineteenth century saw a tremendous wave of evangelical activity. In New England the revival flowed from Yale College and a group of ministers who continued the traditions of the Great Awakening. Timothy Dwight, as president of Yale, preached the necessity of conversion, a serious Christian life, and the rejection of the skeptical attitudes associated with the French Enlightenment. If Dwight was the intellectual captain of the eastern phase of the revival, Lyman Beecher, his chief lieutenant, was its active embodiment. The eastern revival had two goals. It first attempted to salvage traditional Reformed theology by allowing a greater place for human freedom and divine justice, thus reconciling Calvinism and democracy. Second, it emphasized the necessity of moral reform. Beecher became a leader in the campaign against both dueling and the use of alcoholic beverages. In both there was the desire to buttress the traditional religious order of New England, including its established Congregational Church.

> The vast majority of those affected by the revival associated themselves not with any of the older colonial churches but with newer popular denominations.

The Awakening was far different outside of New England. In both the trans-Appalachian West and the post-Anglican South, the evangelical revival aimed not so much at supporting an existing order as filling up a cultural and psychological vacuum. And there it was anything but conservative. At the famous gathering at Cane Ridge in Kentucky in 1801, some twenty-five thousand people gathered to hear the preaching. The emotional excesses exhibited there—commentators spoke of running, jerking, and even barking by those under the sway of the Spirit—became legendary. Even more important, the vast majority of those affected by the revival associated themselves not with any of the older colonial churches but with newer popular denominations. Benefiting most were the Methodists, who from their organization in 1784 to 1844 grew in size from fourteen thousand to over a million members, making them the largest church in America. The Baptists likewise gained, growing tenfold in the decades after the Revolution. New religious communities also sprang up, such as the Christian A sociation, founded by Alexander Campbell, which attempted to capture the unity and simplicity of primitive Christianity.

By 1815 one could identify two distinct branches of American evangelical Protestantism: one centered in New England and tied to the status quo, and the other southern and western and more populist in nature. They were also divided politically. The northern evangelicals (mostly Congregationalists) were Federalist and anti-Jeffersonian, while the Methodists and Baptists were Democratic and Jeffersonian. Methodists and Baptists could not forget that it was Jefferson's Statute of Religious Freedom that freed them from persecution by an Anglican establishment, and they had little sympathy for defenders of the New England established churches. But in 1817, when the old New England Standing Order (or Congregational establishment) began to give way, these two branches of evangelicalism began to draw together. The abolition of the New England established churches made all communities in the United States "denominations," or voluntary religious communities with equal status before the law. As equals, evangelicals of various stripes could work together, and one immediate result was the triumph of evangelicalism over rational religion. Unitarianism became confined to eastern Massachusetts. Deism died out, and the religion of reason lost it sway.

What would characterize America as a result of the evangelical successes was the rejection of any established church and the claim that America was nevertheless a Christian nation. Christianity rested in the people themselves. This was the purpose of the First Amendment's call for the separation of church and state. As Supreme Court Justice Joseph Story explained, the amendment was not intended to prostrate Christianity "but to exclude all rivalry among Christian sects, and to prevent any national ecclesiastical establishment." For much of the next century these evangelical denominations would be the stewards of moral instruction.

Repositioning Christianity

Movements like evangelicalism attempted to respond to the social forces released by the French Revolution, but there were other challenges to meet, particularly on the intellectual level. For a century Christian writers had hitched their wagon to the star of reason, but now reason seemed to be of little help. Where could they turn?

They were aided by a vast change taking place at century's end in the way persons saw the world. By the 1780s sensitive men and women were divining that the Enlightenment emphasis on reason, order, and design hid as much as it revealed about reality. There was a deeper reality to nature than the metaphor of a well-running watch suggested, and there was a deeper reality to human beings than as accumulators of objective knowledge. The revolt against the limitations of the Enlightenment is known as Romanticism. It was a far-reaching movement with many manifestations, but almost all of its embodiments emphasized certain key points. The first was the recognition that there were realities stronger than reason, which was so valued by the Enlightenment. The Romantics were unwilling to reduce experience to either rationalism or scientific observation. Reason provided only surface knowledge. Intuition and feeling could sense realities that reason could not. A second theme was a new understanding of both nature and nature's God. For Newton, the great truth behind nature was that it was like a great machine: balanced, ordered, and predictable. It was as intricate and meticulously planned as a fine watch—hence, a favorite metaphor of God as the Great Watchmaker. For Romantics, however, the world was more like an organism than a machine. It was not dead and mechanical but vital and alive, and the divine was to be seen in this vitality. Behind nature was some Spirit or vital force, and that vital force also existed in human beings; hence, not only was nature alive, but human beings were part of it. To sense this connection was to experience the power of God, and it came through *feeling*. Finally, if nature was alive, it *changed*. It grew. The history or development of a person or thing was the essence of that person or thing. This gave a new value to history, and certain eras such as the Middle Ages that had been denigrated during the Enlightenment now took on a new value as an age of faith. A Gothic cathedral with its stained-glass windows and sense of mystery seemed closer to the spirit of religion than the whitewashed churches of the Enlightenment.

Religion then became a question of faith—strong, deep faith—and not of rationalization and proof. At the end of a celebrated work in which he showed the inadequacy of all proofs for the existence of God, the philosopher Immanuel Kant famously concluded, "I have had to deny knowledge in order

> Kant famously concluded, "I have had to deny knowledge in order to make room for faith."

to make room for faith." He went on to suggest that our sense of the existence of God came not from our abstract reasoning but from intuitions flowing from our moral nature, which he called "practical reason." But where was such faith to be grounded? For the French Catholic François-René de Chateaubriand (1768–1848), it rested in the cultural power of inherited Christianity. Chateaubriand in 1802 published *The Genius of Christianity*. To respond to the great eighteenth-century skeptical assault on the faith, one needed to appeal to the power not of reason but of feeling. As he famously described his own rekindling of belief, "I did not yield . . . to a mighty supernatural illumination. My conviction came out of my heart. I wept and I believed." Christianity lay at the heart of all that Europe was. All the beauty and glory of Western culture and life flowed from Christianity. Its power inspired all poetry, literature, and fine arts. To see the reality and truth of Christianity, he urged his readers to open their eyes and hearts to the world around them.

If Chateaubriand anchored Christianity in feelings of the heart that Christian culture inspired, another French Catholic writer, Joseph de Maistre (1753–1821), rested it on its social power reflected in the church. For de Maistre, true society was rooted in authority. Human nature was a curious blend of the sinful and the social. People were marred by sin but had a social nature. Accordingly, they needed some authority to guide them. The philosophers of the eighteenth century erred in believing that humans could be guided by that knowledge reached by human reason. The horrors of the French Revolution showed the folly of such a confidence. Instead humanity must be guided by a communal and habitual sense of what is true and right. This is why they needed great leaders. Kings in the temporal realm and the pope in the spiritual realm were the foundation for true order. Hence the necessity for the church.

Protestant writers followed a different path. Perhaps the most creative and influential Christian invocation of Romantic themes is found in Friedrich Schleiermacher (1768–1834). Schleiermacher's life is illustrative of the various eddies in late-eighteenth-century European thought. Educated in a strong Pietistic environment (which he found too narrow), he explored the Enlightenment religion of reason, Kant, and the new Romanticism. All came together in his famous early work *On Religion: Speeches to Its Cultured Despisers* (1799). Religion was ignored or dismissed, he claimed, because most people did not know what it was. They saw only the externals and rejected them. Orthodox defenders of religion and rationalist critics focused on either knowing (doctrine) or doing (ethics). Yet in its essence religion was neither. Religion was ultimately "a sense and taste for the infinite." It was rooted in the deepest aspect of human existence—the sense of dependence.

This feeling was not something taught but experienced through intuition, and it led human beings to seek that which was independent and infinite, "the immediate feeling of the Infinite and Eternal." Although religion had other important aspects, at its core was a perception or feeling of piety, and "piety cannot be an instinct craving for a mess of metaphysical or ethical crumbs." The quest for the infinite and eternal was common to all religions, but for Schleiermacher what made Christianity unique was the idea of redemption. In Christ there was a perfect "God-consciousness," and he communicated this to the community.

Schleiermacher's reconstruction of religion is an impressive artifice. In key ways he took themes dear to Pietism and reexamined them through a Romantic lens. The intense personal quality, the sense of dependence and awe, the idea of religion as surrender—all were found in earlier Pietism, but they were now universalized and made a part of a new understanding of religion. His influence was enormous, and both proponents and critics have called him the most important theologian of the nineteenth century.

In the English-speaking world the leading proponent of the new Romantic understanding of religion was the poet/philosopher Samuel Taylor Coleridge. Although in his early years he was attracted to Enlightenment religion, the mature Coleridge became a sharp critic. Proponents of rational religion had tried to prove the existence of God through the order of nature, establish the truth of Christian claims by evidence, and anchor Christian morality in prudence. All were an abomination for Coleridge and reduced Christianity to something reasonable and useful. In addressing true Christianity, Coleridge, like other Romantics, began with the question of knowing. For Coleridge there were two ways of knowing: reason and understanding. Understanding was the empirical accumulation of facts and the drawing of conclusions from them. The eighteenth-century evidences for Christianity drawn from the natural theology genre was an obvious example of understanding. But understanding offered only surface knowledge, and surface knowledge was of little use concerning things of religion. Reason acted differently. Reason was actually intuitive insight, an immediate grasp or perception. The art of the poet was reason. The poet did not mechanically describe but attempted to evoke experience in the reader. This was also the nature of religion. Religion was a deep experience of a sense of reality that overwhelmed. But Coleridge did not stop here. Making use of Kant's category of "practical reason," he suggested that religion could not be proved in itself but could be validated by the practical doing of it. The practice of religion was the key.

By 1815 the revolutionary era was over. Napoleon had been twice defeated and was now safely in exile. The powers of Europe carefully redrew the map of the continent to ensure that order and stability would return. Kings and churches were dutifully restored. A Holy Alliance was established to ensure the tranquility of the continent. But the genie had left the bottle. *Liberté, égalité,* and *fraternité* would not disappear, and they would continue to transform the world. Christianity needed to respond.

Chapter 15

Creating a New World
(Nineteenth-Century Style)

*W*hat Charles Dickens said of the France of the 1790s—"It was the best of times, it was the worst of times"—could characterize the paradoxical nature of Christianity in the West during the long nineteenth century (1800–1914). It was a period whose frenetic energy and great accomplishment have merited it the title "The Great Century." Yet it was also an era when Christianity, and indeed religion itself, underwent both frontal attack and quiet erosion to such a degree that others see in it the roots of the secularization of Christendom. Since the present Christian world is in many ways an outgrowth of nineteenth-century trends, this enigmatic century will occupy the next three chapters, which look in turn at social, intellectual, and missionary issues.

If there was one word that epitomized the nineteenth-century imagination, it would be "progress." Things were advancing everywhere.

The world of the Christian West was changing, though the rate of change differed depending on where one looked. The Protestant nations of northern Europe, particularly Britain and Germany, led the way. Southern and eastern Europe lagged behind, and Russia (more and more a part of Europe) brought up the rear. North America paralleled northern Europe, but Latin America was a paradox. Politically it had adopted the language of democracy and freedom and thrown off the yoke of colonialism, yet the postrevolutionary societies continued to resemble their European forebears.

Part of the change was social and physical: a rural, agrarian society was giving way to cities and industry. Another part of the change was political: the ideas of the French Revolution concerning liberty and nationalism were leaving their mark. Still other changes were cultural, where the values and ethos of an expanding middle class were in ascendance. If there was one word that epitomized the nineteenth-century imagination, it would be "progress." Things were advancing everywhere. The technological innovations of telegraph and rail, which transformed communication and travel, emblemized for many a world that was moving at a rate unparalleled in previous history.

Evangelicalism Triumphant

The great religious force in the Protestant lands for much of the nineteenth century was the evangelicalism that had appeared in the previous century. Wherever it took root, evangelicalism advanced its historic agenda of heart-felt religion, mission, and moral reform.

Evangelicalism fueled the explosion of Nonconformity (or non-Anglican Protestants) in England during these years. Methodists, for example, increased fourfold between 1800 and 1860. Congregationalism grew at a similar rate, and by midcentury the Nonconformist churches were as large (or perhaps larger) than the established Church of England. But evangelicalism also made important inroads in the Church of England itself. The first evangelical bishop was appointed in 1815, and by 1840 an evangelical occupied Anglicanism's highest office, the archbishop of Canterbury. By some estimates, at mid-century almost a third of the established clergy were evangelicals. Evangelicals, however, did not simply fill existing churches; they founded new ones as well. In the 1830s, Edward Irving and his supporters (the "Irvingites," as others called them) claimed that the charismatic gifts mentioned in Paul's Letter to the Corinthians had now reappeared. A decade later John Nelson Darby and his followers (Plymouth Brethren) proclaimed that they had unlocked the meaning of biblical prophecy.

During these decades most of the laws barring Nonconformists from full participation in English society were lifted. Their right to perform marriages was granted in 1836; their freedom from taxes that supported the established church was granted in 1868; and their right to attend the historic universities of Oxford and Cambridge was gained in 1871. The triumph of the evangelical spirit was a triumph of duty, self-discipline, and high seriousness. Attendance at the theater was condemned; novel reading (particularly on Sunday) was frowned on; and enjoyment of secular music was debated. Prized was the "British Sabbath," on which all worldly things were studiously avoided. Evangelicals campaigned vigorously to assure that museums and exhibitions closed on Sundays, and as late as 1905 a picture of the prime minister playing golf on a Sunday set off a national debate.

The great strength of English evangelicalism was in the middle classes (though it also reached above and below), and much of its concern for moral reform reflected a middle-class outlook. All obstacles to the gospel, alternatives to the gospel, and occasions of sin were assailed. The evangelical campaign against slavery, led by the statesman William Wilberforce, was fired by the belief that slavery impeded the expansion of the Christian message. The campaign for a ten-hour workday was inspired by the concern that workingmen have enough time for worship. But evangelical humanitarianism should not be underestimated. Elizabeth Fry labored diligently for prison reform, particularly for better treatment of female prisoners. Evangelicals attacked the tacit government acceptance of prostitution. They fought against popular forms of entertainment such as boxing and cockfighting because of the violence and cruelty they entailed. But, as was also the case in America, one of the chief evangelical reform movements was the campaign against alcohol. Attempts to regulate drinking establishments, limit licensing hours, and establish temperance societies (e.g., the Ulster Temperance Society was organized in 1829) became part of an evangelical agenda. Although more successful among Nonconformists than Anglicans, the crusade against alcohol became a mark of Anglo-Saxon evangelicalism.

The explosive power of evangelicalism was not limited to England. Periodical revivals swept through Wales and Northern Ireland. In Scotland, a leading figure was Thomas Chalmers (1780–1847). Chalmers was a theologian and mathematician as well as an evangelical preacher. His life reflected the way evangelicalism quickened Scottish church life. Unfortunately, one of the fruits of the evangelical revival in Scotland was a schism in the established Presbyterian Church of Scotland. The issue concerned who could appoint clergy. According to law, patrons (wealthy laity) had the right of appointment, but in the 1840s the clergy and people of the church demanded a say in the decision-making process. Chalmers led the fight against the patronage system, which was seen as a struggle between the established powers and the upstart evangelicalism. The General Assembly of the Church of Scotland approved the change, but civil courts ruled in favor of the patrons. The result was the "Great Disruption," in which more than one-third of the ministers of the Church of Scotland resigned their livings and founded the Free Church of Scotland, whose first moderator was Chalmers. Within a few years after the death of Chalmers, the Free Church could claim more members than the established church, and it was a vigorous part of British evangelicalism.

Protestant Revival on the Continent

Protestantism on the continent displayed patterns similar to those in the British Isles. The state of the Reformed church of France, Switzerland, and the Netherlands at the end of the eighteenth century was unhealthy. Enlightenment ideas had sapped much of the vigor from them, and magistrates had encouraged their docility. But a new spirit began to arise in the early nineteenth century that was referred to as the *Le Reveil* (Awakening). British (and particularly Scottish) evangelicals and Moravians were the agents of transformation.

By this time Calvin's Geneva was notorious for its irreligion. Its clergy had produced a scandalously rationalistic version of the Bible. Indeed, its reputation had sunk so low that even Voltaire had called its clergy "shamefaced Socinians" because of their willingness to jettison historic doctrines such as the Trinity. Things began to revive, however, in the early nineteenth century. Robert Haldane, a leading Scottish evangelical, visited in 1816 and began an effective campaign of evangelization. Directing his labors particularly to theological students, he introduced evangelical doctrine to many and was said to have shaped a generation of pastors. An early convert was H. A. Caesar Malan (1787–1864), whose missionary work took him to France, Holland, and Germany, as well as Scotland and England. He has been called the father of French Protestant hymnody. Through such labors, continental Reformed churches began to take on a new vitality.

Through this cross-pollination, continental and British Protestantism drew more closely together. Many of the institutions that marked British evangelicalism—Bible societies, tract societies, missionary societies, and Sunday schools—found favor among the Reformed churches of the continent. Yet there remained differences, particularly concerning doctrine and discipline. Reacting to the laxity that had befallen them in the previous century, continental Reformed leaders called for strictness in both theology and polity. Some sought a return to the doctrinal standards of the sixteenth and seventeenth centuries, while others advocated the classical evangelical doctrines of human sinfulness and redemption through the cross of Christ.

Continental Lutherans followed a slightly different pattern. In Scandinavia, Pietism often clashed with the established order, and as a result many Scandinavian Pietists (particularly from Sweden and Norway) migrated to the United States. In what is now Germany, resistance to Napoleon led German Protestants to forge a closer alliance with the political authorities. The linkage with the state, however, would create a crisis in the 1820s. In 1817 the Lutheran and Reformed churches of Prussia were merged through the efforts of King Frederick Wilhelm III, and such a merger was attempted in other German states as well. The "Union" disturbed those who valued the old traditions as well as those who feared government control of church life. These traditional Lutherans opposed the merger and suffered much persecution. At first they were compelled to conform and were denied permission to emigrate, but after 1840 they were allowed to leave. Many migrated to America to form the Missouri Synod and other conservative synods in American Lutheranism.

The continuing effect of Pietism can be seen in the "inner mission" among Germans. The inner mission movement involved both evangelization and philanthropic endeavors, such as a bevy of benevolent organizations that ministered to underprivileged boys, seamen, prisoners, and others. An important part of this benevolent work involved the revival of deaconesses. In 1836, Theodore Fliedner established a community of nursing deaconesses in Kaiserwerth, and their number and ministry quickly multiplied. This first official ministry for women in the history of Protestantism quickly spread to Britain and America.

Evangelicals in Action in America

America was the wonder of the nineteenth century. Visitors like Alexis de Tocqueville and Frances Trollope came from far and wide to experience the new society firsthand. Not the least interesting aspect of the new land was its religious life. Without an established church and without a clergy tied to the social order, American church life had an amazing vitality. The Swiss church historian Philip Schaff noted that in Berlin there were 40 churches almost never full, while in New York there were 250 never empty. The vast majority of American Protestants saw themselves as evangelicals and believed that despite theological differences they shared key beliefs about the authority of the Bible, the way of salvation, and the meaning of the Christian life.

Still another important institution of American evangelicalism was the revival, or an extended series of services aimed at bringing persons to conversion. Methodists, Baptists, Presbyterians, and others all participated in the revival system. The great revivalist of the first half of the nineteenth century was Charles G. Finney. Finney was a Presbyterian but carried his church's theology lightly, stressing the necessity of choice and human freedom. Revivals, for him, were not mysterious workings of the Spirit but tools for the extension of God's kingdom — and like all tools they could be improved. Finney was both popular and controversial and did much to move American evangelicalism away from Calvinistic theology.

Evangelicals, however, saw an America barren of the institutions of Christian culture that filled the landscape of Europe. During the nineteenth century, as a vast population was pouring west at an alarming speed, evangelicals feared that this population was moving from civilization to barbarism. A whole series of benevolent societies were founded to plant ministers and churches among the western settlers. But it was not only churches that were needed; so too were schools, and evangelicals (particularly Presbyterians and Methodists) established schools and colleges wherever they went. Hundreds of denominational colleges were established, though many were short-lived. In addition, by 1860 there were fifty theological seminaries. Finally, as in Europe, a Bible Society was established (1816) to distribute the Scriptures to all.

The spirit of reform, however, was paramount for American evangelicals. Americans at that time knew their classical history well and recognized that the ancient republics collapsed when their people lost their virtue. Great efforts were made to address the manners and mores of the American people. As already noted, temperance (and eventually total abstinence) was a major concern. In the campaign against alcohol, women played a key role, particularly by the second half of the century. The Women's Christian Temperance Union and its famous president, Frances Willard (1839–1898), worked strenuously to rid the nation of alcohol. Other reforms too were pushed: Sabbath breaking was abjured, and an attempt was even made to prevent mail from being delivered on Sundays. Concern was directed to the plight of prisoners, the mentally ill, and children, and even a Peace Society was organized in 1828. Many American Protestants were convinced that Christ would return only after the way had been paved for him by the establishment of the kingdom of God. All the labors for mission, education, and reform hastened the coming of the kingdom.

The exuberance of nineteenth-century American Christianity occasionally broke the bounds of traditional Christianity. In 1818, William Miller, a Vermont farmer, began to speculate on the return of Christ. Using the King James Bible with Archbishop James Ussher's chronology in the margins (which gave calendar dates to events recorded in the Bible) he predicted the return of Christ in 1843–1844. He published his speculation in 1835 and began to lecture on the subject. By the early 1840s the movement had spread and excitement grew. The nonreturn of Christ (known as The Great Disappointment) did not bring an end to the movement. Rather new visions by Ellen G. White led to the reorganization of the believers as Seventh-day Adventists. Their message included Sabbatarianism and food reform.

Even more radical, and successful, were the Mormons. Joseph Smith (1805–1844), the founder of the Church of Jesus Christ of Latter-day Saints, like Miller was a Vermonter but moved as a boy to upstate New York. There in the early 1820s he received a series of visions (according to believers) of a physical God the Father and Jesus Christ that had nothing to do with the metaphysical persons of the orthodox Trinity. They informed him that all the existing Christian communities were in error. Another vision (of the angel Moroni) said that there existed a hidden book on golden plates that was the "fullness of the everlasting Gospel." This book, when translated by Smith, was published in 1830 as the *Book of Mormon*. The book related a second ministry of Christ after his ascension at Jerusalem to the New World, where members of the lost tribe of Israel eagerly received him and his teachings. There Jesus organized a church directly. The book goes on to tell the story of this church and its eventual destruction. What Smith was to do was to restore this church, thus the meaning of the name Latter-day Saints as well as the Mormon term for non-Mormons, "gentiles."

Early Mormonism not only recast the Trinity and followed "another testament of Jesus Christ" but also reestablished Temple worship and claimed continuing revelation through its "prophet" Joseph Smith. These claims made the movement controversial. So too did Mormon political activities that forced them out of various states before finding a temporary refuge in the new city of Nauvoo, Illinois. The restoration of polygamy in 1843 was even more controversial, and Smith was killed in a mob action in 1844. The community reorganized under BrighamYoung (1801–1877), who led them from Illinois to the Great Salt Lake Basin (1846–1848) and there organized a Mormon kingdom. He also supervised the great missionary endeavors to Scandinavia and Britain.

Mormonism, on account of its polygamy, was seen as a scandal by other Americans. It was not until 1890 that the doctrine was removed by a new revelation. But if polygamy had ended, the missionary impulse had not, and by the early twenty-first century it had become a large international church.

Part of the confidence of American evangelicals in the early decades of the nineteenth century was that they constituted a majority of the nation's population. At the time of the Revolution, America was overwhelmingly a Protestant nation. But beginning in the 1830s, European Catholics migrated in greater numbers, and by the 1840s (due to a failure in the potato crop, particularly in Ireland and Germany) the stream became a torrent. By the 1850s no single Protestant denomination was as large as the immigrant

> Whereas the antislavery cause united British evangelicals, it divided Americans.

Catholic Church. The Catholic presence proved to be a check on the evangelical agenda.

No issue tore apart American Christians like the question of slavery. America was so deeply involved in the slave system that religious life could not help but be affected. Early in the century American evangelicals had organized benevolent societies to address the problem of slavery as they addressed other problems, but no simple answer was available. Whereas the antislavery cause united British evangelicals, it divided Americans. White southern evangelicals defended slavery on scriptural grounds, while many northern evangelicals, inspired by writings such as Harriet Beecher Stowe's *Uncle Tom's Cabin*, attacked the inhumanity of the institution. By the 1830s and 1840s the issue of slavery would divide Presbyterians (1837), Methodists (1844), and Baptists (1844). Slavery also helped forge a particular African American form of evangelicalism. African Americans particularly identified with the experience of ancient Israel in slavery in Egypt, and they saw the heart of the Christian message as deliverance from slavery. The experience of white racism had early on led the free African American community of the North to form their own churches, such as the African Methodist Episcopal Church, and these churches became the centers of the African American communities. Eventually slavery would lead to the splitting of the nation and the Civil War. The institution was abolished as a result of the war, and the union restored, but no religious union came about. American Protestantism became profoundly divided between Northern white churches, Southern white churches, and African American churches.

Questioning Evangelicalism

Evangelical Protestantism was the dominant religious system in Britain, on the Continent, and in America, but it was not without its critics. By the 1830s and 1840s there arose voices within the Protestant churches criticizing the evangelical agenda. For these critics the problem with Pietism and evangelicalism was that the church as a corporate being had largely disappeared in a sea of subjective individualism. In Denmark, Nikolai F. S. Grundtvig attempted to restore dogmatic orthodoxy to the Lutheran Church. He stressed the importance of the Apostles' Creed and called for a renewed understanding of church and sacrament. In Germany, Wilhelm Loehe also labored to revive a church consciousness. His *Three Books of the Church* (1845) called for a revival of the ancient liturgical and sacramental traditions, including private confession and anointing the sick. To maintain the importance of the sacrament, he opposed eucharistic sharing between Lutherans and the Reformed. In America as well, one found critics of the excesses of evangelicalism. Some Episcopalians opposed both revivalism and much of the reform agenda of their evangelical neighbors. Perhaps the most systematic critic of the evangelical excesses in America was John W. Nevin, who attacked both the revival system and the abandonment of traditional Reformed eucharistic teachings.

Nowhere, however, was there a more concerted attack on evangelicalism in the name of the corporate church than in England. The Catholic Revival in the Church of England would transform Anglicanism and impact Christianity as a whole.

The repeal of the laws guaranteeing the place of the Church of England in English society led some to fear for their church's well-being. The suppression of Irish Anglican bishops by Parliament in 1833 roused them to action. From the colleges of Oxford arose a remarkable set of individuals, including John Henry Newman, John Keble, E. B. Pusey, and Hurrell Froude. They and their supporters became known as the Oxford Movement. In a series of pamphlets titled *Tracts for the Times*, they argued that the church was a divine institution, and as such it could not be dictated to by political powers. The essence of the church lay in the apostolic succession that linked it to the apostles and gave to it its authority. The church, they continued, had to reclaim this understanding. In a world rapidly becoming antagonistic to Christianity, the church needed to rest secure on the foundations of the ancient church. Evangelicalism was so bound by individualism and subjectivity that it could offer no protection from the attacks of modernity. Along with the doctrine of apostolic succession (and connected with it the idea of a sacramental priesthood), the Tractarians (as they were also known) called for a restoration of the vision of the early church, an emphasis on the objective work of the sacraments, and a vision of holiness that called for the renewal of many practices long abandoned by Protestants. Like the Romantic writers, they looked fondly at the medieval period as an age of faith.

The attempt to revive Catholic doctrine and practice, though attractive to some, was viewed with suspicion by others. The Tractarians were accused of trying to bring the Church of England back to Rome. In 1841 Newman published "Tract XC [90]," which claimed that the Anglican Articles of Religion (long viewed as a bulwark separating the English church from Rome) could be reconciled with such Roman Catholic teachings as transubstantiation and purgatory. It caused an uproar. Newman joined the Roman Catholic Church in 1845, and more than one hundred clergy and students were to follow him. Newman's conversion, however, did not end the Anglican Catholic revival.

Under the direction of E. B. Pusey, the Catholic movement took root in the urban centers of England. There they practiced their vision of Christianity and enhanced it with a panoply of vestments, rituals, and ceremonies not seen in England since the Reformation. In addition they began to establish religious orders for men and women. The successors of the Oxford Movement claimed that Anglicanism was truly a Catholic religion, hence they were Anglo-Catholics and as Catholic as Roman Catholics or Eastern Orthodox. In their elevation of worship, liturgy, and prayer they were to influence not only Anglicanism but other churches as well.

The Crisis of Faith and the Social Response

The story of Christianity in the West in the nineteenth century cannot stop here. The same 1851 survey of English church life that showed that there were as many Nonconformists as Anglicans worshiping on a given Sunday further noted that there were as many persons absent from worship as present. If the churches were enthusiastically embraced by some, they were rejected by others.

Both intellectual factors (to be discussed in the next chapter) and social forces contributed to this secularization, or de-Christianization. The social transformation of the nineteenth century was creating a new world. Many people who had lived a settled agricultural life now found themselves drawn to urban areas. Long-established customs and patterns of life were disrupted, and religion was one of these patterns. Everywhere one looked, one could see the same pattern: the larger the urban community, the lower the percentage of people going to church.

> Laborers, who were quickly developing class-consciousness, felt that the churches were their enemy. God, it was said, was on the side of the oppressors.

But it was not simply the loss of the familiar that threatened the churches. The new urban industrial world saw great discrepancies of wealth and power. Where industrialism emerged, so too emerged conflict between workers and owners, and the churches seemed all too often to be on the side of the owners. Sometimes it was subtle. The beautiful new churches being constructed with the new wealth seemed inhospitable to working men and women, who felt awkwardly out of place. But often Christian leaders openly supported the owners in time of conflict. Laborers, who were quickly developing class-consciousness, felt that the churches were their enemy. God, it was said, was on the side of the oppressors.

By the 1840s many advocates of labor claimed that the church, and religion itself, was an impediment to progress. None was more influential than Karl Marx. Marx famously wrote, "Religion is the sigh of the oppressed creature, the heart of a heartless world, the soul of a soulless environment. It is the opium of the people." Religion gave comfort to the powerless and allowed them to bear their injustice, and only when it was removed could the proletariat arise. Marx furthermore claimed that the values advocated by the church—meekness, humility, otherworldliness—were all designed to maintain the social status quo and must be rejected.

The fear that the church was losing the working classes, and the sting of critiques like that of Marx, spurred some to address the question of the social order. In England, Charles Kingsley and Frederick Denison Maurice began criticizing the individualism and competition that marked English society and called for a "Christian socialism." As Maurice explained, Christian socialism stood over against "unsocial Christians and unchristian socialists." But it was not just England; all of Western society was at a point of crisis. The world of competition must be replaced by God's order. Maurice and Kingsley were more theoreticians than agents, but Christian socialism would become an important movement, particularly by the end of the century when it began to be taken up by others.

Still another response to the problem of the cities was proposed by William Booth (1829–1912). One of the more colorful figures in nineteenth-century British Christianity, Booth had been converted by Methodists but eventually found them too tame. He founded the Salvation Army and dedicated it to evangelism and social rescue. Taking up the costume and language of the military, the Army ministered to the spiritual and physical needs of the urban underclass. Through the work of Evangeline Booth (1865–1950, daughter of William Booth), the movement also became important in America.

In Germany, the Christian response was much more state oriented and utilitarian in nature. Germany only became a unified nation under Prussian dominance in 1871. Its famous chancellor, Otto von Bismarck—who admired Pietism, despised Roman Catholicism, and feared Marxism—believed that the state must take the lead in advancing Christian values if it was to avoid the Marxist threat. His goal was a centralized state that exemplified Protestant Christian morality. Bismarck's chief religious associate was Adolf Stoecker (1835–1908). A court preacher to the kaiser in Berlin, Stoecker held capitalism to be the worship of mammon. He urged protective labor legislation and social insurance to protect the poor. The laws passed through the efforts of Bismarck, and Stoecker did much to modify the aggressive capitalism then rampant. Stoecker, however, not only condemned capitalism but linked it to Jewish influence, thus coupling a vision of a Christian social order with anti-Semitism.

Bismarck's campaign for a centralized state came to clash with German Catholicism. The German church had controlled education for centuries and had exercised political influence by its own political party. Bismarck attempted to attack Catholic independence and to make the Catholic church subject to the state as German Protestant churches were. The result was the *Kulturkampf* (struggle for civilization) that raged during the 1870s and 1880s. Catholic schools became subject to state inspection, the Jesuits were expelled, and diplomatic relations with the Vatican suspended. The infamous "May laws" of 1873 further wrested clerical education into state hands, claimed a state veto on all episcopal assignments, and circumscribed the power of excommunication. Catholic reaction was swift and opposition to anti-Catholic laws vigorous. As a result a number of prominent Catholic prelates were jailed, and many other bishops and clergy forced into exile. Tensions began to ease by the late 1870s as Bismarck recognized that he had more to fear from Socialists than Catholics, but Jesuits were not allowed to return until 1904.

In America the concern for social Christianity arose in the last decades of the nineteenth century as American Protestants saw their cities becoming places of poverty and class conflict. Various attempts were made to address the problem. An "institutional church" movement called for churches to minister to the bodies as well as the souls of people. Medical dispensaries, gymnasiums, and learning centers became associated with city churches. Novels such as Charles M. Sheldon's *In His Steps* called for the ethic of Jesus to become the governing rule for all society. By the end of the century a social gospel movement developed that called forth Christians to labor for the social betterment of the poor and reform of the society. The most famous representative was Walter Rauschenbusch (1861–1918). Such labors, he argued, were not only good in themselves but could help inaugurate the kingdom of God. Proponents of the social gospel worked along with other progressives, such as Jane Addams of the settlement house movement, to help transform the urban social order.

Catholic Responses

But what about the Catholic Church? What were Catholics doing during these years? The aftermath of the Napoleonic era left Catholics divided over how to respond to the new milieu. Liberals wanted the church to be a creative force in the new social world. The calamities of the revolutionary era stemmed from the church's overly close ties to the old social order. When the order was attacked, the church became a casualty. The church should now reject its old privileges and become more democratic. Furthermore it should adopt the principle of progress. A noted liberal champion was Félicité Lamennais (1782–1854). A French priest, Lamennais believed that the church could flourish only when it became liberated from the state. The Concordat of 1801, which tied the church to the French state, should be rejected. Lamennais strove for a union of Catholicism and liberalism, advocating religious liberty, freedom of the press, universal suffrage, and separation of church and state. He took as the motto of his newspaper "God and Liberty." Lamennais's proposals drew ire from the Catholic establishment. His case was brought before Rome, and in 1832 several propositions drawn from his works were condemned. The condemnation eventually drove Lamennais out of the church, but liberals still hoped for a détente between the church and the age. Conservatives were against any such compromise. The egalitarianism of the age was a threat to a hierarchical church, and the call for religious freedom could lead all too easily to an indifferentism in which a concern for truth was lost. The church, they insisted, must stand as an alternative to a liberal age.

The election of Pius IX as pope in 1846 tipped the scales decidedly in the conservatives' favor. Pius was in many ways the first modern pope, emphasizing the personal role of the papacy as a symbol of Catholicism, but he was also a strong opponent of liberalism. For him the threat of liberalism was not simply theoretical but immediate. In the Italian peninsula—which was divided into countless small states—liberalism was linked to an Italian nationalism that dreamed of a united Italy. Standing in its way, and hence caught in its crosshairs, lay the Papal States. To thwart the threat of liberalism became a key agenda in Pius's long pontificate.

One part of the agenda involved clarifying the church's position concerning the new teachings of the age. In 1864 the *Syllabus of Errors* was published, summarizing the church's rejection of modern ideas and trends. Rationalism and indifferentism were condemned, along with socialism, communism, and Bible societies. The spirit of the document is perhaps best captured by the last thesis on the list: the idea that the "Roman Pontiff can and ought to adjust himself with progress, liberalism, and modern civilization."

The pope's war on liberalism also entailed a clarification of devotion. Pius was a great champion of devotions to the Virgin Mary. In 1854 he had proclaimed the teaching of Mary's Immaculate Conception, or that she was free from original sin. If only to herald the new dogma, in 1858 a peasant girl from Lourdes in France, Bernadette Soubirous, received a series of visions of the Virgin, in one of which Mary proclaimed she was the Immaculate Conception. There a spring appeared from which it was claimed flowed miraculously healing water. The shrine achieved official ecclesiastical approval in 1862. Lourdes quickly became one of the most important pilgrimage sites in Europe.

Perhaps most important, Pius pushed to define the authority of the papacy. Ultramontanism (literally, beyond the mountains), or an emphasis on the authority of the pope, had been formulated by some Catholics during the Napoleonic era. The travail of the revolutionary years had done much to discredit Gallicanism, or the idea that national churches were autonomous. Conservatives began to argue that only an elevated papal teaching office could preserve Catholic truth against the modern world. They got the chance to act on their ideas at the First Vatican Council (1868–1870), called by Pius to address questions of faith and dogma. There the doctrine of papal infallibility was formally defined over the opposition of those who argued that such an elevation of papal power was ill advised. When the pope spoke officially (ex cathedra) on a question of faith or morals, and when he taught from the deposit of divine revelation, his teaching was infallible. The centuries-old debate over the authority of the papacy was finally decided. Some refused to accept the definition, and the Old Catholic Church was formed.

There was, however, an irony in this. As the definition concerning infallibility was being promulgated, the French troops that protected the Vatican from the forces of the Italian nationalists were withdrawn. The Italian peninsula was united, and the pope, who would not accept the confiscation of the Papal States, became a "prisoner of the Vatican" and would not leave the papal residences. This situation would continue until 1929, when a concordat was finally agreed upon between the church and the Italian state. As spiritual authority waxed, political authority waned.

The question of accommodation with modernity was not merely a European debate. In America, Catholics debated how much the church could cooperate with American culture. Could it participate in the public school system? Should it encourage the assimilation of its immigrant members (and risk the loss of their faith) or support the continuation of ethnic identities? By the 1890s American Catholics were divided over these questions. Two wings of the church were clearly discernable: the "Americanists" led by John Ireland, archbishop of St. Paul, and the conservatives led by Michael Corrigan, archbishop of New York. The debate came down to whether the active virtues of humanitarianism and democracy were superior to the passive virtues of humility and submission to authority. In 1898 the Vatican intervened, and the Americanists were rebuked.

Rerum Novarum and Catholic Social Thought

But while Roman Catholicism was hardening its opposition to the social and cultural developments of the nineteenth century, it was also working out a creative answer to the crisis of the industrial order. In this regard Catholics were aided by history: the rise of urban life swept Protestant northern Europe decades before it befell Catholic Europe. Roman Catholics accordingly had crucial time to formulate a response. This took the form of the papal encyclical *Rerum Novarum* by Leo XIII, the successor to Pius IX. The encyclical noted that the present economic crisis pitted unbridled capitalism, which dehumanized workers, against socialism, which subjugated family and property to the state. It was the responsibility of the church to set forth an alternative to both. There was, it continued, an interdependence in society among the different groups, and there needed to be cooperation rather than competition. The state, instructed by the church, must ensure this cooperation and had the further responsibility to protect the rights of the poor. The encyclical called for two specific reforms: Workers should be given the right to associate in trade unions, and a just wage, allowing workers to live in dignity, ought to be established.

The Catholic vision of the just society was an alternative to both capitalism and socialism, and it would be reiterated throughout the twentieth century. In the call for both the right of association and the just wage Leo reached back to the Catholic Middle Ages to criticize the modern economic order. Workers' associations hearkened back to the medieval guilds, and the just wage rested on the idea of natural law as propounded by persons like Thomas Aquinas. The motivating force was not the sense of progress that so captivated many Protestants but the vision of a lost world.

Western Christians hurried throughout the century to labor, preach, and reform. The extent of their endeavors was staggering. How long their accomplishments would last remained to be seen.

Chapter 16

The Great Divide

The historian Henry Adams once observed that a young man coming of age in 1854 stood in all areas of learning except mathematics closer intellectually to the year 0 than the year 1900. The intellectual transformation of the nineteenth century necessarily affected Christianity. At least since the time of Constantine, Christianity had been crucially involved with advances in learning. It had informed philosophy, molded the university, and instructed society in all manner of things. It had been the teacher, and society was its pupil. Now the roles were being reversed.

In part this transformation was a by-product of the expansion of the world. The vast lands of North America were providing all sorts of new geological

> The scientific model assumed that nature was regular and rule bound and that this allowed it to be studied and classified.

information for scientists to consider. Australia, as well, offered strikingly unique examples of flora and fauna that both interested and puzzled students. But there was a trend in the nineteenth century toward the professionalization of areas of learning. The era of the learned amateur—the country parson who liked to collect butterflies and write about his findings—was giving way to the idea that the study of nature had distinctive rules of procedure and categories of evidence. Many of these had been outlined earlier by Francis Bacon in his *Novum Organum*, in which he emphasized that the key to understanding was in determining causality. To advance the study of causality, some scientists proposed the principle of uniformitarianism, the idea that when positing a cause for change, the scientist could only invoke forces of the same nature and degree as could be observed at present. By the 1830s, through the influence of Charles Lyell's *Principles of Geology*, uniformitarianism became an accepted rule for the study of the earth.

Uniformitarianism fit well with scientific presuppositions. The scientific model assumed that nature was regular and rule bound and that this allowed it to be studied and classified. Uniformitarianism pushed this regularity to its logical conclusion. But it posed a problem for Christian thinkers. If nature always followed common rules and was moved by uniform forces, how could one understand divine activity in the world? The laws of conservation of matter and energy proclaimed that neither matter nor energy could be created or destroyed. But if nature were a closed system, how did God enter it? For thousands of years believers had prayed to God for help—for rain in time of drought and healing in time of sickness. Did such prayers make sense anymore?

Darwin and the New Science

The symbol of this new turn in science was Charles Darwin (1809–1882). Darwin successfully brought the principle of uniformitarianism into the study of the biological world, and in doing so he offered an explanation of the development of life that challenged many cherished Christian convictions. Born into a socially prominent household, Darwin at first considered entering the Anglican ministry but decided instead to dedicate his life to science. Much impressed by popular eighteenth-century works of natural theology, which saw in nature a reflection of God's order and plan, he resolved to do a like volume incorporating all the new knowledge about nature. Accordingly, he set sail in 1831 on the HMS *Beagle*, a ship that was to be engaged in a scientific exploration of the world. In the course of the journey Darwin discovered much that destroyed his confidence in the neatly ticking world of the natural theologian. Upon returning in 1836, he began formulating a theory of the transmutation of species. In 1859 this theory was published as *On the Origin of Species*.

Darwin's work rested on the principle of uniformitarianism. Earlier scientists had argued that species were distinct and created directly by God. Darwin provided a new explanation involving evolution. Species changed over time, and one species emerged from another. The mechanism of this evolution was "natural selection": in the competition for limited resources, some creatures, finding themselves better adapted, succeeded while others failed. These successful attributes were passed down to future generations. The shaping of species had nothing to do with direct divine action. It all rested on the law of natural selection.

If this were not enough to trouble traditional believers, Darwin's theory banished from the world two ideas that were primary for the old natural theology. The first was teleology, the assumption that the world reflected the design of God. Darwin argued that there was no master plan; evolution was merely the response to environment. The course of evolution did not move majestically forward like a finely

> Science and religion worked hand in hand in explaining reality. Darwin challenged all this.

crafted ship but was haphazard, inefficient, and wasteful. The second loss was theodicy, the explanation of how a good God could allow evil to exist. Deeply engrained in Christian minds was the belief that the world was fundamentally good, because a good God made it, and that evil ultimately served a greater good. For Darwin, the control factor of existence was competition and destruction; there was no ultimate goodness lying behind it. The world for Darwin, to use the language of the poet Alfred Lord Tennyson, was "nature, red in tooth and claw." Where Darwin's principles triumphed, the world looked like a different place.

Finally, on a most basic level Darwin is reflective of the emerging new consensus that it was scientists who provided knowledge about the nature of the world. From time immemorial, religious figures had claimed an authority vis-à-vis the natural world. The book of Genesis had an account of creation, the origin of evil, and a world-changing flood, and each had been used to explain the world. Even when in the seventeenth century a scientific model began to take shape, great care was taken that no outright contradiction should stand between what the Bible said and what science found. Science and religion worked hand in hand in explaining reality. Darwin challenged all this.

The debate over Darwin has taken on legendary status and has become a crucial part of the telling of the story of the "battle between science and religion." Whether such a "battle" indeed took place is a point of contention among historians, but it is clear that some of the new scientific claims threatened traditional Christian understandings. One of Darwin's supporters, the scientist John Tyndall, argued that before it could be asserted that God had answered a prayer for healing, the case must be tested by scientific methodology to determine whether the prayer had had any effect. The traditional practice of praying for healing or good weather was now scientifically suspect. .

God and History

It was not merely natural science that was changing in ways less conducive to religious claims. Other fields of knowledge were changing as well, none with more explosive consequences than the field of history. The telling of stories about the past is as old as humankind, so in one sense history is endemic to the human experience. But just as natural scientists claimed that by refining their questions and following strict methods they could establish a better picture of the world, so too did students of history claim that with scientific methods they could provide a more accurate picture of the past. Leopold von Ranke, professor of history at the University of Berlin, emphasized the importance of primary sources critically analyzed for their credibility, an objective approach to the material studied, and the importance of psychological penetration in order to capture the past. Although himself a Protestant, Ranke, in his *History of the Popes*, removed the discussion of the papacy from institutional bickering and interpreted the office within the changing structure of European politics. Earlier "history," he suggested, had been more about apologetics and special pleading, but a modern historian should employ a scientific model and strive for objectivity.

Underlying the new historical approach was the same uniformitarianism that had found favor in the natural sciences. History was influenced by such uniform forces as nationalism, economic and social pressures, and the power of ideas, but never by God. God was absent from Ranke's history as well as Darwin's nature.

> From the perspective of the new history, the Bible's claim to accurately represent the past seemed somewhat wobbly.

The problem was that Christianity was tied far more closely to its history than to the natural world. The Bible was a book that claimed to set forth the outline of history from creation to the end of time. In it, God revealed God's truth in history through actors: Abraham, Moses, the prophets, and, most particularly, Jesus. It also recorded God's direct involvement in history: splitting the Red Sea, guiding the Israelites, and turning water into wine. Christians were far more vulnerable to attacks on their history than on any scientific claims. From the perspective of the new history, the Bible's claim to accurately represent the past seemed somewhat wobbly. The discovery of the Rosetta Stone in 1799 allowed scholars to decipher the long-puzzling Egyptian hieroglyphics. They presented a picture of ancient Egypt far different from that found in the book of Exodus. Read from the new historical perspective, some of the stories found in the Old Testament, such as those of Samson and Joshua's holding the sun in the sky, seemed not to pass the test of credibility. Indeed any "nature miracle" in which God affected the physical world must be suspect.

The new history was also leaving its mark on the study of ancient texts. The critical study of ancient literature suggested that works formerly seen as unified had actually been composed out of many separate parts. It was the scholar's task to identify what these sources were in order to establish a better picture of how the work came to be. But if this was the modern approach to ancient texts, how would it shape the understanding of the Bible?

Varied Responses

Nature, history, and the Bible all looked different by the middle decades of the nineteenth century. The claim that Christianity rested on a bedrock of certainty could no longer be assumed. The foundation was shakier. Many of these doubts, to be sure, were not new. Such criticisms had been heard occasionally in the seventeenth century and more frequently in the eighteenth century, but they usually came from outside critics and could be dismissed. But now such questions were being raised by persons within the religious community itself. What response could be offered?

One was to abandon Christianity. Sometimes this involved recasting religion without revelation. In France, Auguste Comte (1798–1857) founded the "religion of humanity" or positivism. History, he argued, moved through stages: from a theological stage where truth was tied to God, to a metaphysical stage where it was tied to philosophy, to the present positivist stage where truth is grounded in the laws of the world as we know it. In the United States, some Unitarians formed the Free Religious Association, which jettisoned both an appeal to revelation and any identification with Christianity. Others found faith to be no longer possible. T. H. Huxley, who defended Charles Darwin against his ecclesiastical critics, coined a term to describe this situation—"agnosticism." The modern person could never know with certainty that God existed. He or she must live in doubt, since to profess belief while having doubt was to dishonor truth. Many poets spoke of the end of the nineteenth century as a time of the general erosion of faith. The words of Matthew Arnold became the song of many:

> Wandering between two worlds, one dead
> The other powerless to be born
> With nowhere yet to rest my head
> Like those on earth I wait forlorn.

One of the most popular novels in the English-speaking world in the last third of the nineteenth century was Mary A. Ward's *Robert Elsmere*, which told the story of a minister losing his faith in a revelation based on miracles and falling into unbelief.

But for others, the challenge of the new knowledge led to a reconceptualization of much of the core of Christianity. The nature of Scripture, the work of theology, the idea of what it meant to be a Christian, and the question of who Jesus was—all became areas of exploration and heated debate.

The attempt to interpret the Bible in light of history while preserving it as a book of faith became the task of many students of Scripture. One obvious implication of the historical method was that older copies of manuscripts were on the whole more reliable than younger ones. For centuries Christians (if they did not merely rely on the Latin Vulgate) assumed the accuracy of the inherited Hebrew text (the Masoretic Text, from the work of Jewish rabbis between the sixth and tenth centuries) and the inherited Greek text (the *textus receptus* compiled by Erasmus from late Byzantine sources). Yet during the course of the early nineteenth century, earlier manuscripts were regularly discovered that called into question the accuracy of the traditional texts. Better texts called for new translations of the Bible, and in England the Revised Version (1881–1885) was published to bring the Bible up to date. Despite the assurance in the *New York Times* that the translators "have not changed the plot," new translations suggested that the Bible was less an unchanging foundation than had been earlier assumed.

Even more significant was the attempt to use the tools of history to examine the biblical texts themselves. The discovery of the Epic of Gilgamesh in the 1880s revealed an earlier nonbiblical account of the flood story that bore strong parallels with that found in Genesis. Scholars began to suggest that repeated biblical stories, such as the two creation accounts, suggested that there may have originally been two separate sources brought together by a later editor. The pattern in the Gospels, in which Matthew and Luke seem to elaborate on Mark while modifying some of the rigorous statements Mark records of Jesus, suggested as well that the Gospels were interrelated and that Mark was the earliest. All these factors led to a movement known as "higher biblical criticism," which proposed a revolutionary understanding of the composition of the Bible. The Pentateuch, the first five books of the Old Testament, was composed from four distinct sources. Some of these were old, but texts elaborating on law and priesthood, these scholars argued, were late. In the New Testament, the oldest Gospel was Mark, and Matthew and Luke had based their Gospels on both Mark and a (now-lost) "Q" text, which was a collection of the sayings of Jesus. The historicity of the Fourth Gospel (John) began to be questioned. But why, others asked, were there multiple Gospels? The German critic F. C. Baur suggested that the Gospels reflected the struggle in the early church between Jews and Gentiles. Matthew, which represented Jesus as the new Moses, was the Gospel of the Jewish Christians. Luke was that of the Gentile Christians, and John was a later synthesis. Baur's ideas were considered radical and were rejected for the moment, but others continued to work to get behind the biblical texts in order to reconstruct the social world that had produced them.

This method of reading the Bible as one read other ancient writings inevitably raised the question of whether there was anything eternal about the Bible. Nineteenth-century Protestant writers (higher biblical criticism was a Protestant endeavor) suggested two places to look. The history of Israel might have been a learning experience in which immature understandings of God were gradually refined, but in the Prophets, with their message of morality and justice, an eternal touchstone could be found. In the New Testament the figure of Jesus became this touchstone. Jesus transcended the ages. Yet since the ultimate confidence was in Jesus, not in the Gospels recording his life, many considered that the task of the scholar was to get behind the Gospels and discover the historical Jesus. Sometimes this took a radical turn. D. F. Strauss in Germany and Ernst Renan in France penned lives of Jesus to argue that his early followers fundamentally misinterpreted him and made him something he was not. The early church had turned a wise man into a supernatural figure. Another radical reading of Scripture was offered by Elizabeth Cady Stanton (1815–1902) and others in *The Woman's Bible* (1895, 1898), in which the higher criticism was used to criticize the biblical picture of women.

A New Theology

By the final decades of the nineteenth century these ideas from evolution, higher biblical criticism, and other intellectual trends came together in a movement known as liberal theology. It gained favor throughout the Protestant world, and despite twentieth-century criticisms, liberal theology still shapes the lives of many Christians in the West. The guiding principle is that God is love, and that Jesus was the manifestation of that true love. God's love is not abstract and abstruse but like that of a loving parent. The German theologian Albrecht Ritschl (1822–1889) made the point most forcefully. God is love, and Jesus is he who brings believers into relationship with God. From this starting point earlier Christian dogmas were reevaluated. Since the Middle Ages the meaning of the death of Christ had been understood as reconciling sinful humanity to God by paying the debt of sin. However, if God is love, the cross could not be a payment of a debt, since no loving parent would ever demand such a thing. Rather it was an example of the sacrificial power of love that revealed God's true nature. Likewise a belief in a final judgment had been foundational to Christianity since the very earliest ages. At that judgment the faithful would be rewarded with heaven, and the sinful would be condemned to hell. But if God is love, love must be the most powerful force in the world. A loving God, it was claimed, would not rest until all persons were reconciled. Hell had no place in true Christianity. The Christ who revealed this God, these writers went on, was not some metaphysical abstraction but a deeply human being. Hence there was a rejection of the Chalcedonian division between Christ's divinity and humanity. Such a Christ did not need miracles to persuade—his very person persuaded—hence, there was a de-emphasis on the miraculous. As the historian Adolph von Harnack explained, Jesus' teaching involved three truths: the kingdom of God, the fatherhood of God and the infinite value of the human soul, and the commandment of love.

> Liberalism saw its task as identifying the permanent kernel of Christian truth and separating it from the transient husk.

Schleiermacher's emphasis on the universality of religion also led to reconsideration of other traditional beliefs. If the religious impulse was inherent in humanity, the process of Christianization ought not to involve introducing a new element but in drawing out a latent religiosity already present. In America, Horace Bushnell in 1847 penned *Christian Nurture* and argued that the nurturing of religion through the institution of the family was a more authentic form of Christian growth than the conversion experience advocated by evangelicals on both sides of the Atlantic. The idea of growth and development in turn made the role of culture more important. A Christian culture brought forth Christian persons. Finally, the idea of a universal religious sentiment allowed some persons to see parallels between Christianity and the other religions of the world. The religious impulse lay at the heart of all religions and in key ways connected them. The religious world was not divided (as it had always been believed) between those who were right and wrong but was filled with peoples in different cultures responding in their way to a common religious impulse. Some might be more advanced (and these persons were sure that Protestant Christianity was the most advanced expression of religion), but all were acting on their innate religious sentiment.

Evolution also contributed to this new theology. Liberal theology not only accepted the idea of evolution but embraced it as the foundation for understanding reality. Darwin was right about evolution; all things did change gradually over time, but Darwin failed to see God's hand in it. God did not intervene actively in either nature or history; nature miracles needed to be rejected. But the path of nature and history was directed by an immanent God, working through the laws of nature. This understanding had theological implications. All doctrines reflected the era in which they were promulgated, and all must develop as the world developed. Liberalism was engaged in this growth. It saw its task as identifying the permanent kernel of Christian truth and separating it from the transient husk.

Finally, the belief in evolution merged with the nineteenth-century confidence in progress to give to liberalism an understanding of what God was doing in the world. Human beings were active agents in bringing about God's will. Their actions would help bring about the promised kingdom of God. But the kingdom was now understood in ethical terms; it would be that time when the world would be governed by the loving teachings of Jesus. The social gospel movement mentioned in the previous chapter was a manifestation of this new liberal belief that human labors could ethically transform the world and bring about God's kingdom.

Roman Catholic Modernism

Protestant liberalism was one way of reshaping Christianity to meet the challenges of the modern world, but it was not the only way. By the 1890s a small group of Roman Catholics also began to call for dialogue with the modern world. Hearkening back to the Middle Ages could not solve the challenge of the age. For Catholic modernism (as the movement came to be known), it was essential that the church, in the words of the English laywoman Maude Petre (1863–1942), "should know how to receive and absorb and direct that swelling tide of thought and action which raises creation to God." There were clear parallels with Protestant liberalism. In Louis Duchesne (1847–1922) one found the use of historical-critical methods to challenge traditional legends long cherished by the church. Alfred Loisy (1857–1940) also took up the cause of higher biblical criticism. He questioned the Mosaic authorship of the Pentateuch and believed that the New Testament was composed from earlier sources. In 1902 Loisy published *The Gospel and the Church*. Although critical of some aspects of Protestant liberalism, particularly an absence of any doctrine of the church, he argued that the key to Christianity lay in development. If the church is a living organism, it must be willing to change. Dogmas that stifle growth must be avoided. The message of Loisy and the other modernists was clear—if the Catholic Church was to have a place in the modern world it had to jettison the defensive and dogmatic attitude it had taken in the nineteenth century.

The Conservative Reaction

But not all Christians could or would go down the path of liberalism and modernism. For them, the older ideas and understandings need to be defended, not modified. And at the same time liberal Christians were calling for reformulation, conservatives were calling for the preservation of the fundamentals of the faith.

An obvious example was Rome's response to Catholic modernism. From early on, modernists found their position precarious. Loisy's writings on Scripture cost him his post as an official Catholic teacher, and *The Gospel and the Church* (along with others of his works) was put on the Index of Forbidden Books. But Pope Leo XIII hesitated to take decisive action against the modernists as a group. His successor, Pius X, had no such hesitation. In 1907 he issued the bull *Lamentabili*, which condemned sixty-five modernist propositions, such as "Divine inspiration does not extend to all Sacred Scriptures so that it renders its parts, each and every one free from error" and "Scientific progress demands that the concepts of Christian doctrine concerning God, creation, revelation, and the Person of the Incarnate Word and Redemption be readjusted." Two months later he issued the encyclical letter *Pascendi*, which condemned "agnosticism and immanentist-evolutionary principles and all theory or dogma and biblical criticism flowing from it." All priests were required to sign an antimodernist oath. With this, modernism ceased to exist (at least publicly) in the Catholic Church. Rome became for decades a bulwark against the liberal agenda.

Within Protestantism the conservative reaction was on the level of both theology and piety. By the last decade of the nineteenth century many voices were raised defending the inherited understanding of the faith and challenging liberal presuppositions. On the Continent, the Dutch politician-theologian Abraham Kuyper (1837–1920) was a vigorous supporter of conservative religion. In the political realm his Anti-Revolutionary Party fought for equal rights for conservatives (both Catholic and Protestant), particularly in the realm of education. The Free University of Amsterdam was established as a bastion for conservative Calvinism. Kuyper also fought liberalizing tendencies within the Dutch Reformed Church and helped organize independent churches. His theology of neo-Calvinism saw God continually influencing the world. In Britain the issue was fought out over loyalty to the traditional creeds. Discomfort with talk of miracles and divine intervention made liberals particularly critical of the claim that Jesus was born miraculously to the Virgin Mary. For them, the virgin birth smacked of ancient myths of gods siring children with mortals; it appeared to make Christ somehow less human. The story, they argued, was a prescientific age's attempt to explain the unique relationship between Jesus and God the Father. But the doctrine of the virgin birth had a prominent place in the ancient creeds, and conservatives such as Charles Gore (1853–1932), a leading Anglo-Catholic, argued that candidates for the priesthood who could not affirm the creeds should not be ordained.

But the central field of contention was the Bible itself. Although there were in Germany some writers who opposed the new higher criticism, such as E. F. Hengstenberg (1802–1869), on the whole it was accepted. Its reception in the English-speaking world was more critical. When it was introduced to England in 1860 (in the volume *Essays and Reviews*), it was roundly condemned. By century's end higher criticism found gradual favor there, although modified and stripped of its more radical claims. In America, however, an alternative position developed. The center of conservative Protestant teaching was Princeton Theological Seminary, and there a remarkable series of Presbyterian theologians fought a vigorous campaign to defend the truthfulness of Scripture and the objectivity of the Christian faith. They walked a fine line—admitting that the Bible contained human and historical elements (since inspiration, for them, did not overpower the biblical writers), while still claiming that divine inspiration guaranteed the inerrancy of the text. In contrast to the liberal claim that the Bible was fallible in its words and only inspired in its spirit or thrust, the Princeton theologians claimed that the Bible was fully inspired down to the level of the words. The position came to be known as the Hodge-Warfield doctrine, named for its authors Archibald A. Hodge (1823–1886) and Benjamin B. Warfield (1851–1921). The question of the nature of biblical inspiration was bitterly debated in many circles of American Protestantism. Conservative advocates also took care to defend doctrines such as the virgin birth and the penal or substitutionary doctrine of the atonement, which liberals were rejecting.

But it was on the level of piety that the strongest antiliberal work was done. As liberals were calling on Christians to enact Christ's moral vision and thus bring about the kingdom of God, conservatives began to preach and teach a very different view of the future. Biblical prophecy, they argued, showed a future marked not by progress but by crisis. The world was heading ineluctably to a great crisis, and only at that point would Christ return to establish the kingdom of God. This teaching was known as premillennialism (since Christ was to come before the thousand-year reign of the kingdom of God), in contrast to the earlier teaching of postmillennialism. Although such speculations may seem abstruse, they had major consequences. Postmillennialism offered a vision of hope for the future and encouraged reform, since reform would bring the kingdom closer. For premillennialists, the kingdom would be brought about not by reform, or any other human action, but by Christ's supernatural intervention. The Bible teacher C. I. Scofield did much to popularize the teaching of premillennialism, particularly through the publication of the *Scofield Reference Bible*.

A concern for the end times could lead to even more radical claims. An expectation of the imminent return of Christ, as we have seen, led to the founding of the Seventh-day Adventists in the mid-nineteenth century. Another Adventist group, the Jehovah's Witnesses, also emerged at the end of the century. Both groups predicted an imminent return of Christ and advocated that those who did not accept this belief should be rejected. Both also saw the message of Christ's coming as a call to separate from the political powers of the larger society.

But perhaps the most important conservative movement, and one that would have great impact on twentieth-century Christianity, was the revival of interest in the "gifts of the Spirit" found in Paul's First Letter to the Corinthians. It had long been assumed that these "charismatic gifts" had passed away and that healing, prophecy, and speaking in tongues were no longer part of the church. But during the last quarter of the nineteenth century, many questioned whether this assumption was true. During the 1870s a strong interest awakened among Protestants in divine healing, and a great international conference on the subject was held in London in 1885. Indeed, an interest in religion and healing led to the emergence of still another religious movement from the fruitful soil of America: Christian Science. Founded by Mary Baker Eddy, Christian Science brought healing back into Christian consciousness as it had not been for fifteen hundred years. Unlike most persons interested in divine healing, who saw healings as modern miracles, Mary Baker Eddy believed that healing came about through the illusions of sin and sickness.

Pentecostalism would become a major force in the Christianity of the Southern Hemisphere. Its focus on the direct connection between the Holy Spirit and the individual made it an ideal religion to transcend cultures.

By the 1890s there also arose among American Protestants an interest in the "gift of tongues." The speaking of either a known language by a person ignorant of it (xenoglossia) or of an unknown language (glossolalia) was claimed to be the biblical mark of one truly baptized in the Spirit. The modern Pentecostal movement was born on the first day of the first month of the twentieth century (January 1, 1901) in a small Bible school in Topeka, Kansas. There Charles Fox Parham and his students began to speak in tongues. The movement quickly spread and gained international publicity four years later in the Azusa Street revival (Los Angeles, California) under William J. Seymour. Throughout the decades it continued to spread. The doctrine of the Spirit, Pentecostals professed, allowed for a greater role for female leadership than in traditional churches. Women such as the Canadian-born Aimee Semple McPherson (1890–1944) played a major part in spreading the Pentecostal message.

Pentecostalism would be important for two reasons. If it gained popularity in the United States and other Western societies, it would through the course of the twentieth century take on even greater importance in the non-Western world. It would become a major force in the Christianity of the Southern Hemisphere. Its focus on the direct connection between the Holy Spirit and the individual made it an ideal religion to transcend cultures. It attracted large numbers of people from all races. It was particularly attractive to those on the margins of society. By the end of the twentieth century there would be more Pentecostals worldwide than traditional Protestants.

A second importance of Pentecostalism is that no group contrasted more dramatically with liberalism. Liberals avoided miracles and wonder; Pentecostals proclaimed them. Liberals believed that God spoke in a whisper through culture; Pentecostals believed that God created new voices. Liberals argued that the church should be open to the spirit of the age; Pentecostals claimed that we were living in the age of the Spirit. In the twentieth century these two divergent tendencies would become competing models of Christianity.

However, formal division still lay in the future. Unlike Roman Catholicism, whose hierarchy could sharply distinguish itself from liberalism, the decentralized polity of Protestantism did not allow for such neat demarcations. Liberal-leaning and conservative-leaning believers continued to coexist in the same churches for decades. Indeed, many found themselves awkwardly in the middle, uncomfortable with either extreme. But new shapes of Christianity had formed, and over time they would help bring about the collapse of the Latin interlude.

Chapter 17

The "Great Century"

*T*he great twentieth-century historian of missions, Kenneth Scott Latourette, christened the nineteenth century the "Great Century." Whereas he could cover the expansion of Christianity between 500 and 1500 in a single volume, it took him three large volumes to treat the nineteenth century, for, he observed, Christianity expanded in those years as it had not done since the age of the apostles. The spread of Christianity was tied to the expansion of European influence. By the end of the century virtually no part of the inhabitable world was outside of the European sphere. European ideas, products, and principles triumphed everywhere, and Christianity was part of this phenomenon. The missionary impulse inspired much of the spirit of the times. Hymns such as Reginald Heber's, whose famous first line proclaimed, "From Greenland's icy mountains, from India's coral strand" bespoke the general hope and confidence. Yet amid the activity, the complications noted in earlier chapters also surfaced in the great missionary endeavor. What was essential in Christianity, and what should be exported? What should Christianity be outside Christendom, and what was the relationship between Christianity and Christendom?

The Heritage of Nineteenth-Century Missions

The great nineteenth-century missionary movement has not sat well among succeeding generations. Particularly during much of the twentieth century, it was seen as a failed endeavor, devoid of sensitivity to other religions and cultures. Worse, it was viewed as the handmaid and stalking horse for imperialism. "From Greenland's Icy Mountains" became less seen as the anthem of the movement, and Rudyard Kipling's poetic text "Take up the White Man's burden / Send forth the best ye breed / Go bind your sons to exile / To serve

227

the captives' need" was seen as a more accurate description. Even more than with the expansion of Christianity in the sixteenth and seventeenth centuries, the missionary movement of the nineteenth century has been seen and condemned as a tool of Western imperialism.

Yet there is ambiguity and irony in the historical record, and the identification of Christianization and imperialism is complicated. For example, when Christianity was brought to western Africa in the late 1700s by "Western Christians," the missionaries were not officers of the British Empire but freed black slaves. During the American Revolution, evangelical Christianity had struck a deep chord among those slaves who had abandoned their American masters to fight along with the British. After the war the former slaves settled in Nova Scotia. Sponsored by the English abolitionist Granville Sharpe, they agreed to become missionaries to Sierra Leone. As they arrived in 1792, they marched ashore singing a favorite hymn: "Awake and sing the song of Moses and the Lamb." The Christians of Sierra Leone quickly became active not only in building their community but in sharing their faith with other Africans, and in the early part of the nineteenth century they became the most successful missionaries in West Africa. Not until years later did the settlement become a colony of the British crown.

Contrast this picture with what was happening at the same time in India. In 1793 when an English Protestant missionary reached India after a harrowing voyage, he was shocked to discover that the British colonial government did not grant resident permits to missionaries. The policy of the ruling East India Company was to thwart missionary endeavors so as not to create disturbances among the native populations. Such tensions were bad for business. Missionaries were free to function only in areas not under British control. It was not until 1813 that, through the pressure of English evangelicals led by William Wilberforce, Parliament changed the charter of the East India Company and secured a place for missionaries. Thus one finds freed American slaves evangelizing Africans while British officials worked diligently to exclude Christian activity. The nineteenth-century expansion was more complicated than it seemed. Although the missionary activities were inextricably linked with European imperial expansion, and with it the subordination of native cultures, one can find many similar instances of indigenous communities taking an active part in evangelization and of Western imperial officials showing ambivalence about what their policy toward missionaries should be.

A further complication was that the expansion was fueled not merely by Western Christians; during these years Russian Orthodox missionaries carried their faith eastward, along with the expanding Russian Empire. They evangelized Asian Siberia, Alaska, and the west coast of North America to what is now San Francisco. In Asia the spread of Christianity occurred through both migration and mission. Millions of European Russians resettled in Siberian Russia (some voluntarily, others not) in the second half of the nineteenth century. Likewise, missions such as that of Archpriest Gregor Sleptsoff were established to minister to the non-Christian population. In the area between the Urals and Lake Baikal, villages were established for the new converts. The mission to the native peoples of Kodiak Island in Alaska, beginning in 1794, was also successful. Monks were the chief instruments of these missionary endeavors, and monks also did important work in China and Japan.

The surging Western interest in missions was largely tied to the evangelical revival. Although in the eighteenth century Moravian missionaries were at work in India, by the turn of the century many others were taking up the cause. The London Missionary Society was founded in 1795, the Netherlands Missionary Society in 1797, the Church Missionary Society in 1798, the American Board of Commissioners for Foreign Missions in 1810, the Basel Missionary Society in 1815, and many others would follow. Catholic missionary activity in the nineteenth century would largely pass out of the hands of the Spanish and Portuguese and into those of the French.

India

Of the great mission fields, India was the first to receive systematic attention. The eighteenth century had witnessed a great deterioration of the Indian Christian community, particularly its Roman Catholic segment. During these years, according to some estimates, the Roman Catholic community declined from two million to under five hundred thousand, and many of these Catholics knew little about their faith. The suppression of the Jesuits and the peculiar political structure of the Indian church both proved detrimental. Without the Jesuits, the mission field was robbed of its most dedicated clergy, and the old *padroado* system, under which Portugal maintained strict control of the Indian church, stymied change. The revival of Indian Catholicism would come about only with the end of the *padroado* system and the subsequent mission work by religious orders such as the revived Jesuits, Benedictines, Salesians, and Oblates of Mary Immaculate.

But more dramatic was the growth of Protestantism. Protestant personnel and resources from Britain, the Continent, and America poured into south Asia. Groundwork was laid not only by the Moravians but also by the "English chaplains," clergy of the established Church of England hired by the

East India Company to minister to its employees. Inspired by the evangelical spirit, some began to see it as their responsibility to preach to the native populations as well. David Brown (1762–1812), one such chaplain, inspired many, and his letters back to England led to the formation of the Church Missionary Society, which would be the leading English missionary society. Henry Martyn (1781–1812) was another key figure. A fellow of St. John's College, Cambridge, he was inspired to give up his academic position for the mission field. In his diary he wrote, "Now let me burn out for God." His prayer was granted, but before his death at age thirty-one, he taught himself Hindustani and translated the New Testament and the Book of Common Prayer. Ill health forced him to leave India, but on his way to England he stopped in Persia, where he learned that language and translated the New Testament and the Psalms. There he died, a candle burned at both ends for the sake of sharing the Christian message.

It was, however, William Carey (1761–1834) who inaugurated a new era in mission. Some have called him the father of the modern missionary movement. A shoemaker turned Baptist preacher, Carey became convinced that Christianity needed to grow beyond the confines of Christendom. In 1795 he set out on a mission to India. Denied the right to settle in Calcutta by the East India Company, he took up residence in the Danish settlement of Serampore. There, along with two other colleagues (they were known as the Serampore trio), he began his labors. Progress was slow, and they quickly realized that success would depend on native evangelists. In Serampore, Carey began two endeavors that would characterize nineteenth-century Protestant labors in India. The first, as has already been seen in the case of Henry Martyn, was a determination to put the Bible into the language of the people. Working with native speakers, Carey proceeded to translate the New Testament (and other Christian literature) into more than thirty of the various languages of the Indian subcontinent. The second was social reform, particularly a campaign against *sati*. Hindu custom dictated that widows join their husbands' funeral pyres. If they balked, the community was expected to force them. Carey found the practice horrible and labored for twenty-six years to have it outlawed. The British government long hesitated to interfere in local religious practices but finally in 1829 passed an edict of prohibition. When it was sent to Carey (because of his linguistic prowess) to be translated, he jumped at the opportunity, even (perhaps for the first time in his life) missing Sunday church worship. As he explained, "If I delay an hour to translate and publish this, many a widow's life may be sacrificed." The translation was done within the day.

A concern for education and a concern for the rights of women would mark nineteenth-century missionary labors. Representatives of the Church of Scotland led the way in education. Alexander Duff (1806–1882), the first foreign missionary of that church, quickly concluded that the key to missionary success lay in education. Western ideas, he argued, would wean Indians away from their old faiths in a far more effective and less threatening way than direct proselytization. Instruction should be in English, he insisted, since that language better conveyed the new ideas. His school combined education in science and religion. Supported by influential Hindus, Duff's school attracted the highest level of Hindu society. He also founded a medical school and hospital in Calcutta. Duff's school was so successful that the British Raj would use it as a model for other schools. Westernization and Christianization went hand in hand.

> By the end of the nineteenth century, the literacy rate for Indian Christian women was ten times higher than the national average for women. Missionaries also fought against prostitution and early marriages for women; they labored against polygamy and defended the right of widowed women to remarry.

Duff also pressed hard for schools for Indian women, who had never had a place in formal education. Success was dramatic. By the end of the century, the literacy rate for Indian Christian women was ten times higher than the national average for women. Missionaries also fought against prostitution and early marriages for women; they labored against polygamy and defended the right of widowed women to remarry. One of the most famous Indian Christian women was Pandita Ramabai (1858–1922). Born into the Brahmin caste, she was learned in both Sanskrit and Hindu. Widowed at a young age, she became attracted to Christianity and was baptized in 1883, whereupon she dedicated herself to the well-being of Indian women. She established a home for widows, a school for orphaned girls, and other institutions. Her works attracted support from around the world.

British policy became more sympathetic to missionaries after the 1857 mutiny of the Sepoy (native Indian troops under British command). With the suppression of the mutiny, India became ruled directly by the crown. Although still technically neutral on religion, the new administration created an order that allowed missionaries to flourish. This resulted in a rapid increase in Christianity during the second half of the nineteenth century. As had been the case in the sixteenth century, those at the bottom of the caste system, the untouchables (i.e., the Panchamas or Dalits), and those ethnic tribes that had never been incorporated into the caste system became the most eager converts. A mission to the Nadars of Tamilnado (which itself was led by an outcaste) established a strong Christian community there. Successful also was a mission to the tribes of Chola Nagpur. A mission to the Dalit community in Telugu also led to mass conversion.

Still another aspect of late nineteenth-century Protestant missionary activities was the growing presence of women. In the last two decades of the century the number of women missionaries increased two and a half times. Women proved to be much better missionaries to other women than were men. Female medical missions also developed, and these also became very effective. As one person noted, "The quickest way to break the barriers into the zenanas [or the women's quarters in Indian homes] is by neither evangelism nor education but by healing the sick. Then education and evangelism will follow." At first the female medical missionaries were amateur nurses, but with Ida Scudder (1870–1960), professional female medical practice became available.

By century's end Christian missionaries could survey their progress. The Christian community now numbered 2,735,000 members. Over the century the number of Catholics doubled while that of Protestants increased fivefold, and Christians made up almost 2 percent of the Indian population.

The missionaries and teachers had shared the heritage of the Christian West, but the results were ambiguous. Rammohun Roy (1772–1833), who had befriended Alexander Duff in his attempt to create schools, ultimately did not use the new knowledge brought by the missionaries to abandon Hinduism but rather to reform it. His Bramo Samaj movement emphasized the fundamental monotheism of Hinduism (Brahman was the reality above all gods) and called for reforms such as the prohibition of child marriage and polygamy, which had been attacked by the missionaries. Roy illustrated that one need not become a Christian to benefit from the new teachings and insights. Other reformers (also responding to the missionary challenge) called for Hinduism to return to its roots and purify itself to better stand up against Christianity. Finally, the spirit of nationalism that was so much a part of nineteenth-century European culture could not for long be kept out of India, and Indian nationalists began to chafe against both British rule and its Christian religion.

Advance in East Asia

India may have been the "jewel in the crown" of the British Empire, but it was the Far East, particularly China and Japan, that were the great attraction for visionaries of Christian expansion in Asia. The size of their populations, the antiquity and refinement of their cultures, and the fact that both had for a millennium fascinated Western Christians made these lands the great target for missionary endeavor.

As we saw in chapter 12, Catholic Christianity flourished in Japan in the sixteenth and seventeenth centuries, only to be crushed as an alien movement by the Tokugowan shoguns. It had seemingly long disappeared when Commodore Matthew Perry sailed his four American ships into what is now Tokyo Bay. He represented the American government and desired the opening of Japan to the West. The ruling powers were impressed by his technology and his guns, and a debate resulted over how to respond. Some urged a continuation of the policy of isolation, but reformers argued that the future of Japan lay with Western progress. By 1868 the old shoguns were swept aside, and the new Menji emperors pushed the nation toward reform.

The new openness to the West reopened the question of Christianity, still legally branded as "the detestable sect." Russian Orthodox, Roman Catholics, and Protestants all attempted to establish missions. The Russian Orthodox focused on the northern island of Hokkaido, and a small Orthodox church was organized. Roman Catholicism reentered when France and Japan established a treaty of commerce in 1858. Catholics had long been eager to return to Japan and in fact had an informal missionary presence as early as 1846. In 1860 a Catholic chapel was opened in the port city of Hakodate, the first Christian house of worship erected in Japan since 1614. In 1863 Roman Catholic priests reentered the old Christian stronghold of Nagasaki, and soon, to their amazement, Japanese began to come to them who had secretly kept the faith in the face of persecution for almost 250 years. These "hidden Christians" testified to the power of faith against persecution and reinvigorated Catholic efforts in Japan. But the resurfacing of these Christians also rekindled anti-Christian persecution.

It was not until 1873 that the last anti-Christian edicts were lifted, and Christian growth began in earnest. Much of the growth was within the Protestant communities. Americans were actively involved in the mission to the Japanese, but many of the greatest accomplishments were through the work of Japanese converts. The displaced samurai class was the group most open to receiving the new faith. Samurai students came together to form what later became known as the student Christian "bands." These societies produced important Christian leaders, such as Niijima Jo, who would found Doshisha University, the oldest and most famous of the Japanese Christian universities.

During the 1880s there was some speculation that Japan might become a Christian nation. Christianity was viewed as the wave of the future and the channel of scientific and technological advance. Furthermore, it was the ticket into Christendom, or the society of Europe and America. One of the leading figures in New Japan, Fukuzawa Yukichi, the educator and founder of Keio University, had earlier opposed Christianity but by the 1880s urged his compatriots to adopt Christianity so as to join the great nations of the world. He had little interest in religion per se, and his comments were largely political in nature, but they reflected the surging interest in Christianity and all things Western. By the 1890s, however, the interest in Christianity began to ebb. The nationalism and suspicion of outsiders that had doomed the earlier Portuguese efforts began to curb Christian growth again. Western scientific knowledge continued to be valued, but Western cultural institutions, including the churches, became suspect. Increasingly the task of westernization was removed from foreign missionaries and taken up directly by the imperial Japanese government. In response, some Japanese Christians attempted to distance themselves from the foreign missionaries. In 1901 Kanzo Uchimura founded the *Mukyokai* or "No Church" movement, which stressed the Japanese nature of the faith. As he wrote in a celebrated poem, "I love two *J*s and no third; one is Jesus and the other is Japan." By the beginning of the twentieth century Japanese Christians represented only about 1 percent of the population. Because of the high proportion of educated and professional people who were Christian, the influence of this group would be greater than its numbers, but the missionary dream of a Christian Japan would never materialize.

The Challenge of China

China was the great prize, but it would be no easy one. China possessed no depressed and marginal classes like India to provide an eager audience for Christian evangelization. Confucianism was more consistently supported by the emperor and lined up against Christianity than was Hinduism in India. There was no British Raj to protect missionaries. The eighteenth-century Catholic malaise had also weakened Chinese Christianity even more than it had other Asia churches. Well into the 1840s no missionary could legally reside in the land, so by 1800 there were a mere 187,000 Christians in all of China. Finally, a wave of persecutions between 1805 and 1811 virtually ended the two-hundred-year connection of Catholic missionaries to the imperial court.

A new era of missionary activity began in 1807 with the arrival of the British Protestant missionary Robert Morrison (1782–1834). Denied passage east by the antimissionary East India Company, Morrison sailed west to America and from there made the long journey to the Chinese port of Guangzhou (Canton), the only port then open to foreigners. Although missionary activity was outlawed, Morrison soon found three Chinese Catholic priests secretly at work, even though they knew that if found they would suffer strangulation. For two years Morrison kept a low profile and learned the native languages from a Chinese student. This too was dangerous, for Chinese subjects were forbidden, under pain of death, to teach their language to foreigners. Morrison's mastery of Chinese (both Mandarin and Cantonese) soon allowed him to translate first the New Testament and eventually the entire Bible, and to compose both a Chinese grammar and Chinese-English dictionary.

> The cost of the success of Christian missions in China was high: Christianity was firmly linked to foreign oppressive power

Morrison eventually concocted a plan to get around the rigid antimissionary legislation. Outside of China there was a large Chinese diaspora. Among these populations missionaries could learn the language, do translation work, and establish Chinese-speaking Christian communities. This became known in missionary circles as the Ultra Ganges Mission. Morrison was helped by another British missionary, William C. Milne.

With the end of the Napoleonic wars, a trickle of missionaries to the East began—both Catholic and Protestant—but until the 1840s they faced fierce opposition and made few gains. The situation changed through one of the most shameful of episodes in the East-West encounter. To pay for its trade with China, Britain insisted on bringing in opium and selling it to the Chinese. The emperor (and many of the missionaries) denounced the practice. The result was the first Opium War (1839–1844), which was followed by a second war (1856–1860). The British were triumphant in both. As a result, China lost control of its borders. Both opium and Christianity could now pass freely into the forbidden empire. As a result of the first war, five ports were opened, and foreigners were able to study Chinese and build houses, schools, and churches. The second war resulted in the right of foreigners to travel legally outside of the treaty ports, and Christians were granted protection and freedom of worship. A new period of Christian expansion now began. The cost, however, was high: Christianity was firmly linked to foreign oppressive power.

Imperial anti-Christian policy had always been political in nature; Christianity was feared as a threat to the stability of the empire. These fears at times materialized, never so vividly as in the Taipei Rebellion (1851–1864). The central figure in the rebellion was Hong Xiuquan. After failing the examination for entrance into the imperial civil service, a dispirited Hong discovered tracts written by an early Chinese Christian convert. He became convinced that a vision he had earlier received, of an old man with a gold beard and an "elder brother," had been a vision of Jehovah and Jesus. The elder brother also called him to bind and whip Confucius (whose teachings informed both the imperial civil service and the exam Hong had failed). Baptizing himself, he began to preach and attract converts. He soon proclaimed that God and Christ had appointed him "Taiping" and commanded him to cleanse China of its sins, expose the errors of Confucius, unseat the emperor, and proclaim himself the new emperor. Christians were unsure what to make of him. Early on, Hong went to Canton and studied with a Baptist missionary, who however refused to baptize him, believing his faith was too unformed. But some Christians, including many Westerners, viewed his cause as divinely inspired. He and his followers captured the ancient city of Nanjing, and for more than ten years Hong and his followers controlled a large part of the Chinese empire. Hong's teachings were, in the words of one scholar, "an explosive mixture of Bible truth, Chinese mythological fantasy, and imperial egocentricity." In Nanjing, adultery, the repeated use of tobacco, and ignorance of the Ten Commandments all became capital offenses. In 1864 the rebellion was finally put down—ironically, with the help of British troops under the command of the devoutly evangelical general C. G. Gordon.

The opening up of the interior of China pushed the missionary endeavor into high gear. Catholic missions were under the protection of France, and numerous religious orders, both male and female, came to China to labor. In addition to preaching, Catholic missionaries stressed the importance of the corporal works of mercy. During periods of famine they administered poor relief, though they often required catechetical instruction in order to get it. They established orphanages for the many abandoned children and homes for the aged. Roman Catholics placed a lower priority than did Protestants on the role of education in evangelization. Catholic schools were primarily for believers, and advanced education focused on raising up an indigenous priesthood. In this concern for creating a native clergy they were relatively successful, and the number of Chinese priests increased from 148 in 1848 to 721 in 1912.

Protestant missionary activity by the last quarter of the century was beginning to reflect conservative/liberal divisions within the Protestant churches concerning the nature of Christianity. The more conservative approach can be seen in the China Inland Mission, under the direction of J. Hudson Taylor. China Inland Mission flowed from the great traditional evangelical heart of Protestantism, and it was confined to no one denomination. Taylor, born into a devout British evangelical household, from early childhood dedicated himself to the cause of Chinese Christianity. He first entered China in 1853, when he learned the language and gathered a small community. Discouraged and in ill health, he returned to Britain in 1860. The thought of a handful of Protestant missionaries toiling in such a vast land (in 1865 there were only ninety-one missionaries in China) troubled him. To arouse concern, he published in 1865 *China's Spiritual Need and Claims*, and in the same year he founded China Inland Mission.

China Inland Mission was distinctive in a number of ways. It was undenominational. Any sincere evangelical could serve as a missionary. It was international. Although drawing most of its support from Britain, the British dominions, and America, it had supporters throughout the Protestant world. It was organized as a faith mission. Funds were not solicited nor debt permitted; God was trusted to supply all needs. Missionaries were required to conform to the social and living conditions in China. They were expected to blend in. Finally, its aim was not to establish churches, or even make converts, but to spread the gospel quickly and then move on. Others, it was maintained, could gather the fruit. The CIM (as it came to be known) grew to become the largest missionary society at work in China.

Other Protestants stressed a different course of action. They believed that the key to Christianization lay in modernization, and in this regard education was key. It could transform in a way that simple preaching could not. A leading representative of this approach was the Welsh Baptist Timothy Richard (1845–1919). After the devastating famine of the 1870s he urged the introduction of Western science, and he claimed that the best way to propagate Christianity was to create Christian colleges in the capitals of each of the provinces. Although his plan never materialized, a Christian college movement did emerge in the 1880s. In 1891 Richard became secretary of what would become the Christian Literature Society, which attempted to introduce China to the best of Western civilization. Like Matteo Ricci centuries earlier, Richard became the confidant of many powerful and important Chinese leaders.

For people like Richard, China was at a crossroads. The old imperial system was on its last legs, and the Christian West was in a unique position to influence China's future. The continuing opposition to Christianity and the Western presence was witnessed in the Boxer Rebellion (1899–1901), in which scores of missionaries and thousands of native Christians lost their lives. Nevertheless the hope of a new China, integrated into Christendom, shone bright. Through their strategic role in education, Protestants (although numerically far fewer than Roman Catholics) believed they could shape

China's future. Particularly in the years from 1905 to 1914, when China took great steps toward modernization—indeed, overthrowing its emperor and replacing him with a republic headed by a devout Methodist (Sun Yat Sen)—Protestants believed that the future of China belonged to them. In addition to schools and colleges, hospitals were built. Between 1895 and 1914 most of the best schools and a large majority of the Western hospitals and medical schools were run by Protestant missionaries. In addition, the YMCA (Young Men's Christian Association) became an important institution, shaping the hearts and minds (as well as the bodies) of China's future leadership. In contrast to Roman Catholics, who stressed building churches, and evangelical Protestants, who focused on conversion, these Protestants envisioned a cultural revolution, inspired by a liberal Protestant ideal that would influence China as a whole. Enlightened Christian ideals emanating from Christian-trained elites would transform the nation.

The Exceptionalism of Korea

As we shall see, these great hopes were to prove ephemeral and ultimately embarrassing. Here the contrast with Korea could not be greater. China was the great prize for all; Korea was a minor peninsula of little importance. Korea had scarcely any place in the great missionary dream of a Christian Asia. Indeed, it was Korean converts and not foreign missionaries who brought Christianity to Asia at the end of the eighteenth century. According to tradition, Lee Seung-hoon was baptized in Beijing and returned to Korea to spread the (Catholic) Christian faith. Roman Catholic missionaries occasionally arrived, but persecution was great. The Christian community suffered persecution in 1801, 1815, 1827, 1839, and 1846, and most cruelly in 1866–67 when more than two thousand were killed. Only as a result of trading treaties with Western powers did the situation eventually ease.

In 1884 Protestants established their first permanent mission. The missionary, the American Horace N. Allen, was also a physician, and he had the good fortune to heal the wounded son of the king. He was rewarded by permission to open a Royal Hospital, the first public building in Korea under Christian control. Christian growth over the next decade was modest, but in 1894 there was a political change that would have great religious significance. The Sino-Japanese war of 1894–95 put Korea under Japanese control. The national despair at falling under colonial rule (though officially colonial rule would not commence until 1910) created an anger that was directed not against the Christian West but against Japan. Conversely, the small Christian community became a rallying point for hope in the face of defeat. Almost immediately, mass conversions began to occur. Through the labors of people such as Samuel A. Moffett (1864–1939) and countless Korean Christians themselves, Korea started a path that would eventually make it, along with the Philippines, the most Christianized nation in Asia.

Africa, Colonization, and Christianity

Two factors are preeminent when the story of Christianity in Africa during the "Great Century" is considered. The first is colonization. During the course of the nineteenth century Europeans carved up Africa in a way that left independent only Liberia on the west coast and Ethiopia in the east. France, Belgium, Germany, Italy, Britain, and Portugal competed as to who would get the greater part of the vast continent. Each nation brought its own religious policy and preference. The second factor is a difference between Sub-Saharan Africa and Asia: in Africa religious life was far less systematically developed than in much of Asia. There were no great religions with elaborate philosophical systems to match the Hinduism, Buddhism, Shinto, and Confucianism that in Asia provided organized opposition to Christian missionaries. Indeed, by the end of the century the folk religions of Africa began to collapse under the weight of Christianity and Islam. Yet here also lay an ironic twist of fate: the absence of formal religious opposition would allow for a blending of older African religious practices and Christianity in a way not seen in other mission fields.

Colonization did not benefit the old Christian churches of Africa. The ancient Coptic Church complained bitterly that when the British assumed control over Egypt, they kept Copts out of high office, made them work on Sunday and rest on Friday, and taxed them for schools in which Islam was taught, all to placate the Muslim majority. Ethiopia throughout the century confronted Protestant and Roman Catholic missionaries trying to push the ancient church's loyalties in one direction or the other, and, by the end of the century, Italian military forces attempting to incorporate Ethiopia into its African empire.

> The Western missionary campaign in Africa raised anew the question of the relationship between Christianity and Western culture.

Nor in the long run did colonization benefit the independent churches planted by Sierra Leone missionaries. Sierra Leone had been the center of

African-to-African mission in West Africa. But the church there belonged to two worlds. It was thoroughly sympathetic with England. It was said to be "more English than the English themselves," but it was also part of a native African culture. At first this combination proved advantageous. The West African climate proved deadly to white European missionaries, so Africans led their church in a way unlike other areas of the continent. A Yoruban (or west Nigerian) African, Samuel Crowther (ca. 1809–1891), was ordained a priest in the Church of England in the early 1840s and by 1864 was made the first African-born bishop in Anglicanism. The establishment of an African hierarchy led some at the time to advocate the "euthanasia" of Western missions and the transference of authority to independent African communities. For more than twenty-five years Crowther labored in his missionary responsibilities, only to be summarily demoted at the end of his career. As West Africa was more integrated into the British Empire, white clergy assumed a greater role, and the idea of a black African representing the imperial church was no longer acceptable. There would be no more black bishops until the twilight of the era of colonialism.

The Western missionary campaign in Africa raised anew the question of the relationship between Christianity and Western culture. Johannes T. van der Kamp (1747–1811), a Dutch missionary working for the London Missionary Society in South Africa, caused a scandal by suggesting that converts need not adopt Western clothing. Instead he urged missionaries to adopt African custom and dress. The alternative (and dominant) view was pithily expressed by a Norwegian missionary: the wearing of trousers and a hat are "the basic characteristics of a Christian." The issue would be debated throughout the century, and the question of Christianizing versus Europeanizing would regularly recur.

We may either smile or be scandalized at such debates, but to judge missionaries by present-day standards would be unfair. For many, the advancement of Christianity and modern European culture were indeed connected. The mid-century missionary and explorer David Livingstone (1813–1873) claimed that the great curse of Africa was the slave trade. Like many British evangelicals, he saw it as Britain's responsibility to root out the slave trade through which it had once so profited. Yet suppressing slavery was not enough. Slaving was the basis of much of Africa's economy. Only by tying Africa to Europe's economy could progress be made. For Livingstone there were three great interlocking goals: "the development of commerce, the elevation of the native . . . [and the] abolition of the trade in slaves." Livingstone dedicated his life as both a missionary and explorer to these ends.

The second half of the nineteenth century (particularly the period after 1885) would see the number of missionaries increase dramatically. They came from a variety of sources. Livingstone, whose adventures became well-known, inspired many well-educated British graduates to join the mission field, and the University Missions to Central Africa (UMCA) together with the Church Missionary Society (CMS) became the leading British organizations. The White Fathers, founded by C. M. A. Lavigerie in 1868, were a Roman Catholic order dedicated to African missions. A number of African American churches also launched missionary endeavors. The African Methodist Episcopal Church began missions to South Africa, and other African American churches worked in the Congo. By 1910 some ten thousand men and women (four thousand Protestants and six thousand Catholics) served as missionaries.

Many of the trends noted concerning Christianity in Africa come together in the story of the church in Uganda, where Christianity in Africa would have one of its great successes. H. M. Stanley, the associate of David Livingstone, had appealed for missionaries to Uganda in order to provide an alternative to the Muslims who were trying to convince the king to bring his dominion over to Islam. Anglican missionaries from the CMS and Roman Catholic missionaries from the White Fathers quickly responded to the call. Despite a persecution that produced more than forty martyrs between 1885 and 1888, Christianity took root, fueled by the grassroots energy of local converts. The establishment of a British protectorate in 1894 led to the political dominance of the Christian (and particularly Anglican) church. Mass conversions continued, and in the period between 1890 and 1914 the Christian community grew to more than 15 percent of the population.

However, by the end of the nineteenth century a new phenomenon could be seen in the separation of African Christians from missionary churches in order to found their own, independent churches. Particularly in West Africa and South Africa, where Christianity had long taken root, tensions developed between Africans and white missionaries. David Brown Vincent, a Yoruban, led Lagos Baptists to establish the independent Native Baptist Church. Rejecting not only missionaries but also his European name, he took the name Mojola Agbebi and spent his remaining years advocating for an indigenous African Christianity free from Western missionaries. Africans, too, would have their say in the debate between Christianity and Europeanization.

Implications of the Missionary Encounter

The Western Christian encounter with the religions of the world would provoke at least two very different responses, both of which would intensify over time. Both were associated with renowned public gatherings. The interest in missions led to periodic international missionary conferences, and in 1910 the World Missionary Conference convened in Edinburgh. Out of the conference emerged a concern for church unity. Divisions that seemed so heated in Christendom did not seem as important in the mission field, and indeed these divisions were viewed as a scandal and a stumbling block for evangelization. The twentieth-century ecumenical movement (to be discussed in chap. 19) is usually dated from the Edinburgh conference, where it was said that the delegates came speaking about the churches and left speaking about the Church.

The second response can be seen in an event that happened seventeen years earlier. To celebrate the beginning of the third American century, the people of Chicago organized a grand world's fair, the Columbia Exposition, to display the wonders of the nineteenth century. The exposition included the World Parliament of Religions, where representatives of dozens of faiths gathered for two weeks to speak of religion and the world. The message of the parliament was cosmopolitanism, or the fostering of understanding of the world's religions. Most assumed that such an endeavor would be led by Christians, but listeners were surprised to hear from an Indian speaker, the representative of Hinduism, Swami Vivekenanda, that it was in Hinduism that all the streams of faith would meet. Hinduism was ancient; it was accepting; and it alone could absorb the great diversity of the world's religions without breaking. "All have a place," Vivekenanda assured his listeners, "in the Hindu's religion."

The words of Vivekenanda would echo for decades, posing a question that represented a second fallout of the great missionary encounter: What made Christianity superior to other religions? In the celebratory grandeur of the Chicago exposition, the question did not have a biting edge. There Western culture seemed secure. But things were changing.

SECTION 6   Wrestling with Modernity

Chapter 18

The End of Innocence

To all external appearances, the sun shone bright on Christian civilization as the world entered the twentieth century. European power and civilization seemed to be at its zenith, and the affairs of the world seemed to be under control. Confidence in progress was everywhere, and progress (as everyone understood) meant that the world was becoming more European. To be European still meant to be Christian, at least in some diluted form. It was true that church attendance had peaked in Britain and was comparatively low in many of the nations of western Europe, but the institutions of Christianity still held a position of honor. The critics—both intellectual and popular—were held in check by a social and political hegemony that still valued the respectability that religion offered. But the story of Christianity in the first half of the twentieth century would not represent the continuation of nineteenth-century themes. Rather it would have to respond to a series of conflicts and crises that would shake the world and prove to be a mortal blow to a European-controlled Christianity. The days of the Latin hegemony were numbered.

The Effects of World War I

Nothing destroyed the inherited confidence as much as the destructiveness of the First World War. Europe had been largely at peace since the Napoleonic wars, and one of the signs of the moral progress in which Europeans took such pride was the belief that large-scale wars were a thing of the past. Society had become too complicated and interrelated to allow for such conflicts, and the meliorating power of Christianity would not allow it. Yet war broke out, affecting not only Europe but, because of colonial expansion, much of the world. World War I was a conflict unlike any others in the past. Entire societies were mobilized; battles would now be fought not by small professional armies but by mass conscripted forces. To support these forces, economic resources had to be harnessed in a way heretofore unimagined. The nations of Europe looked to their churches to provide the moral justification, and on the whole they did not fail. Yet the massive destruction of men and materials was shocking. At the beginning young men enlisted with an idealism and a sense of a noble cause, inspired by the idea of Christian sacrifice. As one said, "I think I can say deliberately, that no household will be acting worthily if . . . it keeps back any of those who can loyally bear a man's part in the great enterprise on the part of the land we love." But bloody battles like the Somme and Verdun peeled away such idealism. With the loss of idealism went much of the trust in the power of Christian society.

If the war disillusioned Europeans, it had even greater impact elsewhere. The war shattered the image of European superiority. Britain and France called on their colonies to provide manpower for the struggle on the Western front, and these people experienced Western society at its very worst. In Africa, others were enlisted for battles between German and British colonies. Still more were forcibly drafted as porters to do manual labor, and the death rate among these laborers approached 10 percent. John Chilembwe, an African missionary in what is now Malawi, wrote in disgust, "A number of Police are marching in various villages persuading well-built natives to join the war. . . . In time of peace, everything for Europeans only. . . . But in time of war it has been found that we are needed to share hardships and shed blood in equality." Chilembwe was to lead an uprising against colonial rule. Although it was crushed, Chilembwe's story shows how war fanned the fire of anticolonialism.

Another aspect of the disillusionment can be seen in the case of the United States. As the war continued, many began to argue that America must abandon its long-standing tradition of isolationism and side with the Allies. Woodrow Wilson, a Presbyterian parson's son who was deeply committed to Christian morality, saw the war in spiritual terms. It was the war to end all wars, and he called the American people to undertake the task of making the world "safe for democracy." Clergy and laity flocked to the cause. But in its aftermath the war was seen more as a political struggle than a moral crusade, and the religious leaders who had so

> A sense dawned that Christianity had lost its vitality. Having put so much emphasis on moral uplift, duty, and character, it seemed out of touch with a war-shattered world.

fervently embraced the effort were now seen as dupes. An illusion of innocence was destroyed.

In Europe, however, it was not merely illusions that were destroyed. A whole order collapsed. The Hapsburg dynasty, which had ruled its empire in Central Europe as Catholic monarchs for six centuries, was cast aside, as was the German kaiser. But the destruction of the old order was most sweeping in Russia. Political crisis in 1917 led to the abdication of the czar and the establishment of a provisional government that augured a new age for the Russian Orthodox Church. Religious liberty was granted, and for the first time in its history the church was able to govern itself. The triumph of the Bolsheviks in 1918, however, undid all this. They quickly confiscated all church property, discontinued state salaries for clergy, made civil marriages mandatory, and made it a criminal offense to teach religion to minors. Resistance to this policy led to the deaths of an estimated 1,000 priests and 40 bishops. The situation eased somewhat after 1923, when the patriarch Tikhon declared his political loyalty to the Bolshevik regime. Yet another wave of persecution soon occurred during which thousands of churches were closed and another 28 bishops, 1,214 priests, and countless laity met their deaths. Although by the mid-1930s persecution subsided, the Russian church was but a shadow of its former self.

The triumph of communism in Russia affected more than that nation. It elevated communism as a major challenge to traditional societies. Communism offered a social vision that rejected the treasured assumptions of the nineteenth century—middle-class hegemony, individualism, property, and religion. For many, it became an attractive ideal in a world in which the old vision was broken. Indeed, for vast numbers, communism replaced Christianity as the way to see the world. To others, however, it was an evil that was to be opposed at all costs. Roman Catholicism saw communism as one of its chief threats and did what it could to oppose it. Anticommunism lay behind Pope Pius XI's support of Benito Mussolini in Italy. Mussolini in turn helped work out a solution to the "Roman problem," which had made the pope a "prisoner of the Vatican" since 1870. In exchange for the papacy's giving up its claims to the Papal States, the Roman church was to be paid a lump sum and given political sovereignty over Vatican City.

During the 1920s there was a perceived sense that there was something wrong with the inherited Christian faith. Yet the problem was viewed differently in different places. As we will see, it would have major political implications on the Continent. In the English-speaking world there was a sense that Christianity had lost its vitality. Having put so much emphasis on moral uplift, duty, and character, it seemed out of touch with a war-shattered world. In the famous words of the novelist F. Scott Fitzgerald, his genera-tion had grown up to find "all Gods dead, all wars fought, all faith in man shaken." Particularly among intellectuals, there could be seen a turning away from religion with its merely naive hope and its stifling morality. In the world of writers such as D. H. Lawrence and Aldous Huxley in Britain, and Fitzgerald and H. L. Mencken in America, the Christian religion was either belittled or ignored. The influence of Protestantism in higher education was radically shrinking (unlike that of Catholicism, as we shall see). In part this was because much of the expansion was through public institutions, where religious claims were more tenuous, but there was a perception that students in the 1920s had little interest in religion. As one commentator observed, "Their grandfathers believed the Creed; their fathers a little doubted the Creed; they have never read it." Furthermore, the culture of the times flouted traditional Christian mores. The new interest in sexuality—loosely attributed to Sigmund Freud—mocked nineteenth-century Victorian views of modesty and chastity. The automobile helped to turn Sunday into a day of travel and leisure rather than devotion, and the worldview offered by the new moving pictures was anything but traditional. Adherence to the church, measured either by attendance or economic commitment, began to drop.

Crisis in the Protestant World

In attempting to respond to these challenges, English-speaking Protestants became bitterly divided. The liberal-conservative split that had developed at the end of the nineteenth century grew wider. In England there were pitched battles between modernists and traditionalists over miracles in general and the virgin birth in particular. In America the conflict was even more intense. During the 1920s militantly conservative Protestants became convinced that the churches had to affirm certain core beliefs. The inerrancy of Scripture, the miraculous birth of Jesus and the resurrection, and the sacrificial nature of his death were considered fundamental (hence the movement became known as fundamentalism), and those who refused to affirm these doctrines should be excluded. Only by holding firmly to its inherited faith could the church stand with certainty against a changing world. In contrast, liberals (also known as modernists) called for a greater openness and a toleration of doctrinal dif-ference. The church, they argued, must be open to the world in which it lived. The result was a violent conflict over the soul of the great Protestant churches. In the northern states the battle was largely fought over theology, but in the South the symbolic issue was Darwinism. For many conservative

Southerners, Darwinism reflected all that was wrong with modern society. It offered a soulless materialism that threatened not only Christianity but also democracy. They campaigned to have the teaching of evolution banned from the public schools. In 1925, a celebrated confrontation—the Scopes Trial—took place in Dayton, Tennessee, where the famous Democratic politician William Jennings Bryan fought to uphold the ban on evolution. The trial, which was widely reported, seemed to manifest the intellectual limitations of fundamentalism, and it tarred the movement with rural and anti-intellectual stereotypes. As a result, the fundamentalist campaign failed, and it was they who were forced to leave the older churches. Retiring to their own small religious communities, they licked their wounds and awaited another chance to challenge religious liberalism.

The sense of crisis among English-speaking Protestants was not merely cultural. It also involved an awareness that the centuries-old conflict with Roman Catholicism was changing. The nineteenth century—with its emphasis on individualism, freedom, and morality—might have been designed to highlight Protestant virtues, and Protestantism was generally seen as Christianity's most vigorous branch. By the twentieth century the tide had turned. The complicated and internationalized world meshed well with the hierarchy and order of Rome. Moreover, the large-scale migration of Irish to Britain, and Irish and other Catholics to America, made for a significant Catholic presence in historically Protestant lands. In response, American Protestants had passed a series of immigration laws that effectively closed the nation's open borders to mass migration. They also added a constitutional amendment banning the use of alcoholic beverages as a way of enforcing traditional Protestant morality.

The attraction of Roman Catholicism could be further seen in converts like G. K. Chesterton and in scholars such as the medievalist Christopher Dawson. It seemed as if, alone within the English-speaking world, Catholics were confident in their religion. Never having completely swallowed the nineteenth century, they had less to spit out when the nineteenth century was rejected.

Theological Reconstruction

If in the English-speaking world there was a vague sense that traditional Christianity had lost its vitality and the churches were only a shell of what they once had been, on the Continent the sense of crisis was more immediate. Particularly in Germany, where Christianity and nationalism had been carefully joined under the aegis of Christian culture, the effects of the First World War were devastating. Oswald Spengler's famous volume *The Decline of the West* reflected an attitude held by many. The vaunted Western culture was collapsing. What would replace it?

In Paul's letter to the Romans Barth found a God far different from that of the God of liberalism.

Such questions were the seedbed for a new theological movement. Known by a variety of names—crisis theology, dialectical theology, and most commonly neo-orthodoxy—it entailed a wholesale questioning of the social and intellectual assumptions of liberal Protestantism. At its center was Swiss theologian Karl Barth (1886–1968). Barth had studied with the leading proponents of the dominant theological liberalism of the early twentieth century and had eagerly accepted their teachings. But while serving as a pastor of a small Swiss church, he experienced two painful realizations. The first came when he saw his venerable professors eagerly proclaim the rightness of the German cause during the First World War. Barth was later to describe this as the "twilight of the Gods." He claimed that these men had compromised their Christian faith by linking it to the German cause. The second realization was the recognition that the theology he had so carefully learned proved of little use when it came to telling his flock what the Bible meant. Another approach was needed, and he found it by reading the Bible with fresh eyes. In his memorable image, he clutched on the Epistle to the Romans "like a drowning man clutched to a rope." There he found a God far different from that of the God of liberalism. "I wrote what I found," he continued, "and I discovered the rope was attached to a bell heard all over Europe." The bell was his famous commentary *The Epistle to the Romans*, first published in 1918.

As we have seen, the liberal agenda featured a belief that the Christian faith should be based on the historical Jesus. The scholar was to use modern tools—linguistic, historical, and psychological—to identify this true Jesus. It was expected that this labor would produce an understanding of Jesus in keeping with what human beings intuited about God from other sources, such as philosophy, mysticism, and intuitive experience. Barth, however, insisted that a new starting point was needed. Theology must begin with the otherness of God. "The Bible has only one theological interest," claimed Barth, "interest in God himself. . . . He is not a thing among other things, but the Wholly Other." Nineteenth-century liberalism had tried to imagine God in human categories but had failed. God was not merely human nature writ large. If God was truly other, then God could be known only through God's own terms or through God's own self-revelation. To approach God through the revelation, or the word, of God was to eschew the nineteenth-century agenda of finding God in experience, philosophy, or moral value. When Barth visited America, he was asked if he could summarize his faith. He smiled and stated (in English), "Jesus loves me this I know, for the Bible tells me so." Although he did not do so, he could have added that what separated him from a liberal figure such as Schleiermacher was that for Schleiermacher the first phrase could stand alone, but for Barth, the first phrase ("Jesus loves me this I know") could exist only because of the second ("for the Bible tells me so").

But for Barth the word of God could not be objectified. Since God was never an object, his self-revelation could never be an object. Rather, revelation was dynamic: the word of God spoke through the text, breaking into the mundane world. And the human response to this divine address was faith. In this Barth was influenced by the writings of the nineteenth-century Danish philosopher Søren Kierkegaard, especially his insistence that the infinite qualitative difference between God and humanity could not be bridged by reason or habit but by a leap of faith.

Finally, Barth claimed that the nineteenth-century fixation on culture and religion was a failure. Culture was for him a finite thing, a human creation that was always under judgment by God. Yet there was an innate human tendency to idolize it—to believe that culture was a ladder to the divine and that by cultural advance civilization moved closer to God. Culture, for Barth, was not an end in itself; only God was. Religion, however, had the same pitfalls as culture. Religion, too, was not an end in itself but rather was true only when it proclaimed the Wholly Other. The church was the church only when it professed and proclaimed that God, never when it was merely existing and mirroring its culture.

Protestants such as Barth were not the only ones who believed that the modern world required Christians to do some fundamental rethinking. Beginning in the early twentieth century, some Roman Catholics began to assert that the liturgy of the church, as then practiced, did not live up to its potential for Christianizing the world. Although the liturgical revival had its roots in the nineteenth century, it was given its chief impetus by Pope Pius X in his promulgation reviving Gregorian chant (1903) and his promotion of frequent Communion (1905). The movement found particular favor in Benedictine monasteries in France, Belgium, and Germany. Its proponents believed that liturgy lay at the center of the Christian life and should be an action in which all the people participated. The chief theologian of the movement, Odo Casel (1886–1948), saw the Eucharist as the reenactment by the church of the mysteries of Christ. On the social level, liturgy united the people, making them a community rather than a group of atomistic individuals. This was a powerful vision in the environment of dehumanizing society. From its continental roots the liturgical movement spread to other lands, and in America it was popularized by Virgil Michel at St. John's Abbey in Collegeville, Minnesota. One practical manifestation of the new stress on the social aspect of liturgy was Pope Pius XI's dedication of the Feast of Christ the King to emphasize the all-embracing authority of Christ in the world.

Still another place the crisis of the West was visible was on the mission front. The nineteenth century had seen the greatest expansion of Christianity since the time of the apostles, but by the 1920s that great surge was being reassessed. Criticism came from all corners. A tidal wave of anticolonialism swelled in the European colonies. In India, Mohandas Gandhi and others campaigned for independence from Britain. In China, Western missionaries, particularly British, were subject to attack as symbols of a foreign presence in the land. Within the Western churches there was a growing awareness that the missionary endeavor was not as simple as it seemed. Literary figures like Pearl Buck attacked the presumptuousness of missionaries. In contrast to the confident enthusiasm of the Edinburgh World Missionary Conference of 1910, the 1928 conference meeting in Jerusalem was more hesitant and unsure how missionaries should relate to the cultures in which they operated. This concern led to the famous report of the (American) Laymen's Foreign Missions Inquiry, *Rethinking Missions* (1932). The report called for a greater appreciation of the great religions of the world and proposed that the task of the missionary was not to uproot older religious traditions but to help men and women come to a truer interpretation of their own faith. Based on this new reassessment, the churches took steps to be more open to native cultures and to empower native church leadership, as well as making the mission churches self-supporting. Unfortunately the policy led to even more cultural clashes. In places like China there were few cultural parallels for the support of churches. As a native Chinese explained, when one contributed to a Confucian temple, one received in recompense a share of the food and decorations offered. When one gave to a church, one received nothing in return.

Economic Crisis

To the troubles caused by the First World War was added by 1929 a new economic crisis. The Great Depression caused dislocation and wide-scale unemployment in almost every land. Its financial impact was to reduce the support for Christian institutions worldwide. Church budgets were slashed, schools and seminaries closed or consolidated, mission programs trimmed, and ministries reduced. The economic crisis seemed to many to be but a further sign that the nineteenth-century era of the hegemony of capitalism, the middle class, and liberal democracy was over. But there was uncertainty as to what would replace it and what role religion would have in the new order.

In 1931 the Catholic Church again addressed the social order. *Quadragesimo Anno* (literally forty years after *Rerum Novarum*) continued to proclaim an economic alternative to both socialism and capitalism. The encyclical called for the extension of property ownership to workers, a fairer distribution of the fruits of industrialism, and cooperative associations of occupational groups, reminiscent of the guild system of the Middle Ages. The truly ordered state, the encyclical taught, was not based on individuals in competition but rather on group cooperation for the common good. The encyclical would embolden Catholics to see in their tradition a solution to the economic crisis of the West. Some conservative European Catholics questioned liberal democracy and called for its replacement with strong central government. Catholic radicals who were committed to relieving poverty, such as Peter Maurin and Dorothy Day in America, used the encyclical to advocate for organized labor.

In America the Depression impelled some Protestant intellectuals to question the value of the old theological liberalism. Reinhold Niebuhr (1892–1971), like Karl Barth, was trained in theological liberalism, but also like Barth he found that theology to be of little use to his congregation. The modern social and economic order was harsh and cruel, bearing little resemblance to the idealistic vision of his teachers. Returning to teach at Union Theological Seminary in New York, Niebuhr in 1932 published *Moral Man and Immoral Society*, which offered a stinging critique of the old social gospel. Proponents of the social gospel had assumed an ethic of love would ineluctably transform the social order. Their error lay in mistaking love for justice. For Niebuhr, love was an individual ethic, but societies were incapable of altruistic love. The central *social* virtue was justice, which at times must rely on force. A realistic Christian social ethic had to recognize the inescapable tension between love and justice. The practical message of Niebuhr was that Christians must not shy away from confrontation.

The liberal failure to respond realistically to society, Niebuhr argued, stemmed from an inadequate theory of human nature. Here too, for Niebuhr,

> Proponents of the social gospel had assumed an ethic of love would ineluctably transform the social order. According to Reinhold Niebuhr, their error lay in mistaking love for justice.

idealism triumphed over realism. Liberals did not take seriously the nature of human sinfulness. Sin, argued Niebuhr, was endemic to the human experience, and for the first time in decades he and others began to address the importance of the Christian doctrine of original sin. A belief in original sin allowed humans to make sense of a world that seemed to have gone astray and to see how grace could still operate there. The movement of American neo-orthodoxy, reflected by Niebuhr at Union Seminary and his brother H. Richard Niebuhr at Yale, did much to revitalize both Protestant theology and social thought.

But it was in Germany that the crisis of war and depression would have the most disastrous effects. The criticism of liberal democracy also involved a criticism of the Versailles Treaty. Imposed on a defeated Germany by the Allies, the treaty blamed Germans for the coming of the war, took away parts of the German homeland, and ordered severe reparation payments that stripped the nation of much of its prewar wealth. The general resentment over the treaty prepared the way for the rise of Adolf Hitler and Nazism. Hitler held up the hope of a purified and reinvigorated Germany that would overthrow the Versailles Treaty and reassert its place in the world. Individualism, liberalism, and Judaism, he trumpeted, were the evils that stood in the path of a restored Germany. The economic crisis swept Hitler and the Nazis into power in 1933.

Clouds of War

Controlling religious dissent was central to Nazi success. In 1933 a concordat was signed with Rome by which Hitler pledged to respect church rights in Germany and the Roman Church agreed to recognize the legitimacy of Hitler's government. Even before taking control of the government, Hitler had begun to organize a pro-Nazi party within German Protestantism. His call for Lutherans, Reformed, and other Protestants to drop their theological differences and form a unified Protestant church, "the Evangelical Church of the German Nation," found willing listeners. Many German Protestant pastors were accustomed to linking God and country and were sympathetic to his appeal. One pastor who was not sympathetic was Karl Barth. For Barth, the idea of such a national church elevated nationhood to the level of the divine and was ultimately idolatrous in its placing of a human institution as the core of the faith.

Yet Hitler did not simply want the Protestant churches united; he also wanted the "German Church" to be purged of all "half-Germans" and particularly those with Jewish blood. Opposition arose, and although the constitution for the reorganized church was adopted, the opposition organized itself as well, particularly after the full scale of Hitler's reforms was revealed: The Jewish Old Testament was to be dropped; the New Testament was to be revised to clarify the German ancestry of Jesus; the apostle Paul and Augustine were to be rejected because of their Jewish sense of sin; and separate churches were to be established for Jewish Christians. In response, the dissident clergy organized the "Confessing Church." In 1934 the Confessing Church issued the Barmen Declaration, which affirmed the sovereignty of the word of God and condemned the political ideology rooted in extreme nationalism, which attempted to corrupt it. In the religious conflict that followed, more than seven hundred Protestant pastors were arrested by German authorities, and more than a thousand were threatened.

The political climate of the 1930s indicated that still another great war might be in the offing. Not only was there the remilitarization of Germany and its advance into the Ruhr and Austria, but there were also the activities of Italy, which invaded Ethiopia in 1936, and of Japan, which began gobbling up China in 1931. What should the Christian response be? Many were convinced that response should be to work for peace. Disillusionment over the First World War ran deep, and there was a general sense that the churches had been hoodwinked into blessing the carnage. Pacifism seemed to be the true way of discipleship. There was also a tendency to see the causes of German aggression as arising from the injustices of the Versailles Treaty. By rectifying those injustices peace could be assured. Such was the idea of "appeasement," and many thoughtful Christians on both sides of the Atlantic were sympathetic to German grievances.

But the calls for pacifism and appeasement did not take account of the increasingly harsh Nazi anti-Semitism. Both the Confessing Church and Roman Catholics criticized Nazi policy that encroached on the traditional rights of the church, but both groups were largely silent on Hitler's Jewish policy. But there were some early voices that insisted that Christians could not be silent. Among Roman Catholics, the Carmelite nun and philosopher Edith Stein (1891–1942), herself a convert from Judaism, believed the persecution of the Jews violated the heart of Christianity. Writing in 1933 to the pope to urge him to speak out, she asked, "Isn't the effort to destroy Jewish blood an abuse of the holiest humanity of our Savior, of the most blessed Virgin, and the apostles?" Stein was to die in Auschwitz. Among Protestants, the most challenging voice was that of the German theologian Dietrich Bonhoeffer (1906–1945). A friend and colleague of Barth's in the Confessing Church, he wrote, "Only he who cries out for the Jews may sing the Gregorian chants."

Later he would be hanged for participating in a failed plot to assassinate Hitler. In America, Reinhold Niebuhr also took up the cause. Absolute pacifism in the face of Nazi policy was still another example of sentimental idealism that ignored the reality of the world. Niebuhr tirelessly argued for a realistic Christian response to the world's crisis. Although other factors besides Nazi anti-Semitism contributed to Niebuhr's critique of pacifism, he consistently argued that Christians could not ignore the plight of the Jews.

> In contrast to a totalitarianism that worshiped power and belittled humanity, the Christian ethos with its doctrines of sin and grace took on a new attractiveness.

When war finally broke out in September 1939, it affected Christians throughout the world. In Asia, the churches, still psychologically linked with Europe, were caught up in the events. This was most dramatically seen in China and Japan. As war clouds gathered, Japanese and Chinese Christians did what they could to establish fraternal relations between the two nations, but it was not to be. When the Japanese invaded first Manchuria and later China itself, missionaries found themselves in difficult straits. Not only did the Japanese view them as representatives of foreign powers, but also, as was the case in the brutal "Rape of Nanjing" (1937–1938), they were often on-the-spot reporters of Japanese atrocities. With the attack on Pearl Harbor and Japan's entrance into war with America and Britain, many missionaries were interned, and missionary institutions were destroyed. In Japan, Christians distanced themselves sufficiently from the Western churches to survive, but in China the war was calamitous to the Christian community. The war, furthermore, was not simply a temporary blow to the Western missionaries. The ease with which Japan overran the colonies of the vaunted European powers demonstrated how fragile the European presence was in Asia, and that fragility encouraged the hope of independence from colonial powers and Western hegemony.

In the Christian West the war paradoxically revitalized the churches. The threat of war had led Joseph Stalin to grant much more toleration of religion in the Soviet Union than had been the case earlier. The death and destruction, both present and imminent, reminded many of the lasting value of the historic Christian worldview. In contrast to a totalitarianism that worshiped power and belittled humanity, the Christian ethos with its doctrines of sin and grace took on a new attractiveness. As the first bombs of the war began to fall, Reinhold Niebuhr, in his Gifford Lectures, which were later published as *The Nature and Destiny of Man*, argued for the superiority of the Christian worldview over those that had succeeded it. Throughout the historic Christian West, churches began to feel a revived sense of relevance whereas earlier there had been despair.

New Realities

This sense of hopefulness would be strengthened in the years following the war. With the war's end in 1945, it could be said that there were three victors. In things military, the United States and the Soviet Union clearly emerged as the chief powers. The nations who had been so active in the extension of European influence throughout the world became second-tier powers. Within a year, however, the United States and the Soviet Union would begin to see themselves in a struggle over who would dominate the postwar world, and a Cold War pitting East against West was the result.

If the Soviets and the Americans were the "winners" militarily, Roman Catholicism was clearly the "winner" ecclesiastically among the world's churches. The scope and complexity of both the Second World War and the Cold War were such that only a strong institution and a multinational presence could provide any meaningful leadership. Here Rome had the advantage. The long-standing Vatican tradition of diplomatic involvement, which seemed horribly out of date in 1900, by 1945 seemed crucial to the well-being of the world. The establishment of the Vatican as a sovereign nation (a fruit of the concordat with Mussolini) allowed it once again to be a center of diplomatic negotiation and intrigue. Nations such as the United States, which had scorned the Vatican's political pretensions in the nineteenth century, began to make moves to send official ambassadors. In the succeeding struggle against communism, first in Europe and then in places like Vietnam, and eventually in the attempt in the 1980s to tear down communism itself, the United States would see the Vatican as a key partner. Once Stalin allegedly asked in scorn how many divisions the pope commanded. He and his Soviet successors would learn. It is not too much of an exaggeration to say that Rome came out of the war as the only European power with its international "empire" stronger.

To the above, however, two caveats should be added. First, Rome was not alone in recognizing that the complicated postwar world necessitated a far greater degree of unanimity. As we will see in the next chapter, Protestants would organize their own world body to speak with a united Christian voice in global affairs. Second, the renewed significance of Rome as a political as well as a religious force meant that it would be subjected to closer scrutiny than the other Christian churches. To take on a more political role opened it up to political criticisms. The charge would regularly be made that the Vatican and Pope Pius XII had not done all that they could have either to denounce Hitler or prevent the Holocaust.

The events of the first half of the twentieth century had changed Western Christendom forever. They also, as we shall see, quickened a dramatic shift in Christianity.

Chapter 19

The Modern Quest for Unity

*I*n the course of the same twentieth century that witnessed economic crisis, two wars in the heart of the old Christendom, and a perceived loss of control, a paradoxical countermovement was taking place. For it was now that, for the first time since the age of Constantine, the Christian churches reversed their longtime spirit of divisiveness and began to seek unity. The first six decades of the century would see a great interest in ecumenism, or the return of the churches to a common household. The concern for unity was certain; its relationship to the age, more complex.

Nineteenth-Century Roots

By the nineteenth century the centrifugal nature of Christian development had reached its apex. The ascendancy of the liberal state, with its ideals of individual freedom and the separation of church and state, dislodged the Constantinian idea of a single state church. Indeed, many sang the praises of a divided Christian community. Just as the dispersal of the apostles in the first century fostered evangelism across the world, so too did a divided and dispersed church help present-day Christians spread the gospel. But in the nineteenth century counter trends arose, trends that suggested that Christian influence was greater in union than in division.

The basic form of nineteenth-century cooperation was the voluntary society, the ad hoc collaboration of individuals for a common purpose. Emerging in the English-speaking world, such groups provided a model for many of the benevolent organizations of the times. On issues of mission and service, Christians could unite on a common basis across denominational lines. The YMCA movement, founded in England in 1844, quickly took root around the globe and emphasized this interdenominational character. Voluntary societies stressed the participation of individuals as individuals. The closest one came to an organization that might represent Christians in a more general context was the Evangelical Alliance. Formed in 1846 through the labors of individual Protestants in England, France, Switzerland, the United States, and Germany, the Alliance brought together members of fifty-two branches of the church of Christ. But from the start it viewed itself as a union of individuals and not churches and stated that its goal was "cultivating brotherly love, enjoying Christian intercourse, and promoting such other objects as they [i.e., its members] may agree to prosecute together."

By the last third of the century, however, calls for a stronger type of union were being voiced. In America, the Episcopalian William R. Huntington published *The Church-Idea*, which proposed organic church union. Writing in an American context in which divisions limited Protestantism's effectiveness, Huntington called for unity based on four principles: the authority of Scripture, the ancient creeds, the two sacraments (Baptism and Eucharist), and the historic episcopate. These four principles were later adopted by Anglican churches and became the basis for the Lambeth Quadrilateral. Although the Quadrilateral proved to have little attraction in the short run, it did reflect a tendency in the last third of the nineteenth century for international branches of churches to federate. In 1867 the different national branches of Anglicanism came together in the international Lambeth Conference, and within forty years Presbyterians formed the Alliance of Reformed Churches (1875); Methodists, the Methodist Ecumenical Conference (1881); and Baptists, the Baptist World Conference (1905).

> Characteristic of the twentieth century was a larger vision of Christian unity that would strive to undo the great divisions within the Christian community.

Still another phenomenon was the reunion of church families that had divided over nontheological reasons. A number of these occurred in the United States. Lutherans overcame ethnic divisions to begin to reunite. Methodists and eventually Presbyterians during the twentieth century overcame divisions caused by the Civil War. The most significant reunion may have been in Scotland, where the Church of Scotland, as we have seen, had divided into several churches in the nineteenth century over the question of ministerial patronage. By 1929 all had come back together with the exception of a small number of critics, and 90 percent of Scottish Presbyterians were again part of the established church.

What would characterize the twentieth century, however, was a larger vision of Christian unity that would strive to undo the great divisions within the Christian community. In this regard there was a desire to transcend the nineteenth-century preoccupation with individuals and the ideal of cooperation and to reclaim the idea of the church as a body itself.

Much of this impetus came from the mission field. The missionary endeavors had been fertile grounds for the idea of Christian unity. The vast expanses of the non-Christian world both necessitated de facto cooperation and made the old divisions—based on disagreements that were both chronologically and geographically far removed from the new Christian communities there—seem somehow less significant. By the late nineteenth century the need for unity in missions began to foster grassroots movements concerned with overcoming divisions. In 1895 the student Christian movements of several nations came together to form the World Christian Student Federation. The movement's expectation and confidence was reflected in its catchphrase "The evangelization of the world in this generation." Participants included many future leaders of the ecumenical movement: John R. Mott (1865–1955), Nathan Söderblom (1866–1931), William Temple (1881–1944), and W. A. Visser't Hooft (1900–1985).

Edinburgh and Beyond

These hopes came to a head at the Edinburgh Missionary Conference of 1910. As we have noted, the Edinburgh Conference is usually seen as the birth of the twentieth-century ecumenical movement. From its start, Edinburgh reflected a different spirit from earlier missionary conferences. Unlike other meetings in which membership was open to all, the delegates came as representatives of missionary organizations; hence for the first time delegates had the power to speak not only in their own names but in the names of their organizations. Furthermore, they came together not merely for support and encouragement but for consultation and the planning of next steps. Most important, one of the main foci was the promotion of Christian unity. Still another important difference was the participation of the "younger churches." Although only 17 of the more than 350 delegates were from the churches of Africa and Asia, they had a public role that had never theretofore been granted to representatives of non-Western churches.

The confidence of the representatives lay not merely in their belief that they could evangelize the world in their generation but also in their belief that historic ecclesiastical divisions could be overcome. The optimism cannot be divorced from the confidence that subsumed much of the Christian West in the decade and a half before the outbreak of World War I. It was not merely (nor, it can be argued, even principally) a confidence in Western culture but rather in the sense of progress that was being unfurled. The advancement of things social, material, and physical stemmed from an ability to direct creative thinking to problems and harness energies heretofore never mobilized. The confidence in organization and creative thinking marked the modern genius of the twentieth century. These were values and beliefs held by the West, but not inherently tied to the West. Intelligence and organization could overcome obstacles that had stymied earlier generations. Indeed there was a not-so-subtle critique of the nineteenth century. In its glorification of individualism and competition, nineteenth-century Protestant Christianity was inefficient, and much energy was dissipated and lost. But it was not only competition that was the culprit. The earlier century also lacked the expertise that was now present. Without proper research—research at the hands of experts—proper goals could not be assessed or difficulties overcome. One sees this in the relationship between the new scholarship and the ecumenical vision. One of the accomplishments of the great flowering of learning within the Protestant world was a systematic reassessment of many of the traditional issues that had divided the Christian world. Many of the cherished beliefs that had undergirded denominational identities—the essential nature of Episcopal ordination, the sacraments, and the fine points of Reformation doctrine— began to be reexamined by scholarly experts concerned with getting behind these later divisions and discovering a basis for Christian unity. Organization and expertise could produce unity, and unity would allow the church to fulfill its mission more effectively. It was perhaps fitting that one of the leading supporters of the ecumenical endeavor in America was the philanthropist (and devout Baptist) John D. Rockefeller Jr., whose family's great wealth was derived from the Standard Oil Corporation. Standard Oil was considered to be one of the wonders of its time; in it competing companies had been combined to create a unified corporation that was vast, rationally organized, and immensely powerful. Just as Standard Oil brought efficiency and dynamism into the business world, so too, Rockefeller believed, Protestant influence would be strengthened by unity.

The effects of the First World War strengthened the recognition of the value of unity. Just as the nations of the world came together to form a League of Nations, some now called for a "League of Churches" to offer a common Christian voice in the world. Such a League of Churches would serve still another function. Throughout the first half of the twentieth century church unity was seen as something that would strengthen the Protestant witness. During this period Rome stood aloof, insisting that unity could be brought about only through a return of non-Catholics to Rome. Protestant leaders were all too aware that Rome did speak with one voice, hence its tremendous influence. Protestant unity, they hoped, could create an alternative common voice.

In some places in the world there was marked success. Beginning in 1902, Canadian Protestants began to work toward unity. The original hope had been to link all major Protestant families, but Anglicans and Baptists demurred. Eventually, in 1925, Methodists, Presbyterians, and Congregationalists did move forward and hammered out a basis of union—balancing Calvinistic Presbyterianism, Arminian Methodism, and a number of different polities to form a new United Church of Canada. A minority of Presbyterians, however, balked at the compromises and refused to join.

Perhaps the most ambitious attempt to overcome the divisions of the Reformation took place in India. In 1919 a group of Indian Christians proposed to unite the non–Roman Catholic churches of India. "We believe," they stated, "that the challenge of the present hour . . . calls us to mourn our past divisions and turn to our Lord Jesus Christ to seek in Him the unity of the body expressed in one visible Church." The plan called for combining churches of different governing schemes—congregational, presbyterian, and episcopal—into a common body. Union was to be achieved through a united ministry without any reordination, but with the inclusion of the historic episcopate. The plan sparked a vigorous debate within Anglicanism. Some argued that the historic episcopate was essential for a true church and could not be compromised. Others claimed that the possibility of overcoming division and creating a unified Christian witness justified the plan. The Church of South India was finally organized in 1947, bringing together Anglicans, Methodists, and a number of Reformed bodies.

International Organizations

On the international level, various groups that were intended to serve as vehicles for unity only slowly took shape. By the second decade of the century, three such centers were active. The International Missionary Council (IMC) was constituted in 1921. The early twentieth century had witnessed strains on the vast missionary endeavor. The First World War had separated many German missions from their home support, creating "orphaned missions." Furthermore, the victorious allies threatened to confiscate missionary property to pay for war reparations. Leaders of the IMC, like John R. Mott, worked to support German missionaries and preserve their property. The IMC was particularly active in giving voice to the younger churches and their concerns over questions such as race relations and the economic issues of industrialism and rural societies. At its second international meeting in Tambaram, India, in 1938, representatives of the younger churches outnumbered those from the churches of Europe and North America.

Life and Work, which had its roots in the Edinburgh Conference, also was concerned in coordinating the church's involvement in society. The leading figure was Nathan Söderblom, archbishop of the Lutheran Church in Sweden, who had worked unceasingly for an end to the war. Life and Work believed it was possible for Christians, while still divided by doctrine, to bring Christian principles to bear on social and economic conditions. The church needed to address the whole of humanity. The aim was "to formulate programmes and devise means . . . whereby the fatherhood of God and the brotherhood of all peoples will be more completely realized through the church of Christ." The first great Life and Work conference was held in Stockholm in 1925.

Faith and Order, the last of the three, also came out of Edinburgh. It was instigated by the American Episcopal bishop Charles H. Brent and was concerned with the theological issues dividing the churches. Faith and Order was quickly taken up by a number of American churches and quickly became a great interest of many Anglo-Saxon church leaders. Particularly among Anglicans, there was the hope that Faith and Order could expand the vista of Christian unity to include not only Protestants but also Roman Catholics and Eastern Christians. In this they were unsuccessful. Despite the exchange of a number of polite letters, the pope, Benedict XV, made it clear that Rome would not participate. The Eastern churches, both Orthodox and Oriental churches such as the Armenians and the Copts, did express interest, and in 1920 the Ecumenical Patriarch of Constantinople issued an encyclical letter calling for closer intercourse and mutual cooperation between the churches. The enthusiasm of Anglo-American representatives unfortunately aroused the suspicion of German and other continental representatives, who feared that the English and Americans were loose in doctrine, and at the first meeting of Faith and Order, in Lausanne (1927), little was accomplished.

Many, however, realized that the ecumenical quest was hampered by the movement's own disunity. The existence of disparate organizations made it difficult to speak with one voice. Theological changes in particular helped to bring Life and Work and Faith and Order together. Nineteenth-century liberals had assumed that the moral and ethical teachings of Jesus could be traced back to the historical Jesus lying behind the Gospels. Ecclesiology, from this perspective, was a later addition to the authentic teachings of Jesus. By the 1920s a new school of biblical criticism, known as form criticism, began to challenge this dichotomy of ethics and ecclesiology. The form critics insisted that the foundational basis for all Christian claims ultimately rested on the preaching (literally, the kerygma) of the primitive church. One could not get behind this proclamation of the early community to recover a historical Jesus. And in this original preaching the church was not an afterthought but was essential. The faith existed from the beginning in community and could not be divorced from it, and hence any sharp distinction between life and work and faith and order was ultimately false.

Just as life and work rest ultimately on faith and order, so too did others note that faith and order were barren without their manifestation in the life and work of the church. The church and the world were enmeshed. One sees this new attitude in the way in which the liturgical movement of the early twentieth century began to expand its scope. Liturgy was not an end in itself, nor was it an option. As the English writer A. G. Hebert proclaimed in *Liturgy and Society* (1935), worship was a part of the mission of the church to the world: "The sacraments and the liturgy exist in order to give to human life its true direction in relation to God, and to bind men in fellowship with one another."

The emphasis on the role of the church was not merely an abstruse theological or liturgical issue. The rise of totalitarianism and extreme nationalism directly challenged the claims of Christianity. The issues raised by the German Christians' blending of Christianity with Nazism threatened the autonomy of the church. The Barmen Declaration had proclaimed, "We reject the false doctrine [that nationalism can dictate to the churches] as though the Church were permitted to abandon the form of its message and order to its own pleasure or to changes in prevailing ideological and political convictions." But such challenges confronted not only the Confessing Church but all Christians. Was there any power that could stand in the way of raging nationalism? Only a united church, it came to be understood, could challenge such forces. The cry became "Let the church be the church," which meant a church united both in faith and life and in work and doctrine. In 1937 both Life and Work and Faith and Order met (the former in Oxford and the latter in Edinburgh), and the leading figure at both was the Anglican archbishop of York, William Temple. The fact that the Nazi government, by refusing travel visas to them, prevented any German Confessing Christians from attending only highlighted the sense of crisis. Temple strongly urged the need for a body that would provide a "voice for non-Roman Christendom."

> Was there any power that could stand in the way of raging nationalism? Only a united church, it came to be understood, could challenge such forces.

Both conferences agreed to move forward and unite their organizations. Delegates were clear that what was needed was not a "super church" but a common voice.

Moving toward Protestant Unity

A provisional committee was established to help move the two organizations toward unity, but the beginnings of the Second World War put plans in hiatus. Armed conflict brought an end to international meetings, and the staff of the organizations, already reduced during the economic crisis of the 1930s, was reduced even further. Yet the provisional committee did do important organizational work during the war. It supported orphaned missions and aided as much as possible war refugees and prisoners of war. One thing it did not do was to speak out concerning the war and the atrocities that were occurring. Christians were loath to condemn either directly or indirectly the actions of their own nations. Nor would they condemn others. The ecumenical movement was seen to be still weak, and there was a fear that judgmental words across national boundaries would do great damage. As William Temple noted, "If we speak corporately we may find we have erected fresh barriers to the reconstruction of the fellowship."

Just as the vast complications of the war effort contributed to the confidence in organization and expertise on the political level, so too did it among ecumenists. Indeed these two values were rooted in an early-twentieth-century matrix of political progressivism and liberal theology; however, they not only survived the changing times but also prospered. Liberal theology may have been challenged by neo-orthodoxy, and progressive optimism replaced by a sense of realpolitik, but a confidence in organization and expertise remained. With the end of the war and the vast problems facing a prostrate world, they became even more important. The staffs of professional committees grew by leaps and bounds as experts became necessary to direct resources for the reconstruction.

The aftermath of World War II, unlike the situation after World War I, saw Protestant churches rally quickly to the ecumenical cause. Unity, it must be noted, was in the air. The United Nations was outlined at meetings at Dumbarton Oaks in the fall of 1944, and a charter was drafted in San Francisco in April 1945. The complexity of the postwar world called for a new sense of international cooperation. Protestant church leaders recognized the same was true in the religious world. Indeed the crisis was even greater in religion than in statecraft. The world, they feared, was moving toward a social order based on technology and force without any real direction from Christianity. The secularism that had blossomed during the interwar years seemed to be growing even stronger. The old League of Nations had at least some religious dimensions, but the new United Nations was a far more secular organization. Moreover, the old Christian nations that for a thousand years had given the churches a privileged place in the halls of influence were waning in influence. Britain was beginning the process of disassembling its once-proud empire, and India received its independence in 1947. Power was shifting to nations such as the Soviet Union, which had little sympathy for Christianity. As Christendom declined, many sought hope in the belief that the time was ripe for a renewal of Christianity—a renewal that would not cling to old structures but adapt itself to the emerging world.

Thus in 1948, some 351 delegates, representing 147 churches, assembled in Amsterdam. Faith and Order and Life and Work formally came together to form the World Council of Churches. Rarely had there been a more celebrated gathering. Although Roman Catholics refused to attend on theological grounds, and representatives of the leading Orthodox churches could not send representatives because of increasing East/West political conflict, Protestants put their best forward as either delegates or consultants. Karl Barth, Reinhold Niebuhr, and many others contributed to the undertaking. The very best of the Protestant world came to Amsterdam to plot the course of the church in the postwar world.

Yet what was this course to be? Although the talk was of the new churches, delegates overwhelmingly represented the older churches. Debate swirled over what position the churches should take in the great East/West struggle. Europe was rapidly dividing between a Soviet/Communist sector and a Western sector. For the American delegate John Foster Dulles, both a devout layperson and leading political figure, the responsibility of the World Council, like that of the United Nations, was to back the great moral principles of Christian civilization as reflected in the West: "If in the international field, Christians are to play their clearly indicated part, their churches must have better organization, more unity in action, and more emphasis on Christianity as a world religion." In contrast, the Czech theologian Joseph L. Hromadka, whose nation now lay behind the Iron Curtain, called for the World Council to avoid any identification with the West and take a position of neutrality in the political struggle.

In the entire swirl of debate it is easy to miss the continuing reliance on organization and expertise. It is not without significance that John D. Rockefeller provided funds for both the residence of the United Nations in New York and an Ecumenical Institute and Training Center in Bossey, Switzerland.

The creation of the World Council of Churches was mirrored on the national level by the founding of the National Council of Churches of Christ in the United States in 1950. In it representatives of mainline Protestant (and some Orthodox) churches met to address issues of the church and society. After 1960 the National Council's meetings took place in still another monumental building provided by the munificent Mr. Rockefeller.

The Path of Rome

During the first five decades of the twentieth century Rome held itself aloof from the broader ecumenical currents. Division and disagreement, it was claimed, were marks of Protestantism and could be overcome only by a restoration of unity with Rome. In 1928, the encyclical *Mortalium Animos* made it clear that the official Roman position against ecumenical cooperation had not budged: "It is clear that the Apostolic See can by no means take part in these assemblies, nor is it in any way lawful for Catholics to give such enterprises their encouragement or support." It is not that there were not attempts. At Malines (Belgium), Anglicans and Roman Catholics came together during the 1920s to discuss their differences, but the discussions faded away because of ecclesiastical pressure.

The Vatican's suspicion of ecumenism was intertwined with its general rejection of things modern, but by the 1940s things were beginning to change. Proponents of the Catholic liturgical movement found some tentative common ground with similar stirrings within Protestantism. More important, the 1943 encyclical *Divino Afflante Spiritu* removed some of the most onerous antimodernist shackles on Catholic biblical scholarship.

In the decade and a half after the end of the Second World War, the Roman church seemed to be at the height of its influence. It was larger and wealthier than ever, and papal power was at its zenith. Papal infallibility was invoked in 1950 to define the doctrine of the bodily assumption into heaven of the Virgin Mary. The Roman church also strategically aligned itself with the cause of the West in the struggle with communism, thus increasing its influence. It was growing throughout the world, including in Africa and Asia. A Catholic hierarchy in China had been established as early as 1919, and on "Mission Sunday" in 1939 Pope Pius XII had consecrated twelve missionary bishops—celebrating the sending forth of the twelve apostles—to serve the churches of Africa and Asia. Things seemed secure. But when Pius XII died in 1958, after a reign of nineteen years, the College of Cardinals was unsure of what direction the church should take. They compromised by electing seventy-seven-year-old Angelo Roncalli to serve, as it were, as a caretaker pope. Roncalli, however, showed his independence by taking as his papal name John XXIII, a name that had been discredited for more than four hundred years as that of an antipope. If this were not enough, in January 1959 he called for a Second Vatican Council.

The Impact of Vatican II

The calling of Vatican II was a momentous event. In the last decades of the nineteenth century Rome had turned its back on the intellectual and cultural trends of the emerging modern world (though not its social problems) and presented itself as an alternative to the modern matrix. Rome was the bulwark against which both Protestantism and the modernist impulse crashed. The militant attitude it had adopted at the time of the Counter-Reformation continued to shield it from its critics. But by the 1950s there were some Catholic voices (albeit quiet ones) who began to call for a reassessment of this strategy. Much of the struggle at the council was over the degree to which Rome could and should change.

As it turned out, the struggle pitted conservative forces lodged in the curia, the administrative offices of the Vatican, against the progressive forces of many French, German, and northern European bishops and their theological advisers. The former were determined that the council do little if any fundamental reexamination of Catholic teaching and practice.

After three years of preparation, the council gathered in September 1962 with more than two thousand bishops attending. John XXIII's opening address stressed the renewal and updating of the church—his term was "*aggiornamento*," the opening of the windows to let in light. Only in this way could the church engage the world. The council would meet in four sessions over three years. Ten commissions were established to deal with the different issues. Almost immediately the bishops rejected both the agendas and proposed staffing of these commissions by the curia. A fierce battle was waged over a proposed document on the sources of revelation. Key bishops opposed the curia's attempt to have the council reaffirm earlier teachings concerning the relationship between Scripture and tradition, and specific claims about the authorship and dating of biblical books. Liberals believed such assertions would tie the church to the sixteenth century and cut itself off from new understandings of the Bible. The deeply divisive nature of the debate led John XXIII to instruct that the proposal be withdrawn. Instead the focus became the liturgy.

At this point a move came to focus the discussion on the idea of the church: first in its inner mystery and then in its relation to the world. This was accepted, and many of the council's statements reflected this concern. The death of John XXIII in 1963 led to the election of Paul VI, and in his opening address as pope he, too, emphasized the themes of the renewal of the church, the unity of all Christians, and dialogue with the world. During the next three sessions the chief deliberations concerned the liturgy, the nature of the church, ecumenism, religious liberty, and the church and the world.

The schema on liturgy incorporated important insights of the liturgical movement. The liturgy was the "summit" and "foundation" of the church's activity and was in its essence common prayer. To enforce this, the document discouraged private masses and encouraged the use of the vernacular for scriptural readings and lay responses in the Latin mass.

> *Lumen Gentium* moved the church away from a monarchical self-understanding to envision itself as a circle with the pope in the center, not a pyramid with the pope on top.

Lumen Gentium (Light of the Nations) was the statement on the church, and it too broke with the past. Moving away from the military metaphors that had shaped Latin Christianity for centuries, *Lumen Gentium* raised up biblical metaphors. The church was both the "body of Christ" and the "people of God." A key word in the document was "collegiality." The document moved the church away from a monarchical self-understanding to envision itself as a circle with the pope in the center, not a pyramid with the pope on top. That bishops should be involved in governing was clear, but the document was ambiguous regarding the limits of collegiality, particularly when Paul VI issued an addendum to the schema, suggesting limitations on the principle of collegiality in relation to papal authority.

Ecumenism and religious liberty were originally to be covered in a single statement but grew to such great importance that they became separate decrees. Both statements clearly distanced the church from some of its earlier positions. The idea of ecumenism was closely connected with John XXIII's vision of *aggiornamento*. One of the first things he did after calling the council was to appoint a Secretariat for Promoting Christian Unity (1960). He furthermore broke with a long papal tradition by exchanging greetings and visits with non–Roman Catholic patriarchs. The decree on ecumenism gave form to these actions. It declared that the church included not only Catholics in communion with Rome but non-Catholic Christians linked in baptism and faith. Christian unity could be brought about only by spiritual and religious renewal. The true goal was not the return of individual Protestants to Rome but the return of all separated churches.

The decree on religious liberty, or the "Declaration on Religious Freedom," was even more momentous. The traditional Roman position on the primacy of truth and the denial of any rights to religious error meant that officially Rome granted no rights to other religions. This had been a long-standing point of tension with Protestants and was one of the reasons that in places like America it was claimed that Catholic politicians could not be trusted to defend the rights of non-Catholics. In the years after the Second World War, some American Catholic theologians, such as the Jesuit John Courtney Murray (1904–1967), argued that such was not the only Catholic point of view and that religious freedom could be justified on Catholic grounds. Although silenced by the Vatican in the 1950s, Murray's ideas were taken up by key American bishops and triumphed at the council. The document taught that no political power had the right to coerce the conscience. In every individual there was a privileged sanctuary in which the state had no business.

Finally, the Pastoral Constitution *Gaudium et Spes* (Joy and Hope) spoke of the relationship between the church and the world. Here, too, older language was eschewed, and a concern was made to present Catholic teaching in terms the world could understand. The dignity of all persons was affirmed, and racial discrimination, poverty, and hunger condemned. It was asserted that Catholics should work with all persons of goodwill and that the church should engage in honest dialogue with separated brethren, those who believed in God and even those who oppressed the church.

The Second Vatican Council was a landmark event in both what it accomplished and what it inspired. It ended one era of Western Catholicism and inaugurated another. Through its many pronouncements the Counter-Reformation was finally ended. Not only in the decrees on ecumenism but in countless other places, Rome stopped aligning itself against the Reformation and began to stress points of commonality. Likewise, not only was the Counter-Reformation over but so too was the civil war with modernity that had begun in the nineteenth century with the defeat of the Catholic liberals. *Aggiornamento* suggested a new relationship with the world.

But all this left Catholics with one immediate question and another lingering, even larger one. The first concerned the relationship between the teachings of Vatican II and earlier conciliar positions. Were the council's pronouncements to be read in continuity with the longer record of Catholic teaching, or was Vatican II to be seen as a new beginning, overturning much of the past? More important, to what world was the church to be open? Just as the Vatican fathers proclaimed that the church must be open to modernity, the modern (as we shall see in the next chapter) began to turn to questions of gender, sexuality, and power, which were far different from the issues of war, peace, social justice, and intellectual adjustment that preoccupied the first half of the twentieth century. Indeed we may say that the ecumenical agenda consisted largely of an ecclesial response to modernity as defined by the early twentieth century. Many Western Christians had come to believe that the church could do so by employing the tools of organization and expertise.

Could the churches also adapt to the new modernity, or postmodernity, of the later twentieth century? That would become the new question.

SECTION 7   # Facing Postmodernity

Chapter 20

A New Christian World

By the early 1960s it looked as if the Western churches had triumphed in their struggle with modernity. North America, and to a lesser extent western Europe, was still experiencing a post–World War II religious revival. Churches were filled, seminaries were bursting, and the place of religion seemed secure. The Protestant theological revival loosely known as neo-orthodoxy seemed to validate the importance of theology for the modern situation, and the great undertaking of the Second Vatican Council showed that even Rome was willing to address the modern world without fear. True, Western churches had suffered a painful wound with the apparent collapse of the Christian movement in China after the triumph of communism in 1950. Decades of missionary labors there seemed to melt away like a castle of sand. But the increasing participation of developing nations in such institutions as the World Council of Churches offered evidence that Christianity was successfully transitioning to a postcolonial world. Western Christianity might be aging, but it still oversaw the expanding Christian world like a benevolent patriarch. Yet all was not what it seemed. The decade of the 1960s would witness the beginning of a profound translation of the axis of the Christian world. The center of gravity that had lodged in Western Christendom for a millennium finally began to shift.

New Forces and Issues

Watersheds are difficult to recognize (particularly at short distance), and there is an all-too-human proclivity to deem an afternoon shower a flood if one has seen it oneself. But the 1960s do deserve to be called a watershed. There are few decades whose tone changed so dramatically from beginning to end. The confidence of the early years of the decade was not merely religious; rather, a sense of "new frontiers" (to borrow a phrase from the times) emboldened many. In America, a young, first-ever Catholic president, John F. Kennedy, epitomized this optimism. In retrospect, the spirit of the decade was something like an ancient Greek myth in which the hero is defeated by the very qualities that made him a hero. To be able to fly, as in the case of Icarus, created the temptation to fly too close to the sun. The success and popularity of Christianity was decried by commentators. The Anglican bishop John A. T. Robinson published the widely popular book *Honest to God*, which complained that the old language about God cloaked the real meaning of God for the modern world. The old language was speedily rejected, but none was found to replace it. Critics like Gibson Winter in *The Suburban Captivity of the Churches* claimed that people were going to church for all the wrong reasons. The criticism was heard, and attendance dropped precipitously. Paul Van Buren argued in the *Secular Meaning of the Gospel* that only by translating the gospel into secular categories could it survive. The secular triumphed, and the gospel waned.

> Lying behind the easy Western talk of individual rights and freedoms were some ugly presuppositions.

But more than all this, in the 1960s many began to question foundational assumptions that marked the careful marriage between Christianity and Enlightenment and that had been a hallmark of Western society for a century and a half. Since the time of Francis Bacon, the West had prided itself in its ability to harness nature and use it as a tool for human advancement. The rational control of nature had led to the accumulation of wealth and the betterment of life. Yet by the 1960s voices began to emerge claiming that such a dominance of nature defaced and endangered the natural world. Rachel Carson in 1962 published *Silent Spring* and asserted that technology was poisoning the earth. Others claimed that nuclear power was threatening the world's very existence. The old Western belief in technology was now suspect. Involved with this was a new interest in religions and culture—such as those of Asia and of Native Americans—that had a different understanding of the relationship between humanity and the natural world.

Also coming under fire were some of the political assumptions of Western society. Lying behind the easy Western talk of individual rights and freedoms were some ugly presuppositions. One was a racism that presupposed a hierarchy of races. Racial prejudice all too easily coexisted with popular rhetoric of brotherhood and equality, most dramatically in the United States. The civil rights movement had gathered speed from the 1950s and by the early 1960s had become a central aspect of American consciousness. Many Christian clergy, both black and white, took up the cause, seeing it as a true Christian social action, and Baptist minister Martin Luther King Jr. gave particular voice to the struggle for civil rights for African Americans. But by the second half of the decade others came to believe the problem lay deeper. Old institutions that had tolerated such prejudice were discredited when light was shown on them. In *The Autobiography of Malcolm X*, for example, Malcolm wrote movingly of how only with Islam had he ever experienced a sense of solidarity among different races. Racism was not merely an individual failing but endemic to the society. To root it out required a major social restructuring. So, too, did the existence of sexism. A new wave of feminism appeared and challenged the patriarchal nature of Western society. Both women and persons of color claimed that Western culture had been structured to disempower them, and both demanded its reconstruction.

Nor did morality escape attack. Scholars have spoken of a great shift in consciousness, long in coming but reaching fruition in this decade, whereby the old Puritan values of inner discipline, work, and delayed gratification gave way to a new Romanticism stressing personal self-fulfillment and authenticity. Much of traditional morality had served to buttress a consciousness rooted in personal discipline, above all in matters of sexuality. The "sexual revolution" made famous in the 1960s cast aside the old social structure of sexuality. Instead it saw sexuality as a central part of personal identity and a key part of self-fulfillment. Women in particular claimed autonomy over their bodies and their sexuality. Birth control, premarital sex, abortion, and other sexual issues became battlegrounds where new understandings clashed with old. The older morality, its critics claimed, was as much a hegemonic construct as were the disempowering ideas of race and gender. Replacing it became a generation's manifesto. These changes, along with the growing presence of women in the job market, gave to women an unprecedented autonomy.

Shifting views of sexuality inevitably led to discussions of the proper role of women in the church. For as long as it could be recalled, women had actively supported the church community far more consistently than had men, yet with few exceptions they had been excluded from ordained leadership. The injunctions of the apostle Paul about women had served as a justification for an all-male clergy. In the period after the Second World War, this began to change. As women began to take on a more public role in the larger society, so too did they begin to assume leadership in the churches. By 1965, Lutherans in Germany and Scandinavia, Congregationalists in England and Scotland, Methodists in America, as well as others allowed for women clergy. Among Roman Catholics and Catholic-leaning churches, women's ordination proved more troublesome. Between 1970 and

1990 Anglicans in the United States, Canada, New Zealand, Brazil, Kenya, and Uganda all decided to ordain women to the priesthood, and eventually the episcopate, and in 1993 the Church of England approved the ordination of women to the priesthood. The debate, however, exacerbated tensions between traditionalists and liberals. Although there was large public support in many circles for the ordination of women in Roman Catholicism, it was rejected by the Vatican.

Like the question of race, the issue of gender was not simply about inclusion. Feminist scholars noted that deeply imbedded in Christian language and doctrine was a structure giving support to male hegemony. These patterns of language and doctrine needed to be reassessed if the church was to be open to women. The title of former Roman Catholic Mary Daly's famous 1973 book *Beyond God the Father* reflected the degree to which some feminists believed that Christianity was flawed at its core. More reformist-minded feminist scholars, such as Phyllis Trible and Elizabeth Johnson, sought to criticize and revise traditional categories.

Even more controversial was the question of homosexuality. The willingness to rethink traditional taboos and to realize that many taboos functioned as forms of oppression by the powerful led to the reexamination of same-sex relations. Such relationships had long existed, but they had been seen as being (at least officially) antithetical to Christian teaching. Inspired by black and feminist theology, many were convinced that the time had come to rethink the old taboos against same-sex relationships. It began to be argued that homosexuality had long existed in both church and society, and as such it ought to be recognized as part of the natural order of things. Particularly within the older Protestant churches of the English-speaking world, a strong campaign developed to bless homosexual unions and to allow practicing homosexuals the right of ordination to the ministry. This issue led to deep division within the religious communities.

These cultural shifts, which one writer called the "Great Relearning," have helped contribute to what has increasingly been called the postmodern worldview. *Postmodernism* is a notoriously slippery term, but many of its practitioners believe that much of what is taken as reality is a social construct, often for the betterment of persons in power. A "hermeneutic of suspicion" was needed to deconstruct traditional understandings.

Old-Line and Evangelical Protestantism

Although the shift from modernity to postmodernity has been halting, it would have a major impact on a large part of Western Christianity. Perhaps its greatest effect was on Protestantism. "Protestantism" had always been a loose coalition of religious groups with many differences, held together by some fragile assumptions. "Faith alone" and "Scripture alone" had been the rallying cries of the sixteenth century. But the stress of the 1960s raised key objections to both faith and Scripture. What was the end of belief? What was the God in whom one believed? Radical Protestant writers argued that the traditional God of Christianity was no longer a possible object of belief. "God is dead," wrote key theologians, and along with God died the practice of religion. The neo-orthodox consensus fell apart, and Protestants were left with no agreed-on theology with which to confront the challenges of the era. Some proposed that a new social gospel, more radical than its early-twentieth-century predecessor, must become the center of Christian life and give new purpose to the old religious world. Many clergy and laity flocked to reform and protest movements concerning race, war, and other issues, in part to show the relevance of religion to the world. But the idea of God as an object of faith became far looser than in the past. Likewise the secularization of the 1960s influenced how the Bible was to be read. If all traditional sources of authority were suspect, why should one exclude the Bible from suspicion? Critics pointed out that many of the ills confronting the West—from environmental havoc to sexism—were rooted in the biblical narrative. The Bible, like other sources of authority, must be read with suspicion.

The crisis in Protestantism was not merely intellectual but also social. In the United States, for example, Protestant unity was emphasized as a counterweight to perceived Roman Catholic threats. The Roman Catholic Church may have had more members than any other denomination, but taken together Protestants were more numerous. The old English-speaking denominations—Presbyterians, Methodists, Congregationalists, and Episcopalians—had a key social role as the spokespersons of this Protestant majority. The decline of Protestant-Catholic tensions as a result of Vatican II meant that Protestant unity was not as important. Now internal tensions fragmented instead of unifying Protestantism. African American churches had always played an important (albeit silent) role in the Protestant majority. With the rise of the civil rights movement, the historic African American churches were thrust into the forefront. But now they were no longer perceived (by themselves or others) as Protestant churches but as *black* churches. Race rather than Reformation theology became the chief badge of identity. Women made up the majority of Protestants in the pews, but when as a result of the feminist movement a new set of women scholars, church leaders, and spokespersons began to emerge, gender and not Protestantism became the central defining category. As a result, the old English-speaking Protestant churches that had proudly spoken of themselves as the "mainline" found themselves bereft of their old social importance.

Such was the case with still another rupture within the Protestant world— the public emergence of a distinctive Protestant evangelical community. As noted earlier, the early decades of the twentieth century witnessed a bitter debate within the Protestant churches between those who urged the churches to adapt to the new ideas of science and history that had arisen in the last third of the nineteenth century and those who opposed these changes. The conflict emerged as a battle between liberalism and conservatism or between modernism and fundamentalism. By the end of the 1920s, the conservatives had in most places (the American South was a noted exception) been defeated, and they retired to form separate religious communities. From the 1930s to the 1960s a liberalism chastened by neo-orthodoxy held sway in the historic "mainline" churches.

> Conservative Protestants chose to begin calling themselves "evangelicals" (the term was falling into disuse among other Protestants) to identify themselves and to distance themselves from the tarnished fundamentalists.

The conservative community began to reemerge after the Second World War. They chose to begin calling themselves "evangelicals" (the term was falling into disuse among other Protestants) to identify themselves and to distance themselves from the tarnished fundamentalists. Preachers like Billy Graham showed the continuing appeal of traditional conservative Protestantism in twentieth-century America. Graham's worldwide evangelistic crusades attracted crowds in the tens of thousands. Furthermore, conservative Protestants continued to stress traditional concerns such as foreign missions, of which liberals were becoming more wary.

The crisis within mainline Protestantism in the 1960s provided the opportunity for evangelicals to return to the public stage. While many of the older Protestant communities were beginning to reassess painfully and haltingly their teachings and practices in the face of the changing culture, evangelicals responded by rejecting the radical elements of the new culture. The world needed conversion and personal religion rooted in the experience of God, and not secular theology and a dead God. Others pushed this experientialism further, and an interest in the charismatic gifts of the Holy Spirit began to take root in churches and fellowships not historically Pentecostal. God may have been dead for some, but for these evangelicals God was very much alive and speaking through the Spirit. Rather than viewing the Bible through suspicion, evangelicals considered it the inerrant word of God and a guide to truth. Biblical prophecy took on new relevance in books like Hal Lindsay's *The Late Great Planet Earth* (1970), where it was claimed that prophecy was a tool for understanding the events happening in the world. By the 1970s people began to note that the older Protestant "mainline" churches were declining in membership, some quite precipitously, while those churches emphasizing a born-again experience and the authority of the Bible were in fact growing. Evangelicals began to make their presence felt not only in areas such as evangelism and mission but also in the intellectual tasks of theology and biblical interpretation. Protestantism was giving way to evangelicalism as the key religious force in American society, a trend that attracted both interest and criticism.

These changes would have an impact on the great ecumenical organizations that had been the pride of the Protestant world. Both the World Council of Churches and the American National Council of Churches were products of high Protestantism and a modernist confidence. Both suffered as a result of the cultural and religious changes. They appeared to be elitist and out of touch with the grassroots religious life that was developing.

Roman Catholics in Turbulent Times

In the maelstrom of the 1960s, Roman Catholics attempted to institute the changes authorized by the Second Vatican Council. These changes affected almost all aspects of Catholic life. The liturgy was translated and modernized; altars were moved so that priests could celebrate Communion facing their congregations; old personal devotions were eschewed in favor of new models of collective worship; organs gave way to guitars in the mass. "Kumbaya" rather than Gregorian chants came to characterize Catholic worship. Long-standing barriers between Catholics and other religious groups were jettisoned, and the practical fruits of ecumenism could be seen in cooperation, education, and dialogue. Even traditional disciplines like the Friday abstention from eating meat, which had long served to distinguish the Catholic community, were terminated. In short, many of the traditional moorings of Catholic self-identity were removed.

But as noted in the previous chapter, there soon appeared serious divisions over the meaning of the council. Some saw the council as inaugurating a new era for the Catholic Church. Language of "collegiality" and the church as the "people of God" suggested an opening and democratizing of the church. By the late 1960s some priests and laity claimed that collegiality should be the decision-making mode for all church matters. The Catholic Church in the Netherlands, in particular, lobbied for such changes. Its bishops set up a National Pastoral Council, which allowed for delegates elected by the laity to pass legislation for the church.

Catholics wrestled with both formal and practical questions. The formal questions often involved the issue of authority. The decrees of the Second Vatican Council did not fundamentally undo the hierarchical nature of the church. Bishops were still superior in their dioceses, and Rome still claimed authority over national churches. But critics who saw radical implications in the council's statements publicly called for change. Canon lawyers argued that there should be maximum participation by all in decision-making processes, and others called for the restoration of the ancient practice of direct election of bishops by the faithful instead of their being appointed by the Vatican. The primate of Belgium, Leon Suenens, called for the abolition of the papal nuncios who watched over the national churches and for a greater shift of authority to the national councils of bishops.

On the practical or pastoral level, issues of sexuality confronted Catholics as they did Protestants. Over the centuries Roman Catholicism had become identified by key teachings on sexuality. Clergy (all of whom were male) were required to abstain from sexual activity through a vow of celibacy; marriages were seen as indissoluble, with no divorce permitted; and the sexual act was judged to be primarily for the procreation of children, so artificial means of birth control were forbidden. All these teachings, if not invariably observed, had been seen as foundational to Catholic life. Yet the new winds of thought flowing in the 1960s began to dislodge building blocks of the Catholic past. The Dutch Pastoral Council in 1970 called for a reexamination of mandatory celibacy, and opinion polls regularly showed that the position had strong support in other local churches. Similarly, by the end of the 1960s many were calling for the reexamination of the traditional ban on the ordination of women.

Issues of authority and sexuality came together in 1968 in the controversy over birth control. The Catholic Church's traditional opposition to artificial means of contraception was increasingly out of step with other religious communities (and the public at large) who recognized the right of their use in family planning. In the 1960s birth control came to be seen as part of women's autonomy and the ability of married couples to express their love. In 1963, John XXIII appointed a papal commission (later confirmed by Paul VI) to review the ban on contraception. A majority of the members seemed to favor the legitimacy of contraception, but their opinions were put aside. Instead, in July 1968 Paul VI issued the encyclical *Humanae Vitae*, which condemned almost all forms of contraception. *Humanae Vitae* outraged many. For those cherishing the idea of collegiality, the decision of the pope to override the members of the commission seemed arbitrary, prelatical, and out of keeping with the spirit of Vatican II. Moral theologians condemned the pronouncement's rejection of all personal considerations from the decision. Feminists saw it as a blow to the autonomy of women, and environmentalists considered it irresponsible in the face of a predicted population explosion that threatened the globe. Still others believed that it reflected the inability of the Catholic Church to see even marital sex as a positive thing. Altogether, many Catholics saw the encyclical as placing the church firmly against the spirit of the age and condemned it. More important, vast numbers of Catholics simply ignored it and perhaps for the first time in their lives rejected an official teaching of the church. A single encyclical had gravely weakened the authority of the church. The title of a 1969 study of the American Catholic Church, *The People versus Rome*, aptly reflected a new crisis in worldwide Catholicism.

In contrast to the perceived official conservatism of Rome, other theological movements began to emerge. Perhaps the most important was liberation theology. Coming into prominence at the Second Conference of Latin American Bishops at Medellín, Colombia, in 1968, liberation theology (represented by writers such as Gustavo Gutiérrez, Jon Sobrino, and Leonardo Boff) sought to link theology to the crushing economic situation of the poor in Latin America. Inspired by Marxist principles, liberation theologians claimed that it was the responsibility of the church to side with the poor in the face of oppression by the small class that controlled land, wealth, political power, and traditionally ecclesiastical power in Latin America. Rejecting a purely spiritual understanding of salvation, they argued that social liberation was integral to Christian salvation. The exodus—or the deliverance of God's people from slavery—became an important motif for understanding the church's liberating mission. Only by grounding itself in the experience and praxis of the poor could theology claim to express the will of God. Institutionally, liberation theology found expression in the development of small "base communities" composed of between fifteen and twenty families that combined prayer with political action. It was claimed that there were more than seventy thousand such communities in Brazil alone. Liberation theology lashed out at the political and economic oppression it found, and its supporters were politically active in many countries. The two religious orders most supportive of it were the Jesuits and the Maryknolls. Both had been historically dedicated to mission, and both had been active in China. The perceived collapse of the Chinese missionary endeavor and the swallowing up of the church by Maoist communism convinced them that a more radical approach was needed if the church was to have a voice in the developing world.

The years between 1965 and 1978 saw liberals and conservatives struggling within the worldwide Catholic Church. As liberals called for deeper and more radical changes to bring the church in line with the "spirit of Vatican II," some archconservatives rejected the entire corpus of Vatican II as misguided. Marcel Lefebvre, archbishop of Dakar, argued that the council had fallen into heresy. He and his followers called for the rejection of the council and the restoration of the Latin mass decreed by the Council of Trent.

Throughout all these years Roman Catholicism suffered from a crisis of ministry. During the decade of the 1970s, for only the fourth time in the entire history of the church, the number of Catholic priests declined. In the United States from 1962 to 1974 the total number of seminarians decreased by over 31 percent, and religious orders suffered similar losses. Many left the priesthood to marry. For some, the changes in the church had called into question the meaning of a clerical calling. In a Vatican survey, of 368,000 parishes in the world, 157,000 had no resident priest.

Catholic Realignment and Its Impact

Paul VI's troubled pontificate ended with his death in 1978. After the very brief pontificate (thirty-four days) of John Paul I, the cardinals elected Karol Wojtyla, cardinal archbishop of Krakow, to the papal office, and he took the name John Paul II. The election of John Paul II was in a sense a response to the perceived crisis in the larger Catholic Church. The youngest pope of the twentieth century, Wojtyla was also the first non-Italian pope in 450 years.

His experiences—as a factory worker, philosopher, poet, and opponent of both Nazis and Communists—had brought him into closer contact with the currents of the secular world than was common for earlier popes.

> For John Paul II the church could no longer rely on the power of state support; the only power now was moral suasion. But he soon showed how powerful that moral suasion was.

John Paul II's papacy, which would last twenty-seven years, had a major effect not only on the Catholic Church but on world Christianity as well. A participant at Vatican II, he rejected both the reactionary position of those like Archbishop Lefebvre and the liberal view that the council was the birth of a new Catholic Church. Rather, through a series of encyclicals he attempted to integrate the teachings of Vatican II into the longer traditions of Western Catholicism. He reined in liberation theology, squashed grassroots agitation for the ordination of women while calling for a more conservative Catholic feminism, and restored devotions—such as those concerning the Virgin Mary—that had lost favor in the years after the council. He was also influential in issuing a new catechism and a new collection of canon law.

Many of John Paul's efforts were directed toward reviving the sense of a spirit of mission in the church. He quickly became the most peripatetic pope in history, visiting every continent save Antarctica. He placed particular interest in appeals to youth and in reviving clerical and religious vocations. Still another focus of his labors was the advancement of Catholic social teachings. The church, for him, could no longer rely on the power of state support; the only power now was moral suasion. But John Paul soon showed how powerful that moral suasion was. Claiming that the fundamental error of the modern world was the denial of the universality of human rights, he was tireless in using the church to defend human dignity. His triumphal visits to his native Poland, as well as his behind-the-scenes negotiations, contributed to the toppling of the Communist regimes of eastern Europe. He used the message of human rights to challenge both left-wing and right-wing authoritarian regimes in Latin America, as well to attack the materialism and "culture of death" of Western culture. His message was given particular focus in the ministry of Mother Teresa (1910–1997). She and her Sisters of Charity served the very poor in Calcutta, ministering to them in their sickness. Her witness became an international phenomenon and epitomized the Catholic reverence for life. The moral influence of the Catholic Church rose during the pontificate of John Paul II and was higher than it had been for centuries.

But in the pontificate of John Paul II one observed a crucial shift in Catholic Christianity. Not only was he the first Polish pope, but through his words and actions he made it clear that the vital center of the church no longer lay in western Europe. In Latin America, Asia, and Africa, he pointed to the vigor that was no longer apparent in the old centers of Christendom. The shift was visible not only in his travels but also in his appointments. Through him, the Roman curia (traditionally made up largely of Italians) became far more international in nature, and non-Europeans played key roles in other parts of his governance. The new Catholic spirit could also be seen in his commitment to ecumenical and interfaith concerns. Although not abandoning dialogue with churches of the Reformation—indeed, a "Joint Declaration on Justification by Faith" was issued by Lutherans and Catholics in 1999—the thrust of his activities was elsewhere. He placed particular emphasis on restoring the breach with the Eastern Orthodox, and in the encyclical *Et*

Unum Sint suggested ways forward. He also labored to normalize relations with the non-Chalcedonian, or Oriental, Orthodox churches. His interest in clarifying Christian teaching and defending the rights of the unborn led him to open up dialogues with evangelical and Pentecostal churches, even as relations with some of the older Protestant traditions noticeably cooled.

The episcopate of John Paul II was controversial. Many, particularly in the older centers of Western Christianity, found his agenda counterproductive. Indeed, within the Western societies there began to emerge a new post-Reformation division, in many ways following the fault lines created by the social and cultural challenges of the 1960s and 1970s. Many old-line Protestants (though by no means all) and liberal Catholics argued that the churches must enter into the new social and cultural world, while Catholics sharing John Paul's vision and evangelical Protestants argued that such a move was wrong. The old Reformation divisions over sacraments and grace (not to mention even more ancient divisions concerning the nature of Christ) were giving way to new divisions based on issues of sexuality, gender, and equality. This division viewed the church in very different ways. During the latter years of John Paul's episcopate, the church was deeply damaged by a series of sex scandals involving priests and minors. Conservatives viewed these cases as part of the moral laxity of the heritage of the 1960s and episcopal irresponsibility in the face of the scandal and called for greater discipline. Liberals saw in them an autocratic ecclesiastical hierarchy out of touch with the people and asked for greater institutional transparency. But all viewed them as a terrible misfortune.

The Shifting Center of Christianity

Yet the disagreement was no longer a Western debate. It was not merely John Paul II who recognized that the center of Christianity was rapidly shifting away from the old Christendom. Everywhere church growth was advancing in the non-Western world. The collapse of communism in eastern Europe and the Soviet Union unleashed a burst of energy in the religious communities there, which many had assumed to be all but dead. Church growth has been so fast in Russia that it is estimated that 70 percent of the population will identify themselves as Christians by 2025, and in Slovakia and Moldavia even higher percentages are predicted. Significantly, in the debate over the European Union Constitution, it was the nations of eastern Europe, until recently under Communist yoke, who argued for the recognition of the continent's historic Christian identity against the opposition of the western European nations that had historically made up the core of Christendom.

Even greater changes were taking place in Latin America. "Christian-ized" by Spanish and Portuguese colonization, Latin America appeared to present the most solidly Catholic culture of any continent. Yet as early as the nineteenth century, many observers noted that the inherited Catholicism rested uncomfortably on many of the social forces present in the continent. In the second half of the twentieth century, Latin America experienced a tremendous increase in Pentecostal churches. Pentecostalism has exploded throughout the developing world, as we shall see; some estimates place its membership at two billion, making it the largest non–Roman Catholic Christian movement in the world. But what has been different about Latin America is that Pentecostalism has taken root in a society that had been Christian-ized for centuries. Scholars have drawn parallels between Pentecostal growth in Latin America and the emergence of Methodism in eighteenth-century Britain. Methodism, as we saw, was a response to both modernization and an economic order that was undermining traditional social structures. Like Methodism, Pentecostalism has stressed the virtues of betterment, self-discipline, and aspiration, traits that have allowed an extremely poor, displaced population to negotiate a position in the modern world far more effectively than it could have done through traditional Catholic religion or Marxist ideology that some had predicted would triumph. In places like Bra-zil, Pentecostals and other evangelicals now make up more than 16 percent of the population. Some have dismissively called this the "Americanization" of Latin American religion, but it may be more fruitful to see it as an example of how a breakdown of the traditional social order spurs the growth of alter-native religious responses. Furthermore, Pentecostalism's emphasis on the direct power of the Spirit allowed it to embrace many of the black religious traditions of Afro-Brazilians.

At the end of the colonial era Christianity rapidly expanded throughout Asia. Nowhere was the growth so dramatic as in Korea. As previously noted in chapter 17, the annexation of Korea by Japan placed Christianity in the role of chief defender of Korean nationalism. The activities of Presbyterian and Methodist missionaries (largely from the United States) created modern educational institutions. The division of Korea into north and south after the Second World War, with North Korea dominated by communism, further enhanced the role of Christianity in South Korea. All these factors contrib-uted to phenomenal growth in South Korea. Beginning with only 1 percent of the population in 1900, Christians by 2000 were the single largest religious group in South Korea, claiming over 40 percent of the population. The larg-est of the Christian groups were the Protestant churches of the Methodists and Presbyterians, but a significant percentage of the Christian population did not emerge from the Western religious matrix. Korean Pentecostalism, grounded in a long-standing shamanistic tradition that elevated direct contact with the Spirit, flourished as an indigenous movement. Furthermore, independent churches, inspired by new prophets, blended new teachings with traditional beliefs. Foremost of these was the Unification Church, founded by the Rev. Sun Myung Moon. Its proponents believed that Moon was the messiah, returned to set up the divine order; in this way they parted company with traditional Christianity. The movement became greatly popular, attracting converts in a number of nations, including the United States. But Unification members were not alone in desiring to extend their faith. Korean missionaries spread all over Asia, and in the diaspora of Korean communities throughout the world, Korean Christians served as a leaven for local religious life.

In the second half of the twentieth century Christianity grew rapidly in other parts of Asia. One such area was India. Despite the centuries of labor by both Catholic and Protestant missionaries, the Christian community in 1900 made up less than 2 percent of the population of the subcontinent, and forces such as Indian nationalism were hostile to Christian growth. Many predicted that independence, and with it the virtual disappearance of foreign missionaries, would further stymie Christian growth. Yet in the second half of the twentieth century, Christianity in India (now excluding Pakistan and Bangladesh) has grown from four million to more than fifty million members. The bulk of these are members of neither historical Catholic nor Protestant churches. The Church of South India in 1995 had fewer than three million adherents, and even Roman Catholics counted for less than a third of the identified Christian community. The largest group of believers is listed as "crypto-Christians," persons who identify themselves as Christians but belong to no church or religious community. This phenomenon derives from the peculiarities of the Indian social order. Because it rejected the caste system, Christianity had long appealed to those at the margins of the Hindu caste society, particularly the Dalit, or "outcastes." In recent decades the Indian government has attempted to reverse the inhibitions against Dalits (now called "scheduled caste persons") by granting them special status vis-à-vis education, employment, and benefits. To convert to Christianity formally would threaten these benefits, since as Christians they would no longer be identified within the caste system. Still another nine million identify with Christianity primarily through radio ministry.

The most difficult Asian church to assess is that of China. Long believed to have been crushed by the Communist takeover, the rumors concerning its death (to borrow a famous line) were somewhat exaggerated. Here, too, the growth rate has been phenomenal. From less than one-half of 1 percent of the population in 1900, Chinese Christianity by 2000 was said to be 7 percent of the population, or more than sixty-eight million members. Yet even more than in India, the Chinese pattern defies Western categories. Ninety percent of Chinese Christians are said to be members of semiclandestine independent churches. The rise of these independent churches stems from the traditional Chinese distrust of foreign operators. As we have seen again and again, Chinese political leaders have looked with suspicion on religious movements they could not control, particularly those connected to outsiders. First appearing in the early twentieth century, indigenous autonomous churches emphasized the freedom of Chinese Christians from foreign missionaries. When the Chinese Communists came to power in 1949, they attempted to sever the Chinese churches' connection to all outside bodies and to bring them under the authority of the new government. The independents balked at governmental control and instead became semiclandestine. As a result they underwent strong persecution. With the relaxation of persecution after the death of Mao Zedong in 1976, these long-simmering independent churches mushroomed in growth. They have spurred a Christian growth that is predicted by 2025 to include 9 percent of the population.

> The ability of Pentecostal Christianity to creatively absorb cultures and tap into native spirituality has also been a boon to the growth of African Christianity.

Yet the place where Christianity has truly exploded is Africa. In the course of the twentieth century the Christian community climbed from fewer than 10 million members to upward of 360 million members, and even greater growth is predicted. The unparalleled vitality of Christianity in Africa rests on several factors already noted. The collapse of African native religions in the face of modernization proved a fruitful ground for evangelism. Moreover—and in contrast with their Muslim missionary rivals—Christians have emphasized the creative interplay between African culture and the Christian gospel. Twentieth-century missionary theory recognized the importance of the incarnation for Christianity, that is, that the divine could truly become embodied in the human. This belief emboldened Christians to allow their faith to be translated into new cultures in a way that other religions (such as Islam) could not. In the absence of major political obstacles, the indigenizing principle gave to postcolonial Christianity astonishing vitality. By the early twentieth century, independent Christian movements inspired by local prophets (like those in Korea) distanced local Christianity from the churches of the imperial West. Earlier in the century William Wade Harris had shown the way. He was followed by prophets such as Moses Orimolade of Nigeria and Johane Maranke of southern Africa. In places like South Africa, independents outnumber traditional Christians, and in other African nations they are almost as numerous. Finally, the ability of Pentecostal Christianity to creatively absorb cultures and tap into native spirituality has also been a boon to the growth of African Christianity.

One particularly important force in the growth of African Christianity was the "East African Revival." Beginning in Uganda, it eventually spread to Kenya, Tanzania, Rwanda, and Burundi. The revival reflected a coming together of Protestant British holiness and traditional African religious practices. Its message was personal holiness and "full submission" to the Holy Spirit. A meeting in 1929 of the English Joseph Church and Ugandan Simeon Nsibambi convinced both that a new infilling of the Spirit was necessary for a full Christian life. A central aspect of the revival was the public confession of sins, long a practice in many African tribal cultures. Africans and Europeans would confess together, and the force was electrifying. As one African noted, "I have never before seen any white man admit he had any sins." The revival grew in strength during the 1940s and 1950s, drawing meetings (by now almost exclusively African) of hundreds of thousands. The revival provided a spiritual stability in the stressful period between colonization and independence. It also proved to be one of the sources of resistance during the Ugandan dictatorship of Idi Amin (1971–1979). The resistance came with a price that included the assassination of Ugandan Archbishop Janani Luwum in 1977.

African Christianity has not only been a phenomenon in itself, but it has served as a source of revitalization for larger Christianity at the end of the modern era. We have already observed how John Paul II commented on the liveliness of African Christianity during his frequent visits to sub-Saharan Africa. This liveliness is visible in numerical growth. By the end of the twentieth century some judged Roman Catholicism to be the majority religion in Angola, Gabon, Burundi, Rwanda, and the Congo, with double-digit presence in many other lands. On another level, African Christian witness in the face of adversity, whether apartheid in South Africa or the civil war in the Sudan, has impressed Christian communities (as well as others) around the world.

The rise of African Christianity has been particularly momentous for the Anglican Communion. Nineteenth-century missionaries and colonial magistrates positioned Anglicanism to be a leading Christian community in Africa. Anglicanism has been the chief beneficiary of the East African revival and has swollen its numbers. The rapid growth of other African Anglican churches—particularly in Nigeria, the Sudan, and South Africa—has transformed the international communion, making it perhaps the most African of all the historically Western churches. Church leaders like Desmond Tutu, archbishop of Cape Town and leader in the fight against apartheid, have become world-famous figures.

During the decades when Christianity in Asia and Africa mushroomed, an opposite trend was being experienced among the churches of the Middle East. Increasing Muslim-Christian tension made the lot of Christian communities in predominantly Muslim societies particularly difficult. Persecution has led to a wide-scale migration of Christians from nations such as Lebanon, Iraq, and Egypt. The lands where Christianity was born and had its earliest existence are less Christian now than they have been since the third century.

A New Christian World

The emergence of a vast non-Western Christian population has changed the face of Christianity and reshaped the politics of the Christian community. For the first time since the start of the second millennium of the Christian era, the face of Christianity has again become brown. The great historic churches of Europe and North America are not only minorities within the Christian world, but they are static or declining in the face of real expansion in Asia, Africa, and South America. Furthermore, as we have seen, the churches of the Southern Hemisphere (with the important exception of Roman Catholicism) are different not only ethnically but theologically. Pentecostal and independent Christians now outnumber the children of the Protestant Reformation. The great European churches are being overtaken by new Christian movements. More important, these Christian communities of the Southern Hemisphere often have different agendas from those of the older communities. Critically aware of the economic issues facing their regions, they often combine a radical sense of economic justice with a deep suspicion of some of the cultural trends concerning sexuality and gender that have captivated many Western Christians.

These churches, broadly speaking, are only marginally aware of the great social and cultural struggle that

In the great debates within the world Christian community at the beginning of the twenty-first century, the churches of non-Western societies tack in their own directions, making their insights and opinions felt.

the West and its churches experienced during the course of the twentieth century. They do not own, nor necessarily want to own, the intellectual and cultural refittings that have been a result of that struggle. In the great debates within the world Christian community at the beginning of the twenty-first century, they tack in their own directions, making their insights and opinions felt. Whether it be on questions of sexuality or social justice, their voices, although challenging to some Western Christians, are unmistakable. Lagos and Seoul are Christian centers that claim a place at the table of fellowship and discussion, as Antioch and Edessa once had done.

The new churches have transformed the Christian world. As we have seen, for the first thousand years of the Christian era, the Christian world saw centers of regional Christianities cooperating, competing, and jostling with one another. Only after the year 1100 CE did Western growth and decline elsewhere allow Western Christians to lay claim to the center stage of the Christian world. This was the "Latin era" of Christianity, with the West clearly at the center. The second half of the twentieth century has proved that this Latin era has passed. Indeed, it was but a Latin interlude in the long history of Christianity. An era of competing regional Christianities has returned.

Chapter 21

Growth and Challenge

*T*he twenty-first century has been a time of growth and trial for world Christianity. Although no longer dominating the Christian world as it had done for centuries, Western Christianity still shaped much of the agenda. Indeed, two of the most influential figures in setting the tone of Christian discourse during these years have been the pope and the president of the United States. The first may seem obvious, and the second, odd, but together their impacts have been distinctive.

The Papacy

On the death of John Paul II in 2005, Joseph Ratzinger, prefect of the Sacred Congregation for Doctrine of the Faith, was elected pope. His chosen papal name, Benedict XVI, gave to some an indication of his agenda. Benedict of Nursia in the sixth century had offered a rule of life to give order to a disorderly time, while Benedict XV had labored to bring peace during the time of the First World War.

Benedict's policies in many ways followed those of John Paul II, and indeed Benedict championed the beatification of his predecessor. He continued to emphasize the fullness of Catholic doctrine and the relevancy of Catholic life. But one of his particular concerns was the revival of the church in Europe. As a distinguished theologian he spoke out against the "dictatorship of relativism" that was disordering Western society as the Germanic invasions had during the time of St. Benedict. Relativism undermined the Catholic understanding of objective truth. The denial of truth, particularly moral truth, was the central problem of the twenty-first century in Benedict's view, for relativism recognized nothing as definitely good and could see no goal higher than one's ego and desires. Benedict was a traditionalist by nature, and he advocated elevating the use of the Tridentine mass (technically the mass of 1962) and the use of Latin. He also had a confidence in the unity of faith and reason and had a strong aesthetic sense, doing much to emphasize the role of beauty in Catholic worship and to emphasize the church's continuity with ancient truths.

But whereas John Paul II had been outgoing and charismatic, Benedict was reserved and humble and could not generate the electricity that his predecessor had. Furthermore, almost immediately in his pontificate the clerical sexual abuse scandals that had emerged in the United States mushroomed into an international scandal. The discovery that sexual abuse had occurred for decades in the church in Ireland and was carefully covered up by the Irish hierarchy caused a crisis that shook both the Irish church and the nation. In 2010 Benedict issued a pastoral letter of apology to the Irish people. Scandals emerged in Australia, Belgium, Germany, Switzerland, Norway, the Philippines, and other countries to such an extent that the Catholic Church everywhere came under suspicion. If this was not enough, early in Benedict's tenure it was discovered that the founder of one of the leading conservative Catholic orders (the Legionaries of Christ), Marcial Maciel Degollado, had for years serially abused underage seminarians as well as fathered several children. In 2006 the Vatican was forced to remove Maciel from his ministry, and in 2010 the Vatican appointed a cardinal to oversee the reform of the order. The fact that the Legionaries and Maciel himself had been praised by John Paul II as late as 2004, despite charges against him, made these events particularly shameful.

These scandals all predated Benedict's pontificate, and indeed he was an early critic of Maciel, but they nonetheless broke out on his watch, and his papacy was tainted by them. All this put a strain on Benedict. Already elderly (seventy-eight) when elected, by the second decade of the century the mental and physical stress of the office were too much for him. In February 2013 he announced his intention to step down as pope, citing a "lack of strength of mind and body." A pope voluntarily resigning his office had not occurred since Celestine V in 1294, and it raised the question about the status of the former pope. An office of "Pope Emeritus" was created, and in March 2013 Benedict XVI stepped down.

> The name Francis indicated some of the most striking characteristics of the new pope.

His successor, Jorge Mario Bergoglio, was a break from the past in a number of ways. As cardinal archbishop of Buenos Aires in Brazil he became the first pope from the Americas. He was also the first Jesuit pope. And he was the first pope to choose a completely new papal name since the tenth century! The name Francis indicated some of the most striking characteristics of the new pope. Like St. Francis in the thirteenth century he emphasized simplicity and informality in his person and a discomfort with the wealth of the church. Whereas Benedict had reintroduced the traditional red shoes as a mark of papal dignity, Francis quietly discarded them in the name of simplicity. Whereas John Paul II and Benedict had used a "popemobile" for their public appearances following the assassination attempt on the former, Pope Francis has plunged into large crowds without security. These symbolic acts and other actions have generated some of the excitement that followed John Paul II, but it is impossible to predict where Francis's papacy will lead.

American Trends

In its own way the American presidency also sets a religious tone. The election of George W. Bush in 2000 was widely perceived as being dependent on the votes of conservative Protestant Christians. And throughout his eight years Bush spoke (though not always acted) in a way supportive of the worldview and agenda of conservative Protestants and Catholics. He often spoke of his personal faith as being crucial to his political vision. On issues such as stem cell research he was consistently pro-life; he opposed government funding of abortion; and he insisted that the federal government uphold marriage as traditionally defined. He also emphasized that America was a nation under God, which made America exceptional. All these positions endeared him to his conservative Christian base while alienating an increasingly secularized liberal America.

But by the midyear election of 2006 lower turnouts by evangelical voters suggested that some evangelicals were cooling to the close relationship between evangelicals and the Republican Party. Politics, some people such as David Kuo (a former Bush evangelical adviser) argued, sullied evangelicalism and kept believers from focusing on faith and its moral imperatives.

The election of Barack Obama in 2008 profoundly changed the religious atmosphere in America. Although nominally a member of the United Church of Christ, Obama is arguably the most secular president in 130 years, and his election was another blow to the self-confidence of conservative evangelicals. Furthermore his domestic agenda was a reversal of Bush's. He openly challenged the notion of American exceptionalism, so important for Bush. More important, he supported gay marriage and the responsibility of governmental funding of abortion, and in some details in his health plan he impinged on the concerns of conservative Catholics. The decision to mandate Catholic institutions to provide contraceptives, sterilization, and morning-after abortifacients to their employees shocked the Catholic hierarchy, and some talked about a war against the Catholic Church. In response Catholic bishops issued missives in January 2012 to be read to the faithful at mass, condemning this policy.

> Although evangelicals and Catholics continue to be the most vibrant sectors in American Christianity, their percentage in the society is becoming smaller.

But despite the stand of the hierarchy Obama not only won reelection in 2012 but carried the vote of American Catholics. In doing so he exposed a division within the American Catholic public. Whereas earlier commentators had noted a division between mass-attending Catholics and non-mass-attending (often called "cultural) Catholics, the former being more conservative, the 2012 election also showed a new pattern. White Catholics followed their bishops, Latino and (perhaps) Asian Catholics did not. Thus Obama's reelection was in the face of strong opposition from both conservative evangelicals and the Catholic hierarchy.

These political trends are reflective of a drift in American religious life. Although evangelicals and Catholics continue to be the most vibrant sectors in American Christianity, their percentage in the society is becoming smaller. By 2013 approximately 20 percent of the American public did not identify with any religious group. They are the "nones." Their strength is greatest in the group of the population known as the millennials (those born since 1980). Often these persons describe themselves as "spiritual but not religious." Others are openly (and militantly) atheistic. Some commentators have predicted that this moving away from organized religion is indicative of a drift toward secularism such as Europe had experienced since 1950. Various explanations have been offered to explain this phenomenon. Some have suggested it is a reaction to the divisive nature of religion in American politics and society over the last three decades. Others have argued that it has flowed from the decline of families with children. Families have historically been the nursing ground of religion for both children and parents, and the decline of family life has dried up this source. Still others have argued that American religiosity was only a temporary phenomenon, and the trend toward secularism was inevitable. Whatever the cause, the trend has alarmed many of the churches that had assumed that America was immune from European-style secularism.

There has been some talk that this trend will provide an opportunity for the revitalization of old-line Protestantism. The historic Protestant churches, it is argued, have the flexibility to reach these "spiritual" individuals. To date this has not happened in any significant way, and the older churches of the Methodists, Presbyterians, Episcopalians, and the United Church of Christ have seen their membership decline and age. The plight of old-line Protestantism is perhaps best seen in the fate of the National Council of Churches of Christ. During the 1950s it was the meeting ground where all the then-mainline churches met to address questions of church and society. It was perhaps the flagship tenant of the monumental Interchurch Center in New York City built by the munificent and deeply religious John D. Rockefeller Jr. to house ecumenical Protestantism. By 2013 the National Council, made less and less relevant by the decline of old-line Protestantism and the rise of other churches, had become so weak that it could no longer pay the rent at the Interchurch Center and was forced to seek out humbler office space in Washington DC.

One further ramification of the presidential election of 2012 was that it placed the issue of Mormonism before the American public in a dramatic way. Mitt Romney became the first Latter-day Saint to be a presidential candidate of a major party. In the course of the campaign, the public for the first time learned that the Mormon community not only had over sixteen million members internationally but was also the fourth largest church in America. Romney's faith forced the Christian community to confront the question of the relationship between Mormon beliefs and those of classical Christian orthodoxy. Many conservative evangelicals (particularly in the South) found themselves in a dilemma: they agreed with Romney's politics but questioned whether his church was in fact a true Christian body. The effect of Romney's faith on the election is still unclear.

The Global South

In the global South, growth and persecution in the Christian world have gone hand in hand. Christianity has continued to flourish in these nations, and this growth, seen in both evangelical and Roman Catholic churches, has continued to make it the most vital religious movement in the world.

One example is the Protestant growth in Brazil. Only 5 percent of the population in 1970, "Protestants" by 2010 made up 22 percent of the population. Over forty million persons identified themselves as such. But the Christian presence in Brazil is indicative of the complicated nature of this new

Christian world. These "Protestant" Christians agree on a belief in Christ, but after that there are profound differences between old-line Protestants, classic evangelicals, and various forms of Pentecostalism. But the influence of this Protestant community has extended to the realm of politics. A Pentecostal (Assemblies of God) candidate for governor received 19 percent of the vote for governor in a recent election.

Korea has continued to be a major force in the Christian world. Although some have noted that church growth (among Protestants) if not actually declining is growing at a slower rate than in the 1980s and 1990s, this has not stymied their activism. It has been estimated that whereas in 2000 there were eight thousand Korean Protestant missionaries at work in the world, by 2007 there were over fifteen thousand.

But some of the most remarkable growth continues to be in Africa, and there Roman Catholicism has been a major actor. By the year 2010 there were over 175 million Catholic Africans, the vast majority (almost 172 million) in Sub-Saharan Africa. Sixteen percent of the population of Africa was now Catholic, and Catholics grew by almost 21 percent between 2005 and 2010 alone. The Catholic Church ran fifty-five thousand schools and twenty universities, and in some countries it was the second largest institution, second only to the state governments themselves. Pope Benedict referred to the African church as the "immense spiritual lung" of humanity and appointed a higher percentage of Africans as cardinal than any of his predecessors. Indeed, the strength of African Catholicism was so great that for the first time in modern history two African prelates—Francis Arinze of Nigeria and Peter Turkson of Ghana—were seen as serious candidates to succeed Benedict as pope.

But if growth has been one side of the picture of non-Western Christianity, persecution has been the other. Many have noted that the twentieth century was the greatest century of Christian persecution in history. Nazis, Stalinists, and other petty tyrants murdered millions of Christians. Such persecution has only continued in the twenty-first century, leading Pope Benedict to declare that Christians are the most persecuted group in the world today. The Vatican has recently claimed that one hundred thousand persons have been killed annually because of a relationship with the Christian church. Much of this has taken place in regions dominated by Islam. In the Middle East, home of Christianity, this persecution has been particularly severe, and an ethnic cleansing of indigenous Christian communities seems to be taking place. Christians in Syria, Lebanon, Turkey, and Iraq have been particularly affected. The "Arab Spring" of 2012 has been particularly devastating to the ancient Egyptian Coptic community, heirs of the great christological debate of the fifth century. Christians in other parts of the world suffer similar persecutions. The civil war in the Sudan has taken a terrible toll on the Christian community. In Indonesia and Pakistan persecution has increased. In Northern Nigeria Christians have been caught in the attempt to impose Sharia law that imposes drastic penalties on those who convert from Islam. In places like China Christians who do not adhere to the accepted (i.e., Communist controlled) churches also face state persecution. Some of these persecutions have been government sponsored; others, government permitted, while in other places governments have simply ignored them.

Roman Catholics and evangelicals have led the battle against such persecution and attempted to aid Southern Hemisphere Christians, but the "Christian" nations of the West have been relatively silent. This silence itself may signify the continuing decline of Christianity as a force in the Western world. But despite all these travails Christian communities continue to thrive.

Epilogue

*T*he great historian Sydney Ahlstrom used to advise his students to avoid making predictions: history is the study of the past, and a historian can claim expertise in that field, but predictions lie in the realm of the future. And then he would add smiling, "History has no future." Yet after enduring a two-thousand-year story, the reader has a right to expect some indication of where the story is heading. What is offered here, accordingly, is not a prediction but some observations on the present state of Christianity and where these trends (if they continue) may be leading the Christian world.

> The biblical world is alive for the churches of Asia and Africa in a way it is not for the Christians of western Europe and North America.

In its third millennium the Christian world displays a vitality and sense of division unparalleled since its earliest centuries. Many speak of the emergence of a new Christian order, with the churches of Asia and Africa taking the lead. It is there that the Christian world is expanding and profoundly shaping the lives of millions of individuals. In part the church is growing there because the population itself is growing, but the growth is not merely numerical. It also reflects intensity and commitment. Commentators have noted that the biblical world is alive for the churches of Asia and Africa in a way it is not for the Christians of western Europe and North America; the latter are separated from the biblical milieu by the Enlightenment and modernity. The supernatural elements of the Scriptures—the angels and demons, healings and possessions, miracles and manifestations—resonate in the traditional cultures of the Southern Hemisphere, where God is understood to be still active. Further, just as we saw that during the early Middle Ages in the West the themes of the Old Testament—with its emphasis on holy conflict,

301

peoplehood, and ritual purity—hit home more than did the more peaceable themes of the New Testament, so too in Asia and Africa is the Old Testament greatly prized. Issues and ideas that have little more than academic interest in the Global North, such as whether God communicates through dreams, have a keen immediacy in the Global South. Global Northern and Southern Christians, it may be said, are divided by a common Bible.

One reason the Old Testament themes seem relevant is that the Christian communities of the Global South live in conflict. In Africa and large parts of Asia, Christians and Muslims are in strenuous competition. Both growing, these two great religions are battling over which will be the dominant religious force in the twenty-first century. Religious conflict breeds militant faith, and this has been the case among Global Southern Christians. Here too the contrast between Global North and South has been sharp. The Christian North's focus on tolerance, mutual understanding, respect for others, and the rejection of proselytism gives to it a far different ethos than that of the militant South.

All of this has inevitably led to intra-Christian conflict between Global North and South. The most dramatic case has occurred in the Anglican Communion. The Western Christian tendency to reassess traditional injunctions against homosexuality in light of concerns for justice and self-authenticity has not sat well with a Global Southern Christian belief in the authority of the Bible. The decision by the American Episcopal Church in 2003 to ordain a publically professed noncelibate homosexual, V. Gene Robinson, as bishop of the diocese of New Hampshire, and the move by some dioceses of the Anglican Church of Canada to approve same-sex blessings, created a firestorm in the Anglican Communion. Churches in Africa and Asia quickly condemned the actions as an abandonment of the authority of Scripture. They further claimed that such actions exacerbated Christian/Muslim tensions in their lands, putting individual Christians at risk. As this book goes to press, the fate of the worldwide Anglican Communion is uncertain. Indeed there has been an attempt to create an alternative Anglican community or a "Fellowship of Confessing Anglicans," independent of the Archbishop of Canterbury and the liberal-leaning Western Anglican churches. In part, the conflict is unique to this one communion in which autonomous national churches, possessing the sole right to legislate for themselves, are linked together in a communion that claims the right to offer guiding principles. Such a combination of centralization and decentralization is a recipe for discord. But many see in the Anglican controversy the firstfruits of a continuing conflict between Global Northern and Southern Christianity. In the twenty-first century the issue of homosexuality looks profoundly different in Lagos, Nigeria, than it does in London, England, and the changes of the past half-century have made it such that one can no longer assume that the attitudes of London are central and those of Lagos marginal. Where there is no center, there are no margins.

But as I have tried to suggest, the idea of a "new Christendom," although crucially influenced by the Christian expansion in Africa, Asia, and Latin America, is also being shaped by three other factors. The first is the perceived stagnation of Christianity in the historic Christian West. That part of the church that led the Christian world through Reformation, Enlightenment, modernity, ecumenism, and countless other concerns seems to have lost its vigor. Both in numbers and spirit the Western churches appear to be floundering. Critics both within and without see them as aging, failing to appeal to youth, out of touch with their grass roots, and largely ineffective. The change has been dramatic. Until the past century the churches of Europe and North America had spread their vision of Christianity around the globe, both by missionaries and by migrants, but the tide has become reversed. Now Global Southern Christians flock to the old lands and carry with them their churches; churches in Korea and Africa send missionaries; and some Western churches even depend on Global Southern Christians to provide them with clergy.

A second factor is the perception that the remaining vigor to be found in Western Christianity is with those conservatives who displayed a more ambiguous response to the modernization and secularizing trends of the past two hundred years, one far more

> Some sociologists have claimed that conservative religions of dogmatism more successfully maintain strength and coherency in the modern world than do liberal religions of accommodation.

critical to the social and intellectual revolutions of the 1960s. For much of the previous two hundred years it was assumed that it was the liberals in the conservative/liberal split who were on the side of the future and it was the conservatives who were fighting the inevitable. From the perspective of the twenty-first century this is no longer certain. The passing of "Protestantism" and the rise of evangelicalism that has occurred in America can be seen as part of a larger phenomenon. The end of the previous century witnessed a sharp revival of fundamentalism in many of the major religions of the world. Some sociologists have claimed that conservative religions of dogmatism more successfully maintain strength and coherency in the modern world than do liberal religions of accommodation. To some, the liberalism that emerged in Europe and America in the second half of the nineteenth century now looks as antiquated as the Victorian parlors where it was first taught.

The final factor shaping the idea of a new Christianity is developments in Roman Catholicism since 1978. The success of John Paul II in moving the Catholic Church off the Vatican II debates and restoring a sense of spirit and mission has further served to push the religious center of the Christian world away from mid-century assumptions. Traditional teachings on doctrine, morality, and devotion have been promoted, and Roman Catholicism, like evangelicalism, has distanced itself from both the nineteenth-century liberal agenda and the 1960s revolution.

The results of these three interlocking trends can be seen in a number of places. Evangelicals and Roman Catholics are closer to Global Southern Christians in their view of the Bible and a willingness to see the divine actively present in the world. The supernaturalism of miracles, healings, and deliverance unites (to a degree) Catholics and evangelicals with Christians of the Global South even as it distances them from other parts of the older Christian West. It is among these groups that talk of a new Christianity is not simply an observation but a fervent hope. Also holding these disparate groups together is the belief that Christianity took a terrible misstep with its acceptance of modernity, secularization, and the 1960s revolution. Mark Noll, an American evangelical historian (now, significantly, teaching in a leading Roman Catholic institution) posed the question in a recent book *Is the Reformation Over?* He notes how shared assumptions have brought together evangelicals and Catholics, communities who until recently viewed each other as the "Whore of Babylon" of the book of Revelation and the arch-enemy of true Christianity, trying to destroy it from within. It is not too much to say that part of their newfound unity is that both groups now believe that the true whore of Babylon is the liberal spirit found in much of the old church life of the West. But the unity foreseen is not like that envisioned by the mid-twentieth-century ecumenists who founded the World Council of Churches. It is more dynamic and ad hoc. A group such as "Evangelicals and Catholics Together" is almost a throwback to the old nineteenth-century vision of the voluntary society, where individuals, not churches, are at work and where the goal is action and not communion.

On the surface the pattern outlined above seems set for the foreseeable future. The election of Francis at first glance seems to show a continuity with the recent past by conforming to the teachings (if not the spirit) of his two predecessors.

But if the long story of Christianity shows one thing, it is that surprise is the stuff of history. Few in 1950 would have predicted the revolution that has taken place over the past sixty years. In the same way, the future may astonish us. Many of the Christian communities of the eighteenth century were as moribund as Western Christianity seems today, yet they took on new life in the nineteenth century. Similarly, the conservative coalition that lies at the heart of the new Christianity is less solid than it appears at first. A change in papal policy or a crisis in the evangelical community could change the dynamics of world Christianity. The latter in particular is something to watch for, since, as scholars note, the category of "evangelical"—made up of such diverse groups as conservative Calvinists, Pentecostals, large independent churches, and many others—is at least as problematic as the old category of "Protestant." That internal tensions could lead to a collapse of the evangelical umbrella is not impossible. Predicting the future course of Global Southern Christianity is also anything but certain. Whether African Christianity (now on the forefront of the clash in global Christianities) is paradigmatic of all of Christianity in the Global South or a special case remains to be seen.

But there are still other questions. What will be the religious future of Latin America, where Catholics and evangelicals, not having heard that the Reformation is over, battle for influence? Has liberation theology there really seen its day, or is it merely existing below the radar of the Vatican? What will be the impact of the large number of "crypto-Christians" and "radio Christians" in places such as India, where Christian identity and church identity are separated in a way that is new to Christian history? Will the more informal grassroots nature of their structure increase or decrease their influence on Indian society and the larger Christian world? All these issues could affect the course of Christianity in the twenty-first century.

And there are larger questions. If the influence of Western Christianity is on the wane worldwide, the same cannot be said for Western culture. Its individualism, consumerism, and other marks continue to influence the entire world. For most of its history Western influence and Christianity have been connected, but now they are separate. What the impact will be is any person's guess. Already there are signs that feminism (a Western idea) is beginning to influence some Christians in the Global South.

Finally, is a global diversity, which is now the case within Christianity, the end of the Christian story, or is it, too, to be a passing phase? Could a new unity emerge eventually, perhaps one centered on a new idea of the papacy?

The future may have its share of surprises. But if the past offers any clues to the future, the movement that began with the simple question "Who is this man?" will continue to shape the lives of many—and the course of history.

Time Line for the History of Christianity

c. 6 BCE	According to the Gospels, Jesus is born in Bethlehem.
c. 29	Jesus begins his ministry of teaching and healing.
c. 31	Jesus enters Jerusalem and is crucified.
c. 35	On the road to Damascus Saul sees a blinding light.
c. 50	Council of Jerusalem
c. 64	According to tradition, both Peter and Paul are martyred in Rome.
c. 90	Traditional date of the death of John, the last disciple
c. 112	Ignatius of Antioch's writings
c. 112	Trajan offers council on the persecution of Christians.
c. 150	Justin Martyr's writings
c. 155	Martyrdom of Polycarp
c. 190	Irenaeus of Lyons's writings
c. 200	Clement of Alexandria's writings
c. 203	Martyrdom of Perpetua and Felicity
c. 240	Origen's writings
c. 301	Armenia becomes the first nation to accept Christianity.
303	Diocletian persecution
312	Battle of the Milvian Bridge and the vision of Constantine
316	Constantine favors Catholics over the Donatists in North Africa.
c. 320	Pachomius in Egypt organizes first community of Christian monks.
325	Council of Nicaea; Arius is condemned.
330	New city of Constantinople inaugurated
c. 356	Athanasius writes *Life of Antony*.
381	Council of Constantinople; Trinity is affirmed.

381–384	Pilgrimage of Egeria
c. 413	Augustine writes *The City of God.*
431	Council of Ephesus; Nestorius is condemned.
c. 450	Patrick begins the tradition of Celtic Christianity.
451	Council of Chalcedon; Monophysites are rejected.
530	Benedict founds a monastery in Monte Casino and writes a rule.
537	The church of Hagia Sophia in Constantinople is dedicated.
543	The church in Nubia is organized.
554	Split between Armenian and Orthodox Christians
589	Council of Toledo adds the filioque to the Nicene Creed.
590	Gregory is elected pope.
597	Augustine with monks from Rome reaches Canterbury.
632–709	Expansion of Islam
726	Emperor Leo II inaugurates the iconoclastic controversy.
732	Charles Martel checks Islamic advance at the Battle of Tours.
753	Pope Stephen II anoints Pepin in the abbey church of St. Denis.
800	Pope Stephen II crowns Charlemagne emperor.
962	Pope John XII crowns Otto as Holy Roman Emperor.
1054	Mutual excommunications establish the East-West schism.
1075	The investiture controversy begins.
1078	Anselm offers the ontological proof for the existence of God.
1095	Pope Urban II preaches the first crusade.
1210	St. Francis informs Pope Innocent III of his wish for a life of holy poverty.
1216	Fourth Lateran Council
1216	Dominicans are formally established.
1260	Battle of Ain Jalut ends Mongol/Christian hope of conquering the Middle East.
1265–1274	Thomas Aquinas composes the *Summa Theologiae.*
1302	Boniface VIII issues the papal bull *Unam Sanctam.*
1309	Clement V moves the papacy to Avignon.
1375	Catherine of Sienna urges the return of the papacy to Rome.

c. 1376	John Wycliffe writes, criticizing the contemporary church.
1379	Two popes now exist: a Roman one and an Avignon one.
1402	John Huss offers a radical reform of the church.
1414	Council of Constance is called to address the problem of multiple popes.
1415	Council of Constance condemns and executes John Huss.
1417	Council of Constance disposes of existing popes and elects a new one.
1453	Fall of Constantinople
c. 1475	Moscow becomes the "Third Rome."
1504	Diocese of Santo Domingo in the Americas is established.
1516	Erasmus publishes his edition of the Greek New Testament.
1517	Martin Luther protests the selling of indulgences and sets forth his 95 Theses.
1519	Huldrych Zwingli in Zurich begins preaching directly from the Bible.
1520	Luther's writings are burned in Rome.
1521	Ignatius Loyola begins reading the lives of the saints.
1525	Conrad Grebel baptizes an adult, beginning the Radical Reformation.
1529	Luther and Zwingli at the Colloquy at Marburg cannot agree on the Eucharist.
1530	Augsburg Confession defines the Lutheran faith.
1531	Aztec Virgin of Guadalupe appears to Juan Diego in Mexico.
1534	England's Parliament issues the Act of Supremacy separating the English church from Rome.
1536	John Calvin issues the first edition of his *Institutes*.
1540	Pope Paul III establishes Ignatius Loyola and his followers as the Society of Jesus.
1541	Colloquy at Ratisbon fails to heal the Protestant-Catholic division.
1542	Francis Xavier reaches Goa, the start of his ministry to the East.
1545	The Council of Trent is called.
1549	First edition of the English Book of Common Prayer

1558	Elizabeth becomes Queen of England and attempts a "compromise" between her Protestant and Catholic subjects.
1562–1563	Teresa of Avila begins her reform of Spanish monasticism.
1570	Pope Pius V excommunicates Elizabeth.
1572	St. Bartholomew's Day massacre of French Protestants
1582	Matteo Ricci arrives in China.
1593	Henry IV accepts Catholicism so as to secure the throne of France.
1598	Edict of Nantes secures right for French Protestants.
1614	Edict is passed expelling the Jesuit missionaries from Japan.
1619	Beginning of the Thirty Years' War
1630–1640	Mass migration of English Puritans to the New World
1648	Peace of Westphalia recognizes a religiously divided Europe.
1675	Philipp Spener publishes *Pia Desideria*.
1685	Protestants leave France after the revocation of the Edict of Nantes.
1738	John Wesley finds his heart "strangely warmed" (beginning of Methodism).
1740s	The Great Awakening occurs in America.
1773	The Jesuit order is abolished by Pope Clement XIV.
1795	William Carey begins his mission to India.
1795	Thomas Paine publishes *The Age of Reason*.
1799	Friedrich Schleiermacher publishes *On Religion*, a work shaped by Romanticism.
1801	Cane Ridge revival in America; the Second Great Awakening in America
1807	Robert Morrison begins his mission to China.
1814	Jesuit order is reestablished.
1833	Beginning of the Oxford Movement in England
1844	Young Men's Christian Association (YMCA) is founded.
1854	Pius IX declares that the Immaculate Conception of the Virgin Mary is an article of faith for Catholics.
1857	David Livingstone calls for "commerce and Christianity" in Africa.
1859	Charles Darwin publishes *On the Origin of Species*.
1864	Pius IX issues the *Syllabus of Errors*.

1865	The China Inland Mission is established.
1870	Vatican I defines papal infallibility.
1870	With the loss of the Papal States the pope becomes "prisoner of the Vatican."
1870s	*Kulturkampf* takes place in Germany.
1891	Leo XIII issues *Rerum Novarum* explaining Catholic view of labor.
1901	Beginning of the modern Pentecostal movement
1906	The Azusa Street revival
1910	Edinburgh Missionary Conference; beginning of modern ecumenical movement
1918	Karl Barth publishes his *Commentary on Romans*.
1925	The Scopes trial in America
1929	Lateran Treaty between the Vatican and the state of Italy establishes Vatican City as a free state.
1934	The Barmen Declaration of the Confessing Church in Germany challenges Adolph Hitler.
1947	The Church of South India is established by the union of Protestant churches in India.
1948	The World Council of Churches is established.
1949	Billy Graham begins his active public ministry.
1959	Pope John XXIII summons a second Vatican Council.
1960	Beginning of the charismatic movement in non-Pentecostal churches
1962–1965	The Second Vatican Council meets in Rome.
1963	Martin Luther King gives his "I Have a Dream" speech.
1968	Pope Paul VI issues the encyclical *Humanae Vitae*, condemning all artificial methods of birth control.
1976	Some in America declare this as "the year of the evangelical."
1977	Ugandan Archbishop Janani Luwum is assassinated for criticizing Idi Amin.
1978	Karol Wojtyla is elected pope and takes the name John Paul II.
1980	Conservative evangelicals emerge as a powerful political force in America.
2002	Revelations of cover-ups of sexual abuse of minors by Catholic priests in America ignites a major crisis.
2003	V. Gene Robinson elected as the first openly gay bishop in the Anglican Communion, causing a crisis.

2003	Muslim persecution of Christians in the Middle East intensifies with the fall of Saddam Hussein in Iraq.
2005	Joseph Ratzinger is elected pope and takes the name Benedict XVI.
2010	Benedict issues an apology to the people of Ireland about the Irish church's long cover-up of clerical sexual abuse of minors.
2010	Beginning of the "Arab Spring" leading to increased persecution of Christians in the Middle East
2011	Decades of Christian-Muslim conflict in Sudan leads to the establishment of South Sudan as an independent, largely Christian nation.
2013	Benedict resigns the papacy.
2013	Mario Jorge Bergoglio is elected pope and takes the name Francis.

Suggested Readings

*T*here are innumerable excellent surveys of the entire sweep of the history of Christianity as well as selected parts of the narrative. The following list is not an attempt to reproduce those sources (which can be found in many other places). Rather, the following are (on the whole) some recent and/or less-known sources that I have found particularly useful.

SECTION 1: SHAPING A CHRISTIAN TRADITION

Fredriksen, P., *From Jesus to Christ: The Origins of New Testament Images of Christ* (New Haven, CT: 1988); Sanders, E. P., *Jesus and Judaism* (Philadelphia, 1985); White, L. M., *From Jesus to Christianity* (New York, 2004); Meeks, W., *The First Urban Christians: The Social World of the Apostle Paul* (New Haven, CT, 1983); Hurtado, L., *How on Earth Did Jesus Become God? Historical Questions about Earliest Devotion to Jesus* (Grand Rapids, 2005); Pagels, E., *The Gnostic Gospels* (New York, 1979); Clark, E., *Women and the Early Church* (Wilmington, DE, 1983); Stark, R., *The Rise of Christianity: A Sociologist Reconsiders History* (Princeton, NJ, 1996); Bradshaw, P., *The Search for the Origins of Christian Worship: Sources and Methods for the Study of Early Liturgy* (New York, 1992); Wilken, R. L., *The Spirit of Early Christian Thought: Seeking the Face of God* (New Haven, CT, 2003); Lane Fox, R., *Pagans and Christians* (New York, 1987); Wilken, R. L., *Christians as the Romans Saw Them* (New Haven, CT, 1984).

SECTION 2: EMBRACING THE WORLD

MacMullen, R., *Christianizing the Roman Empire* (New Haven, CT, 1984); Barnes, T. D., *Constantine and Eusebius* (Cambridge, MA, 1981); Williams, R., *Arius: Heresy and Tradition* (Grand Rapids, 2002); Anatolios, K., *Athanasius: The Coherence of His Thought* (London, 1998); Brown, P., *Augustine of Hippo: A Biography* (Berkeley, CA, 1967); Moffett, S. H., *A History of Christianity in Asia*, vol. 1 (New York, 1992); Brown, P., *The Rise of Western Christendom: Triumph and Diversity, A.D. 200–1000*, 2nd ed. (Malden, MA, 2003); Binns, J., *An Introduction to the Christian Orthodox Churches* (Cambridge, 2002).

SECTION 3: THE SHIFTING CENTER

Lynch, J. H., *The Medieval Church: A Brief History* (London, 1992); Bolton, B., *The Medieval Reformation* (New York, 1983); Cantor, N., *The Civilization of the Middle Ages,* rev. ed.

(New York, 1993); Bynum, C. W., *Jesus as Mother: Studies in the Spirituality of the High Middle Ages* (Berkeley, CA, 1982); Browne, L., *The Eclipse of Christianity in Asia: From the Time of Muhammad till the Fourteenth Century* (Cambridge, 1933); Huizinga, J., *The Autumn of the Middle Ages* (Chicago, 1996); MacCulloch, D., *The Reformation* (New York, 2003); Cameron, E., *The European Reformation* (Oxford, 1991); Ozment, S., *The Age of Reform (1250–1550): An Intellectual and Religious History of Late Medieval and Reformation Europe* (New Haven, CT, 1980).

SECTION 4: CONTESTING BOUNDARIES

Mullett, M. A., *The Catholic Reformation* (London, 1999); O'Malley, J. W., *The First Jesuits* (Cambridge, MA, 1993); Dunn, R. S., *The Age of Religious Wars, 1559–1689* (New York, 1970); Hastings, A., *The Church in Africa, 1450–1950* (Oxford, 1994); Moffett, S. H., *A History of Christianity in Asia*, vol. 2 (New York, 1998); Mecham, J. L., *Church and State in Latin America* (Chapel Hill, NC, 1966); Campbell, T. A., *The Religion of the Heart: A Study of European Religious Life in the Seventeenth and Eighteenth Centuries* (Columbia, SC, 1991); Hempton, D., *Methodism: Empire of the Spirit* (New Haven, CT, 2005); May, H. F., *The Enlightenment in America* (New York, 1976).

SECTION 5: PLACING CHRISTIANITY IN A NEW WORLD

McManners, J., *The French Revolution and the Church* (London, 1969); Reardon, B. M. G., *Religion in the Age of Romanticism: Studies in Early Nineteenth-Century Thought* (Cambridge, 1985); MacLeod, H., *Religion and the People of Western Europe, 1789–1970* (New York, 1981); Chadwick, O., *The Victorian Church*, 2 vols. (London, 1966–1970); Chadwick, O., *The Secularization of the European Mind in the Nineteenth Century* (Cambridge, 1975); Desmond, A., and J. Moore, *Darwin* (New York, 1991); Barth, K., *Protestant Theology in the Nineteenth Century: Its Background and History* (Valley Forge, PA, 1972); Noll, M., ed., *The Princeton Theology, 1821–1921: Scripture, Science, Theological Method from Archibald Alexander to Benjamin Breckinridge Warfield* (Grand Rapids, 1983); Neill, S., *A History of Christianity in India, 1707–1858* (Cambridge, 1985); Latourette, K. S., *A History of the Christian Missions in China* (New York, 1929); Ward, K., and B. Stanley, *Church Mission Society and World Christianity, 1799–1999* (Grand Rapids, 2000); Sanneh, L. O., *West African Christianity: The Religious Impact* (Maryknoll, NY, 1983).

SECTION 6: WRESTLING WITH MODERNITY

Hutchison, W., *Between the Times: The Travail of the Protestant Establishment in America, 1900–1960* (New York, 1989); Busch, E., *Karl Barth* (Philadelphia, 1976); Hastings, A., *A History of English Christianity, 1920–1990*, 3rd ed. (London, 1991); Brendroth, M. L., and V. L. Brereton, eds., *Women and Twentieth-Century Protestantism* (Urbana, IL, 2002); Rouse, R., and S. C. Neill, eds., *A History of the Ecumenical Movement, 1517–1948* (Philadelphia, 1954); Schenkel, A., *The Rich Man and the Kingdom: John D. Rockefeller Jr. and the Protestant Establishment* (Minneapolis, 1995); Latourelle, R., ed., *Vatican II: Assessment and Perspectives*, 3 vols. (Mahwah, NY, 1988).

SECTION 7: FACING POSTMODERNITY

Marwick, A., *The Sixties: Cultural Revolution in Britain, France, Italy, and the United States, c. 1958–c. 1974* (New York, 1998); McLeod, H., ed., *World Christianities, c. 1914–c. 2000* (Cambridge, 2006); Ellwood, R. S., *The Sixties Spiritual Awakening: American Religion*

Moving from Modern to Postmodern (New Brunswick, NJ, 1994); Allitt, P., *Religion in America since 1945: A History* (New York, 2003); Jenkins, P., *The Next Christendom: The Coming of Global Christianity* (New York, 2002); Weigel, G., *Witness to Hope: The Biography of John Paul II* (New York, 1999); Hassett, M. K., *Anglican Communion in Crisis: How Episcopal Dissidents and Their African Allies Are Reshaping Anglicanism* (Princeton, NJ, 2007); Walls, A., *The Missionary Movement in Christian History: Studies in the Transmission of Faith* (Edinburgh, 2000).

Index

320 Index

Baptists (*continued*)
Baptist World Conference (1905), 260
Martin Luther King as, 277
and slavery, 204
Bardasian (or Bar-desenes), 49
Barlow, Joel, 190
Barmen Declaration of the Confessing Church, 255,
265, 311
baroque architecture, 146
Barth, Karl, 250–51, 253–55, 267, 311
Basel Missionary Society, 229
basilicas, 57, 108, 129
Basil of Caesarea, 68
Baur, F. C., 218–19
Bavaria, 147
Beecher, Lyman, 190
Beguines, 106
Belgium, 148, 239, 251, 268, 282, 294
colonialism of, 239
Benedictines, 99, 105, 229, 251
Benedict of Nursia, 89, 293, 308
"The Rule of Benedict," 89, 105, 308
Benedict XV, Pope, 264, 293
Benedict XVI, Pope, 293–95, 298, 312
Bergoglio, Mario Jorge. *See* Francis, Pope
Bernadette Soubirous, 210
Bethlehem, 6, 55, 307
Beyond God the Father (Daly), 278
Bible, 143
Alexandria church and, 70
Antioch church and, 70
Apocrypha and, 31, 84, 145
authority of, 130, 135, 144–45, 260, 302
Barth on, 250–51
Calvin on, 135–36, 143
Constantine and copies of, 55
core of, 70, 130
Council of Trent, 145
defining Scriptures, 31–32
divine inspiration and inerrancy of, 223, 248,
281
evangelicals and, 280–81
form criticism of, 264–65
Greek text of, 4, 126, 218
Hebrew text of, 4, 218
higher biblical criticism, 218–19, 221
historical method of study of, 218
history in, 216
Hodge-Warfield doctrine, 223
humanism and, 126–27
Ignatius Loyola on, 143
Irenaeus on, 30–31
King James Bible, 202
Latin Vulgate text of, 218

Luther and, 130, 143
Marcion's expurgation of, 30
missionaries' translations of, 230, 235
nature of, 218
New Testament, canon of, 32
nineteenth-century interpretation of, 218
Old Testament God in, 30
Old Testament of Christians, 31
Old Testament themes of, 301–2
Origen and, 47–48
Paul's epistles in, 32
Pentateuch in, 218, 221
Protestant Reformation and, 145
reason in interpretation of, 152
Reimarus on, 175
Revised Version (1881-1885), 217
Scofield Reference Bible, 224
sola scriptura, 130, 144–45
Stanton's *Woman's Bible*, 219
supernatural elements of, 301
unity of, 135
the *Woman's Bible*, 219
Wycliffe and, 115
Zwingli and, 130, 143
See also Hebrew Scriptures; New Testament;
Old Testament
Bible societies, 200, 202, 209
birth control, 277, 282–83, 296, 311
bishop of Rome, 41, 55, 68, 72–73, 88–89
patriarchs and, 88–89, 101, 107, 121, 264, 270
the successor of Peter, 36–38
See also papacy
bishops
American colonies and, 166
authority of, 146, 282
Catholic prince bishops, 185
Church of England and, 152
consecration of, 67–68
Constantine and judicial authority of, 55
Council of Trent on, 144, 146
in early Christian community, 15, 25
Eucharist and, 28
Ignatius on, 28
missionary, 268
office of, 25, 28
ordination rites, 33
as representatives of God, 28
as successors to apostles, 28, 30, 33, 36
See also under specific locations, e.g.,
Alexandria
Bismarck, Otto von, 207–8
black churches, 204, 241, 279
blacks. *See* African Americans; slavery
body of Christ

CPSIA information can be obtained
at www.ICGtesting.com
Printed in the USA
FSOW01n0642301214
4240FS